THE POLITICS OF LAND IN VANUATU

For the people of Vanuatu

THE POLITICS OF LAND IN VANUATU

from colony to independence

Howard Van Trease

Institute of Pacific Studies
of the
University of the South Pacific
1987

USP Library Cataloguing in Publication Data

Van Trease, H.N. (Howard N.)
The politics of land in Vanuatu: from colony to independence/Howard Van Trease. — [Suva, Fiji] : IPS, USP, 1987.

xiv, 313 p.; 21 cm.

Bibliography : p. 289-301
ISBN 982-02-0004-0

1. Land tenure — Vanuatu 2. Ni-Vanuatu — Land tenure 3. Land settlement — Vanuatu I. University of the South Pacific. Institute of Pacific Studies II. Title

HD 1125 .z63 V284 *333.309934*

Published by the
Institute of Pacific Studies of the University of the South Pacific

Reprinted by Fiji Times Ltd 1991

Cover design by Uday Singh
Typeset by City Typesetters, Suva
Text set in Megaron 10/11½
Printed by Fiji Times Ltd.
No royalties are paid on this publication.

CONTENTS

List of Maps

Figures

ACKNOWLEDGEMENTS

In carrying out the research for this book I have incurred debts of gratitude to a number of individuals. In particular, I gratefully acknowledge the help and encouragement of Professor Ron Crocombe, whose wide knowledge of the Pacific has been an invaluable source of information and inspiration. My special thanks go as well to Keith Woodward, formerly Political Adviser in the British Residency, whose support in the early phase of my research, time spent in discussion and comments given during the final drafting stage were extremely helpful.

To the people of Ataripoe/Alovwaru on Malo, Loonelapen on Tanna and Fila Island and to the three individuals who assisted me in my field work — Nikenike Vurobaravu, Joe Natuman and Willie Lokin — I owe a special debt of gratitude. I also appreciate very much the assistance given by the staff of the Vanuatu Library and Cultural Centre and the excellent maps provided by the draftsmen of the Survey Department.

ABBREVIATIONS

ADCO	—	Advisory Council
ANHC	—	Australian New Hebrides Company
BDA	—	British District Agent
BRC	—	British Resident Commissioner
BRCF	—	British Residency Confidential Files
CCNH	—	Compagnie Calédonienne des Nouvelles-Hébrides
CFINH	—	Compagnie Francaise Immobiliere des Nouvelles-Hébrides
CFNH	—	Compagnie Francaise des Nouvelles-Hébrides
CO	—	Colonial Office
COA	—	Commonwealth of Australia
CPC	—	Constitutional Planning Committee
FDA	—	French District Agent
FO	—	Foreign Office
FOR	—	Foreign Office Records
FRC	—	French Resident Commissioner
HC	—	High Commissioner
JPH	—	Journal of Pacific History
JPS	—	Journal of the Polynesian Society
JRAI	—	Journal of the Royal Anthropological Institute
JSO	—	Journal de la Société des Océanistes
MALNATCO	—	Malakula Native Company
MANH	—	Mouvement Autonomiste des Nouvelles-Hébrides
NHNP	—	New Hebrides National Party
PMB	—	Pacific Manuscripts Bureau
PPG	—	People's Provisional Government
PRNH	—	Plantation Réunies des Nouvelles-Hébrides
RFSM	—	Residence de France. Synthèse Mensuelle
SFNH	—	Société Francaise des Nouvelles-Hébrides
SPADES	—	South Pacific Action for Development and Economic Strategies
UCNH	—	Union des Communautés des Nouvelles-Hébrides

UPNH	—	Union de la Population des Nouvelles-Hébrides
VP	—	Vanua'aku Pati

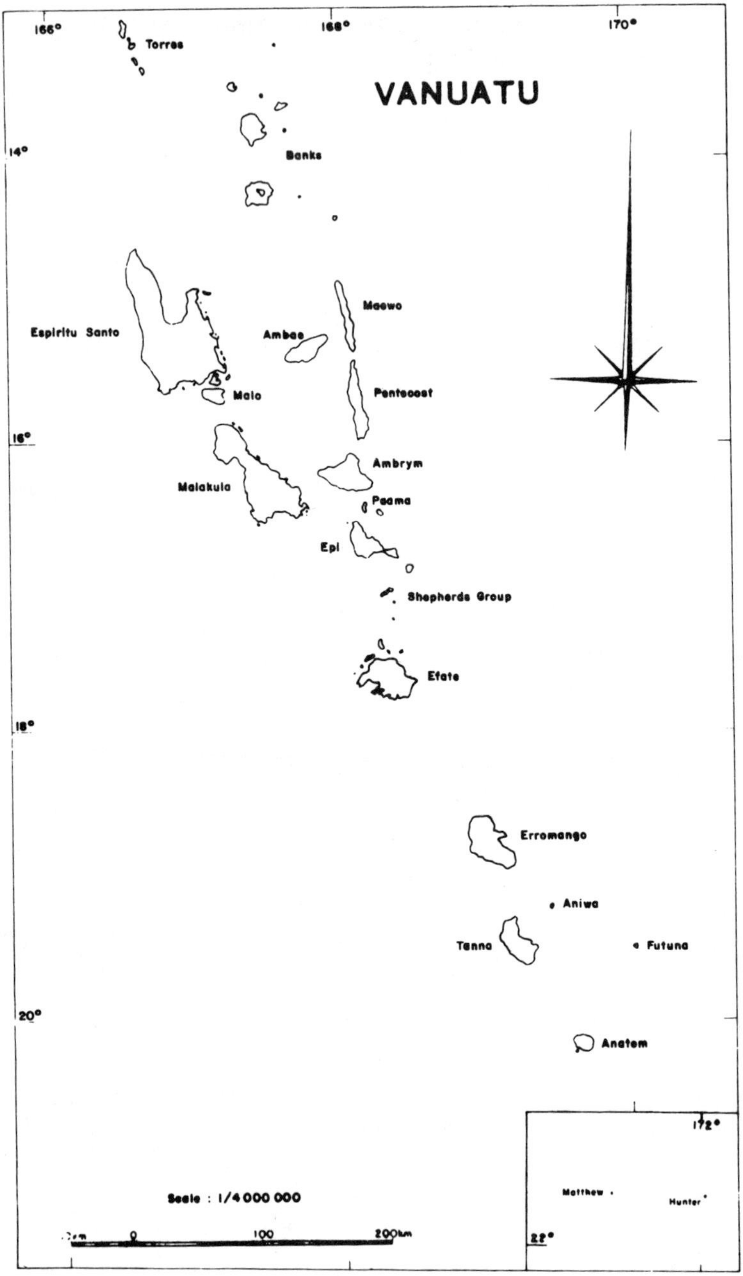

Figure 1: Vanuatu

INTRODUCTION

> Land to ni-Vanuatu is what a mother is to a baby. It is with land that he defines his identity and it is with land that he maintains his spiritual strength. Ni-Vanuatu do allow others the use of their land, but they always retain the right of ownership.
>
> Hon. Sethy Regenvanu
> First Minister of Lands

The relationship between ni-Vanuatu and their land and the fundamental distinction between proprietary rights and various kinds of use rights, was not always understood by the first foreign settlers who came to Vanuatu in the mid-19th century. As a result, the early period of European contact was marked by frequent disputes and much violence. Part I begins, therefore, with a broad survey of traditional land tenure principles. Using land as the focus for this historical survey helps understanding of the underlying issues which shaped Vanuatu's recent past. For example, the way in which ni-Vanuatu manipulated Europeans in the early contact period gives insight into the power relationships of the time. The degree of violence reflects the fact that ni-Vanuatu are still in a position to influence what land was acquired, by whom and on what conditions.

The balance of power shifted in favour of Europeans in the late 1880s when the governments of Great Britain and France agreed to regular naval patrols, with the specific order to protect the lives and 'property' of their nationals. The backing of gunboats enabled settlers to expand and consolidate their control over land they claimed. Because the two foreign powers were competing for influence in Vanuatu in the last decades of the 19th century, the question of European land claims took on special significance. Little of the land had been occupied or developed, but France used the fact that the vast majority of claims were by French individuals and companies to justify its goal of pushing out the British and achieving full political control. Centuries of competition and rivalry, however, plus pressure from missions, the Australian Government and business interests, led the British to aim at restraining French ambitions, while trying to avoid any further colonial responsibilities themselves.

With land as the focal point of discussions, the two governments finally agreed in 1906 to establish a joint Condominium administration. Viewed by both the British and the French as progress towards a final solution, it was in fact a victory for neither side. Although the British aimed to establish a system of land registration which would correct past abuses and curtail future European encroachment on ni-Vanuatu land, the French view prevailed and a system was established which provided the mechanism to confirm most claims. This facilitated registration of vast tracts of land, mainly by French claimants. While British administrators in Port Vila were soon protesting to London, the French aimed to achieve political control through title to thousands of hectares of valuable land.

Part II covers the period of ni-Vanuatu resurgence and protest against excessive land alienation. During this period the full impact of the dual administration became apparent. The two colonial powers had different attitudes to their future roles and doomed Vanuatu to a chaotic transition from colony to independent country. When, in the 1960s, Jimmy Stephens and his followers in the Nagriamel movement began to protest against the expansion of European planters into uncleared bush areas, British officials realized that if appropriate land reform was not forthcoming, land could become an uncontrollable political issue. The British counselled general reform to the Condominium structure with the aim of advancing the country towards independence.

French officials, on the other hand, viewed the early land protests as a threat to their continued presence. They were determined to remain in Vanuatu and therefore committed to protecting the land interests of the French settler and business community. The French were slow to understand that control of vast tracts of land which local people viewed as having been stolen from their ancestors was not a sound basis for continued influence and control. By the 1960s, French land holdings had become a political liability rather than an asset. Moreover, in the changed circumstances following the Second World War, ni-Vanuatu came to realize that they could again begin to influence the course of events in their country. European land became a symbol of colonial domination and the focal point of the nationalist movement aimed at achieving independence.

In the 1960s the French resisted land reform and adopted a policy of spending large sums on education and social services aimed at creating a French-speaking Melanesian majority loyal to and dependent on France and supportive of her continued presence in Vanuatu. They did, however, introduce a programme of returning undeveloped bush land to Melanesians to diffuse the growing protest against European land alienation. The French hoped that by giving up bush land, ni-Vanuatu would be willing to allow European occupation of developed properties. By the 1970s, however, when the programme was implemented, the issue was no longer land, but independence.

Section III deals with the 1970s, when pressure for reform and independence came to dominate the political scene. The French Government responded by manipulating the Francophone/Anglophone division within the Melanesian community which its policies of the previous decade had encouraged. But despite French efforts, the overwhelming majority (62%) voted in 1979 for independence under the leadership of Father Walter Lini and the primarily Anglophone Vanua'aku Pati.

Ni-Vanuatu of all political groups agreed on the main principles embodied in the Constitution, including the provision for all alienated land to be returned to indigenous ownership. While leases were possible for foreigners, there was no guarantee that former owners would be granted leases. French settlers and businessmen — especially on Santo — found these conditions unacceptable. They joined with Jimmy Stephens and his semi-cult Nagriamel movement, which in turn had the support of right-wing American business interests looking for a 'new country' in which to invest. Together, they fomented a rebellion against the democratically elected Lini Government. With the vast, sparsely populated island of Santo as the prize, the French Government could not resist a last attempt to consolidate the position of France and actively supported the break-away Vemarana Confederation. The British would do nothing to re-establish law and order in Santo — as required under the provisions of the 1914 Protocol — and the French would not turn against their own friends and supporters. Only with the aid of the Papua New Guinea Defence Force, with Australian logistical support, was the Government of Vanuatu able to regain control over rebel areas following independence.

On 30 July 1980, the Constitution came into effect and all formerly alienated land was returned to Melanesian ownership. The Government prepared legislation to enable non-indigenous people to lease ni-Vanuatu land, illustrating the principle expressed by the first Minister of Lands, the Hon. Sethy Regenvanu: "Ni-Vanuatu do allow others the use of their land, but they always retain the right of ownership". Had the French been willing to concede this point years before, instead of retaining their outmoded, 19th century attitudes regarding colonial power and influence, Vanuatu could have been saved the violence and disruption associated with independence.

1

Ni-Vanuatu Land and Foreign Intruders

The islands of Vanuatu had been known to outsiders for over two hundred years before they began to receive regular visits by Europeans in the early 19th century. The northern islands were first sighted in May 1606, by the Spanish explorer de Quiros, who anchored at Big Bay and named the island Espiritu Santo. Bougainville sailed through the group in 1769, and in 1774, Captain Cook gave the islands the name they would carry until independence in 1980 — the New Hebrides. Except for Quiros, who dreamed of expanding Spain's empire in the Western Pacific and made an unsuccessful attempt to establish a settlement (a New Jerusalem) on Santo at the mouth of the river which he named the Jordan, none of the explorers attempted to acquire land or stay long enough to have any significant impact on the islands or their people.

Nor, indeed, were the early explorers given an especially friendly reception. Violent confrontations occurred between Quiros' men and the people of Big Bay[1] and both Bougainville[2] and Cook[3] were forced to make hasty departures on several occasions to avoid hostilities. The islanders, with few exceptions, were not interested in the trinkets and trade goods offered by the ships' crews in exchange for provisions; they were probably more worried about the apparent threat the strange white figures posed. Many Pacific people viewed the first Europeans as "returning ancestral ghosts".[4] Captain Cook interpreted the hostility encountered at Tanna as simply opposition to an assumed invasion:

> Is it not as reasonable for them to think that we come to invade their country as to pay them a friendly visit; time and some acquaintance with us can only convince them of the latter; these people are in a rude state, and if we can judge from circumstances and appearances, are frequently at War not only with their Neighbours, but amongst themselves, consequently must be jealous of every new face.[5]

Vanuatu's reputation as inhospitable to visitors became widespread after the publication of Cook's journals. Occasional visits by whaling vessels or traders on their way to the eastern Pacific must have occurred, but it was fifty years later before foreign interest in Vanuatu increased again.

Starting in the early 1800s, the islands were visited more regularly by Europeans wishing to trade, proselytize and convert the local people to Christianity or to settle permanently among them as planters and businessmen. All required access to land and — during the early contact period — all were compelled to negotiate directly with custom owners, whether for temporary occupation to extract sandalwood or for more permanent, long-term rights to establish trading and mission stations and plantations. Although their superior weapons gave Europeans a short-term advantage, longer term occupancy depended on the willingness of the local inhabitants to allow them to stay. In the early 19th century, ni-Vanuatu were still dominant in ther own environment and the few foreigners who ventured into the islands were compelled to accept the situation.

Traditional Principles of Land Tenure

Much of the violence in the early contact period was due to the lack of understanding or awareness by Europeans of the complex land tenure systems of Melanesian societies and a general feeling of racial and cultural superiority, which would have led them to underrate the rights and wishes of local people. Cook's assessment of ni-Vanuatu reactions (above) was probably accurate. Europeans must have been seen as intruders into a world which for ni-Vanuatu had order and meaning and in which land formed a vital and integral part of the culture. The natural inclination of any people, when their existence is threatened, is to fight. European attempts to encroach on their lands would have been interpreted by ni-Vanuatu as just such a threat warranting violent retaliation.

Land in Vanuatu has always been highly valued and its allocation and use carefully regulated. Before Europeans arrived, however, it did not have monetary value and most evidence indicates that the sale of land did not usually occur.[6] Some recent land transactions have been cited as evidence for permanent transfer of land for cash or kind in ancient times, but such instances are usually accompanied by references to extensive land alienation, and may indicate new attitudes and practices.[7] It is now impossible to conclude categorically one way or another, but there is widespread belief among ni-Vanuatu today, which is important in understanding the modern politics of land, that the sale of land was not possible in pre-contact land tenure systems.[8] Partly it is a semantic problem, for whereas it was common in many Vanuatu societies for the transfer of land rights to be accompanied by the transfer of valued goods, never were goods the only factor — and usually they were a subsidiary factor conferring the transfer and/or compensating other relations for the advantage accruing to the individual or group who acquired the primary rights.

Traditionally, land was valued because of what it symbolized at least as much as for what it produced — it was the source of identity for individuals and groups as well as the basis from which almost all subsistence requirements were met. When he married, a man needed land on which to build a house, make gardens and plant fruit trees, and access to bush and forest lands for hunting and foraging. The shifting cultivation practised in Vanuatu made it necessary to have access to much more land than one used at any one time — a fact not understood in later years when the colonial administration reserved only small amounts of land for use by ni-Vanuatu, while registering large areas in favour of foreign settlers. A small section would be cleared for gardening, used for one or two seasons and then allowed to lie fallow for a number of years, the length of time depending on soil fertility and the amount of land available relative to population.[9] Moreover, stone tools, the fact that techniques of food preservation were limited and the absence of large scale trade and marketing systems meant that there was little need for an individual and his family to bring large amounts of land into direct use. Except as displays of wealth or gifts on special occasions, there was little incentive for excess production nor the means to achieve it given the available technology.[10]

In pre-contact times, land was vested in groups which were based on common descent, residence in a particular area and participation in various activities. The group was the land — its ancestors were buried in it. Through membership in the group, the individual derived his or her social status, power, livelihood, name and rights to land. At birth an individual acquired specific rights through both the mother and father, usually with an emphasis on one side or the other, depending on whether the society was matrilineal or patrilineal. However, while the emphasis was on the acquisition of primary rights through a single matrilineal or patrilineal kin group, an individual was in fact linked by birth and marriage to one or more groups through which additional rights to land could be obtained:

> What one acquired at birth was certain rights immediately, and various potential other rights as time went by. In practice no rights were unconditionally guaranteed, though nominally some were. The extent to which potential rights were activated depended on a number of variables.... in the various unwritten codes and customs of the Pacific peoples, potential rights frequently grew over time as a function of the participation in particular activities. That is, land rights waxed and waned as an integral part of other social and demographic processes.[11]

Since the principles on which land tenure systems were based were not written, and genealogical records were left to memory, decisions relating to land rights were made in the context of existing social and political circumstances, which reflected changes occurring within the society and in the system itself.[12]

Since it was usual for women to shift residence and land use at marriage, female offspring normally acquired only usufruct rights, while primary rights were held by males.[13] Women did, however, sometimes assume a custodial right over land when no male heirs existed to inherit primary rights.[14] Most important, however, was the role which women played as the link through which husbands, sons, brothers and other male affines might gain usufruct rights to needed land.[15] In the central islands of Vanuatu, for example, a woman brought with her into marriage, rights to specific parcels of land which she and her husband could use during their lifetime.[16]

Vanuatu's extreme cultural diversity — 118 languages in the present population of 130,000 — resulted in a great deal of variation between and within islands in social organization and thus land tenure systems, though there were basic similarities in certain regions. In the islands north of the Shepard Group, where hierarchical grade-taking systems operated, membership in a clan or kin group entitled male members to relatively free access to land within the area associated with the clan or kin group, subject to the approval of group elders.[17] There was seldom any permanent allocation of land to individuals, each having access to land according to need, with a constant process of redistribution at birth, death and in accordance with changing requirements during the life-cycle between. While boundaries between clans were usually well established, those between members of component groups, and particularly of individuals, were often less clearly defined, since they were not considered permanent but subject to modification or renegotiation in each generation. This aspect of customary land tenure is often overlooked by ni-Vanuatu today, who have grown up in a time when land has taken on a new value — as a source of cash through the production of marketable commodities. Thus the need to demarcate boundaries has become much more important, since how much land an individual controls can have a direct bearing on income.

A clear example of a community in which individual rights over land were relatively weak compared to the larger kin group is West Ambae.[18] The most important social group consisted of those males descended from a known ancestor several generations earlier, along with their wives and children, who resided together in a named locality. Ideally, all male members were related though it was not uncommon for outsiders to join the group and in time become fully integrated:[19]

> Titas Liu, who is about forty years old, told me that in his father's and grandfather's time all members of the carpel [extended family] jointly cultivated all of the land cleared by their joint ancestors. There was no internal partition and each man made his gardens where it best suited him. [Note that while much of the heavy work was shared, each man made individual gardens.][20]

With the widespread planting of coconut trees for the production of copra, the traditional land tenure system on West Ambae has been radically changed.[21] As is common throughout most of Vanuatu, trees belong to the individual who planted them and become part of the inheritance of the original owner at his death.

The situation on East Ambae was different in that individuals belonged to matri-clans, dispersed over a wide area. A man might exercise land rights in a number of localities through links of kinship in the families of his father, mother and wife.[22] While patrilineal inheritance was the preference, upon the death of a man, land that he used became the focus of conflicting claims by various individuals:

> Some appeal on the grounds of close agnatic connection or of common residence in a named locality regardless of genealogical connection; others base their claims on the bonds and obligations between matrilineal kinsmen, and yet

> others on the scale of their investment in the deceased's funeral.[23]

Thus the rules governing inheritance on East Ambae demonstrate the flexibility of the use rights of the individual, which facilitated progressive redistribution depending on social and political circumstances. Proprietary rights were vested in the descent group.

On North Pentecost, where society was also organized into matrilineal clans, the system was complicated by the fact that a woman normally moved at marriage to the village of her husband. Thus children were born into a locality where they did not have primary land rights. Sooner or later, therefore, it was necessary for a young man to move to the area from which his mother's family originated in order to gain access to his own clan's land. One incentive to young men to make this move was the desire to rise in the chiefly grade-taking system. A man could theoretically take grades in the men's house of any village, but the support of his mother's brothers — his own clansmen — was necessary to rise to high rank. A young man, therefore, had to physically move to the village from which his mother originated and establish himself within the community and his family in order to activate rights to land to which he was provisionally entitled by birth.[24]

Southwest Malakula society was divided into patrilineal clans through which one gained rights to land. Among the Seniang people of Southwest Bay, the land belonging to each clan was clearly demarcated as were sections within the clans associated with smaller kinship groups. Individual male members of the patrilineages, however, did not necessarily inherit rights to specific pieces of land:

> We are told that these plots, which include both cultivated and uncultivated ground, appear to be in a constant state of subdivision, repartition, and rejunction according to [the degree to which] the kinship groups owning them swell or diminish.[25]

While kinship provided an ideological framework, containing some options and preferences, economic and social factors determined the actual land rights of component individuals.

The system of land tenure operating in the central bush area of Santo reflects the characteristic in the northern islands of the dominance of group rights over those of the individual and the flexibility which allowed an individual access to land from a number of different sources. The numerous cultural groups were organized matrilineally with the tradition that a man sought his wife from the line of his father.[26] The system of inheritance, however, has been described as patrilocal and patrilinear, which seems incongruous given the pattern found elsewhere in Vanuatu, whereby matrilineal group membership usually included access to land as well.[27] The fact that ideally males sought wives from the line of their father could indicate a system in which the male members of two intermarrying kin groups acted as custodians in alternate generations for the land of their sons, which they had inherited from their fathers.[28] Thus, what might appear as patrilineal inheritance was in fact a matrilineal system obscured by the traditional Melanesian predominance of males over females.

Whatever the precise rules of inheritance might have been, the system for acquiring land rights was extremely flexible:

> Every five or six years approximately, when the huts rot, the village is re-established a little way away or sometimes a considerable distance away from the previous location; sometimes even, the village breaks up with the different elements going off and joining other groups. In fact, the local matrilineal tradition, which governs relationships between individuals, has the effect that the group one feels bound to is primarily that of the mother, and where people live tends to reflect this. One notices that very few people live where their fathers used to live and, even when they do, the father tends to have come from elsewhere. Thus each head of a family is almost always living on land which he does not own. His land is some way away and he goes to it from time to time to pick the fruit from the trees (especially coconuts). Every dwelling, therefore, involves bargaining and a verbal agreement with the real custom owner, who himself can be living a very long way away, dependent on the good will of a third party. This all leads to a kind of system of compensation which could very well be one of the factors determining the unity of the group among bush-dwellers. In fact, the individual does not feel so much a part of his actual dwelling place, which is temporary, as he does of any area where custom allows him to live.[29]

It is clear, therefore, that rights derived from membership in one's own and links to other kin groups were far more important to the individual Santo bushman, than inherited rights to specific pieces of land.

The observations of R.H. Codrington in the 19th century regarding the land tenure system in the Banks Islands also illustrate the principle of predominance in determining land rights over that of the individual. On Mota Lava, where clan membership was matrilineal, Codrington points out that a man normally inherited rights to land through his mother's brothers. It was possible, however, for an idividual to inherit patrilineally land which his father had cleared and planted. Such land, however, in the next generation would usually become the common property of the man's sister's son.[30] Thus, individual inheritance was the exception rather than the rule and, when it occurred, applied only to the one generation. Thereafter, the rules of matrilineal group rights came to dominate.

In the islands south of Epi, land tenure was less flexible than in the north. The allocation of land rights was related to titles or names bestowed on individual males, which carried with them control over specific parcels of land. While land was clearly linked to a larger kin group, certain individuals were given primary rights of use and the power to grant access to other members of the clan. A man without a title, in effect, had no land.[31] Family ties through birth and marriage, however, would have provided non-title holders with easy access to enough land to meet their needs. While a title might in itself have carried with it high status, without people dependent on his generosity, a chief would not have been in a position to project his potential power and influence. Thus the bestowing of a title would have carried with it for the recipient the obligation and necessity to grant his clansmen and others usufruct right to the land he controlled.

Common throughout the Shepard Group, Efate and surrounding small islands, was the existence of matrilineal clans. Each clan had its own *farea* (meeting house) and *mwalala* (dancing ground), though on Efate where the concept of the village was more explicit, all clans represented in a village could use the same dancing ground.[32] The most important titles in a community were those associated with the clans, handed down matrilineally, with preference given to the sons of the sister of the dead chief.[33] In pre-contact times, the control of land would not have had the same political significance as it does today, since the power of a chief was derived from his ability to influence the use of land rather than to control it directly. Of more importance in demonstrating the power of a chief would have been his ability to extract tribute from his inferiors.[34] In any case, direct control over large tracts of land for purely economic gain was unnecessary in pre-contact times — a man needed control over only enough land to meet his immediate subsistence and social requirements, though he might gain in status and wealth from having control over more lands which he could delegate to others.

In addition to the high status associated with the matrilineal clans, there existed a larger number of less important titles within the *farea* which were passed down patrilineally and also gave the holder rights over specific parcels of land.[35] Indeed, the greatest percentage of land in the central islands was associated with these lesser titles. Thus there was a patrilineal emphasis in the acquisition of land rights but with clear matrilineal possibilities as well.

This matrilineal/patrilineal duality may indicate that the islands of central Vanuatu have been undergoing a process of reconciliation between two separate cultural influences. There is clear evidence, for example, that on Efate in the cases of Mele and Fila Island, a later intrusion of Polynesian peoples brought into the Melanesian milieu the language and, conceivably, certain patrilineal aspects of the social structure with important implications for the land tenure system. One of the languages spoken on Emae is also of Polynesian origin, though different from that spoken by the Fila Island and Mele people.[36]

If such outside influences did bring a patrilineal emphasis to central Vanuatu it would appear that the new-comers did not dominate the original culture completely, but were forced to adapt to the system into which they moved. This could explain, for example, the predominance of the matrilineal clan system together with certain patrilineal aspects of the social structure, e.g. the lesser titles associated with the transfer of land rights. What makes the central islands of Vanuatu unusual with regard to allocation of land rights is not the existence of both matrilineal and patrilineal traditions — most Pacific cultures provided the possibility to acquire rights to land through either side — but the fact that both the matrilineal and patrilineal traditions were reinforced through clearly defined political institutions, i.e. the chiefly titles, with the patrilineal tendency appearing to predominate, while the basic underlying principle of the society was matrilineal. This could support the theory of another cultural intrusion.

Another possible explanation for this apparently unusual patrilineal emphasis is that it results from missionary influence in the 19th century. Some early missionaries — in particular, Peter Milne of Nguna — sought to suppress the matrilineal tradition because it appeared to him to be contrary to the Scriptures.[37]

On Fila Island, the rules regulating marriage provided a mechanism for dealing with the two opposing traditions with significant implications for land tenure. It was very important that a man should marry a woman from the clan of his father, so that he could pass on to his sons, rights to land to which they were entitled by virtue of their clan membership and which he had held in trust for them. The man's sons would also inherit custodial rights to the clan land of their father which their own sons would be entitled to inherit in due course. So important was the rule that a woman from outside would first be adopted by the clan of the man's father before the marriage could take place.

Marriage regulations on other islands in central Vanuatu do not exhibit this same rigidity. Early missionary reports reveal that a man was only prohibited from marrying within his own matrilineal clan and with any close relative.[38] Indeed, one must be careful not to over emphasize the importance of Polynesian influence. Patrilineal inheritance of land rights may simply be the effect of patrilocal residence, which is common throughout the area, and the practice of men passing on to their sons parcels of lands which they had cleared and cultivated.

Further south, on the island of Tanna, descent and inheritance of land rights were patrilineal. However, like the central islands, primary rights to land were bestowed on individual males through a process of name-giving. Associated with the clan into which an individual male child was born were a series of names linked to specific parcels of land. The name given to a male carried with it primary rights to the particular piece or pieces of land. However, land was closely identified with the clan and a man, therefore, acquired his rights to land by virtue of his membership in the clan.

While kinship was of prime importance throughout Vanuatu in determining land rights at birth, other factors could influence an individual's access to land at different times or in different circumstances. If a man found it necessary to ask to use land to which he did not have primary rights — for example, for making a garden — there would normally have been little difficulty. On West Ambae, for example:

> It was seldom difficult for a member of a large and expanding group that was experiencing acute shortage of land suitable for cultivation to find another group to which he was closely related that had a surplus. If, as was frequently the case, a donor group was short of members, then the granting of usufructuary privileges was commonly accompanied by change of residence. When this occurred the immigrant gradually became absorbed within the host community and, as his own status changed, so too did the rights that he had to the land. In other words, temporary rights of usufruct gradually changed to those of full co-partnership.[39]

Moreover, granting access to land on a temporary basis was a common method of creating and strengthening distant family and community relationships. In any case, the amount requested would have been small and used for only one or two seasons, then left to revert back to bush and to the original owner.

Another method for outsiders to acquire rights to land, which appears to have been widespread in the central and northern islands of Vanuatu, was the practice of taking over the funeral expenses of a deceased person in return for rights to land.[40] Such was the case on East Ambae[41] and on Fila Island:

> A stranger can become part of the system, or a man from the local area can round off his own property, by the possibility of receiving from the son of the dead man a piece of land called in custom *kasia tekava* (wipe off the sweat). For that he would have to provide, . . . the cooked food necessary for all the funeral ceremonies, right up to the 30th day's dancing.[42]

Such an arrangement required the consent of the dead man's sons,[43] thus it would have been very unlikely that a total outsider would have been able to move into a community and acquire land.

Tree crops presented a slightly different situation with regard to the acquisition of land rights in that they required a much longer time to mature. It was common throughout Vanuatu that trees belonged to the man who planted them and were considered personal property which could be inherited, even if the land on which they were planted was not that of the original owner.[44] In pre-contact days such a situation would not usually have created any great difficulty since the amount of land involved would have been slight and the trees would have had no commercial value. Indeed, the existence of such trees would have provided the basis for a more enduring link between the two groups involved and thus would have been viewed in a positive sense. Ni-Vanuatu have continued to recognize the customary ownership of trees as distinct from the land on which they were planted, and this explains to some extent their willingness in recent years to accept European occupation of developed plantations, while disputing the original sale.

While the acquisition of land rights was relatively easy, one must also be aware of the reciprocal process of loss of land rights — sometimes suddenly as in defeat and flight, but much more commonly imperceptibly. The absence of action to preserve rights (e.g. use, assertion of claims, participation, etc.) was in fact a process of reduction of rights. On West Ambae, for example, prolonged absence would over time weaken the rights of an individual in favour of others who had continued to reside within the community and participate in its activities.

> Unless non-resident agnates regularly return to work their

> land, and to interact and co-operate with resident parishioners, they soon cease to be known as members. Their land rights are said to go 'cold'. After two or three generations the two groups usually consider inter-marriage to be permissible, and when the genealogical connection is forgotten there is nothing else, such as clan name, by which the bond can be remembered.[45]

An individual's continued rights to land, guaranteed at birth, depended on his following the rules of custom governing his particular society and meeting the social obligations demanded of him by his family and community.

Today, easy communication and increasing incomes allow ni-Vanuatu who work in urban centres — indeed, spend all their lives there — to retain land rights in their home islands by making frequent visits and contributing to important social occasions, e.g. births, deaths and marriages. This has important long term implications with regard to land distribution, since it can mean that people living in the islands may find it difficult to gain access to needed land, as they could have in the past when a kinsman departed. Urban dwellers can continue to fulfil certain custom obligations which enables them to control land which they in fact often do not use and most likely never will.

From the above discussion, a number of principles emerge as primary features of traditional land tenure systems in Vanuatu: the emphasis of rights of various levels of groups over those of individuals (but with the clear recognition of both), the almost universal practice of granting temporary rights rather than absolute alienation, the predominance of male over female rights and the concept that land rights could be perpetuated or acquired through the application of physical labour. Furthermore, underlying the total structure was the implied notion of extreme flexibility, allowing for alternative solutions to almost any situation in which the overt rules of custom created undue obstruction for the individual in gaining access to the necessary land to enable him and his family to meet their daily needs.

Traders and Missionaries

In 1825, Peter Dillon, an Australian trader, made a voyage to Vanuatu in search of sandalwood, which he discovered in large quantities on Erromango. He found it impossible, however, to establish a trading relationship with the islanders, as they did not "attach the least value to any of our goods".[46] This apparent dis-

Trader Donald McLeod at his station on Efate. (Photo by Rev. Lawrie 1981-1984, Vanuatu Cultural Centre Photo Archives, courtesy Mitchell Library Sydney).

interest in foreign trade goods indicates that ni-Vanuatu contact with Europeans and knowledge of the technologically revolutionary items offered, must still have been very limited as late as the 1820s. Europeans, therefore, were still seen as a threat to be repelled and ni-Vanuatu, being dominant in the environment, were able to hold the invaders at bay.

In 1829 and 1830, several more attempts were made to obtain sandalwood from Erromango using workers recruited from Tonga and Rotuma, but with similar results. Small amounts of sandalwod were taken, but the difficulty of establishing a working relationship with the people of Erromango made it virtually impossible to undertake full-scale extraction. Work parties were attacked and forced to withdraw.[47] Discouraged by the results, and due to the drop in the price of sandalwood in China, no further attempts were made to harvest sandalwood from Vanuatu for more than a decade, since large-scale cutting required at least the tacit approval of the islanders to whom the wood and the land on which it stood belonged.

It was not until the early 1840s that European trading vessels again sought sandalwood in Vanuatu waters, though no doubt casual contacts were made by the occasional whaling vessel or transiting trader. In June and July 1842, sandalwood ships were reported trading at Aneityum and Tanna, and by 1847, Vanuatu was experiencing a boom period with never fewer than twenty trading voyages from Sydney alone per year.[48] Although violent incidents continued, ni-Vanuatu had come to value the trade goods offered for sandalwood and were willing to tolerate the foreign intruders long enough to allow work parties ashore to cut the wood and to make the exchange. The situation changed so much that several enterprising traders had been able to establish semi-permanent stations on several islands, which they used as bases from which they operated smaller vessels and collected sandalwood for shipment. The first was James Paddon who, in 1844, established a sandalwood station on Aneityum. In addition to serving as a transhipping point, Paddon's establishment became a popular base of supply for whalers and traders in the area.[49] By supplying provisions to Paddon, therefore, the people of Aneityum came to enjoy a certain prosperity through regular access to what were now becoming highly valued European trade goods. Paddon and others established stations during the 1840s and 1850s, on Tanna and Erromango and by the 1860s, on Santo, where interest shifted following the discovery of good stands of trees and the depletion of accessible supplies on the southern islands.[50]

The upsurge in trade from the 1840s onwards clearly indicates that ni-Vanuatu had come to accept Europeans in their midst as long as their presence was seen as advantageous. The local inhabitants were now eager to obtain the metal tools, tobacco, cloth, muskets, liquor, etc. offered. On Santo, when the desire for such goods declined and was replaced in part by a demand for traditional pre-European forms of wealth — especially pigs — Europeans responded by trading for pigs on other islands, to exchange for sandalwood.[51]

The acceptance of trading stations necessitated the temporary occupation of small sections of land. Paddon paid an axe, a rug and a string of beads for the island of Inyeuc in Analgauhat harbour, which the Aneityumese considered to be haunted[52] and, therefore, of no practical use to them. As the demand for foreign goods increased, the trade expanded to other commodities, especially copra. A British naval officer commented, in relation to Ambae and Ambrym, that most traders made some payment — sometimes a small quantity of tobacco — for the *use* of the land in which their dwellings and stores stood, "but this is probably not supposed to entitle the payer to ownership of the land, but merely to its use as long as he may remain."[53] Such arrangements, which in later years sometimes included additional land on which traders planted coconuts for the production of copra, often became the source of major disputes between ni-Vanuatu and the heirs or subsequent owners of the trading establishments.

As Vanuatu became better known through trade contacts and its reputation as an area whose population was yet 'untamed', another group of outsiders with quite different objectives began to arrive. From their bases in Polynesia, missionaries of the London Missionary Society sought to spread Christianity and 'civilization' to the people of Vanuatu. Their initial reception was no different from that experienced by the first traders. After leaving three Samoan catechists at Port Resolution on Tanna, John Williams and his party sailed to Erromango where he and one of his colleagues were killed. Several Samoan and Cook Island missionaries stationed over the next couple of years on the other southern islands met the same fate or became sick, some dying from malaria, to which they had no immunity.[54]

Some ni-Vanuatu were interested in the material goods of the missionaries, but almost no progress was made in these first attempts to attract local converts. They allowed the missionaries to stay, however, because they were interested in their personal possessions which, though meagre compared to the traders, may still have appeared significant to ni-Vanuatu of that time. Moreover, ni-Vanuatu probably assumed that the missionaries had the power and the knowledge to acquire more goods, even if the supply on hand was limited. The Rev. George Turner who worked on Tanna in 1841 and 1842:

> ... tried to get some of them to come and live with us as servants, but could not succeed. They would crowd about, and be ready to do any little job, but, in an hour or so, they wished payment in the shape of fishhooks, or strips of print, and then must be off to their home again. .... By giving a prize of some beads to the boy who said his lesson best, we for a time got a number of them daily to school.[55]

An outbreak of dysentery on Tanna in late 1842 was blamed on the missionaries, forcing them to flee. By 1845, the only missionaries left in Vanuatu were on Aneityum, where the first Presbyterian Europeans took up permanent residence in July 1848.

Despite problems the missionaries had with the resident trader, James Paddon, they experienced considerable success. By 1856, it was estimated that all but 200 of the 3,000 Aneityumese had been converted to Christianity.[56] By then, attempts were again under way to establish missionaries on the other southern islands. There was much greater success this time, but as Rev. J.G. Paton commented, regarding the stationing of mission teachers on Aniwa: it may be that it was "mats, buckets, blankets and iron tools"[57] that they really wanted.

There is evidence, therefore, that missionaries were allowed access to land by various communities, not because of acceptance of the new religion, but because the missionaries represented access to the powers of the white man, often material more than supernatural. In July 1870, for example, the Rev. Watt negotiated with Chief Mariwota of Tikilasoa village on Nguna for a piece of land.[58] A 'deed of sale' was drawn up, describing in detail the boundaries and transferring as well all "trees and stones" on the property. Goods given in exchange were:

> Sixty yards of calico, one dozen 4½ in. knives, one half dozen 6 in. knives, one 9 in. knife, one American tomahawk, one pair of scissors, a half pound of beads, and a small chest.[59]

The deed was signed by Wota, Bonal and Amos — those men who apparently held primary rights to the land.

The missionaries' house and buildings were quickly erected, but it was nearly two years before any Ngunese could be persuaded to come regularly to the mission station.[60] While the missionaries had been pleased with the ease at which they acquired land on Nguna and carefully drafted a document to avoid future problems regarding ownership, they did not realise until later that they were allocated land that the people of Nguna did not use because it was the bush of the spirit called Taloa:

> Right in front of the piece of ground which was bought for the Mission site on Nguna, and only about twenty yards from the shore, lies a reef of coral, visible as a large rock in the middle, with a number of smaller ones round about. The rock was the chief abode of the demon Taloa, the surrounding smaller rocks represented his harem, the shellfish and crabs on the reef formed their diet, while the beach and among the shrubs and trees was their recreation ground, where the wives of the spirit arrayed themselves in blossoming branches of a sweet-smelling evergreen shrub — a kind of jasmine, called *Nasara*.[61]

The most important factor in the acceptance of missionaries to reside appears to have been the acquisition of valuable trade goods, which they acquired at no real cost, since they were not interested in using the land exchanged. Indeed, the Ngunese apparently perceived the arrangement as temporary. They avoided the missionary "lest they should share in the fate that they considered certain to overtake him."[62]

A similar land arrangement was concluded between missionaries and the people of Erakor Village on Efate. The site agreed to for the mission station was a small island in the bay, thought to be haunted, and thus unused by the local inhabitants:

> The village of Erakor lies in a low confined situation, and is apparently very unfavourable for health, but in the centre of the bay there lies a beautiful island, slightly elevated and covered with wood, on this we fixed as the site of the mission premises, the chief and people cheerfully gave up the island to the mission.[63]

On the island of Mataso, as well, local people freely granted the mission rights to land:

> Mr Milne bought two or three acres of the sandy land at the waist of the island for a mission station. Several coconut trees growing on the west side also were bought. Payment was made as follows to the chief: 2 American tomahawks, 1 hatchet, 3 butcher knives, 1 clasp knife, 18 yards of calico, 6 yards cotton print, ¼ lb beads, totalling £1 3s 4d.[64]

The "sandy land" would have had relatively little economic value to the islanders, thus the exchange of trade goods meant a clear gain.

The land at Port Resolution, acquired for the Presbyterian

Mission by Nesbit and Turner in 1842, and which they were forced to abandon eight months later, shows longer-term acceptance of at least some such arrangements, for in 1849:

> The land purchased by Turner and Nesbit was still regarded by the Tannese as belonging to the Mission, in spite of the owners having long before been driven away. A deputation sent at this time was cordially received and a few chiefs extracted a promise that Missionaries should come and live among them as soon as possible. It was years, however, before this could be accomplished.[65]

The missionaries, therefore, did not keep their end of the bargain, which may explain why Paton had to re-negotiate with the local inhabitants regarding the site of the mission when he arrived on Tanna in 1859:

> He had much difficulty in securing permission to occupy the site of the Mission Station once tenanted by Turner and Nesbit. The bargaining was keen to secure an exorbitant price. The savages argued that although the ground might have been sold, the trees on the ground had not been purchased and the fruit on the trees had not been paid for.
>
> The Missionary's desire to create a favourable impression at the outset caused him to submit to what was practically the re-purchase of the ground . . .[66]

Although the above account refers to the land as having been purchased, events indicate that that was not how the Tannese perceived the arrangement. Indeed, in 1862 Paton experienced a situation which became common throughout Vanuatu. He was forced to leave Tanna due to deteriorating relations between himself and the local people due in part to problems over land:

> Part of the quarrel was due to the old question of ownership of land. The complaint was again raised that the land on which the Mission house was built belonged to one party while the other party claimed it. Great talking arose. The inland chiefs were full of wrath that their claims should be disallowed, and a suggestion was made by one band of warriors as they marched into the centre of the Mission grounds that the Missionary should say the word and let them sweep away their opponents.[67]

During this period Tanna presented an especially difficult situation because of the frequency of tribal warfare and movement of people. With whole tribes being conquered and displaced by groups from other parts of the island, the question of land rights in some areas was in a state of confusion and dispute.

The above examples indicate that in the early years of contact with Europeans, ni-Vanuatu were willing to grant to traders and missionaries the right to use their land, when they perceived the arrangement as resulting in a net gain in material goods. Furthermore, in the mid-19th century, ni-Vanuatu were dominant relative to Europeans in determining access to their land. Europeans were compelled, therefore, to accept the temporary nature of their rights, despite attempts at regularizing land transactions in European terms by acquiring the marks of local people on pieces of paper.

Planters

The first recorded sale of land in Vanuatu for development as a plantation occurred in 1867 on Tanna. Henry Ross Lewin purchased for £800 in trade goods, 324 hectares on which he established a small cotton plantation.[68] More Europeans followed, but relations with the local people were so poor that the settlers were:

> living in a state of most unpleasant suspense as the natives may shoot them any day. They have already killed three for which they have not been punished and it is more than likely that they will do more damage soon.[69]

Rev. John Geddie, the resident Presbyterian missionary on Aneityum visited Tanna in 1871, and predicted trouble over land:

> The natives on the west side of Tanna have sold much of their land to white men... It is very doubtful if these land transactions were properly understood by the natives, and they will at no distant time be a fruitful source of trouble.[70]

By 1871, Lewin had been killed, ending European settlement on Tanna for the time being. European planters eventually returned, but in small numbers. Geddie's description of the situation was an exaggeration — land alienation was never extensive on Tanna. The disturbed situation between tribal groups, the relatively large population and lack of good harbours would all have reduced Tanna's attractiveness for permanent European settlement.

The situation was more settled on Efate in the early 1870s, however, and a number of Europeans negotiated land purchases around Havannah Harbour. The early buyers were predominantly British subjects from Australia and New Zealand, sometimes via Fiji. Their arrival in Vanuatu coincided with a general increase in the European planter population throughout the Pacific, which began in

French planter on Ambae (Aoba) circa 1900. (Photo: National Library of Australia, Canberra, held in Vanuatu Cultural Centre Photographic Archives).

the 1860s when the American Civil War led to a sharp rise in the world price of cotton. Many of the early Efate deeds included detailed boundary descriptions, which suggest that an effort was made by the original buyers to ensure that local vendors understood the transaction.[71] Sixty years later, however, when the Joint Court began hearings for the registration of land on Efate, applications involving many of these early purchases proved to be extremely complex and difficult due to the number of overlapping claims. The original purchases of Robert Glissen and others at Sivery, for example, give quite detailed boundary descriptions.[72] But adjudication of the application for registration of the land at Sivery[73] involved eight separate overlapping claims including a caveat against the whole of the application by the Native Advocate on behalf of the chief of the village of Sivery, who claimed that the land in question:

> was not sold by the natives of Siviri, who were the legal owners, but by Nasthalo, a native of a neighbouring island who pretended to be the chief of Siviri.[74]

The caveat was rejected by the Court as were all native caveats against applications for registration of land on Efate. It is clear, therefore, that the careful documentation of details relating to land purchases did not guarantee that the transactions were in fact as clear-cut as the European buyers would like to have believed, nor that they would necessarily be accepted by future generations.

There was much less violence associated with the early alienations on Efate than on Tanna, due in part to the decline in large-scale inter-tribal fighting by that time, and to the lower population density, which made it easier to accommodate foreign occupation. In addition, the attempts to come to mutually acceptable agreements with ni-Vanuatu landowners — though there is evidence that local residents did not perceive the land transactions as implying permanent alienation — must have contributed to the maintenance of a relatively peaceful situation. In addition, except for the warehouses and cotton gin built by Benjamin Hebblewhite as a representative of the Sydney firm of Scott, Henderson and Co.,[75] most of the early settlers began on a very small scale. They usually resided on their land, but lacking labour and capital were only able to develop a small portion of their properties, which often included extensive areas of uncleared bush. Moreover, since the main crops in the 1870s were seasonal — cotton, maize and sugar — early settlers would not have appeared especially threatening to ni-Vanuatu, compared to later years when local people saw Europeans planting large areas in coconut trees, which implied long-term occupation.

EFATE ISLAND

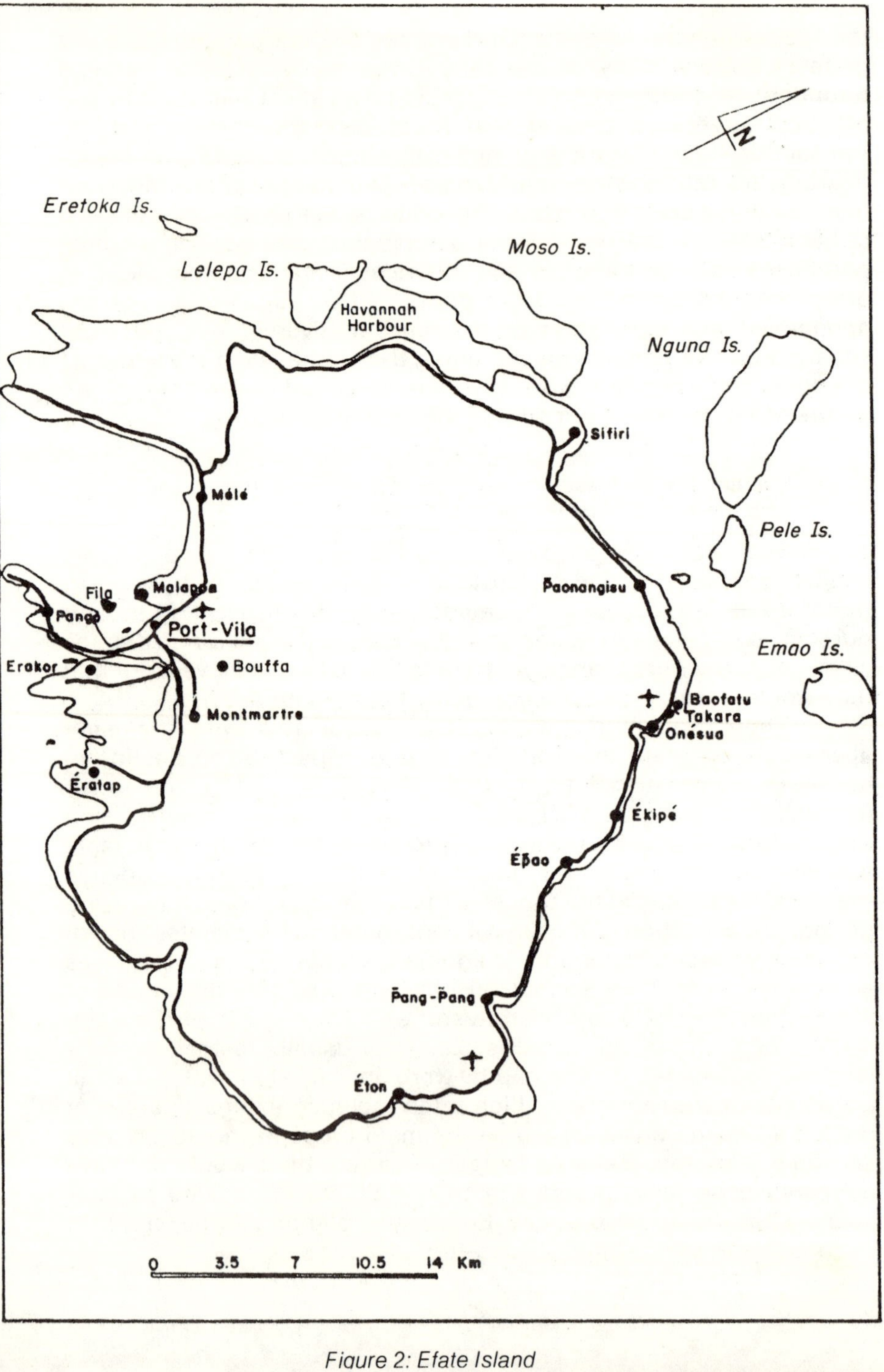

Figure 2: Efate Island

By the end of the 1870s, the once flourishing community of planters around Havannah Harbour had dwindled to a handful. Factors contributing to their failure included the inability of British planters to recruit sufficient labour following the decision in 1874, by the British High Commissioner for the Western Pacific, to cease issuing licences to British traders to recruit labour in the Solomon Islands and Vanuatu.[76] British planters also suffered from the collapse of the world price of cotton,[77] a series of hurricanes in the late 1870s, and the ravages of malaria.[78] The expansion of British interests was also inhibited by the attitude of the British Government to the permanent settlement of their nationals in the Western Pacific area. Following their experience in Fiji, where the large numbers of primarily British settlers had exacerbated internal rivalries and necessitated the Government's acceptance of Fiji as a colony in order to prevent civil war, Great Britain was reluctant to see the same process repeated in Vanuatu.[79]

The first Western Pacific High Commissioner (and Governor of Fiji), Sir Arthur Gordon, considered that a check on land transactions was essential to avoid fraudulent claims which would only lead to trouble. For this reason he directed naval officers in 1881 to inform British land purchasers that their claims had to be registered with the Western Pacific High Commission in Fiji and that such claims were to include reliable information on the nature of local land tenure, "which usually assumes its absolute inalienability by any single individual of [or] even the whole mass of those holding an actual life interest in it."[80] Gordon hoped to limit land transactions by forcing European purchasers to respect native custom, which did not include the concept of permanent alienation.

The notice to British residents, however, seemed to imply that such registration would result in the granting of title and official protection. A British naval officer, Capt. A.G. Bridge, reported to the High Commissioner in May 1883 that:

> though I was especially careful to impress on British subjects in those islands in general and particularly on those who brought papers to me to be registered, that it was not to be assured that the Registration would convey any guarantee of the title, it did appear that — in spite of this caution — the claimants as a rule believed, or at all events hoped, that their claims would in some measure be strengthened by it.
>
> They seemed to be persuaded that registration of the papers connected with land claimed by them would at least give them a right as against any subsequent purchasers (of British nationality) of the parcels which they asserted that they had

> already bought from the natives; and that — in the event of annexation of the islands by a foreign power — the fact of their claims being registered would tend to improve their position....
>
> I am inclined to think that the recommendation to register claims has had the effect of rather encouraging purchases of land; though, it may have tended also to make purchasers a little more exact in their proceedings with the native vendors.[81]

The Colonial Office reacted in September 1883 to such reports by instructing Gordon's successor, Des Voeux, to refuse registration of land transactions as it:

> would be liable to be construed as a confirmation of them by the Imperial Government, carrying with it some obligation to uphold such transactions, and possibly to give special protection to the purchasers....
>
> ... Her Majesty's Government will accept no responsibility in regard to transactions relating to land in the Pacific Ocean, not being in British territory.[82]

Since this policy did not prohibit British subjects from continuing to make land purchases, and no international agreement existed governing individuals of other nationality, there was nothing to prevent the situation with regard to land alienation from deteriorating further.

The decline of British economic interests in Vanuatu coincided with a number of French businessmen beginning to take an interest in Vanuatu as a source of labour for the rapidly expanding nickel mines in New Caledonia and as an area for plantation development. In 1880, Ferdinand Chevillard began clearing land near Vila harbour for what was to become one of the finest plantations in the group, known as Franceville.[83] French planters were soon established throughout Vanuatu, especially on the islands from Efate northwards — Epi, Malakula and Santo — which possessed extensive coastal plains, ideal for large coconut plantations. British planters continued to arrive, mainly from Australia, but from the 1880s onwards, French economic interests became dominant and remained so until independence in 1980.

John Higginson — an "English born financier with Australian experience, naturalised French citizen and Anglophobe *par excellence*"[84] — was the key figure during this period in laying the economic foundation for what he hoped would be the eventual annexation of the islands by France. He came to New Caledonia in

John Higginson aimed to secure Vanuatu for France through the acquisition of hundreds of thousands of hectares of land.

1859, by the 1870s was actively involved in the development of the mining industry and became interested in Vanuatu as a source of labour, due to the difficulty in recruiting local Melanesians to work in the mines.[85] He saw Vanuatu as "a natural annex to New Caledonia."[86] When in 1878, agitation from the Australian colonies for the annexation of Vanuatu by Britain led the French Government to suggest an exchange of notes with Great Britain agreeing to respect the independence of Vanuatu, Higginson was "stupified".[87] From this time onwards, he became actively involved and saw himself as the driving force in the struggle against Britain for control in Vanuatu.

In his memoirs, he quotes President Jules Ferry, as having told him personally in 1881 during a visit to Paris that:

> For the moment... the French Government is unable to do anything for the New Hebrides question; you alone can move forward — act, and we will help you.[88]

The next year, in October 1882, Higginson founded the Compagnie Calédonienne des Nouvelles-Hébrides (CCNH) with the publicly declared goal of bringing about French political control in Vanuatu through the acquisition of land on which French citizens would be encouraged to settle. Higginson's declared aim was:

> to carry out on a large scale what the English up to then had done only on a small scale: to buy land in the same way as they did; to encourage our French compatriots to establish regular communications with New Caledonia and the various islands of the archipelago; to supplant especially the many English ships which never cease recruiting these island populations for Australia and Fiji; to re-establish the flow of Kanak immigration, without which New Caledonia will be condemned to complete impotence; in brief; to follow exactly the policy of the English and by continuing acquisition of territory to succeed in putting into French hands and in consequence into the hand of France, the ownership of the whole archipelago.[89]

Thus began one of the biggest land grabs in the history of the South Pacific.

Higginson began by purchasing every available existing title. He found many eager sellers — all British. Donald McLeod, a notorious trader and suspected blackbirder[90] sold his land on Efate and at Port Sandwich on Malakula (which Higginson estimated to be about 100,000 hectares) and then became the company's representative at Port Vila.[91] Higginson also began a programme of direct purchases from ni-Vanuatu. In October and November 1882, his agents Barthelemy Gaspard and Charles Peterson Stuart, on board the ship *Caledonienne,* purchased an estimated 95,460 hectares of land (about 8% of the total land area of Vanuatu) on the islands of Malakula, Epi and Efate.[92] Most of the transactions were conducted on board ship. Unsuspecting islanders were enticed aboard with promises of trade goods or liquor, then persuaded to affix their marks on pieces of paper transferring vast amounts of the coastline, designating the hills as back boundaries.[93] Lieutenant Martin D'Arbel, who was on board the *Caledonienne* reported to the Governor of New Caledonia on the "fairness" of the land transactions and the "accuracy" of the coastal boundaries.[94] Although he admitted that descriptions of the back boundaries might not be exact as it had been impossible to penetrate into the interior "he assured the Governor" that "names of villages and mountains had always been entered on the deeds, which would serve to locate boundaries at a later date."[95] The Governor of New Caledonia ordered the captains of French warships operating in Vanuatu waters to certify the dates of the purchases, thus giving them official Government recognition.[96]

Needless to say, these land transactions were not worth the paper on which they were written. No attempt could have been made during the 14 day voyage to investigate the legitimacy of the vendors or the accuracy of the boundaries, nor to explain the implications of the transactions. Given the nature of the traditional land tenure systems of Vanuatu, it is clear that ni-Vanuatu who signed the deeds could not have understood what they were doing or were themselves unscrupulous in selling land to which they had no rights. In any case, it would have been very difficult to permanently alienate land or, at least, such transactions would have required the consent of the group of related individuals with rights to the land.

Higginson faced competition in the mid-1880s from an Australian company set up in 1884 by W.E. Morgan, the brother of his partner John Morgan. The South Sea Speculation Company, as it was known, used similar techniques to acquire land to gain control for trading purposes.[97] In 1886 and 1887, operating from the schooner *Fairy Queen,* the company's agents laid claim to land on Epi, Ambae, Ambrym, Emae, Pentecost, Malakula and Santo. Like the transactions concluded several years before by Higginson's agents, the claims were for vast areas of land, the boundaries of which were usually described in only the vaguest of terms. The company bought land on the north end of Malakula described as:

> commencing at the north east point called Latatarre extending along the coast for a distance of two miles in an easterly direction, from the south west point called Lomamaris

> running in a southerly and easterly direction for three miles. The inland boundary to be a direct line joining the extremities of either coast line and frontage to be the sea beach including all bays and rivers and the Bay of Wabeau lying between the points Latatarre and Lomamaris.[98]

The deed, dated 7 August 1885, was signed by Loowarian, Nataraway and Matatil, who were paid £15 in merchandise.[99] Such a vast area must have contained the rights of hundreds of ni-Vanuatu.

In addition, the Morgan brothers purchased a number of claims from other Europeans operating on a smaller scale, but using the same methods. On the west coast of Epi they bought a claim for land at a small bay called Esakiel, the boundaries of which were described as:

> Bearing from La Meuse Island South Point NW by W and running about one mile S by W and N by E by compass with all flat land, hills and valleys right up to the top of the furthermost hills visible from a boat one hundred yeards [sic] from the sea beach.[100]

The above description is typical of the way in which land speculators in the 19th century conducted their negotiations. Soon after registering the claims with the Western Pacific High Commission in Suva, the Morgan family sold them to Higginson. They may have anticipated the French military occupation of the islands in 1886 and feared outright annexation[101] or they may simply have sought to make a quick profit at the expense of the French and registered their claims in Suva as a means to increase their value.[102] An Australian journalist travelling through Vanuatu in 1887 reported his views on the Morgan brothers' operation:

> British subjects settled in Noumea have acquired large tracts of land in the New Hebrides which they have sold to the French Company after registering the titles in Fiji. In the last case which came under my notice, that of the Morgans, land was sold to the Company [Higginson's CCNH] before the natives had been paid for it by the vendors to the said company, which seems a proof that it was nothing but a speculation, the British flag being used to cover transactions with the natives which would not be acknowledged in any other part of the world.[103]

Whatever the reasons, Higginson was able to add thousands of hectares to the hundreds of thousands he already claimed to have purchased, making his company — at least on paper — the most important economic force in Vanuatu at that time.

There is no evidence that ni-Vanuatu viewed this new group of white men with any particular apprehension. Since the encounters were brief and involved the acquisition of trade goods at no apparent cost, there was no reason to oppose the foreigners. The land speculators of the 1880s usually just sailed away after obtaining the marks of islanders on pieces of paper and did not attempt to settle on the land they had purchased. Indeed, reports indicate that ni-Vanuatu viewed these men as particularly gullible. They did not hesitate to sell the same piece of land again and again, receiving each time a new supply of trade goods in return. Reporting on land purchases of the CCNH to the Governor of New Caledonia, a French naval commander wrote:

> The land possessions of this company are simply fictitious and they know it so well that they leave the use of it to the vendors without demanding the least due. They are not able to take possession of their purchases as that would require a considerable army. If the Kanaks were really dispossessed of the lands they sold, they would starve to death. For the simple sale is a mere formality which earns them guns, ammunition, pipes and tobacco. Thus they do not hesitate in selling the same piece of land two or three times over . . .[104]

Only when the CCNH sought to establish permanent settlers on their claims did ni-Vanuatu begin to realise what was happening and react with violence. By that time, however, it was often too late to block European settlement.

Higginson moved quickly to fill his newly acquired land with French settlers. He became a founding member and first President of a society established in France in October 1883 to bring colonists to Vanuatu — the Société Francaise de Colonisation.[105] Higginson's company made 10,000 hectares of prime land available to the Society,[106] and between 1885 and 1887, sent 28 families from France to settle in Vanuatu — 64 people in all — to whom the CCNH allocated a total of 680 hectares of land. There was, however, much dissatisfaction among the settlers:

> nothing had been organized in Noumea nor at Sandwich for the reception of the unhappy expatriates, almost all of whom arrived without resources — some old and feeble — people whose previous occupation had not prepared them in anyway to clear virgin land in a very harsh climate.[107]

They were, moreover, soon complaining about the operation of the company: low prices paid for produce, irregularity of shipping and difficulty in getting labour.[108]

The increasing activity of the CCNH in the early 1880s began to arouse the concern of the Presbyterian missionaries, who viewed the growing economic importance of the company as the prelude to possible French political control. Through their spokesman in Australia, the former resident missionary, John G. Paton, the Presbyterians mounted a campaign to bring to the attention of the British Government what they viewed as the growing threat of the French presence in Vanuatu:

> We have been informed by one of the missionaries in the island of Efate in the New Hebrides, that the French are purchasing large tracts of land in Pango Bay in that island & appear as if they intend to take possession of the whole island.
>
> They profess to have purchased the small island of Iriviki [sic], in Filli [sic] Harbour, which was bought many years ago by the Missionaries, as a mission station, and occupied as such for 3 or 4 years. Of this property the missionaries have the title deeds....
>
> We fear that if this spoliation of British property be overlooked, none of our mission property in the islands will be safe, & *if* France shall take possession of these islands, the result will be utterly destructive to the native population as well as of our mission.[109]

Failing to arouse the British Government to positive action, the Presbyterians in Victoria and New South Wales attempted to generate support for the establishment of an Australian company to compete with the CCNH. However, the refusal of the British Government to allow the registration of land titles purchased by British subjects in Vanuatu and the landing of French troops in 1886, discouraged Australian investors.[110]

Acting independently, resident missionaries moved to thwart French land purchases by acquiring land in the names of various missions to be held in trust for their island converts. The practice, in fact, had begun before the land rush of the 1880s. In September 1871, the people of Aniwa transferred the whole of their island to the Presbyterian mission:

> This is to certify that... we the undersigned chiefs and people of Aniwa do voluntarily and unanimously sell to the Revd John Gibson Paton Missionary on Aniwa, for the New Hebrides Mission, every inch and part of this our island...
> We are afraid of the destruction of life and property that have followed the settlement of Traders and Planters on the

> islands of Tanna, Erromanga [sic] & Efate, and have been thus led to desire to sell our island to the Mission, that the missionaries may be able to help prevent any of them from settling on our island of Aniwa.
>
> On the agreement that, excepting the parts of this island previously sold to the mission, on which the mission premises and church and the mission schools and teachers houses at villages are built, the mission will not take it from us so long as we need it for ourselves, but protect it from all foreigners for us and our children...[111]

The chiefs of all the districts signed the deed and received trade goods in return. One of the most important pieces of land acquired by the mission was the over 1,400 hectares of prime land at Erakor village close to Vila Harbour, which undoubtedly would have been acquired by European planters and speculators had the mission not come in between.[112]

By the end of the 1880s, the efforts of the Presbyterian missionaries to persuade Australians to expand their operations into Vanuatu finally succeeded. A group of wealthy businessmen agreed to contribute £100 each towards the establishment of what came to be known as the Australasian New Hebrides Company (ANHC), which was registered in Sydney in 1889. By 1891 there were 39 shareholders, including James Burns and Robert Philp of Burns, Philp and Company who already had a trading operation in the group. The directors of the company acted without pay and all shareholders were told that they would not receive dividends nor, in all probability, the return of their capital investment.[113]

A subsidy of £1,000 per year was secured from the New South Wales Government to run an inter-island steamship service and the Presbyterian Mission agreed to lay up its ship *Dayspring* and contribute a yearly subsidy of £1,500 to the company in return for an agreement to service all the mission stations in the group. Using an inter-island steamer as a floating trade-store, the ANHC quickly built up a successful business, selling goods to settlers and ni-Vanuatu and buying copra and other produce in return. French as well as British settiers preferred dealing with the ANHC rather than the CCNH, because of its more efficient service and generally lower prices.[114]

Trade was only one aspect of the Company's operation. Another was:

> to acquire by purchase, barter, lease, licence, reclamation or otherwise, portions of land and territory in the... New Hebrides group or in any other island...[115]

The ultimate aim was to encourage the settlement of British subjects in Vanuatu. In this regard, the Presbyterian Mission gave the Company its full support, declaring at its annual meeting in 1890, that "British subjects should be encouraged to settle in the group as traders and planters".[116] The Presbyterian missionaries were not now opposed to European land purchases in Vanuatu per se, but only to the French, whom they viewed as a negative influence due to their refusal to limit the sale of liquor and firearms. As a concession to the Mission, the ANHC refused to sell liquor, even to Europeans, or to barter firearms for land. It was, nevertheless, extremely successful in the early years of its operation.[117]

Starting in mid-1889, agents for the ANHC began purchasing large tracts of land on Santo and Epi as well as scattered parcels on Efate and Tanna.[118] As with earlier land transactions, it is unlikely that the ni-Vanuatu vendors understood the true meaning of the deeds they signed, nor were they by custom entitled to dispose of such large amounts of land. In some cases, however, the Company recognised the right of ni-Vanuatu to continue to occupy and use their land and appear to have made some effort to identify boundaries more carefully than had earlier land dealers. For example, on South Santo, the ANHC registered a deed at the Western Pacific High Commission in Suva for a parcel of land consisting of:

> all the land claimed by the Tangoans on Santo. Commencing at a marked tree on the coast which is the eastern boundary of the French land, about a third of a mile west of Abunan's village, thence running N5°W along the French boundary by blazed trees to a small creek in a westwardly course to Nakere, thence down Nakere to the creek called Wairikiriki passing marked trees by the main path and on the course of the said creek to Tapao to marked trees, thence onward on same course parallel with the coast line to the boundary of the land previously purchased by the Australian New Hebrides Company on the east side of the river Azone, thence running in inland along that boundary to the stream called Waikeze, the bushman's boundary, thence eastward along the bushmen's boundaries to the river called Wailapa, thence southwardly down said river to a marked Rao tree on the west bank, which marks the NE boundary of the P. Servil lot, thence westwardly along the shore four chains and seventy links to the place of starting: being estimated to contain three thousand five hundred acres more or less. The native vendors reserve to themselves their plantations and the breadfruit and coconuts on condition that the surplus fruits shall be sold to the company's agents when settled on

> the land, excepting such as shall be required for use by the resident missionary.[119]

The positive influence of the Mission is evident from the above, though there does not appear to have been any concern that ni-Vanuatu in effect had become tenant farmers, having lost control over their land, in that they were bound to sell their excess produce to the ANHC. Whether this was understood or could have been enforced in the long run is doubtful.

By 1891, the Company's plan to recruit settlers from Australia to develop its land was well under way. Nine settlers had been placed on 24,000 acres on the south coast of Santo. With the support of the Presbyterian Mission and the Federal Council of Australia, ANHC pressure was exerted on the Western Pacific High Commission to alter its policy regarding the recruitment of labour by British subjects. It also pressed the High Commission to take steps to enable British subjects to gain permanent title to their lands. The High Commission, however, would not change its policy on labour recruiting, and the resolution of the land issue was, in the 1890s, still beyond reach.[120] With little capital of their own, the Australian settlers were soon heavily in debt to their sponsoring company, which in 1892 refused to extend any more credit and evicted them after agreeing to cancel their debts.[121] From this time onwards, the ANHC concentrated on developing its trading operation in competition with the CCNH, and soon became the most important commercial firm in the group.[122]

Despite the failure of the Australian settlers and the difficulties faced by those recruited by Higginson, the number of European residents in the group began to increase rapidly. In 1891, there were 51 adult non-missionary British settlers, which was a three-fold increase over 1886, and over 70 French settlers. British subjects were the largest group of Europeans, since British missionaries and their families far outnumbered their French counterparts. With this increase in population, there was a corresponding increase in violence between Europeans and ni-Vanuatu. Between 1882 and 1886, the CCNH reported that 12 of its agents or settlers had been killed on various islands in the group, while others had been either wounded, threatened or forced to flee from their properties.[123] In 1891, one of the ANHC's settlers on Santo was killed soon after his arrival,[124] and there were numerous other attacks against Europeans.

Land was the major cause of the violence. When the French naval officer assured the Governor of New Caledonia that Higginson's company would not be able to take possession of the land they claimed to have purchased without a "considerable army", his interpretation of the situation was accurate. Although ni-Vanuatu on some islands had begun to view the presence of Europeans as less of a threat and certain aspects of European introduced culture as worthwhile and desirable, the potential for conflict still remained. Misunderstandings were inevitable between ni-Vanuatu and Europeans due to the quite different concepts relating to land ownership, transfer and use. As long as ni-Vanuatu were dominant politically, they were able to force Europeans to recognize these differences. In the late 1880s, however, the balance tipped in favour of Europeans — the British and French governments agreed to regular naval patrols in Vanuatu waters to protect the lives and property of their nationals.

2

The Condominium Land Tenure System

Vanuatu's political status at the end of the 19th century was unique in the Pacific. The nationals of Great Britain and France were competing, with neither group able to gain complete dominance. The British had established themselves first and in the greatest number, and by the 1870s it might have been expected that their influence would increase, leading eventually to full political control. Great Britain was the dominant colonial power in the region — being long established in Australia and New Zealand, having acquired Fiji as a crown colony, and with naval supremacy throughout the islands. The British could easily have had their way in Vanuatu, but their policy at that time did not favour acquiring more colonies, especially where the expense of administration could not be easily offset by substantial economic development. They only reluctantly accepted colonial responsibility for Fiji in order to prevent civil war between rival tribal groups, and they wanted to avoid being drawn into a similar situation in Vanuatu.[1] Since settler expansion had contributed substantially to internal disorder in Fiji, British policy aimed to limit their nationals' activity in Vanuatu by restrictions on the recruitment of island labour and in 1881, by ceasing to register land claims of British nationals.

While these policies did contribute to a reduction in British (and Australian) settlers, officials in London could not totally ignore political developments in Vanuatu as they were under constant pressure from British nationals there and in Australia to support British interests. While a number of early missionaries originated from Great Britain, very few 'British' settlers were ever involved in Vanuatu. Great Britain came to be one of the two administering powers, but it was primarily Australian — and to a lesser extent New Zealand — groups and business interests which sought to establish and expand their influence.

The Presbyterian and Anglican missionaries continued to expand and, being firmly established throughout most of the islands, were effective in attracting public support, though they were not always taken seriously by the British Government. As the number of French settlers began to increase during the late 1870s, the missionaries waged a strong campaign to convince officials in London to take positive action to thwart French colonial expansion, which they saw as the major cause of the increased violence and disorder in the islands. They were supported by groups in Australia whose motives were different. The attitude was widespread, extending to the highest levels of the colonial governments, that the British empire should extend into the islands of the South Pacific — an area seen as lying within the sphere of interest of the Australian colonies and the natural focus for their future economic exploitation and control.[2]

While the British Government was not moved by such arguments and calls for annexation, it did adopt the position that no other power should have the islands either. In 1878, an agreement was negotiated with France guaranteeing the independence and neutrality of Vanuatu. In fact, the request for the agreement came from the French Government and reflects far more their concern that the islands should not become British, rather than any worry on the part of officials in London that Vanuatu might be lost to France.[3] In addition, bowing to pressure from Australia and in Parliament, the British Government undertook in 1885 not to allow France to take control of the islands without consulting the Australians and ensuring that their interests were not compromised.[4] Indeed, Australian fears that Vanuatu might fall to France were not unfounded, but it was not until the mid-1880s that French interests in the islands were substantial enough to attract the serious attention of officials in Paris. The land purchases of John Higginson — dubious as they were — made France, potentially, the dominant economic power in Vanuatu. Many French interests (settlers, merchants and officials) wanted to see Higginson's vast paper claims confirmed by legitimate titles, which they believed would confirm the French position and ultimately force the British to withdraw.

The Joint Naval Commission

In April 1886, two French warships were dispatched to Vanuatu by the Governor of New Caledonia following the murder of several settlers. Troops were landed on Efate and at Port Stanley on Malakula. When reports were received by British officials that the troops were erecting barracks in the islands, concern was expressed in both Australia and London that the French intended more than a simple peace keeping mission.[5] The action does not appear to have been authorized by the French Government, and the French Minister of Marine and Colonies instructed the Governor of New Caledonia to hold the positions until further notice, but to take no steps towards annexation.[6]

The French were aware that they could not annex Vanuatu at that time without arousing considerable British opposition, but they were in no hurry to withdraw their forces. Their plan was to use the presence of their troops to force other concessions out of the British. In June, the French Ambassador in London raised the issues of fishing rights off the Newfoundland coast and the extension of the French Protectorate in the Society Islands.[7] When, in July, the British voiced their concern to the French regarding "the prolonged occupation by the French troops of points in the New Hebrides" and the fact that "the object for which they had been landed had not been fully answered", the French Ambassador in London expressed his regret "that during the past few months so few of the pending questions between France and Great Britain had been settled".[8]

In the end, it was the French who in July 1886 proposed that the two governments should begin negotiations regarding the situation in Vanuatu in order to "arrive at an arrangement providing for the security of their respective subjects".[9] The following month, the French Ambassador in London suggested an arrangement to enable the naval officers of both countries "to act as police, so as to avoid the appearance of an occupation".[10] The British responded positively and expressed their hope that the proposal would be carried out quickly in order to effect the withdrawal of French troops, whose presence had created much tension both in Britain and Australia.[11] Discussions dragged on for sixteen months before an agreement was finally reached in November 1887.

One of the complicating factors, which emerged early in the negotiations, was the land issue. In August 1886, the British Government received complaints from a long-time settler on Efate, Donald McLeod, claiming that the officer in charge of the French troops at Havannah Harbour had taken sides against him in a dispute over land along the shore-line of his property, resulting in the destruction of a fence. The issue centred on a difference between British and French law under which the latter did not recognize private ownership of lands within the *zone neutre de bord de mer* — all land 81 metres from the high water mark. At Havannah Harbour, McLeod had built his store and dock on such land and as a result, it was alleged, represented serious competition to the CCNH, the intimation being that it was for this reason that the French naval commander acted as he did.[12] It was also reported that a dispute had developed in the same area between ni-Vanuatu and the CCNH over lands which the local inhabitants claimed had not been sold to the Company, but which its agents had begun to fence.[13] As a result, the British Foreign Office protested to the French Government that:

> Her Majesty's Government do not believe that the Commanders of the French temporary posts in the New Hebrides have been authorized to dispossess any persons, native or foreign of their lands ... and urge that, in view of the importance of the matter, immediate instructions may be sent out by the French Government to prevent any risk of interference with the lands of any persons, native or foreign, on the part of the military authorities or the French Company, pending the constitution of the proposed Joint Commission.[14]

It was the British view that the settlement of land claims was:

> hardly a matter to be dealt with by naval officers, but more connected with civil administration.... these disputes should be settled by Consuls or special officers delegated for the purpose as civil Commissioners, but that their decisions should be enforced by the Naval Commission.... provision being made to that effect in the proposed Regulations.[15]

The documents available do not reveal the French response, if any, to the British protest and suggestions for settling land disputes and no further mention was made of the land issue until late 1887, when negotiations had reached their final stage.

After much delay, a Convention signed on 16 November 1887 provided that:

> A Joint Naval Commission shall be immediately constituted composed of British and French naval officers on the Pacific Stations, charged with the duty of maintaining order, and of protecting the lives and property of British subjects and French citizens in the New Hebrides.[16]

A declaration bringing the Convention into effect and the regulations for the guidance of the naval officers were signed by the two governments on 26 January 1888.[17]

The issue of land arose again following the initial signing of the Convention, when it was pointed out by officials in the British Colonial Office that the wording in two of the proposed regulations was ambiguous and could lead to abuses on the part of the CCNH, supported by the French Government. In the original version, the Naval Commissioner was empowered to act in order to protect the "lives and property" of British and French subjects. It was proposed, and eventually accepted by the French in the final version, that "life or property" should be used in place of "their lives and property", since the original wording confined the duty of the Commission to protecting the lives and property of British and French subjects only. The opinion in the Colonial Office was that the Commission should also "protect the natives from aggression by white persons".[18]

Officials in the Colonial Office also called attention to the 6th regulation:

> The Commission shall have no further or other powers than are expressly delegated to it by these Regulations, and no British or French officer shall interfere in disputes concerning the title to land, or dispossess of their lands any persons, natives or foreigners.

While originally a British suggestion, emanating from interference by French troops in the McLeod dispute in 1886, there was concern that as it stood, "it leaves it open to the French Company to forcibly drive out the natives and then claim the land as theirs".[19] Colonial Office officials, however, did not suggest an amendment and the wording remained unchanged.

The one alteration of the 6th regulation was the substitution of "shall not" in place of "no British or French officer shall". This was proposed by the French and was seized upon by British officials as an indication of:

> a readiness on the part of the French Government to agree to the appointment of a Mixed Civil Tribunal for the settlement of conflicting claims to land, and other differences between French and English subjects.[20]

It is clear from earlier comments by British officials, that such a solution to the land problem was their ultimate goal. However, since no provision was written into the agreement authorizing the setting up of such a tribunal and — as subsequent events would reveal — since the French had quite different objectives from the British regarding the resolution of land disputes, no progress was made until the founding of the Condominium in 1906. In order to get at least some structure in place to provide order — inadequate as it may have been — the British were willing to allow further discussion of the matter to wait. The failure of the two governments to establish a system for settling land disputes was, in the long term, a great advantage for the French — and as future events would reveal, was indeed their intention — since it enabled their nationals to operate with little restraint. French officials saw the agreement as a means to hold off the British long enough to allow their nationals to strengthen their position in Vanuatu. The French Minister of the Navy ordered naval commanders "to combat English influence by all legal means, to eliminate as much as possible British interests from the archipelago and substitute French interests".[21] The emphasis was to be on taking possession of as much of the land claimed by Higginson as possible, through a scheme of subdivision and settlement of French planters.

While laying claim to well over half the land area of Vanuatu, French companies and individuals had in fact occupied only a small portion of their properties. The problem was how to convert these paper claims into plantations. By the 1890s, Higginson had begun to organize the transport of further French settlers to Vanuatu with the intention of developing the land he claimed on islands outside Efate, but he was on the verge of bankruptcy and the French Government was forced to come to his assistance. In 1894, the Government reorganized the Company under the name Société Francaise des Nouvelles-Hébrides (SFNH) and assumed majority interest and control.

SFNH agents operated throughout the group, but Epi became the focus of the Company's operation. Properties were divided on maps into 50 hectare blocks and offered to new *colons.* Upon their arrival they discovered that their boundaries often included villages or gardens planted by ni-Vanuatu, who denied the Europeans access to the lands as they did not recollect selling them. In 1890 ni-Vanuatu were pulling out boundary markers from land surveyed for the CCNH.[22] Numerous disputes arose, and Epi became the *cause célebre* for English missionaries, who by the end of the century were leading the campaign to force the British Government to restrain the French and establish a more effective administration. In 1899, the Presbyterian Mission published what it called a "Memorial on French Aggressions in the New Hebrides", which received wide circulation abroad:

> On the Island of Epi matters have now reached a condition that is simply intolerable. Land, in varying-sized lots, along

> the shore, has been acquired from time to time by the French New Hebrides Company. These pieces of land, according to the unanimous testimony of the vendors, in all cases were strictly coast lands, and did not extend far inland. It now appears that for the purpose of making a French Settlement on Epi, a plan of the French Company's property on Epi has been prepared showing the situation and extent of the said property, as divided into allotments. This plan is secret and no British subject is supposed to see it. This secret plan discloses the astonishing fact that the claim of the French Company includes the whole of the west coast of Epi from the Foreland to and inclusive of Lamenu Point, excepting the property of the late G. Facio and M. Blanc, and stretching inland to a uniform depth of nearly three miles, the back boundary running parallel to the coast. This area includes whole inland villages which have never had any dealings with the French Company.[23]

The tract outlined the various phases in the dispute, including the destruction of schools and a village by French colonists and agents of the SFNH.

The role of the Joint Naval Commission was equivocal in the Epi affair. The British captain held that the Commission had no jurisdiction since it was a land matter, while the French captain became overtly involved, holding meetings to discuss title-deeds and boundaries and openly encouraging the French colonists to resist.[24] The role played by the French naval commander is not surprising, given the instructions issued by the Minister of the Navy in Paris, that they "must not only be the protectors of our nationals in the New Hebrides... this role must be more militant".[25] Thus, while the French flaunted the rules to achieve their objectives, the British dutifully followed orders and did nothing to stop them, even though their actions violated the terms of the Joint Naval Commission. Such would be the pattern of joint administration which would characterize Anglo-French rule in Vanuatu until independence in 1980.

The 1906 Convention

The failure of the Joint Naval Commission to deal adequately with the increasing disorder in Vanuatu in the last decade of the 19th century was due primarily to the fact that Britain and France did not address themselves to the root cause of the violence — the problem of European land alienation. The initial British reluctance during discussions to establish the Joint Naval Commission to allow the naval commanders to deal with land matters — which they realized too late left the door open to widespread abuses against ni-Vanuatu — had the predicted effect. As the case on Epi indicates, French settlers could simply move onto land they claimed and, supported by gunboats there to "protect" them, forceably drive out the local inhabitants.

France's more aggressive policy in Vanuatu was due partly to the fact that by the end of the 19th century, the French Government itself had a vested interest in seeing the position of French settlers strengthened and their land claims validated. By the later 1880s, the CCNH was in financial difficulty and the French Government had agreed to come to its assistance. In 1888, the Company was granted a subsidy in return for establishing a mail and shipping service between New Caledonia and Vanuatu.[26] Higginson's financial problems grew worse and in 1894 the French Government took control of the company, which was reconstituted as the Société Francaise des Nouvelles-Hébrides (SFNH) and promised an annual subsidy of 360,000 francs. Higginson ceased to play an active role in the new company, but retained a small share interest. The new director was to be appointed by the Ministry for Colonies and paid for by the SFNH.[27] In Article 5 of the Convention establishing the SFNH, the French Government officially recognized the land titles of the CCNH in Vanuatu. Thus, the need to validate the claims of the SFNH gave France a clear reason for finding a solution to the land problem. However, because the French were finding it impossible to take control by force, as shown by the increasing violence associated with the establishment of French settlers, other means had to be found.

Responding to pressure from their own nationals in Vanuatu and Australia, the British finally took the initiative to correct the situation. In March 1901, they proposed to the French that the two governments convene a special commission to review land titles. In June, the French agreed in principle, but the start of formal discussions was delayed due to a basic difference of opinion between the two governments regarding the powers and functions of such a lands commission. The British view was that the validity of titles should be tested by enquiring into the manner in which they were acquired, as had been the basis on which the lands commissions of Fiji and Samoa had operated. The French, on the other hand, were intent upon obtaining a procedure which would accept title-deeds at face value and not enquire into the actual transaction on which they were purported to be based. They responded to the British proposal with the suggestion that the powers of the Joint Naval Commission should be extended to settle land disputes. The British view was that in most cases the validity of the title-deeds was the reason for the disputes and thus they continued to press for a full-scale lands commission.[28]

In August 1901, the French finally agreed that a special commission on land titles should be established and in October the British submitted a draft agreement setting out the procedures such a commission might follow, including power to investigate and decide upon "all claims of British subjects and French citizens to land in the New Hebrides, whether acquired from natives or from aliens" and "all the circumstances affecting their validity". No claim would be certified as valid:

> 1. Unless the agreement by which the lands or interest in lands was granted was reduced into writing, and was duly signed by the grantor, or some person duly authorized by him;
> 2. Unless the Commission are satisfied that the proper persons were parties to the transaction by which the land or interest in the lands was acquired, and that it may be reasonably presumed that they understood the nature and terms thereof;
> 3. If based upon mere promises to sell or options to buy, or if obtained by fraudulent or other improper means;
> 4. Where the agreement by which the land or interest in lands was granted contained, at the time it was signed, no description of the lands conveyed sufficiently accurate to enable the Commission to define the boundaries thereof;
> 5. If made without valuable adequate consideration, regard being had to the circumstances existing at the time of the agreement.
> 6. Unless all of the terms and conditions upon which such agreement was made, which ought, prior to the inquiry by the grantee, have been reasonably and substantially performed by him.[29]

In cases where a title was found to be defective, but the land in question had been acquired "in good faith" and "improved or cultivated", the Commission could confirm title "in whole or in part upon the payment by the occupant to the person or persons entitled thereto of an additional sum".[30] This last clause had the potential of neutralizing the power of the six points listed above. However, since little land had been developed by this time, it is unlikely that large tracts of fraudulently obtained land would have been permanently alienated. Clearly, a commission empowered to investigate the validity of all claims and confirm titles in disputed cases through proof of actual occupancy, would have rejected the vast majority of the claims held by French individuals and companies. The French

Government, therefore, retreated to its former suggestion that the powers of the Joint Naval Commission should be expanded to deal with land disputes.[31]

The British continued to press the French for agreement, but no firm commitment could be obtained until, in April 1904, due to the growing threat of war in Europe, the two governments signed a declaration with the intent of settling the outstanding colonial questions existing between them. At the request of the French, a conference was convened in London on 1 February 1906 to look into the nature of the enquiry which should be held into land cases. However, by the time the two governments had agreed to begin discussions, it had been decided — again, at the suggestion of the French Government — that the scope of the conference should be enlarged to deal with the larger question of sovereignty.[32]

At the first meeting, the delegates launched straight into a discussion of the problem of settling land disputes. The British view was that the draft agreement of 26 October 1901, which proposed the setting up of a lands commission to investigate all lands claims, should serve as the basis of discussion. The French delegates, however, argued that the 1901 proposals had been superseded by the 1904 declaration of intent, which they understood as suggesting "the establishment of a Commission to decide disputes between French citizens and British subjects; and not those between European settlers and natives".[33] The French were opposed to investigating undisputed claims and only favoured the establishment of a "Mixed Tribunal to decide contested cases as they arose".[34] Their aim, therefore, was to limit investigations to those small areas in which European settlement had actually taken place and where disputes had arisen. In this way, they would protect the vast areas of unoccupied land included in the dubious claims of French nationals and companies — in particular, those of the SFNH.

Before proceeding further, it was decided that the Commission should first attempt to "elaborate some form of administration which should have the effect of a Condominium or Joint Protectorate without the name".[35] Thus, on the second day of the conference, the British presented to the Commission what was termed a rough "Basis of an Agreement", which served as the framework for discussion in subsequent meetings and, after substantial modification, became the Convention of 1906, establishing the Condominium of the New Hebrides.

Having thus agreed in principle to the establishment of some form of joint administration for Vanuatu, the Commission returned to the problem of settling land disputes. The focus of the discussion was

Article 15 of the "Basis of an Agreement", which laid out a possible procedure for dealing with land claims and incorporated substantial British concessions on several key issues. Most important, the British were prepared to drop the idea of an *ad hoc* commission to settle land claims, proposing instead that the Court, which was to deal with civil suits and criminal offences, should also have jurisdiction over all land matters. In deciding on land claims, the Court would use the same criteria as laid out in the 1901 draft agreement (see above), but "in cases were land acquired in good faith has been improved or cultivated upon a title which is found defective", the British were willing to accept a compromise which would make it less likely that ni-Vanuatu land rights would be protected. They accepted the principle of occupation as conferring validity and substituted in place of the specific criteria laid down for dealing with defective land claims, the principle that the Court should decide such cases by merely following a direction "to effect a just and equitable compromise of all matters in dispute".[36]

Despite these major concessions, the French spoke out strongly against accepting Article 15 as it stood. Even though the British had already agreed not to press for a lands commission and conceded that in certain cases, occupation and improvements took precedent over title-deeds, the French attacked the whole concept of accepting written agreements, basing their argument on the "social conditions prevailing among the New Hebrides natives". In the opinion of M. Picanon, "the natives were mostly illiterate and subsequently unable to sign their names". In addition, he felt that the "untrustworthiness of the native witnesses, their venality, and the impossibility of finding them" would make adoption of the British proposals impossible.[37] M. Picanon's aim was to convince the Commission that there ought to be a fixed period beyond which claims could not be contested under any conditions, that a distinction should be drawn between "legislation for the past and legislation for the future". Once the Condominium had been established, he argued, it would be "possible to determine the conditions under which land would be acquired in the future", but the two governments were "not responsible for what had happened in the past".[38]

At stake were the claims to hundreds of thousands of hectares of land acquired by the SFNH since the 1880s, control of which the French Government sought to legitimize. They knew the proposed Court would reject most of these claims, applying the criteria laid out in Article 15, since only a minute proportion of the land had actually been occupied. The statistics presented to the Commission by the French delegation themselves revealed the nature of SFNH land claims: of the 776,843 hectares claimed by the company, only 434,843 hectares were detailed in title-deeds. The remaining 342,000 hectares was only an estimate — the exact area, the French explained, was not known.[39]

The other key issue, therefore, was the degree of importance which the proposed Court should give to actual occupancy in deciding land claims. The British position was that "effective occupation" should be maintained, since recognizing all land claims where occupation had not occurred would "inevitably lead to insurrections as soon as the claims were asserted". Sir Eldon Gorst stated bluntly that the British intention was "not only to prevent an injustice to the natives, but also to prohibit an undue absorption of great quantities of land".[40] The French argued that "local conditions" rendered this principle "impossible", and wanted all deeds dating more than ten years back and duly registered, accepted without further investigation.[41] The following day, the French presented a series of amendments which they assured the Commission were intended "in every case... to adopt as far as possible the form and spirit" of the original proposals and to "show their good will and conciliatory attitude towards the British contentions".[42] In fact, the amendments amounted to almost total rejection of the British position and the introduction of new concepts designed to enable French nationals — and in particular the SFNH — to acquire full title to the vast amount of land they claimed only on paper.[43]

The French amendments provided for procedures to deal with two categories of land disputes: cases involving registered title-deeds more than ten years old at the signature of the proposed convention, which could only be contested if they were not signed, and all others since that date and in future. For the latter category involving disputes between natives and non-natives, rules were laid down for the Court, with non-native claims being established on evidence of occupancy of three years and material improvements and/or by the submission of title-deeds. This was a significant change in that the French proposed that the Court could accept mere occupation and signs of improvement as grounds for granting permanent title to non-natives — no deed of sale would be required. Under the original British proposals, the claims of non-natives would not be considered without title-deeds. The implication of this new proposal was that a non-native could simply establish himself on a piece of land, develop it and claim title through the Court.

Where title-deeds existed, as the British proposed, disputes would only be admitted if it could be established that the deeds were not signed properly, the vendor did not understand the effect of the sale, the deed was obtained by improper means (i.e. violence or fraud) or the conditions of the deed had not been fulfilled. An obvious omission, however, in the French amendments was the stipulation, included in the British "Basis of an Agreement" that the deed must include a description of the lands conveyed "significantly accurate to allow the Court to define the boundaries".[44] Under the French proposals, the Court would be empowered to investigate and determine boundaries for disputed properties. Given the vague, ill-defined boundaries on the deeds of most French claims, it is clear why they chose the latter course of action.

Like the British proposals, the French also allowed for the confirmation of title when a deed was found defective, but the land had been improved or cultivated. In disputes between non-natives, the Court would be bound by the law of the defendant's country. They also provided for the Court to confirm title when it had decided on the validity of a claim under dispute. The British proposed issuing a certificate, while the French envisaged the setting up of a land register. The functions and powers of the land register, outlined in a new section (Article XVI), included one extremely important clause — the French proposed that in the absence of a dispute, anyone could require the Court to enter in the land register a title-deed, and receive a copy thereof, which would "constitute a conclusive title to land".[45] Since the ni-Vanuatu owners of much of the land under claim would not have been aware that their land had been 'sold', there would be few challenges to registration. This last provision was extremely important to the French in that it would facilitate the confirmation of title to the land claimed by the SFNH. However, even where there were disputes, the proposed system for dealing with land suits was so heavily weighted in favour of foreign claimants that the expropriation of the vast amount of land under claim by French individuals and companies would be assured.

On the following day, 7 February 1906, Sir Eldon Gorst responded on behalf of the British delegation. The British still found it impossible to accept that title-deeds more than ten years old, and registered in Fiji or Noumea, should be validated without question. He argued that British public opinion was "exceedingly sensitive in regard to the treatment of natives" and demanded that they should be dealt with justly:

> extending perhaps beyond the limits of the strict justice applicable as between Europeans, on the grounds that civilized countries ought not to allow their nationals to take advantage, even under the cover of a strict legal transaction, of the weakness and ignorance of savage races.[46]

He pointed out further, that while the British had agreed to drop the idea of a lands commission, they were not prepared to take away the power of the proposed Court to investigate title-deeds "as it may see fit in order to secure substantial justice."[47] Given the fact that by this point, the British had dropped all other objections to the French proposals, Gorst's moralistic comments seem less than convincing.

The French delegates immediately objected to the phrase, that the Court should decide "as it may see fit in order to secure substantial justice", arguing that a precise method of procedure should be substituted.[48] The following day, they voiced further dissatisfaction with Gorst's comments, which they interpreted as an attack on their own motives. M. Saint-Germain pointed out that his delegation:

> acknowledge the lofty sentiments which animate the British Delegates. But they are convinced that their colleagues cannot attribute different intentions to them. Public opinion is not less sensitive in France than in England on the question of the treatment of natives....
>
> But they would also consider it most regrettable that, under cover of a loosely worded text, unscrupulous businessmen could take advantage of native ignorance to sweep away honourable interests, acquired in good faith by English and French subjects.[49]

All the delegates in the Commission — both British and French — knew that it was "unscrupulous businessmen" who had created the land problem in Vanuatu in the first place. It had become obvious that the French proposals were designed to achieve international recognition of the dubious land claims of their nationals at the expense of the indigenous population and to ensure that other European businessmen did not displace their own. Gorst left no doubt as to the degree of the British commitment to the "lofty sentiments" he had so eloquently expressed. But his immediate reply to the French diplomatic double-talk was unfortunately British double-talk:

> nothing could have been further from their [his colleagues and himself] thoughts than to suggest that the French Government or the French nation were less zealous for the welfare and protection of native races than the British....[50]

The French then proceeded to press the British to accept their position regarding title-deeds more than ten years old. The British finally agreed that such deeds should be treated differently from those acquired more recently, and on the following day both delegations presented a new set of amendments.

In the British version — their last show of resistance — it was proposed that deeds more than ten years old could only be questioned if they were not properly signed, had been obtained by improper means (e.g. fraud or violence) or if the land did not belong to the vendor, but to some other individual or tribe.[51] The French version contained the vague provision that a challenge to such deeds would be admitted only if it could be proved by an individual or chief that "he or his tribe possesses an effective right to enjoy and use the contested property, and that this right has been infringed".[52] Both versions included provision for the Court to reserve portions of a claim for indigenous claimants when it decided against admitting a dispute. The French, however, added a catch-all provision, which would still achieve their desired aim of blocking any effective challenge to the majority of their claims:

> Title-deeds which received *de facto* recognition by reason of transactions between non-natives for valuable consideration shall never be disputed.[53]

In other words, if a property had been sold subsequent to the original transaction — even if the original deed were proved to be totally fraudulent — it could not be contested. At this point the British capitulated. Except for a few minor suggestions to the wording, they raised no further objections. On 27 February 1906 the final text was confirmed officially, along with the other articles establishing the Condominium.[54]

In summary, the system adopted for dealing with land claims was set out in a Convention which provided for the establishment of a Joint Court, consisting of three judges: one British, one French and a third appointed by the King of Spain, who was to act as President. The Joint Court had jurisdiction in land matters and clear principles were laid down on which it could make its judgments, with the focus of its attention to be on the title-deeds presented as part of the applications for registration. The Court could register claims based on either three years of occupation, on a title-deed coupled with occupation, or on a title-deed alone. The deeds would not be questioned by the Court — as would have been the case if Britain and France had agreed to the setting up of a lands commission — unless the application for registration of a claim were challenged. As in the Torrens system,[55] proof of impropriety regarding a transaction rested with the challenger.

The grounds on which a title-deed could be challenged were,

however, extremely limited. A title-deed relating to a transaction which took place after 31 December 1895 could be challenged on the grounds that it had not been signed properly, that the vendor did not understand the agreement, that the agreement was obtained by improper means, that the terms and conditions of the agreement had not been fulfilled or that the property did not belong to the vendor or his tribe (Article XXII, paragraph 4). If, however, the title-deed related to a transaction before 1 January 1896, and had been registered in Fiji, New Caledonia or Vanuatu, it could only be challenged on even more limited grounds — by persons who had an existing right to occupy the land in question and whose right would be infringed by registration, and then only if the land had not been sold by one non-native to another in good faith and for valuable consideration (Article XXII, paragraph 5).

Despite the fact that under the Condominium system established in 1906 the registration of European land claims was now all but assured, provisions were included that recognized the existence of native interests. The Convention allowed for the appointment of a Native Advocate to represent ni-Vanuatu before the Court and gave the Court power: "When ever it shall consider it necessary... [to] assign to native claimants reserves of land in proportion to their requirements" (Article XXII, paragraph 3). It is significant that the decision to grant native reserves was left to the Court, to be based on information which it might have or acquire. No principles were laid down to guide the Court in its decisions. The French had insisted on fixing rules and conditions to guide the Court in registering land, but only where European interests were at stake.

The same criticism could be applied to the provision which allowed the two High Commissioners or their representatives (i.e. the Resident Commissioners) to declare as native reserves, land which was not under claim prior to the signing of the Convention whenever they:

> jointly consider that the amount of lands acquired from the natives in one of the islands of the Group is so great that the land remaining undisposed of is indispensable for the needs of the natives, they may prohibit any new sale or grant of land in such island to non-natives (Article XXVII, paragraph 8).

Again, the Convention did not provide principles or guidelines for determining these needs. Moreover, given the great difference in the perceptions of the two governments of the need to protect native interests and the fact that such decisions required agreement, it is obvious that the provision would have little effect.[56]

The priority given to European interests over those of indigenous ni-Vanuatu was also evident in various other aspects of the administrative structure laid down by the Convention. Vanuatu, including the Banks and Torres Islands, were recognised as a "region of joint influence", with each power "retaining jurisdiction over its subjects or citizens, and neither exercising a separate control over the group" (Article I). Within Vanuatu, French and British nationals remained subject to the laws of their respective countries in all matters not contrary to the provisions of the Convention or regulations made under it. The subjects of other countries were given six months to decide under which legal system they wished to live. Natives were defined as "any person of the aboriginal races of the Pacific who is not a citizen or subject or under the protection of either of the two Signatory Powers" (Article VIII). They were prohibited from acquiring within the group the "status of subject or citizen or be under the protection of either of the two Signatory Powers". The Resident Commissioners were, however, given authority over native affairs, including the power to make and enforce regulations binding on the various tribes. Ni-Vanuatu were, in effect, stateless. Moreover, their affairs were made the responsibility of, not one, but two foreign governments with significantly different attitudes — as evident from the above discussion — relating to the treatment of colonized peoples.

The High Commissioners of Fiji and New Caledonia were to be responsible for administration, acting through Resident Commissioners in Port Vila. They were given power to issue local ordinances binding on all inhabitants of the group and to impose penalties to ensure their enforcement. Separate police forces were to be established under the control of each of the Resident Commissioners (Article II). Each Government agreed to finance its own administration, while expenses of a joint nature would be paid for out of local taxes, postal and other joint revenue (Article V). Specific regulations were also included relating to shipping (Articles XXVII-XXX); recruitment of native labour (Articles XXXI-LVI); the sale of arms, ammunition and intoxicating liquors (Articles LVII-LXI); and the establishment and administration of municipalities (Articles LXII-LXVII).

There were two National Courts, presided over respectively by a British and French judge, and criminal cases involving British or French subjects would come under the relevant National Court. The Joint Court had jurisdiction in all land and civil cases, over suits between natives and non-natives and in cases of the former against the latter. Either French or English could be used in the Joint Court, but in cases between British subjects and French citizens, the judgments would be drawn up in both languages. There was provision for the appointment of an official advocate to assist and represent ni-Vanuatu before the Court, the cost of which was to be paid for from the joint budget. The judgments of the Joint Court were to be final —there was no provision for appeal (Articles X-XXI).

Thus in a few weeks, Great Britain and France resolved a problem which had plagued their relations for decades. The French had achieved considerable success in the Conference, as their chief delegate reported:

> If we really wish to consider the vital importance that the question of land tenure has for the New Hebrides... France is consolidating in the most advantageous way its economic predominance, a base for the political supremacy to which it aspires.[57]

While full political control remained beyond their reach for the time being, the provisions dealing with land provided the French with the legal means which they believed would enable them ultimately to attain their goal.

The key section, stipulating that the validity of deeds registered before 1 January 1896 which had passed between Europeans for "valuable consideration" could not be questioned, meant that over 300,000 hectares of land which John Higginson had purchased from other Europeans between 1882 and 1887 could not be contested. In addition, 400,000 hectares which he 'bought' directly from ni-Vanuatu and registered before 1 January 1896, could only be challenged with great difficulty (Article XXII, paragraph 5). Moreover, the administrative and judicial structures which the French delegates negotiated at the Conference were also designed to serve French long-term interests. The powers of the joint administration were curtailed, while those of the national administrations were given considerable freedom of action.[58]

The French were clearly not moved by British arguments during the Conference that the two governments had a moral responsibility to safeguard indigenous interests. Their attitude reflected the prevailing point of view at the end of the 19th century among most European colonialists, that it was inevitable and indeed right that the more 'civilized' nations of Europe should come to dominate the rest of the world. Writing in 1908, the French jurist, Nicholas Politis, argued that the British were in error in suggesting that all land transactions between ni-Vanuatu and foreigners should be investigated prior to registration to determine the legality of the sales. Politis' reasoning was that when a foreigner acquired property in a "civilized country", the laws of that country applied when disputes arose. However, when a dispute arose involving a foreigner in a country where "no local law exists, there is no conflict; the law of the country of the purchaser prevails . . ."[59] In his view, the indigenous people had no right to challenge the legality of European land transactions. He argued further that properly constituted land commissions did not protect the rights of indigenous people and that the British had used such institutions to facilitate the annexation of New Zealand in 1840 and Fiji in 1874: "by using an act of justice, vis-a-vis the indigenous people, to justify the conquest of their country".[60] Politis' point is that the economic base of British settlers was assured by invalidating some of the more blatant cases of fraudulent land transactions.[61] The French considered their position in 1906 as more honest than the British.

Indeed, Sir Eldon Gorst's closing remarks at the Conference raise some doubts about British intentions. He praised the Commission for having reached an agreement which would "promote the welfare of the British and French colonists in those distant islands".[62] He did not mention the welfare of ni-Vanuatu. If he meant his earlier statements about Great Britain's commitment to preventing "injustice to the natives" and prohibiting "undue absorption of great quantities of land,"[63] then the British agreement to establish the Condominium system was naive and short-sighted:

> The whole agreement reeked of arm-chair theory, the questions that practical administrators would have asked were nowhere considered. No one stopped to ask how will it work? No one considered the everyday control of the native populations. An equipoise on paper was what the diplomats needed — a footnote to the *Entente Cordiale;* and then a relegation of the matter to obscurity.[64]

The 1906 Convention would allow the French to achieve what the British knew was their main objective: to validate French land claims. Moreover, the British were aware of the duplicity of French Government policy as demonstrated during the Joint Naval Commission. Gorst had, however, predicted what would happen, in many cases sixty years later: that recognizing all claims to land where occupation had not followed would "inevitably lead to insurrection as soon as the claims were asserted". Indeed, when the balance of political power shifted back in favour of ni-Vanuatu in the 1960s and 1970s, land became the catalyst for the independence movement, just as it had been the issue which had led to their loss of sovereignty in 1906.

The Protocol of 1914

The deficiencies in the Condominium system established by the Convention of 1906 soon became apparent. The limited powers of the joint administration and wide field of action left to the national administrations served the French very well — as they intended. The French planter community expected French officials to do everything possible to assist their settlers to establish themselves on the land which had been allocated by the SFNH — even if there was a dispute — and not to apply too strictly the regulations relating to the recruitment and employment of native labour.[65] In the words of Edward Jacomb, a Sorbonne-trained lawyer who had resigned his post as Assistant to the British Resident Commissioner to set up a local practice, the French Residency was most obliging:

> It has frankly regarded the Group as French, and has with difficulty tolerated the presence of the British Administration at all. Its object has been to push French interests. If they could be pushed without quarrelling with the British Residency so much the better; but they had to be pushed on in some way. It has been perfectly prepared to make personal attacks on members of the British Administration, or to do anything else with this one object in view — the advancement of French interests.[66]

In Jacomb's opinion, the British Residency played into the hands of the French:

> It always pursued a policy of unswerving loyalty to the spirit of the Condominium. No attempt has ever been made to advance the British interests at the expense of the French, either by encouragement of the British settler or by endeavouring to secure a preponderence of influence over the natives. The work at the British Residency has been purely of a routine nature, and the utmost care has been taken never to offend French susceptibilities. Better that a thousand injustices should take place than that the French Resident Commissioner should be annoyed. Its strength has been to sit still.[67]

The pattern which had emerged with the establishment of the Joint Naval Commission was continuing — while the French flaunted the rules, the British stood by, watched and dutifully followed orders.

When, for example, plantation labourers on Efate — assisted by Jacomb — began taking their employers to court for abuses and infringements of the Convention's regulations, the French Resident Commissioner, M. Repiquet, attempted to muzzle the Joint Court. He insisted that the recruitment and employment of labourers was an administrative matter outside the jurisdiction of the Joint Court and argued that the Public Prosecutor had no right to initiate prosecutions against French nationals on such matters unless requested to do so by the Resident Commissioner himself. In any case, if a planter were convicted in the Joint Court, the execution of sentence was left to the National Courts. The result was that British offenders usually had to pay their fines, while French offenders generally did not.[68]

The division of jurisdiction between the Joint Court and the National Courts also hampered the former's operation when it came to more serious offences. Breaches of the regulations relating to employment and recruiting were treated as "infringements" and thus were dealt with by the Joint Court, while the more serious offences of kidnapping, for example, which involved the use of violence, constituted a felony and was therefore a matter for the National Courts. One French judge in particular, J.Calonna, was notorious for supporting the settler community: "anyone who committed a crime against a native whilst furthering the colonising mission of France was assured a sympathetic hearing".[69] In 1911, a Frenchman by the name of Leclerc shot and killed a Santo man. The man, along with 16 others, had been enticed on board Leclerc's ship and was shot while trying to escape. Leclerc was convicted of murder in the French National Court, but was immediately released under the *lois de suris*.[70] A British crew member was convicted by the British judge as an accessory and served his six month jail sentence.[71]

Writing about his experiences as the first British Judge, Gilchrist Alexander described the failure of the French Judges and Residency officials to carry out their obligations to uphold the laws of the Condominium as laid down in the Convention of 1906:

> From all that one heard, offences against the Convention, such as illegal recruiting and the sale of liquor to natives, were of frequent constant occurrence throughout the group. We judges, however, depended on the executive authorities to bring the offenders before us for trial... the infrequent British offender was brought expeditiously before the Court and tried summarily. His fine was levied and paid promptly.[72]

Of the £28.8s fines inflicted on British subjects by the Joint Court between April 1911 and November 1912, £16.19s was collected, the rest being due from one man who had left Vanuatu and another who was penniless in jail. But of the £456.14s 8d imposed on French citizens, only £65.13s 6d was collected.[73]

Land matters were another area in which the French were able to take advantage of the divided authority. The native Advocate — Dr. Borgesius, a Dutch lawyer appointed in 1911 to represent ni-Vanuatu interests in the courts — should have been primarily concerned with land cases. The French, however, made sure there was no transport available and the French Resident Commissioner vetoed a suggestion that he be allowed to travel on the British Resident Commissioner's yacht.[74] Edward Jacomb, therefore, filled the gap. He travelled around the islands gathering information on disputes where settlers were attempting to establish themselves on land which ni-Vanuatu claimed had never been sold. He warned settlers and encouraged ni-Vanuatu to resist European encroachment on their land.[75]

The French planter community was outraged at Jacomb's activities, accusing him in their local newspaper *Le Néo-Hébridais* of "counselling the *canaques* to oppose, by force if necessary, all new land-clearing".[76] Many of the incidents involved new settlers who had been given blocks of land by the SFNH and discovered when they sought to take possession that local people did not accept that the lands had been alienated. Epi was again a focal point of dispute where the murder of the settler, Guittel, evoked an outcry for the administration to instigate much harsher measures to reduce the threat against Europeans throughout the islands.[77] Because of his encouragement of ni-Vanuatu to resist European settlement, Jacomb was accused of instigating the Guittel murder.[78]

Jacomb was motivated to support ni-Vanuatu because of the situation created by the signing of the 1906 Convention. While a system for dealing with the land problem had been established, it was clear that the Joint Court would not be in a position to begin hearing land claims for years. In the meantime, however, the Court had ruled that it had no power to issue injunctions preventing a settler from entering land he claimed.[79] Thus, there was a real inducement for planters to establish and maintain themselves by force on land which they claimed — even if they had no title — since there were no legal means to stop them. In the distant future, when the Joint Court did finally get around to dealing with their cases, the planters could use occupation and improvement in support of their applications for registration. A typical example was reported at a conference of the Protestant Churches held on Paama in June 1913:

> On September 24, 1912, it was brought to the notice of the Joint Court that a French subject, named Courtois, had recently established himself on a 60 acre block of land at Vila Harbour, under concession granted him by the French New

> Hebrides Company, which lands had been from time immemorial in possession of the local natives, and which they had never sold. It appears that when the French company's surveyors placed land marks on this and neighbouring ground after survey, the local natives removed the same, and were thereupon ordered by the French Resident to replace them. When, however, the natives applied to the French Resident for protection against M. Courtois to prevent encroachment upon their land until such time as the Joint Court should be in a position to determine the matter, no answer was vouchsafed; but M. Courtois was left to continue his planting operations unchecked by the French authorities.[80]

Under the circumstances, Jacomb advised ni-Vanuatu to resist by force, if necessary, any attempt to dispossess them of their land — there was no alternative course of action open to them.

The result was that the jails were soon filled with ni-Vanuatu who had, in the eyes of Condominium officials taken the law into their own hands.[81] In reality, however, there was no effective law and order in Vanuatu during this period — certainly no means to protect the rights of ni-Vanuatu — since the Condominium system allowed French officials to condone activities by their nationals, which the British Government would not have agreed to in 1906 when it signed the Convention. But the British — true to form — were unwilling to confront their colleagues with the fact that the spirit of the Convention was being undermined.

The weakness of the Condominium system was further evidenced by the fact that its authority did not extend much beyond Port Vila and its environs. In the islands, the Joint Naval Commission continued to deal with cases of violence and disorder — arresting, detaining and sentencing ni-Vanuatu for offences against Europeans and ni-Vanuatu as well. This was illegal, since the 1906 Convention had set up a judicial system to deal with such problems. For Condominium officials, however, there was no alternative but to allow the naval commanders to continue to operate as they always had, since the Condominium Administration had neither the personnel nor the money to project their power into the islands. In 1911, the two High Commissioners agreed to appoint 'Condominium Agents' as a way to extend the authority of the joint administration. A French Condominium Agent was sent to Malakula and the British stationed a man on Tanna, but their presence did little to reduce the disorder that had become widespread throughout the group.[82]

In 1913, the British finally moved to correct the situation which allowed France to make a farce of the Convention. They called for a conference, which met between June and August 1914, with the intention of changing those aspects of the original Convention of 1906 which enabled French officials to condone the misdeeds of their nationals. The aim of the British was:

> to remedy the evils arising from divided control by increasing the scope and powers of the joint authority, both administrative and judicial, and correspondingly limiting the scope and powers of the National Administrations and National Courts.[83]

Clearly on the defensive, the French delegation:

> laid great stress upon the retention by each Power of the sovereignty over its own nationals expressly recognised by Article I of the Convention of 1906.[84]

Compared to the 1906 conference, that of 1914 was characterized by far more open and frank discussion of the issues and problems, especially by the British delegates.

In support of their argument, for example, that the division in jurisdiction between the Joint Court and National Courts created inequities in the administration of justice, the British raised the Leclerc case and pointed out "the disparity of the sentences... in which the principal offender escaped unpunished".[85] They described another case involving kidnapping and maltreatment of ni-Vanuatu labourers by a French national where the offender had yet to be brought to trial. A French planter by the name of Gauthier had allegedly kidnapped four ni-Vanuatu from the island of Pentecost, held them against their will and:

> employed violence and brutal menace against these natives in the presence of Dr. Borgesius [the Native Advocate, who had gone to investigate the situation] and of other witnesses. Meanwhile no steps had been taken to bring him to trial before the French Court.[86]

Even when the British High Commissioner intervened, it was pointed out, legal manoeuvering prevented Gauthier from being brought to justice. According to the British, the ni-Vanuatu labourers were being held against their will and "if still alive will have been detained for more than one year and eight months", while Gauthier remained free to continue to violate Condominium regulations.[87]

In response, the French argued that in the Leclerc case, "no negligence or weakness is attributable to French authorities", since a suspended sentence was perfectly legal under French law for first offenders. Application of the First Offender's Act, the *lois de suris*, it was pointed out, was left to the discretion of the Court.[88] Obviously, to French authorities in the early days of the Condominium, the murder of a ni-Vanuatu was not thought to be a major offence and warranted giving the guilty party a second chance. Gauthier, the French argued, was still to be dealt with by the Court and thus it was "desirable to await the issue of the trial before forming any opinion..."[89] The French, therefore, chose simply to ignore the issue raised by the British in this instance — and which concerned them with respect to land problems — that the system provided no sure means for authorities to stop obvious violations of Condominium regulations. British officials could do nothing, because Gauthier was a French national, and French authorities chose not to act, since it served their interests to allow their citizens a free hand in the development of their plantations.

The French delegates attempted to counter British accusations of failure on their part to uphold the spirit of the Convention of 1906, by raising the issue of Edward Jacomb's activities as a case in which a British subject had "openly and violently opposed" Condominium authority. Jacomb's "attempt to induce the natives to oppose the registration of French properties, and to incite them to acts of violence, resulting in the destruction of plantations and fences", it was argued, "were perhaps not unconnected with the murder by natives of M. Guitel, a French citizen".[90] The British rejected the accusation against Jacomb and challenged the French to produce evidence to substantiate their charge connecting him to the murder.[91]

Realizing the futility of continuing the discussion of specific cases, which could not be verified or resolved, the meeting moved on to debating what measures could be taken to reduce the violence, in particular that relating to land. The French proposed that Article XXII of the Convention, which related to land disputes, should be expanded to allow for the punishment of individuals or groups found guilty of damaging or destroying visible and material evidence of occupation of land — the issue which had become one of the main causes of violence between ni-Vanuatu and Europeans in recent years.[92]

The British delegates' determination to take a much firmer stand on important issues in the 1914 Conference, was evident in their response. They strongly opposed the French proposals, arguing that the root cause of the problem was the tendency of European settlers to expand the existing developed sections of their properties into neighbouring areas occupied by ni-Vanuatu. The British quoted a letter from the Native Advocate, Dr. Borgesius, to support their point of view. They argued further that ni-Vanuatu resorted to violence because they had no legal means to halt what they saw as encroachment on their land, since the Court had ruled that it had no power to grant an injunction to stop clearing of additional land. This was especially threatening to ni-Vanuatu, since such occupation under the existing regulations could at a later date constitute a solid base in the eyes of the Court for registration of the land.[93]

Under such circumstances, the British "felt great difficulty in protecting occupation of this kind by making forcible interference with it a criminal offence", which appeared to be "the only means open to them [ni-Vanuatu] of asserting their claims...[94] In the opinion of the British, the problem lay in the provision of the 1906 Convention which allowed for occupation of only three years to serve as a basis on which to validate a claim. It was pointed out that it had been expected that the Court would deal with such claims almost immediately, which led to the decision to fix only three years as the period prescription. Rather than punish ni-Vanuatu for what they saw as justifiable action in the circumstances, the British suggested giving the Joint Court the power to issue injunctions to protect *bona fide* occupation, which would relieve ni-Vanuatu of the need to resort to violence.[95]

The solution finally agreed upon made it an offence to interfere with the *bona fide* occupation of both natives and non-natives (Article XXII paragraph 4).[96] In addition, the provision which allowed for occupation as the sole basis of a claim was changed, requiring that the minimum of three years of occupation had to have begun prior to 1 July 1908 for Efate and 1 August 1908 for the rest of the group — the dates on which a joint regulation governing the interim sale of lands by natives to non-natives came into effect (Article XXII, paragraph 2).

The jurisdiction of the Joint Court regarding land matters was strengthened by additions to Article XII, spelling out more precisely to what extent the Court could intervene. The Convention of 1906 stated merely that the Court had jurisdiction "over all suits respecting lands". The revised Protocol of 1914 gave jurisdiction as well in cases involving land which was not yet registered. This new provision enabled the Joint Court to issue injunctions to stop Europeans expanding into areas occupied by ni-Vanuatu (Article XII, paragraph 1).

While the above adjustments were a step forward, there was no way to ensure that ni-Vanuatu would be able to take advantage of provisions designed to protect their interests, both in the original Convention and the Protocol of 1914, unless the position of the

Native Advocate were strengthened. The British therefore proposed a specific duty of the Native Advocate to visit different parts of Vanuatu to collect information on native rights and customs, at the expense of the joint administration. The British also pressed for provision to allow the Native Advocate to represent ni-Vanuatu before the National Courts as well as the Joint Court. With a few minor concessions in wording, the British delegates got French acceptance (Article XVII).

At the last sitting of the conference, on 6 August 1914, what was termed a "land tenure system" was formally adopted. The President of the Joint Court, Count de Buena Esperanza, who had been on leave in Europe and present throughout the conference, had urged the delegates to devise more precise regulations for the Joint Court to follow regarding the procedure to effect land registration. A sub-committee designated to formulate proposals outlined a procedure for applying to register a claim, the requirements of the Court in making such applications public to allow for challenges, and the form judgments should take with regard to delineating boundaries and defining the rights confirmed. A Registrar of Titles was provided for and his duties and procedures spelled out (Articles XXV-XXVII). The delegates were reluctant to prolong discussions due to the deteriorating political situation in Europe — earlier in the week Britain and France had declared war on Germany and Austria — and thus the report was adopted with no apparent debate or changes.[97]

It is impossible to know whether further debate under different circumstances would have had a different result. Clearly, the British were successful in correcting some of the more glaring administrative deficiences, but the negotiations of 1914 did not result in any substantial changes to underlying principles. Thus, despite the compromises the French were forced to agree to, they must have been satisfied that their plans to achieve full political control of Vanuatu were still on track. In 1878, they had forestalled what seemed to be an inevitable absorption of the islands into the British Empire by negotiating an agreement to respect the neutrality of the islands. The Joint Naval Agreement of 1887-88 legitimized the presence of French naval vessels in Vanuatu waters to support French planters, and in 1906, a legal system was established to validate French land claims. While strengthening the role of the Native Advocate and the Court's power, and limiting claims based on occupation, the 1914 conference made no substantive changes to the Convention of 1906.

Indeed, there is no evidence that the British had sought any fundamental changes in the 1914 negotiations. The British delegates urged their Government to accept the new agreement as the best possible under the circumstances: "... given the inherent imperfection of any system of joint control, and the inevitable divergencies in the point of view of the... two countries...."[98] The British viewed the 1914 Protocoi, not as a final solution, but as a next step in the process of evolving a suitable administrative structure for the islands.[99] The British obviously felt they would continue to be able to modify the agreement regulating the joint administration as the need arose. It would seem that their strategy from the start had been to accept a less than perfect arrangement — beginning with the Joint Naval Agreement — rather than no agreement and thus no influence. The British would find, however, that joint rule meant joint agreement for change and that the French would be reluctant to alter a system which served their interests so effectively. Indeed, with minor adjustments, the 1914 Protocol and the provisions regulating land registration, operated virtually unchanged until independence in 1980.

3

The Operation of the Joint Court

Because of the outbreak of the First World War, ratification of the Protocol negotiated between Great Britain and France in 1914 was delayed until 1922. The Joint Court did not begin dealing with land claims until 1927, though it had begun some work before the 1914 Conference. In 1911 it produced Rules of Procedure for registering land claims and in February 1913 it opened a land registry and began accepting applications for registration. At the request of the SFNH, however, the British and French governments agreed in July 1915 to suspend the services of the Joint Court relating to land claims for the duration of the War.[1] Up to that time a total of 232 applications for registration had been received, though no judgments had been handed down. In October 1919, the Joint Court ceased to sit altogether.

Resumption of Joint Court Operations

When Great Britain and France again turned their attention to Vanuatu at the end of the war, a number of uncertainties had arisen about the future of the islands. The French raised the issue of ratification of the 1914 Protocol in March 1921,[2] but it was not until 18 March 1922 that the two governments agreed to its implementation. There was debate among British officials as to whether Australia should take over responsibility or whether Britain should pull out altogether in exchange for islands between the Cooks and Pitcairn. There was also a suggestion that the French should pull out, allowing the British to purchase the land interests of the SFNH. In the end, British officials decided that the best solution was to ratify the Protocol as soon as possible in order to restore a functioning administration in the islands.[3]

The French position was complicated by the fact that in 1909, the agreement which had been negotiated in 1894 between the SFNH and the French Government, giving the government virtual control over the Company in return for an annual subsidy, had expired. Rumours had been circulating for a number of years that it might be possible to purchase the shares in the SFNH of the late John Higginson and articles began to appear in the press in 1921, hinting that Australia was about to acquire the land holdings of the Company in Vanuatu for £500,000.[4] The French Government was anxious to retain control over the Company in order to ensure the future of French interests in the islands and therefore had proposed in 1909 to buy out the Company completely, though nothing was done at that time. Thus the French were alarmed in 1921 by the apparent interest in the Company being shown in Australia and New Zealand.[5] They informed the British Government that the SFNH was bound, despite the lapse of the 1894 agreement, not to dispose of any of its property without the consent of the French Government and urged the British to inform the Australian Government of this fact to preclude their entering into an illegal agreement.[6] In a later note to London regarding the status of SFNH interests in Vanuatu the rights held by the French Government over the Company were detailed:

> 1. The right to veto the sale of territory or leases of greater duration than 40 years.
> 2. The right to place land up to 50,000 hectares at the disposal of persons emigrating under the auspices of the French Government.
> 3. A right of pre-emption on one half of the property of the Society at a price of O.F. 20 per hectare.[7]

The British Government had not shown any real interest in gaining control of the SFNH, but had decided — at least for the present — not to withdraw from Vanuatu and to ratify the 1914 Protocol. This meant that the Joint Court should reopen its land registry and begin accepting applications for registration.

While the French were prepared to ratify the Protocol, they found themselves at a disadvantage with regard to the registration of land claims. It was not possible for the SFNH to prepare applications for land registration while its legal status remained unclear, and due to its serious financial position, it was doubtful that the Company would be able to pay the court fees in respect of its many claims.[8] The problem for the French lay in the fact that once an application for registration had been received by the Joint Court and found to be in order, it was published in the official gazette and notices placed in various locations in Vanuatu to allow anyone whose rights were threatened to lodge a caveat at the Registry. If no caveats were lodged within one year, the Registrar then passed the application to the Court for adjudication. Since the SFNH was not in a position to lodge applications, the Company's vast claims were threatened, especially the developed portions, small though they were. On Efate, for example, there were numerous conflicting claims where deeds had changed hands several times and Presbyterian missionaries were actively engaged in applying for the registration of land as a means of protecting ni-Vanuatu interests. The French Government, therefore, adopted a stalling tactic, refusing to co-operate with the British Government in taking the necessary steps to enable the Joint Court to re-establish its land registration functions.

In May 1923, the former Native Advocate, Dr. Goerman Borgesius, was appointed Public Prosecutor by the King of Spain and took up the position of acting President, since Count de Buena Esperanza was still in Europe. Upon assuming his position, he informed the two Resident Commissioners of his intention to reopen the service of land claims as of 1 October 1923. The British approved, but the French Resident Commissioner refused to co-operate, contending that it required a new agreement between the two governments.[9] There were indeed a number of issues which needed to be settled to enable the Joint Court's registration system to function properly. Count de Buena Esperanza, writing to the British Foreign office in 1921, outlined the inadequacies of the system as he had experienced them as President during his time in Vanuatu before the war. He noted the need for the publication of a Condominium Gazette as provided for in the 1914 Protocol, to enable the Court to publicize applications. This had been slow and inefficient when done through the official gazettes of Fiji and New Caledonia. He also urged the establishment of survey facilities and the appointment of a Registrar of Lands as required under the regulations.[10]

When the President finally arrived back in Port Vila in February 1926, he found that little had been done to enable the Joint Court to resume its land work. The positions of Registrar and Public Prosecutor had not been filled due to problems relating to salaries.

Various British proposals for temporary staff and changing salary payments, had not been supported by the French,[11] who also stalled on approving the budget estimates for the current year for the Joint Court.[12] In April 1926, the Count threatened to resign if some agreement was not forthcoming,[13] and reported that "opposition to resumption of lands work comes from financial interests of the French Company".[14] The French Government was successful in blocking the land work of the Joint Court until 1927.

In December 1926, the British were finally able to get the French to agree to the cancellation of the Joint Order of 20 July 1915, suspending the land work of the Joint Court, but they were forced to accept a compromise to the effect that the Joint Court could only receive and publish applications of registration. It was not to order any registrations, deliver final titles or pronounce judgments on land disputes associated with registration until the two governments had re-examined the question.[15] The Register of Applications was re-opened in April 1927, and an agreement finally worked out in August made a few minor adjustments to procedures, but did not modify the Protocol. The two governments agreed to increase the salaries of members of the Joint Court, authorized the appointment of a Legal Commissioner to act temporarily in the absence of the President, Public Prosecutor or Native Advocate and removed the restriction on the land work of the Joint Court imposed by the Resident Commissioners' Joint Order of 2 December 1926.[16] The Joint Court was thus permitted to deal with land registrations and in 1928 actually granted 22 titles to land on Efate — all but one in respect of uncontested applications.[17]

By this time the French Government had resolved its problem with the SFNH and had set a course of action designed to overcome the fundamental economic weaknesses which had plagued France's Pacific possessions for decades. In 1921, the French Government came upon a scheme to use its very successful colonial base in Indo-China as a source of manpower and capital for the development of its Pacific colonies. Without labour and capital, New Caledonia's nickel and cobalt, and the plantations of Tahiti and Vanuatu, were mere paper assets.[18] In December 1923, what came to be known as the scheme for *une entr'aide coloniale* was officially adopted and approved by the Government Council of Indo-China. After that the plan to revive France's colonies in the Pacific by unlimited Asiatic immigration and Indo-Chinese capital became an integral part of French colonial policy.[19]

The arrangement between the French Government and the SFNH in late 1924 was a manifestation of the above policy. The

Company agreed to lease all its property for 75 years to a holding company, the Compagnie Francaise Immobiliere des Nouvelles-Hébrides (CFINH), with a capital of 4 million francs in 4,000 shares of 1,000 francs each. The Government of Indo-China provided the major financial backing for the new company, appointing a *commissaire du gouvernement* to act as general supervisor of its operations.[20] A consortium of financial institutions and companies was involved including: la Banque de l'Indochine, la Banque de l'Union Parisienne, la Société Financiere Francaise et Coloniale, la Société de Nikel, la Maison Ballande and several individuals. The purpose of the new company was to ensure the development of the land of the SFNH.[21] The French Government placed the same restriction on the new company with regard to dealings in land as it had imposed on the SFNH — the CFINH could not dispose of its lands without the consent of the French Government.[22]

By 1927, therefore, when the Joint Court was again in full operation, the French Government was well positioned to benefit from the land registration system established in 1906 and refined in the 1914 Protocol —the delaying tactics had paid off. Control over the SFNH and its vast, potentially valuable land holdings was now more secure, capital was available to develop plantations and in 1923, the first of over 6,000 Vietnamese labourers arrived in Vanuatu.[23] Where earlier the French Government had merely supported its nationals, it had now become the driving force behind the expansion of French influence and economic dominance in the islands. All that remained was for the Joint Court to transform the paper claims of the SFNH/CFINH into firm titles.

The British were not, however, prepared to allow the expropriation of ni-Vanuatu land to go unchallenged and were determined to ensure that the provisions embodied in the 1914 Protocol to protect native interests were adhered to and if possible strengthened. What the British did not seem to realize was that the French were also determined — more than ever — to achieve full political control over Vanuatu. They would find that enforcing provisions, which were vague and open to differing interpretations as to implementation, extremely difficult, if not impossible. Thus, the Anglo-French duel over Vanuatu, which began in the 1870s, continued with renewed gusto in the post-war period.

The Joint Court in Action

The one aspect of the land registration system which does not appear to have provoked extensive debate between the two

The Joint Court sitting in Port Vila, with the Spanish Count De Buena Esperanza presiding. (Photograph from Alexander, G. From the Middle Temple to the South Seas, London, 1927. Photographer possibly Martin Johnson, who passed through Vila in 1917 and 1919: Vanuatu Centre Research Collection).

governments was the "Rules of Procedure for the Registration of Titles to Land", published by the Joint Court in 1911 and amended slightly in 1927. In this document, the Court set down the procedures to be followed when applying for registration, publication by the Court of applications, the lodging of caveats to applications and the judgment by the Court of both uncontested and contested applications.[24]

An applicant was required to provide particulars of the claim, including all deeds and documents pertaining thereto, and information regarding occupation by other persons. Each application was given a number based on date and time of receipt and entered in the Application Book by the Registrar (Articles 1-26). When the application was in order, the Court ordered publication. A notice in both English and French included particulars of the application (Article 30). This notice was sent to the two Resident Commissioners and published in the official gazette, which appeared for the first time in 1927. The regulations also required the notice to be published by means of placards posted:

> 1. through the Resident Commissioners and district agents respectively: at the office of both Residencies, at the District Agencies of the district in which the immovable (land) is situated;. . .
> 2. through the Registrar: on the doors of the Court House, at the usual places of posting of official notices at Vila. (Article 33)

In addition, copies of the notices were required to be sent to the Native Advocate, other occupants of the property, the owners and occupants of adjoining properties, third parties with interests in the property and any others whom the Court may designate (Article 35). On paper at least, ni-Vanuatu were to be informed of applications for the registration of land which might concern them.

When the publication formalities had been completed, the Joint Court, by means of a decision posted at the Court and in the Condominium Gazette, fixed the date of commencement of a one year period during which opposition to the application for registration could be made. Anyone whose rights were threatened could lodge a caveat, which "may also be presented by or on behalf of natives" (Article 44). If no caveat had been lodged within one year the Registrar passed the file to the Court. If it appeared that "the publication may not have been brought to the notice of the natives" or other interested parties (Article 60), the Court could extend the period for receiving caveats. The Court then had to satisfy itself:

1. That the application is not defective in material particulars.
2. That all persons interested may have had notice thereof.
3. That the rights of all persons under a disability or absent from the Group, or of the natives, or of all other persons interested have been sufficiently safeguarded (Article 61).

When all the conditions had been fulfilled to the satisfaction of the Court, it ordered the registration of the land.

When applications were contested, the Court first examined the caveats. If they were allowed under the terms of Article XXII of the Protocol, the parties were summoned for conciliation. Failing an agreement, the Court proceeded to hear the application. The Rules allowed the Court great liberty in seeking help and gathering information to "order any inquiry, inspections of boundaries, or of cultivation or improvements or facts of operation, and any other proceeding which it may deem necessary..." (Article 93). Such investigations were not a requirement, but an option open to the Court.

Upon conclusion of the hearing, and after taking into account Articles XXII, XXIII, XXIV, and XXVII of the Protocol — those articles relating specifically to land suits between natives and non-natives —the Court made its decision, usually within one month of the last day of the public hearing. If the application did not fall within one of the special cases provided, the Court would declare the registration of the property. Provision was allowed for additional time to be given before final judgment in special cases where a rectification of survey plans or the allotting of native reserves was required.

The British Government would have found few objections to this procedure since a major aspect of the rules was to ensure that claims could not be registered without the knowledge of ni-Vanuatu holding an interest in the land and without their having a chance to contest the registration. What soon became clear, however, once the Court began its work in earnest in the late 1920s and 1930s, was that the safeguards — and those embodied in the Protocol as well — depended almost entirely on the prerogative of the Court and in particular, on the President.

The power of the President to influence the process of land registration was especially evident in the control which he could exercise over the activities of the Native Advocate. As part of the discussions between the British and French governments in the early 1920s, leading to the agreement to restart the Joint Court's land functions, the British raised the issue of the role of the Native Advocate. A deficiency in the Convention of 1906, which they had not been able to correct in the 1914 Protocol, was that of giving the

Native Advocate the freedom to investigate land suits as he deemed necessary. According to the Protocol, he could travel in the islands "to collect information respecting the habitats and customs of the natives...", but only "with the approval of the President of the Court".[25] In 1923, the British approached the French Government, suggesting that the following words be added to the above section of the Protocol:

> and he will also be responsible for the collection of evidence of native claims to land and for the preparation of such claims for submission to the Joint Court.[26]

The French rejected the proposal without any apparent discussion.[27] It served their interests that the role of the Native Advocate should be limited and the French could simply reject the proposal with no recourse open to the British.

It soon became apparent to the British that the interests of ni-Vanuatu relating to land were threatened by this concentration of power in the hands of the President. Although it was never proved, British officials in Port Vila suspected that the Count had come under the influence of the French — in particular the SFNH. In December 1928, for example, the President proposed to the two Resident Commissioners that the Court should set a date for the temporary cessation of reception of applications for registration. He argued that this would limit caveats, since an application served as a caveat if the land claimed overlapped with that of another application. Of special concern to the President were the islands of Santo and Malakula, where numerous overlapping claims existed, but many of the original purchasers had left the group and would only be interested in exercising their rights as land speculators, rather than true developers.[28]

The President was probably correct in his evaluation of the situation, but the British were suspicious of his motives. Several months before his proposal arrived, the SFNH had filed 17 applications for registration of 260,000 hectares on Santo — over two-thirds of the island.[29] The British Resident Commissioner's analysis was that the SFNH was withholding the presentation of its claims until as late as possible in the hope that there would be few oppposing applications.[30]

British officials were concerned that vast areas of land were about to be registered in the name of the SFNH — land which was inhabited by ni-Vanuatu, who did not have the slightest idea that it was under claim. While not opposing the suspension of acceptance of applications, the British suggested that the Court declare all land more than two miles from the Santo coast to be a native reserve, except such areas as were in actual and effective occupation.[31] The President of the Joint Court replied, however, that he was powerless to comply, since the land was already under claim.[32]

The British Resident Commissioner continued to press the President for assurances that native interests on Santo and Malakula would be protected. The Count finally agreed to make every effort to ensure that applications would be brought to the notice of interested parties and that native caveats would be entered *pro forma* by the Native Advocate on behalf of ni-Vanuatu on Santo and Malakula.[33] The British Resident Commissioner reported to the High Commissioner, however, that there was no guarantee that such caveats would be accepted and, in any case, it would be unlikely that the Native Advocate would be able to investigate adequately claims on the two islands due to his heavy workload.[34] At that time, the Native Advocate was also holding the position of Public Prosecutor and, therefore, seldom left Port Vila except on leave.

British officials also suggested to the French that the Rules of Procedure — or perhaps even the Protocol — should be amended to ensure that all interested persons would be heard in relation to land suits. They suggested that an applicant should produce proof that ni-Vanuatu had been notified — that notice of publication be presented to chiefs or headmen in person by an authorized official, e.g. the District Agent.[35] The negative response of the French Resident Commissioner came 22 months later.[36]

Twenty years after the signing of the Convention, British officials were still finding that co-operation with their French colleagues on land matters was virtually impossible. In 1929, the British Resident Commissioner observed that French authorities regard the active British "support of the cause of the native not as springing from any ethical motive but as a means to frustrating their national aims".[37] This was undoubtedly the French view, but the British also allowed national interests to influence their policies. They were willing to compromise in the discussions of 1906 and 1914 to the clear disadvantage of ni-Vanuatu, rather than alienate the French during a period of increasing world tension. While on the whole the British may have pursued more ethical policies towards colonized peoples, in the case of Vanuatu they were also determined to see the struggle through out of national pride *vis-a-vis* the French.

By the early 1930s, British attempts to achieve a just settlement of the land problem in Vanuatu focused more and more on the person and policies of the President of the Joint Court. By 1931, after four years of work, Count de Buena Esperanza was preparing to return to Europe on leave. A strong effort was made by officials in the British Residency in Port Vila to make a case for not allowing him to return. The Acting British Resident Commissioner, Mr. B. Blandy, described him as:

> ... very old... deaf... extremely autocratic. He cannot see any point of view but his own — this with remarkable clearness — and will not listen to any other.... HE IS the Joint Court — the Judges being mere puppets in his hands....
>
> The President is a natural schemer and intriguer.... He has clearly been playing with doubtful 'methods' of survey and 'doubtful' surveyors... this speeding up... by these doubtful methods would mean an abandonment of all standards of accuracy and appears to be exactly what is wanted by the Société Francaise des Nouvelles-Hébrides, whose Director has lately been entertained by the President (a striking honour to a non-official). The latter has been showing him marked deference and respect, and frequently visits him privately.[38]

Blandy also hinted that the Count may have been accepting money from the French, though he does state that "there is no proof — only circumstantial deduction".[39]

These comments, however, may reveal more about the xenophobic nature of Anglo-French society in the tiny beach community than any conclusive evidence of misconduct. There is evidence that in his desire to deal quickly with the growing number of applications for registration of land claims, the Count was driven to adopting questionable methods.

Initially the Joint Court required claimants, as stipulated under the "Rules of Procedure for the Registration of Titles to Land", to supply plans with their applications. The Government of Australia had employed surveyors to prepare plans for its lands, which they completed by about 1917, and had provided their services to both the Presbyterian and Anglican missions. The SFNH also employed surveyors during the period prior to the Joint Court's hearing of claims. In 1924, a surveyor was appointed as part of the Joint Court staff, whose job it was to check and compare plans to detect overlapping claims. If conflicts were discovered, the Court would declare the later claim a caveat to the first. The Convention of 1906 provided for the establishment of a joint Condominium survey service, but during the early years of the Court's operation, surveyors were placed under the direct control of the Joint Court.

When the Court began to deal with the first claims on Efate in

1927, the Court surveyor, Mr. A. Larney, reported to the President that while plans lodged by most British claimants appeared adequate, those lodged by French claimants — mainly by the SFNH — were worthless from a survey point of view. They did not agree with the descriptions of the lands claimed, and did "not contain one necessary detail to assist in re-survey".[40] As a result, the Court decided to have all claims surveyed by its own surveyors, the cost to be passed on to each claimant as part of the registration fee.

As an alternative, the British proposed that claimants should be required to submit proper plans as required under the Rules of Procedure — as the British applicants had done — and let the French bear their own expenses. This would, however, have created difficulties from a public and administrative point of view and was, therefore, not accepted. The issue was that of fees. Between 1906 and 1917, the Australian Government had incurred a cost of over £22,000 in the survey of its lands and was, therefore, opposed to paying for the duplication of what was accepted by the Court surveyor as adequate. On the advice of its solicitor in Port Vila, however, the Australian Government agreed to pay the additional costs.[41] A fee was fixed by the Court, which turned out to be ridiculously low, and was eventually raised due to pressure from the joint administration.

Because there had never been a comprehensive survey of the group, the Court surveyors began by first triangulating the islands before dealing with individual blocks. They fixed the position of key points to which every block later surveyed would be linked. The Court, in short, did the work of a lands and survey department. Because of this added operation, and due to the limited survey staff (only six in 1931) the operation of the Joint Court progressed very slowly. Even uncontested claims were often held up because of the lack of an official survey plan.

During the early 1930s, the way in which the Joint Court surveyors conducted their work also became an issue of some significance. The Australian Government solicitor, Mr. Wallace, raised with members of the Court the fact that when the surveyors went into the field, they were provided with the plans or sketches originally lodged with the applications, rather than the original titles and documents supporting the claim. The official plans were produced, therefore, not from the original deeds, but from the plans which the Court itself had already declared inadequate. Wallace noted:

> The survey by the Court Surveyors is a sham and a delusion. The surveyors are simply going over the *plans* lodged in

> Court by the SFNH — plans which the Court has declared to be unsatisfactory.[42]

The effect of this procedure was to give the authority of the court to plans which often bore little relationship to the actual areas of land described in the original transactions.

The President adopted this method of surveying to speed up registration. It was alleged that he came under the influence of two French surveyors who were sent to Vanuatu by French authorities in France.[43] The French disclaimed any knowledge of the arrangement,[44] but in fact two French surveyors (Messrs. Rollin and Perrin) did arrive and were hired by the Joint Court.[45] It was they who convinced the President that surveying could be done more rapidly by establishing trigonometric points based on plans presented with applications, rather than using fixed trigonometrical points for the islands as a whole.[46] This method aroused strong opposition among British surveyors and led to the accusation that the Court was basing its judgments on faulty evidence.

According to Wallace, the President of the Court was "trying to hide this fact", and was "making deliberately false statements about it".[47] It is difficult to substantiate Wallace's contention of a deliberate attempt at deception,[48] but there is little doubt that the surveyors were conducting their work as he described. The Chief Surveyor responded to an enquiry from Wallace that:

> all our surveys have been made from the plans and sketches deposited by the applicants with their application for a title and not from the deeds of the original purchases from the natives.[49]

Moreover, the surveyors were under strict instructions from the Court, in particular from the President, to follow the procedure described above. On 18 May 1931, Count de Buena Esperanza wrote to the Chief Surveyor:

> It is I, as Chief of the international jurisdiction who am responsible for the settlement of all these questions for which I delegate you for the present, but do not forget that you are an official of the Joint Court, that according to the Convention you are placed under the disciplinary authority of the President and that you have no other orders or instructions to receive except mine.[50]

The Chief Surveyor, therefore, had no other choice but to follow the instructions of the President or run the risk of being replaced.

It appears, however, that Wallace's concern was also due to the fact that many of the Australian Government's land claims, which he had been commissioned to represent, were opposed by the SFNH. In his opinion, "under the present regime no litigant will have a chance who is opposed by the SFNH".[51] He was convinced that the President was in collusion with the SFNH and as a result, the claims of the Australian Government would suffer.[52]

Indeed, the French had reason to press the Joint Court to proceed quickly in registering land. By the early 1930s, the SFNH was again in financial difficulty due to the world depression. The drop in the prices for primary products pushed many French settlers, burdened with heavy loans, to the brink of bankruptcy. In 1929, the CFINH was liquidated with its interests in Vanuatu reverting to the SFNH, which was reorganized with 16,000 shares of which 1600 were held by the Government of Indo-China with a 10 to 1 voting power. In 1930, the French Government agreed to an annual subsidy to the SFNH of 10 million francs[53] and in March 1931, a loan was negotiated between the French Government and a large Paris bank — Crédit National — for 40 million francs to be lent to French settlers and businesses in Vanuatu.[54] Clear titles to large tracts of land were necessary to provide the SFNH — and the Government of France, which controlled the Company — with the collateral to negotiate loans and other financial arrangements.

These measures did not solve the Company's financial problems and in 1934 a further loan was made from the Banque de l'Indochine, which the French Government guaranteed in return for certain concessions from the SFNH. The Company agreed to renounce in favour of the French State all rights to an 81 metre strip of land from the high-water mark along the shore of all its properties with a coastline — the *zone maritime* — and sold outright to the Government for 4.8 million francs, 160,403 hectares of land on five different islands: 82,353 hectares on Santo, 48,992 hectares on Malakula, 13,300 hectares on Efate, 13,958 hectares on Epi and 1,800 hectares on Mota Lava in the Banks Islands.[55]

In the early 1930s there had also been proposals made by the British that the "New Hebrides Problem" might best be solved by dividing the group, or even turning the Islands over entirely to the French Administration with compensation elsewhere.[56] The registration of their claims on the main island of Efate, would have given the French Government a much stronger bargaining position should negotiations have occurred.

It is now almost impossible to substantiate whether or not there was collusion between Joint Court officials and French interests. It is evident, however, that the procedures followed by the Court produced surveys of questionable validity, which the Court then often used as the basis for its decisions. It was common for a judgment to state that the Court "has decided on the advice of the surveyors to reserve"[57] a road or a native reserve. Thus, the reliance placed by the Court on the results of the surveys casts considerable doubt as to the accuracy of many of the early judgments.

Despite such criticisms, however, there was a minority opinion expressed from the British Residency that the Joint Court was run impartially during this period. The Resident Commissioner in 1932, Mr. G.A. Joy felt that the President was basically honest and that any criticism of the overall work of the Joint Court should have been directed towards the Convention of 1906 and the 1914 Protocol, which provided the rules to guide the President:

> The Count has told me on many occasions that the bulk of the French titles outside Efate, known as the 'Higginson Claims' are nothing more than a 'bluff' (his own expression). These claims are controlled by the French Company. The Count's interpretation of Articles 22 and 23 of the Protocol in which his British colleague concurred and which his French colleague had no option but to accept, was aimed at exploding the areas claimed under the Higginson titles. It has already successfully accomplished that end in one or two instances and it will have a profound effect if the French titles to the Northern islands are ever dealt with by the Joint Court.[58]

As evidence of the President's impartiality, the Resident Commissioner went on to point to his refusal to accept the original French surveys provided with applications and argued that the Count had no other option but to refuse the work of the Australian surveyors as well.[59]

The British Resident Commissioner, however, does not explain why the Count then used the original French surveys for making judgments. Nevertheless, the evidence seems to indicate that the President felt a great commitment to the major task assigned to him — the registration of land claims — and may have made compromises in order to fulfill what he saw as his duty. While he may have been susceptible to various pressures from French interests, their desire by the late 1920s and 1930s to see the registration of land proceed quickly would have coincided with his own objective. Indeed, in 1926, when the French were making every effort to stall the resumption of the Joint Court's land functions, the Count was openly critical of French policy. Finding that none of his recommendations had been carried out regarding the hiring of staff for the Court he wrote to the British Colonial Office to complain:

> This confirms what I was already told, viz. that the French Government *does not* want the resumption of the Land Registry, that all kinds of obstructions will be put in motion, so as to hinder the working of our Court, in short to make me despair of any result and resign my functions, hoping that no one would be found to take my place; and thus to allow the new convention to remain a dead letter as far as joint jurisdiction is concerned.[60]

He even threatened to resign if an agreement was not forthcoming to allow the Joint Court to resume its work. Moreover, the President's suggestion in 1927 to limit the period for accepting applications, which would have been an advantage to the French, was probably only an attempt by the Count to speed up the work of the Court. Limiting the number of applications would have reduced the number of caveats, but it would also have speeded up the work of the Court. A more accurate description of Count de Buena Esperanza would seem to be that in his eagerness to accomplish what was turning out to be a more and more impossible task, he unwittingly allowed himself to become a tool of French interests.

By the time Count de Buena Esperanza left for Europe on leave in late 1932, he had finished most of the applications for registration on Efate. It had taken him more than four years to deal with 200 applications.[61] The slow pace was due in part to the requirement of the Court that official surveys should be produced before final judgments could be handed down. Many Efate claims overlapped and a number had changed hands, making registration difficult. In his rush to complete Efate before departing, the Count issued interlocutory judgments pending surveys.[62] The President correctly estimated that at the then rate of progress it would take over fifty years to register all lands claimed. He began to urge British and French officials to consider radically changing the procedures, suggesting that registration be suspended until arrangements could be worked out.[63] If registration continued under the existing system, he proposed that the administration should increase the survey team and allow the Court to grant partial deeds for developed land and interlocutory judgments subject to survey. As an alternative, the Count suggested that registration be suspended and the Court abolished, transferring its other functions to the National Courts.[64]

While both governments were aware that changes were necessary, they could not agree on where or how to begin. Neither side was in favour of suspending registration or abolishing the Joint Court, though the British felt that the system of granting indefeasible titles, which necessitated precise surveys, should be stopped at least temporarily until Condominium finances allowed for an increase in survey staff. Moreover, the British were receptive to the idea of granting partial title to developed areas, but were opposed to interlocutory judgments, which they felt would give French companies hold over land to which they were not entitled.[65] As might be expected, French officials supported those suggestions which would have speeded up registration: augmenting of the Court's survey staff and the granting of interlocutory judgments.[66]

The one point on which the British and French agreed was to increase the staff of the Joint Court. The British felt, however, that changes would have to wait until the world economic situation improved, since the depression had dramatically affected the financial position of the joint administration. Prior to 1930 the Condominium had been self-supporting, but from that year there had been a substantial excess of expenditure over revenue and the two governments had been forced to contribute towards the maintenance of the joint services. British proposals in 1933 to increase customs duties were blocked by the French High Commissioner in Noumea who felt the sacrifice would fall primarily on his countrymen. That was precisely the British intention:

> a community should pay for its own services and that the French beneficiaries by the activities of the Joint Court, etc., were more numerous than the English, which effectively counterbalanced the difference in the incidence of taxation.[67]

Because of the French attitude and because the Joint Court was the most expensive item in the Condominium budget, the British refused in the early 1930s either to increase Joint Court staff or to replace established positions as they became vacant. The financial crisis in the 1930s, therefore, compounded a problem which had plagued the Joint Court since the start of its operation — lack of adequate staff.

It was, for example, 1911 before the first Native Advocate was appointed — the Dutch lawyer, Dr. Borgesius, who for a time also held the position of Acting Public Prosecutor. When he left on leave in 1920, the Joint Court simply closed. The President, Count de Buena Esperanza, was still in Europe, the posts of Public Prosecutor and Native Advocate were vacant, and there was no British or French judge.[68] As Acting President, Borgesius re-opened the Court in 1923, but the positions of Native Advocate and Public Prosecutor remained unfilled and there was no Registrar as provided for in the 1914 Protocol. In 1926, a M. Persyn was appointed Native Advocate and also assumed the position of Acting Public Prosecutor. By 1928, he had become full-time Public Prosecutor,[69] but in 1930 was asked to resign when it was discovered that he was accepting money from ni-Vanuatu to represent them.[70] In late 1928, a Belgian lawyer, Mr. Van Houtryve, was appointed Native Advocate and also acted as Public Prosecutor until his departure in 1931.[71] In 1927 the two governments agreed to establish the post of Legal Commissioner, who was to act in the absence of the President and in 1929, the role was extended to cover the post of Public Prosecutor as well.[72] There is no evidence from the documents that any appointment was ever made and the position was abolished in 1936.[73]

The Joint Court in 1932 was without a President, a Public Prosecutor or a Native Advocate, and the British refused to agree to immediate replacements, despite French pressure.[74] The British succeeded in securing the retirement of the Count, who was 78 years old when he left Vanuatu,[75] and the position of President remained vacant until late 1936, when the King of Spain appointed Senor Manuel Bosch Barrett.[76] During the interim, the British and French judges acted as President and *ad hoc* appointments were made for the positions of Native Advocate and Public Prosecutor as the need arose.[77] In 1935, it was agreed that the Native Advocate's position should be filled by another Belgian, M. Albert Dujardin, even though he did not speak adequate English.[78]

Despite the chaotic staffing situation throughout the 1930s, the Joint Court continued to deal with land suits. In 1933, it turned its attention to the 81 applications from the Southern Islands. Registration of these claims proceeded smoothly, since the situation was very different from that on Efate. All but one of the applications were from British subjects, including 13 from Burns Philp acting for the Commonwealth of Australia, and 24 from Presbyterian missions. The single French application was from the Catholic Mission on Tanna. Except for 5 large properties of several thousand hectares on Erromongo and one each on Tanna and Aneityum, most of the remaining claims were less than 50 hectares and about half of those less than 10 hectares. The influence of the Presbyterian mission in limiting European settlement was evident.

By 1935, the Joint Court had completed registration of claims for the Southern Islands and then turned to the last area where triangulation had been done — the island of Epi. A total of 74 applications had been received, 42 of which were caveated. The history of speculative land purchases in the 1880s was reflected in the series of applications submitted by the SFNH — the Company applied for registration of virtually all the land on the west coast of the island. Representatives of the old Australasian New Hebrides

Company had also purchased land on Epi and thus there were several applications for registration of claims by Burns Philp on behalf of the Australian Government, most of which conflicted with those of the SFNH.[79]

The Court moved very slowly in dealing with claims for Epi due to the amount of surveying required and the number of conciliation hearings necessary to resolve the complexity of overlapping claims and caveats lodged on behalf of ni-Vanuatu by the Native Advocate. The lack of survey staff became more of a problem, since the Court depended on them for much of the information it required for adjudication. Registration came to a halt at the end of 1935, with no judgments at all handed down in 1936, and only 6 at the end of 1937, when the Court's survey staff was increased.[80] Most of the claims for Epi were completed by 1941, when the Joint Court ceased all land work due to the outbreak of the Second World War, though final judgments for several more complicated applications were handed down in the early 1950s.

Protection of Native Interests

In 1906, the British made a significant compromise when they agreed to the establishment of a Court to adjudicate rather than a Commission to investigate and rule on the validity of land claims in Vanuatu. It would seem, however, that they were satisfied that their demands for protection of native interests were met within the articles of the Convention. Provision was made for the appointment of a Native Advocate to represent ni-Vanuatu "in any suit" before the Joint Court. Although not specified, this included land suits as well as criminal cases. On the controversial question of early land purchases, the British succeeded in having included in the Convention the assurance that claims registered before 1 January 1896 could be invalidated, if the Native Advocate could establish which people had what right to the land and prove that the agreement had been obtained by force or fraud, or that the land in question did not belong to the vendor or his tribe.[81] But if the property had "lawfully and in good faith" changed hands for "valuable consideration" prior to that date, then the right of action against the claim would not be admitted by the Court.[82]

The only other provision in the 1906 Convention to protect native interests allowed the Court to assign to native claimants "reserves of land in proportion to their requirements"[83] and the High Commissioners to prohibit the new sale of land on islands where it was considered that "the amount of lands acquired from the natives... is so great that the land remaining undisposed of is indispensible for the needs of the natives".[84]

The "Rules of Procedure for the Registration of Titles to Land" published by the Court in 1911, also provided — at least on paper — the safeguard that ni-Vanuatu would be informed of any applications for registration of land which might concern them. The Native Advocate and District Agents were also to receive notices of applications, and copies were to be posted at various public places including the relevant District Agencies. If it was found that an application threatened the land rights of ni-Vanuatu, the "Rules of Procedure" also provided that caveats could be lodged on behalf of individuals or groups.[85]

It became evident soon after the signing of the Convention in 1906, that the role of the Native Advocate needed to be spelled out more precisely. Some minor changes were made in the 1914 Protocol and efforts were made by the British to strengthen their position prior to the resumption of the Joint Court's land work in 1927. But throughout the 1920s and 1930s, the Native Advocate — when, in fact, the post was filled — spent most of his time in Port Vila, rather than investigating claims in the islands. The Court relied almost entirely on its survey staff to provide information on boundaries and native occupation of properties under application for registration.

Moreover the Native Advocate was often assigned the job of Public Prosecutor as well, and there were times when no one was in the post at all. In 1931, the Acting British Resident Commissioner described the role of the Native Advocate:

> The Condominium system has, in practice, failed to protect Native Land Interests.
>
> Natives as a whole are unaware how they can protect themselves from non-native aggression and would be incapable of understanding the means of availing themselves of it unaided, if they were aware. The Native Advocate is completely out of touch with natives except round about Vila and has never been in touch. No practical means has ever been devised to put or keep natives in touch with him. Up to now the Native Advocate has never made any attempt on GENERAL LINES to protect native interests. He has confined himself to caveats (all local) before the Courts....
>
> There appears to be some kind of purely theoretical protection for natives, but in practice there is none, and I consider that no native lands can be safe from usurpation while the joint system lasts. Our partners will put every

> possible obstruction in the way, though paying lip service to PROTECTION, and every effort will be baulked.[86]

He went on to argue that it was impractical to depend on District Agents because of their lack of legal training and transport difficulties. Moreover, "the French Agents have no desire to help".[87]

This point of view was reinforced by reports from Presbyterian missionaries who lived in the islands and thus saw at first hand how the Condominium system worked. The Presbyterian Mission Synod in August 1934 noted:

> A notice of French land claims for the Island of Ahambe was posted on a copra-house on the South Coast of Malekula in May, 1934. The Ahambe natives do not know French, the language used, which is one only of the official languages of the Condominium. A protest sent to Vila on behalf of the natives received the reply that the time for protest had expired in December, 1933. Notice of the claims was posted up five months after the date of expiry of the time for the lodging of caveats.
>
> Protests against occupation of land by Europeans have been made to District Agents. The natives have been told to wait until the Land Court meets and settles the dispute; and in most cases the natives have been deprived of the land in dispute until that time should come.
>
> No Native Advocate is available to whom the natives can apply. For reasons like these Synod would respectfully urge on the High Commissioner the need of an active legal Native Advocate to move about the Group and to help the natives in land and other difficulties.[88]

The Presbyterians also voiced their disapproval at the appointment of M. Dujardin as Native Advocate in 1936, due to his only slight knowledge of English.[89]

The Presbyterian missionaries were very much aware of the need to register their own land claims — both land on which their mission stations were situated and that which ni-Vanuatu had given to them to hold in trust. Due to the cost of re-surveying, however, the missionaries decided not to file applications for all their claims. Mission officals requested that only where title was necessary for the mission's work and in cases when land required by ni-Vanuatu was threatened, should applications be submitted.[90] The Presbyterian Mission was granted title to 25 claims on Efate and the surrounding islands totalling over 4,000 hectares, 28 claims in the Southern Islands totalling over 4,300 hectares and seven titles on Epi totalling 49 hectares. Included were several large trust properties on

Erromango encompassing over 3,600 hectares and two properties totalling 1,765 hectares held on behalf of the people of Erakor — a village close to Port Vila.[91] The other main Protestant missions — the Anglicans, Church of Christ and Seventh Day Adventists — were not involved in registering their lands at this time, since their activities were concentrated in the Northern Islands, which were not dealt with by the Joint Court until the 1950s and 1960s. They did, however, submit applications for registration.

The land situation of the Catholic Mission was different from that of the Protestants in that there were fewer mission stations and, when they required land, various French individuals or companies were often prepared to meet the mission's needs from their own holdings. A number of Catholic Mission properties were, in fact, acquired after the land had been registered and would not, therefore, have been recorded on the original judgments. For example, in 1977, the Catholic Mission had title to 14 separate properties on Efate and the surrounding small islands, totalling 890 hectares. During the 1930s, however, when land for Efate was originally registered, only seven judgments were handed down in favour of the Catholic Mission for land totalling 128 hectares.[92] Indeed, the Mission's single property on Epi was registered as a substitution on an original SFNH claim.[93]

The inability of the Native Advocate to defend ni-Vanuatu interests was especially clear in the Court proceedings. Nor did he always carry out his duties to the fullest — limited though they were. For example, in 1931, the Native Advocate was granted extra time by the Court to hold an enquiry on the island of Nguna, regarding the boundaries of an SFNH claim to 1,700 hectares, and to ascertain the population of the villages on the island. The enquiry never took place and the Court, therefore, rejected the native caveat lodged on behalf of the people of Nguna — land totalling 567 hectares was registered in favour of the SFNH. At the same time, however, the Court authorized the creation of a native reserve, once surveying had been completed. A reserve of 1,000 hectares was eventually created for a population of 174 Ngunese. The Court also stipulated that any land which was found after the survey to be outside the boundaries of the SFNH property, but claimed by the Presbyterian Mission, should be registered in favour of the Mission.[94] It is significant to note that while the native caveat was rejected, the SFNH claim was greatly reduced and land was reserved for the local population and added to the mission property. Thus the Court, not the Native Advocate, did most in this case to protect the interests of the people of Nguna.

The Court followed a similar pattern in dealing with a number of claims around Havannah Harbour — an area complicated by overlapping claims of the SFNH, early British settlers and the Presbyterian Mission. The Court rejected a native caveat, but after surveying to define boundaries, authorized that any land not included in the other claims should be registered in favour of the Mission.[95] In this case, unlike that on Nguna, a native reserve was not created, but it would appear that the Court viewed registration in favour of the Mission as having the same effect.

The Court was clearly willing to create native reserves when it felt there was justification — as it was authorized to do in the Protocol — but at the same time, it was scrupulous in adhering to the letter of the law regarding registration of claims. Indeed, its job was to effect land registrations and it would not be swayed from that task. In dealing with an application by the SFNH for over 25,000 hectares on Efate, a native caveat was lodged on behalf of the chiefs of the two villages claiming that the land had been sold by people who were not the true owners. Because the caveat raised the question of the capacity of the vendors, it was admitted by the Court. The SFNH argued that the deeds had witnesses and that it was impossible to prove at the present time that the vendors did not have the right to sell the land. The argument used by the Court to reject the native caveat was as follows:

> Whereas the Native Advocate presents as proof only a presumption, namely the impossibility of the purchasers and the vendors to state the boundaries of the land sold, and a proof by all legal means should be ordered by the Court.
>
> Whereas a presumption more or less logical cannot constitute a precise fact which is admissible as proof.
>
> Whereas it falls upon the Native Advocate to make the proof himself and he appears to have charged the Court with making this proof....
>
> Whereas it results that the Native Advocate, who is charged with proving his case, has failed to do so and consequently his caveat must be rejected.[96]

The Court's position was clear — without documented evidence, there was no case. It would not accept the evidence of present-day occupants. The Court did, however, create a native reserve of 327 hectares for the 50 inhabitants of the village of Eton, which the SFNH had recommended with the stipulation that the land should revert to the Company should the tribes become extinct.[97]

The reliance by the Joint Court on documented evidence in dealing with native caveats is especially clear in relation to those applications for registration of land in and around Port Vila. A number of caveats were lodged in 1929 and 1930 on behalf of the residents of Fila Island, against applications for title to land which they were then using, i.e. they did not challenge the registration of land in the developed area of Vila town. In the case of Rodin estate, located at the south end of Vila harbour, the Fila Islanders argued that they had never sold the land, but only allowed Rodin to use it. The Court rejected the caveat on the grounds that the allegation was not supported by any acceptable legal proof, i.e. it based its judgment on Article XXII, paragraph 3 of the Protocol.

Moreover, the Court did not hesitate to apply the provision within the Protocol, which allowed it to exclude all challenges to an application, if the property in question had changed hands between non-natives prior to 1 January 1896 — as provided for under the Protocol (Article XXII, paragraph 6 [A], sub-section b). The Court, for example, used this argument to reject native caveats lodged on behalf of Fila Islanders against applications for the registration of the Anabrou plantation, located to the north of Vila town, even though Fila Islanders were using the land at the time. The Court did, however, create native reserves for Fila Island, including one very controversial case (Judgment 57), in which a reserve was created from land not actually part of the application under consideration (see Chapter 7).

During this period, not a single native caveat was accepted by the Court, though a number were admitted for consideration. Indeed, it would appear that caveats were lodged primarily as a means to get the Court to consider granting native reserves, rather than in any serious attempt to block registration. Since the Court relied completely on documented evidence and ni-Vanuatu would have had nothing but the spoken word of their fathers to support their cases, there was almost no chance for them to succeed.

On Epi, the Native Advocate was instructed by 21 chiefs from the island to oppose all SFNH applications on the grounds that none of the land under claim had ever been sold.[98] Because of the staffing problems of the Joint Court, registration of land on Epi was not completed until after the Second World War, by which time 15 native reserves had been created. The Native Advocate had not given any information regarding location of villages or native occupancy — the Court was left to determine how it should divide the land. There never seemed to have been any question about granting natives reserves —the SFNH was in favour.[99] But at the same time, there was no doubt that the vast majority of the land would be registered in favour of the European claimants.

One of the major criticisms of the Joint Court in later years was, therefore, the way in which it allocated native reserves. As noted above, no procedures or criteria were laid down in the Protocol, and due to the ineffectiveness of the Native Advocate, the Court was left to its own devices to decide if a native reserve should be established and, if so, what its dimensions should be. The reports of the Court's survey team were its main source of information and these tended to be vague and lacking in the precise information required to make an accurate assessment of the needs of ni-Vanuatu living on land subject to registration.

In January 1938, for example, the Court ordered the creation of a native reserve of 242 hectares out of a claim for registration by the SFNH on Epi, known as Bonkovia. The surveyors noted "the existence... of native villages and native gardens; and they have proposed that the land containing these villages and gardens be made a Native Reserve".[100] No mention was made of the number of inhabitants involved, nor does there appear to have been any recognition of the traditional shifting pattern of agriculture, which requires a much larger land area than is under cultivation at any one time. Twenty-five years later, a major dispute arose when the owner of the neighbouring property sought to expand the developed portion of his property and found that it was occupied by the people of Bonkovia, who had themselves expanded outside the boundaries of the reserve which had been allocated to them. Moreover, as became clear during the investigation of the dispute in 1966, the people of Bonkovia were not even aware that the land in question had been alienated (see Chapter 4).

Thus, under the direction of Count de Buena Esperanza, the Court created only 11 reserves during the registration of land claims on Efate and the surrounding small islands totalling some 2,500 hectares. At the same time, it granted titles to more than 70,000 hectares — over 70 percent of the total land area of the islands. In the Southern Islands, only two reserves were created totalling almost 2,000 hectares, but only 15,561 hectares were registered out of a total land area of over 170,000 hectares and — as noted above — 4,300 hectares were registered in favour of the Presbyterian mission, much of which was to be held in trust.[101] On Epi, where 15 native reserves were created, totalling some 6,000 hectares, only 10,000 hectares were registered out of a total land area of 44,505 hectares.

While the Court's record for Efate clearly shows the degree to which European interests took priority over those of the indigenous population, it would be unfair to say that its decisions with regard to the Southern Islands and Epi deprived ni-Vanuatu of an unduly large amount of land, though as later events would prove, ni-Vanuatu did not usually accept the Court's decisions. With regard to Epi, however, the Court did tend to grant Europeans title to the best land — most of the flat coastal strip on the western side of the island — while leaving to ni-Vanuatu the less desirable portions in the interior and along the rugged, northern coastline where, in fact, few Europeans had claims. The Joint Court was not opposed to creating native reserves and, as the above examples demonstrate, it was prepared to carve out sizeable portions of European claims in order to do so. If in later years these reserves proved inadequate for the ni-Vanuatu living on them, it would be more just to criticize the framers of the Condominium land registration system, rather than the Court, which merely followed the regulations.

Moreover, it was a common belief in the late 19th and early 20th centuries, during the period of rapid population decline in the Pacific as a whole, that the indigenous populations of the islands would eventually disappear. In 1906, following a visit to Vanuatu, the High Commissioner for the Western Pacific, Sir Everard im Thurn wrote:

> There can be no doubt that these natives have decreased very greatly in number since the days of Bougainville and Captain Cook, and that this decrease is now taking place at a much more rapid rate; and I greatly doubt, with regret, whether any steps which it would be possible to take would save from speedy extinction the New Hebridean race, with the exception of the few individuals who are gradually being practically absorbed into the European races which have come into these islands.[102]

No one could have anticipated the rapid growth of population following the Second World War and the changing attitudes of ni-Vanuatu. There were, however, a few, like Jacomb and some missionaries, who realized that ni-Vanuatu would some day require more than land for villages and gardens, and would also want to participate in the cash economy of the plantation system — the domain of Europeans when the Condominium was established.

From the efforts made by British officials during the 1920s and 1930s to strengthen those regulations in the Protocol designed to protect native interests, it is clear that they too were concerned about the long term effect of the Court's work. It had become clear with the completion of registration on Efate, that the Court had chosen to interpret the Protocol in such a way that the claims to vast areas of land which ni-Vanuatu did not recognize as having been sold — and which they occupied and would need for the future — were in danger of being confirmed. The Court had registered over 70 percent of the land on Efate, and the same thing was likely to happen on Santo and Malakula, where almost the whole of the two islands was under application. Although the Court would not be in a position to deal with Santo and Malakula for years, the "Rules of Procedure" stipulated that caveats against an application for registration had to be lodged within one year following the publication of the application (Article 44). By the mid-1930s, this one year period had expired for most of the applications for Santo and Malakula. Native interests were clearly threatened. As described above, provisions for guaranteeing that ni-Vanuatu would be able to challenge such claims had proved to be almost totally ineffective. Moreover, by the time the Joint Court did begin to deal with applications for Santo and Malakula, few ni-Vanuatu who had been present when the alleged land transactions had taken place would still be living to give evidence.

By the end of the 1930s, therefore, the British had come to the conclusion that the only solution was to negotiate changes to the regulations in the Protocol under which the Joint Court operated. The British focused their argument on what the British Judge in 1935, W.D. Carew, called the Court's "misconceived idea of its function", which was to give an indefeasible title to land.[103] In Carew's view, the Court had misinterpreted Article XXIV, paragraph 9(A) of the Protocol, which stated that in making its decisions regarding the validity of a claim, the Court had to declare "the situation, extent and boundaries of the immovable". He felt that judgments should be precise enough in regard to the location of the land to enable the Registrar of Titles to register the title. But he argued that the duty of granting indefeasible title should rest with the Registrar of Titles by virtue of Article XXVI, paragraph (B), which defined registration as comprising a transcription of the Court decision on the register and:

> the establishment of a title to the immovable concerned written in the register in both the French and English languages, and stating the situation of the immovable, its description, the extent of its boundaries, and the enumeration of the rights and charges affecting it.

For these reasons, Judge Carew felt that the Survey Department should be independent of the Court as well as the Registrar of Titles, who should be designated the officer responsible for granting indefeasible titles.[104]

Although he did not state it at the time, Judge Carew was proposing, in effect, that the Court should recognize the immediate right of a claimant to occupy his property, but the extent of that right would be determined at a later date when the land would be surveyed and indefeasible title granted by the Registrar of Titles on the basis of occupation and improvements. This was spelled out in January 1939 in a proposal submitted to the French entitled "A New Scheme for the Rapid Determination of Land Claims in the New Hebrides".[105] The British felt that if this system were adopted, the reason for disputes would disappear, since conflicting claims usually concerned rights to undeveloped land. Indeed, the reason for the Joint Court would have disappeared as well. The only thing which would remain to be determined would be boundaries — the work of surveyors.[106]

The proposal, therefore, also outlined a restructured system for dealing with land claims. A modified Joint Court, consisting of British and French judges sitting with an assessor who was a surveyor would determine the validity of claims and deal with civil and criminal matters as well. The post of President was to be abolished. In the event of disagreement between the two judges, cases would be submitted to the Supreme Court of New Caledonia if French law were applicable or to the Supreme Court of Fiji if English law were applicable.[107] The functions of the Registrar would be combined with that of the Claims Clerk of the Lands and Survey Department, which was to be independent of the Court and have increased staff. A clerk would be appointed to do the work of the Registrar in the Land Titles Registry.[108]

In 1935 the French had rejected earlier suggestions for reform from Judge Carew.[109] The British were, however, hopeful that they would accept the new proposals, since the new system would have the effect of recognizing the preponderance of French ownership of land and at the same time achieve British objectives of preventing the registration of hundreds of thousands of hectares of undeveloped land. Moreover, there would be big savings by reducing the amount of surveying required and the advantage that title could be given quickly to developed land, thus encouraging economic enterprise.[110] It was felt that the French might indeed be inclined to accept this new concept of registration due to the fact that the French Government was now interested in acquiring title to land as soon as possible as security for the loan made by the Crédit National for French settlers, which the Government had guaranteed.[111] There is no evidence in the available documents of French opposition to the proposal and in September 1939, the Joint Court issued an order establishing a new method of survey. A traverse was to be made along the coast and large concrete markers placed on which to record bearings. No trigonometric survey was to be done for the Northern Islands. The Court recognized that it would not be possible to penetrate the islands — especially Santo and Malakula — to undertake a normal survey.[112] The momentum for change, however, died with the outbreak of the Second World War. The Joint Court handed down its last judgments in May 1941 and did not resume operation again until 1945. While the British were probably genuine in their concern that the Joint Court was abetting the French in the expropriation of ni-Vanuatu land, it should not have been surprising that such would have been the case given the procedures agreed to in 1906. The British Resident Commissioner, Mr. G.A. Joy, seems to have been an exception in his interpretation of the Joint Court's operation. Writing to the High Commissioner in 1932, he comments:

> The Joint Court in its land jurisdiction is bound neither by British or French law but by the principles laid down in the Convention of 1914 and 1906 and it is open to the Court to set up such land procedure as it considers will best suit the circumstances. I am convinced that little useful purpose would be served if the most brilliant King's Counsel were to plead orally the majority of contested land suits before the Joint Court because I feel sure that the case stands or falls on documentary evidence of title, occupation, transfer, sale and survey. The idea that the Joint Court is a 'French Court', held by a few of the British community but passed round to all, comes about through ignorance of the circumstances and of the law.[113]

It is difficult to imagine that the result of 15 years of work by the Joint Court would have been very much different, even if the Native Advocate had performed his duties more conscientiously and ni-Vanuatu had in fact understood what was taking place with regard to their land. The Joint Court was given the task and the power to register land claimed by Europeans. It did just that.

4

Anglo-French Post-War Land Policies

The Joint Court resumed work in 1945, but made very slow progress. Part of the problem was the continuing uncertainty over the position of President, which had become vacant in 1941 with the dismissal of Senor Bosch-Barrett, and the whole question of reform to the land registration system. In June 1939, the British had sought French agreement to abolishing the post of President and giving Senor Bosch-Barrett six months notice.[1] However, no reply had been received from the French prior to their collapse in 1940 and the British refused to negotiate with the Vichy Government. The British had received a letter from Bosch-Barrett disputing their right to dismiss him without agreement from the French and noting that he had been in contact with the Vichy Government who wanted him to remain in office at half pay and stay in Barcelona.[2] When this information was conveyed to the Free French, the Foreign Office received the reply from General de Gaulle that he was in complete accord with the settlement of the question of the President of the Joint Court as proposed by the British.[3] In 1945, the Court resumed its work without a President, turning its attention to the numerous applications for registration of land on Santo and the surrounding small islands. By the end of 1948, however, the Court had handed down only ten judgments, due mainly to a shortage of surveyors.

During this period the debate resumed between the British

and French governments over reforms to the land registration procedure. The issue of the position of President was raised again when, in June 1945, the British Foreign Office received a letter from Bosch-Barrett stating that he would be able to return to his position, if the Joint Court resumed its functions.[4] In January 1946, the Foreign Office instructed its ambassador in Paris to initiate discussions with the French Government in order to decide if the Protocol should be changed and the post permanently abolished.[5] The French reversed their earlier position and requested that the British agree to a return to the system in operation before 1939.[6] The British were not convinced that the system would work effectively and discussions continued throughout 1948 and into 1949, when the decision was reached to allow the Joint Court to operate without a President. It is not clear from the documents what form the final decision took. No formal change was made to the Protocol abolishing the position, thus it would seem that the governments simply agreed not to recruit a replacement.[7]

Beginning in early 1949, the Court moved to deal with a number of applications for registration on Santo dating back to the early part of the century. The properties involved were large, most were claimed by French individuals or companies, and had usually been subdivided, thus requiring the Court to approve a number of substitutions of owners in each case. This added to the Court's work, since each substitution necessitated a separate survey. Thus in 1949, while handing down 34 judgments, the Court in fact only dealt with 6 applications. Shortage of surveyors hampered the work of the Joint Court for the next decade. In 1958, when most Santo applications had been dealt with, the Court had handed down 324 judgments since the end of the War — an average of only 25 per year.[8] One property, Luganville, claimed by SFNH, was to become the basis of a major dispute in the 1960s, leading to the rise of a semi-cult movement known as Nagriamel led by Jimmy Stephens.

Attempts at Co-operation

In 1959, when the Joint Court began preparations for the registration of the large number of claims on Malakula, the British Residency became apprehensive about the effect this would have on peace and stability. Ni-Vanuatu were becoming increasingly aware of the significance of the work of the Joint Court and the British feared that there would be a strong reaction when local people realized that land which they had always considered their own — on which they had lived and worked for generations — was being permanently alienated.[9]

The British Resident Commissioner, Mr. J.S. Rennie, initiated discussions with his French counterpart, M. Deloney and in mid-1960 they requested their representatives in the islands to assess the "position of native custom relating to land owned by New Hebrideans, in the light of changing conditions, the land law of the Condominium and the increasing interest in the production of cash crops".[10] Reports from the four districts were received in mid-1961.

The District Agents confirmed what the British Resident Commissioner had suspected: that in many areas, pressure on land was increasing due to expanding population, a desire by local people to become more involved in cash cropping and the fact that some of the best land had been or was in the process of being permanently alienated through the registration of European claims by the Joint Court. The British Agent from Central District 2 noted that on Epi:

> The areas on which no claims have been made consist of narrow mountainous strips, between non-native claims, in the centre of the island and the greater part of the sparsely populated and somewhat rugged eastern end of the island.[11]

On Malakula the situation was worse:

> Non-Native applications cover about 80% of the coastline. It is estimated that considerably less than 10% of the area claimed has been developed....[12]

In the Northern District, on Santo and Malo, it was reported that:

> Most of the usable coasted [sic] land is alienated and forms the subject of registrations in the Joint Court. In both [islands] the European coastal land owners are almost exclusively French.[13]

On Efate, the District Agent noted:

> Whilst the natives in many areas may have sufficient land for cash crops and subsistence agriculture they have invariably been deprived of all good cattle grazing lands and water sources. Should the natives desire or need such grazing land in future, it is going to cost them dear unless some of the vast areas of undeveloped grazing land are now ear-marked for expansion for them later.[14]

Statistics collected by British Residency officials revealed that in 1961, about 570 applications for registration were still awaiting adjudication. For the three main islands not yet dealt with by the Joint Court, the land involved was as follows:

Island	Total Area	Under Claim
Malakula	200,000 ha.	149,200 ha.
Ambrym	66,300	5,100
Ambae	38,000	24,900

Most significant to the British was the fact that registration of these claims would affect over 25,000 of an estimated population of 55,000, either because of actual occupation or common interest in the land claimed by Europeans.[15] It was further noted that the greater part of these claims was under application by the French State or the SFNH with lesser numbers by the Commonwealth Government of Australia and the various missions; thus it was beyond the power of the British Government itself to take direct action in order to correct the situation.[16]

The British Resident Commissioner initiated further discussions with his French counterpart to seek agreement on a course of action to prevent a potentially dangerous and disruptive situation from developing.[17] In November 1961, Rennie outlined the problem and made recommendations to the French Resident Commissioner. The main focus of his argument was the judicial process of land settlement, which he felt did not adequately protect native interests, and the inability of the two Resident Commissioners to interfere due to the limitations relating to land matters placed on them by the Protocol. He pointed out that the Protocol and the Rules of Procedure for registration provided means for ni-Vanuatu to challenge claims, but they were unable to protect themselves because of the nature of the provisions, which were weighted heavily in favour of foreign claimants.[18] The danger, Rennie pointed out, was that ni-Vanuatu had in recent years become more aware of the work of the Joint Court and were bound to react negatively if a large number of claims were registered which included significant amounts of land which they did not recognize as having been sold and had continued to occupy.[19]

Furthermore, he pointed out, it was very unlikely that any ni-Vanuatu would be satisfied with the solution provided for in the Protocol, i.e. the creation of a native reserve out of a portion of the land which he and his family claimed, had used and envisaged developing. Indeed, Rennie felt that the judicial process of allocating native reserves was totally inadequate, since it lacked any clear procedure or principle for the Joint Court to follow. He noted that different judges had applied divergent methods and standards and it was apparent that some of the reserves resulting from earlier judgments were now proving inadequate. Rennie was especially concerned about a recent informal intimation by the Court that it would no longer follow the procedure which earlier judges had used, of sending out surveyors to investigate claims, the reports of whom were then used to create native reserves. The Court had indicated that in future no action would be taken to create a native reserve unless a case were submitted by the Native Advocate, showing numbers and location of ni-Vanuatu occupants, and the nature and extent of their occupation.[20] Rennie urged that immediate action be taken — perhaps an adjournment of the Court, which was about to re-convene and begin final hearings on the Malakula claims — in order to allow the necessary research to be carried out for each of the applications.[21] The reason for this expected change of policy by the Joint Court was that, with the creation of a Survey Department under the control of the Joint Administration — until 1961, surveyors had been employed directly by the Joint Court — the judges were no longer empowered to authorize surveys as they saw fit.[22]

Rennie welcomed the French Resident Commissioner's stated intention to return undeveloped French State land to local inhabitants, but noted that the Joint Court was preparing to pass judgments on many applications by private individuals and companies. As the two Resident Commissioners had no power to interfere in the work of the Joint Court, Rennie asked the French Resident Commissioner to consider requesting their two governments to modify the Protocol relating to land and to suspend the provisions pending such revision. He also wished to discuss what steps should be taken to assist and brief the Native Advocate to enable him to better protect native interests.[23]

A spirit of co-operation appears to have prevailed in the discussions which took place ten days later. M. Deloney agreed with the British Resident Commissioner's outline of the situation and felt there were grounds for changing the Protocol, though the difficulties would be considerable. He also expressed the opinion that there was still time to deal with the problems since he had been assured by the French Judge that no final decisions would be made regarding native reserves until adequate investigations had been undertaken. Both Resident Commissioners agreed to address their governments about the problems. Rennie also agreed to take up the question of Commonwealth lands and Deloney to clarify the problem regarding French State and SFNH land. They agreed that surveyors and agricultural staff would assist District Agents to obtain information for the Native Advocate.[24]

By 1961, with the establishment of the Condominium Survey Department and the recruitment of more staff, the Court was finally in a position to resume hearing claims on Malakula. However, as a result of the anxiety of the two Resident Commissioners efforts were made on both sides to minimize the effects. The British Resident Commissioner wrote to the Colonial Office suggesting that the British Government should try to persuade the French to agree to halt land registration by the Joint Court until revisions to the Protocol could be arranged.[25] Rennie's advice was not accepted. The British Government did not think that there was much chance of the French agreeing, since the very important planter lobby would have pressured the French Government to refrain.[26]

On the French side, Deloney put pressure on SFNH, which had some very large claims on Malakula and succeeded in getting the Company to withdraw or substantially reduce most of them. He was also successful in reducing the number and size of the claims held by the French State. He was not, however, very successful in dealing with private individuals and companies, of which there were a number — especially along the east coast of Malakula.[27] One company in particular, the Plantation Réunies des Nouvelles-Hébrides (PRNH) located at Norsup, refused all attempts to reconsider its land claims. As a result, within a few years, it was involved in a dispute with the former owners of much of its developed plantation, the people of Tautu Village, which threatened the continued operation of the plantation and prevented further expansion (see Chapter 6).

As agreed by the two Resident Commissioners, however, a special effort was made to ensure that the Joint Court had adequate details regarding native occupation and future needs relating to land. The chief surveyor, M. Page, and the Native Advocate, M. Pujol, were instructed to tour Malakula to obtain the necessary information. As a result, when the Joint Court began to hear land claims for Malakula in 1962, it pursued a more liberal policy (compared to earlier periods) of creating native reserves on many of the European claims.[28] Between 1962 and 1966, when the Court heard the largest part of the claims on Malakula and Ambrym, it handed down 247 judgments and designated 47 native reserves — the same number of reserves (47) which it had created in the whole of the period since it had begun land registration in 1927 until 1958, during which time it had handed down 681 judgments.[29]

The ratio used by the Court in deciding on reserves was ten hectares for each person, including women and children, in any village which would be affected by the registration of a claim and which might be subsequently short of land if the claim were registered *in toto*.[30] It has since been pointed out, however, that while the

Court often set aside relatively large areas as native reserves, the land was not usually the best available. The case of Tautu village was a particularly bad example. The land designated as Tautu Native Reserve was a long way from the village, in the hills beyond the PRNH plantation, while the Company retained the more desirable undeveloped areas nearby.

On the whole, however, the consequences of land registration by the Joint Court in the early 1960s on Malakula were not disastrous in that, except for the Tautu village dispute with PRNH, relatively few serious incidents relating to land occurred involving disputes between ni-Vanuatu and Europeans. One reason which may account for this is the fact that most of the judgments handed down for Malakula were only interlocutory judgments, which confirmed the principle of ownership, but did not amount to an order to the Land Registry to prepare a title. This was done in order to process applications quickly and included only sketch maps of the properties, the final judgments to be made when formal surveys had been completed. In several cases, when surveyors went to Malakula to complete the final step required by the Joint Court, they encountered opposition from local people and were unable to complete their work. As a result, the majority of the interlocutory judgments were never finalized.[31] Thus, a degree of uncertainty remained regarding alienated land on Malakula, which had the effect of inhibiting European expansion into undeveloped portions of their properties, as occurred on Santo and Efate.

British Policy

Officials in the British Residency continued to be preoccupied with the land problem. In 1964, they arranged for the Land Tenure Adviser to the Secretary of State for Commonwealth Affairs, Mr. Rowton Simpson, to come to Vanuatu. His report stressed the need to bring about reform quickly in order to avoid serious problems developing. He pointed to an increase in the incidence of interference by ni-Vanuatu in the work of survey teams and noted that the feeling was rising among local people that their ancestors had been cheated out of their land,[32] and reported that "a dangerous situation is arising. . . ."[33] His recommendations were, however, quite moderate. He did not, for example, advocate any attempt to undo the work of the Joint Court. Instead, "registered owners should be encouraged in every possible way to set right, voluntarily, the manifest inequalities which have occurred from some of the judgments".[34] Where foreign individuals and companies held surplus unused land, Simpson felt they should voluntarily make land available to ni-Vanuatu who needed it and could put it to use. Where corporations or individuals were unwilling to make land available to the local population, he advocated measures to "compel the owner of land which is unused or misused to make proper use of it".[35]

Simpson favoured the continuation of land registration, but advocated the formulation of a new common land law, which included ni-Vanuatu and would allow them to obtain a recognized form of legal title to their land.[36] He noted that "the more native titles there are on the Registry the less likely is it to be upset"[37] and recommended a joint Anglo-French committee to work out the details.[38]

Of prime concern to Simpson was that whatever system was developed, it should encourage the occupation and proper use of land. He advocated an improved system which would allow ni-Vanuatu to register land if they wished, and assist them in the transition from subsistence to commercial agriculture. He did not take a stand on the question of 'group' or 'individual' registration of native land, but gave examples from Africa and the Pacific where attempts to register native land had been tried and the difficulties encountered in the process. He stressed instead the importance of providing assistance through a programme of agricultural extension in order to allow local people to take full advantage of the registration of their land to improve its use.[39]

Simpson's report was summarized and submitted to the Advisory Council in 1965, the emphasis being on land reform. His recommendations relating to the transfer of unused land to ni-Vanuatu were, however, omitted. The French would only agree to the inclusion of points relating to land reform through possible legislation.[40] But even at that time, ni-Vanuatu members of the Advisory Council were becoming much more concerned with the political side of the land issue — the fact that there was an increasing number of land disputes and that they considered a great deal of land owned by Europeans had not been properly purchased.

The main ni-Vanuatu spokesman on the land issue in the mid-1960s was Dr. John Kalsakau. He and his fellow ni-Vanuatu members on the Advisory Council were anxious to have a land commission established which would look at the disputed properties, to determine what had happened and to right whatever wrongs might have been committed. In 1965, during the 11th session, the following motion was tabled:

> Seeing that there is much unrest among the New Hebridean people over certain registrations of land which were made in the past and where it seems that there was not sufficient

> investigation on the spot where judgment was given, we request that a Lands Commission be set up by the joint administration to:
>
> 1) investigate the position of undeveloped land;
> 2) to recommend what action should be taken in the case of disputed claims; and
> 3) to make sure that in future the local people are given full notice of land claims before they come to the Joint Court for judgment and that their opinions are taken into consideration in the making of judgments.[41]

Kalsakau made it clear that ni-Vanuatu were not trying to evict Europeans wholesale from their land, but to bring about just settlements to disputes because "there is perhaps going to be trouble in the future".[42] Where it could be established that Europeans had acquired land through misunderstanding or fraud — relating to the original purchaser, not the present owners — then it was proposed that a settlement could be reached whereby Europeans could remain on their registered lands by paying compensation or rent to the custom owners.[43] Dr. Kalsakau argued further that if only part of the land had been developed:

> that part which has not been developed should go back to the real owner. The commission will find out the real owner and give it back to him. If whoever is developing that land wants to lease that piece of land from the real owner then he can do so.[44]

The emphasis was on undeveloped land. Ni-Vanuatu in the mid-1960s were willing to recognize that land which Europeans had worked for a long period of time was in a different category from the large areas of undeveloped land, whether claimed or already under registered ownership.

The French Residency and some expatriate members of the Advisory Council felt the suggestion for a land commission was revolutionary and radical.[45] A countermotion was tabled by a number of European members:

> We are disturbed at the increasing number of complaints about land. We realise that these disputes relate to undeveloped land, but feel that they may at anytime threaten developed land and the work of several generations of planters.... We also think that they are likely to discourage the investment of outside capital essential to the development of the country. We, therefore, move that their rights of property should be guaranteed once and for all so that they

> may continue without apprehension the work of our forbears.[46]

Both motions were deferred and never put to the vote. The British Resident Commissioner noted that the subject had not been "brought into the light of day before" and felt that only good would come of bringing it into the open "in the spirit in which it has been approached this afternoon".[47] The French Resident Commissioner agreed "entirely" and was sure that "all our problems will be solved with a smile".[48]

Since the Advisory Council could only advise the two Resident Commissioners, who were unwilling to carry the public discussion of land reform any further, no apparent progress occurred. However, at the Ministerial Conference in July 1966, the British Government raised the issue of land reform along the lines suggested by Simpson and tried to persuade the French Government to agree to a land commission with an advisory and conciliatory role, but no powers to impose settlements. It would suggest ways of negotiating amicable settlements.[49] The French agreed in principle and a skeleton structure was worked out between representatives from the two residencies. In the years that followed, however, the French could never be persuaded to put the plan into action.[50]

In May 1966, however, prior to the Ministerial Conference, the French Residency did agree to the establishment of a land commission to deal with one particular dispute, that involving the Bonkovia property on the west coast of Epi. The British argued that such a commission would serve as a useful experiment as to how a future advisory land commission might function and what it could be expected to achieve.[51] The Commission was to consist of representatives of the two residencies, the Chief Condominium Surveyor, the British Residency Legal Advisor — because the European owner was a British optant — two Europeans (Mr. S.J. Brusch of Ambae and Mr. M.H. Russet of Vila) and two ni-Vanuatu (Mr. Michael Ala of Ambae and Dr. John Kalsakau of Vila).[52] The Commission was to make a thorough inspection of the property, note the extent to which it had been occupied by the registered owner or the local inhabitants, and hear whatever statements the two parties wanted to make.[53] The French would not agree, however, to giving the Commission access to the Joint Court dossier concerning the original judgment and registration of the property.[54] In its investigation the Commission nevertheless found itself involved in trying to unravel the early history of the land transaction which was an important part of the current disagreement.

Bonkovia, of 111 hectares, was registered in 1938 in the name of Finbow Harvey. It had been sold in two portions: the first to a trader

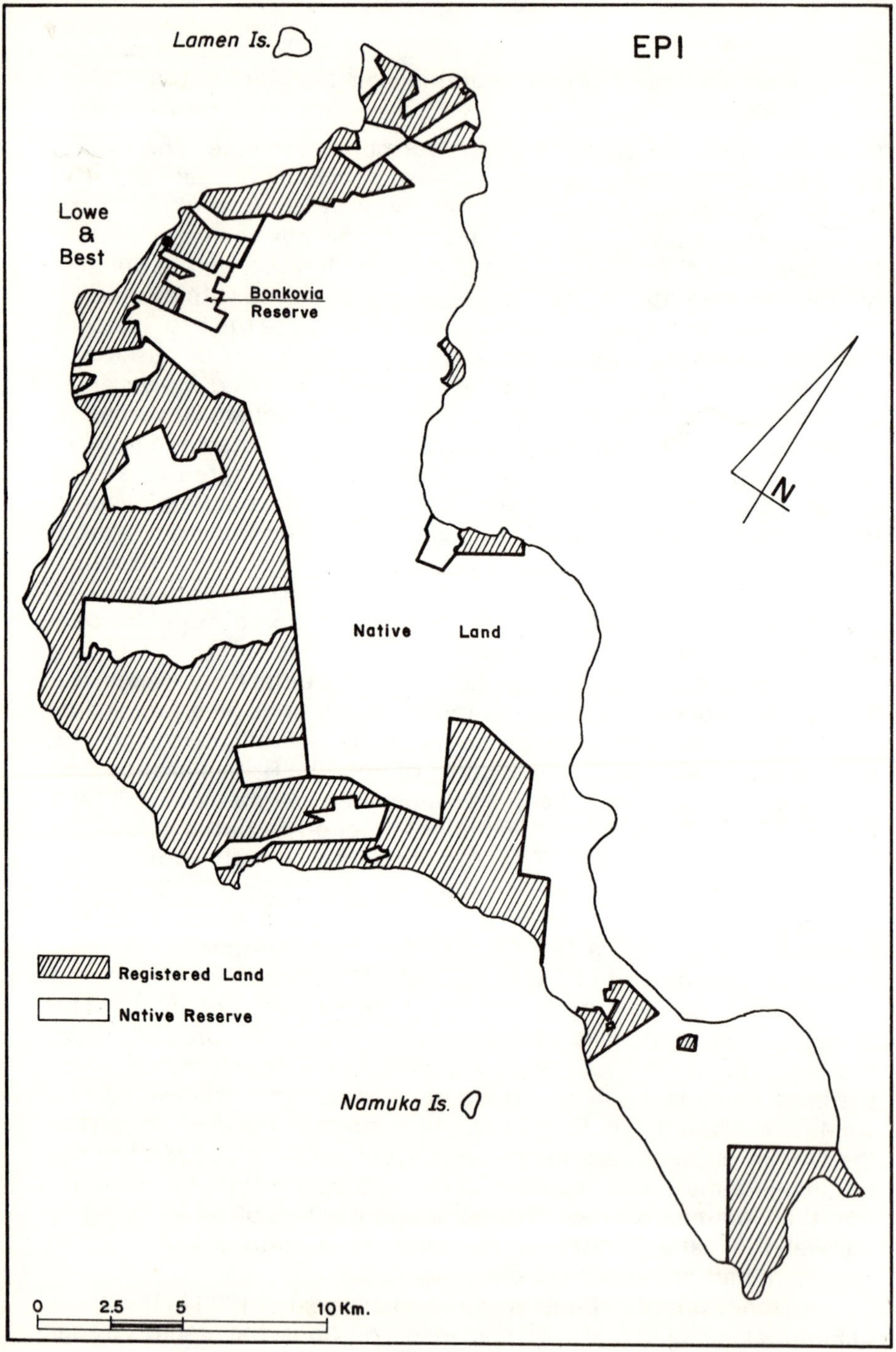

EPI
Lamen Is.
Lowe & Best
Bonkovia Reserve
Native Land
N
Registered Land
Native Reserve
Namuka Is.
0 2.5 5 10 Km.

Figure 3: Epi

named Swallow in 1899 and the second to Swallow by the Rev. Fraser and Henry Trumble a year later. Both deeds had been registered in Fiji in 1901. Swallow established a coconut plantation and store on the coastal area. He later sold the land to Finbow Harvey who lived there until his death in 1951. Harvey applied for Registration of title in 1913 — it was unopposed — and the Joint Court delivered its judgment covering registration in 1938.[55] At the same time, it created a native reserve adjacent to the property.[56] Unworked for seven years following the death of Harvey, it was purchased in 1958 for A$3,000 by Messrs. Tom Low and Roy Best, who asked the Survey Department to verify the boundaries. It was discovered that the people of Bonkovia were using two-thirds of the area of the registered property and had been for several decades. When Best sought to expand planting into the uncleared portion of the property in 1963 and 1964, confrontations began with the Bonkovia people. Best complained to the District Agents and subsequently, in February 1965, representatives of Bonkovia explained their claims to the British Resident Commissioner. In March 1966, the Bonkovians took direct action, removing to their own driers copra cut by Best's labourers, and prevented Best from working the copra on part of his land. As a result of these incidents the two Resident Commissioners agreed to the setting up of the Commission.[57]

The Commission uncovered conflicting facts about the original alienation. They were told that a Presbyterian missionary had suggested that a friend by the name of Cocker should be established along the coast in order to prevent the land from falling into the hands of French land speculators. Cocker was replaced by Swallow, who began planting coconuts, and he was eventually replaced by Harvey. The Bonkovians denied all knowledge of the application to register the land. They confirmed that the coastal strip had been sold, but denied that the inland area had. The Commission noted that none of the European owners had developed inland and recommended that the people of Bonkovia should be assisted through a loan from the Condominium to buy out Low and Best.[58]

The French Resident Commissioner, Mouradian, did not accept the proposed solution, arguing that the Commission had overstepped its terms of reference and was suggesting the establishment of a dangerous precedent:

> ... the Committee ... had gone beyond the time when Registration was decreed, thus exceeding its terms of reference.
>
> ... I have greatly stressed the danger that committees of this

> type might be tempted to carry out the registration procedure all over again....
>
> The solution recommended by the Committee... presents the risk of creating a precedent with important financial and political consequences....[59]

Mouradian was most concerned about the Commission having raised the issue of the original purchase of the property and insisted that Degree of Registration alone should serve as the starting-point of any enquiry.[60] While money was an issue, the French were clearly most frightened by the prospect of a widespread challenge by ni-Vanuatu to registered titles, which they believed the acceptance of the Bonkovia Commission's recommendations would encourage.

Nevertheless, Mouradian finally agreed to the British suggestion that the Bonkovians be assisted in setting up a land purchase co-operative.[61] This was not, however, acceptable to the people of Bonkovia,[62] and the British Resident Commissioner turned instead to the British Government for funds, which were not forthcoming.[63] In the end A$24,000 was used from British Residency funds to re-purchase the developed portion of the property. It was hoped that the Bonkovians would in due course pay for the land, but they were not interested. Their main aim had been to keep control of the undeveloped area, which they had achieved. The British Residency, therefore, retained title and used the profits from the copra plantation to support the operation of a nearby school.[64]

Despite the difficulties encountered in getting agreement on the Bonkovia problem, officials in the British Residency continued to press their French colleagues to consider further land commissions to deal with the growing number of disputes which began to flare up in the late 1960s. In November 1967, the British Resident Commissioner, Mr. Colin Allan, suggested, for example, that commissions be established to deal with the growing number of land problems arising out of the Nagriamel movement on Santo and with the increasing number of land disputes such as that between the village of Tautu and the PRNH plantation and between Fila Islanders and foreign occupants of their traditional lands in the Port Vila area.[65] The French Resident Commissioner responded that French planters had demanded strong action "to protect private property guaranteed by the Protocol" and that his High Commissioner had "ordered me to take appropriate measures".[66] He therefore declined to accept further land commissions to investigate grievances of ni-Vanuatu "since they are meant purely and simply to strip settlers of their land rights in order to divide the land among the natives.... I am now persuaded that the imposition of legal sanctions alone will succeed in intimidating the trouble makers....[67] The French Resident Commissioner argued further that any attempt to encroach on the property rights of settlers would create a long term financial problem for the Condominium by discouraging investments.[68]

The response of the British Resident Commissioner with particular reference to the Buluk/Stephens dispute on Santo reflects the growing exasperation felt by British officials at the intransigence of the French. Colin Allan made it clear that his policy was not to:

> sacrifice the interests of the French or any other planters to the unjustified demands of Chief Buluk or any New Hebridean. I am fully aware of property and public confidence in the governments' determination to preserve law and order. My sole objective is to promote the adoption of a joint land policy which will be seen by both main communities to be fair to all and will therefore bring about the kind of harmonious relations over land that we both consider to be essential.[69]

The British were just as concerned as the French about maintaining investor confidence, but their attitude was that without a land tenure system that relieved ni-Vanuatu fears about the future of their interests, there could be no long-term stability which would attract investment.

The key issue to the British was the right guaranteed to European title holders to expand their plantations into undeveloped areas of their registered properties. Allan explained that:

> the continued unilateral extension of such land occupation, based solely on the legal rights of ownership conferred by the Joint Court without regard to understandable New Hebridean fears will be a gross error that will produce an extremely unhealthy political situation and in the long run, be prejudicial to economic development because of the resulting lack of confidence between New Hebrideans and Europeans and, on the part of the former, in the Government.[70]

The British were not advocating the reversal of Joint Court decisions granting freehold titles to Europeans, but they felt that if compromises were not forthcoming regarding undeveloped portions of European owned properties, these assets and future European investments would be in real danger once ni-Vanuatu were in control of an independent government — a political development which the British could by this time see as inevitable.

With reference again to the Buluk/Stephens dispute Allan was:

> dismayed that during the three years that we have been aware of the Buluk land problem on Santo... we have not yet evolved a policy consistent with the objectives that I have just set out and now find ourselves in a situation where prosecutions of New Hebrideans for offences connected with land are considered necessary. In my opinion this situation would not have come about if we had taken Buluk's original complaint more seriously and taken measures to deal with the essential problem regarding undeveloped land in European ownership.[71]

While the French Resident Commissioner would not accept the idea of a land commission, which held the risk of bringing into question the whole issue of registered titles, he would be prepared to negotiate the settlement of outstanding land disputes on a case-by-case basis:

> I would be prepared at the conclusion of the present court case to open with Mr. Buluk and his friends ... negotiations which I would like to prevent from taking place on the town square ... I shall strive, if I obtain the authorization of my Government, to provide the people entrusted with good office with the assurance of the means to bargain. These means could be land from the domain of SFNH or the French state, for example. The exchanges could play accordingly in favour of the natives or the European owners who might have to give up their extensions.[72]

The French Residency, in fact, began the transfer of such land on Santo even before official approval was given from Paris. It was reported in January 1968, that SFNH land at Port Olry and Hog Harbour had been transferred to local communities to settle disputes hampering the company's operation.[73]

Thus, in the 1960s, British efforts to bring about land reform through co-operation with the French — either in recovering undeveloped land for ni-Vanuatu or by instituting land reform legislation or in setting up land commissions, were almost totally unsuccessful. The only time that the British were able to convince their French colleagues that decisive joint action was required to deal with the land problem came in 1971. In that year, the two governing powers joined forces to block what was clearly becoming a threat to the peace and security of the country — the arrival of a growing number of foreign (especially American) land speculators, attracted by the country's tax-free status and the apparent abundance of freehold land whose owners were eager to sell.

The first report of American businessmen negotiating for the purchase of land in Vanuatu came in September 1966.[74] The French Residency then learned of the sale of the Graziani property at Hog Harbour on Santo in February 1967 to Mr. Eugene Peacock, using a New Caledonian businessman as intermediary.[75] Peacock and others arrived just at the time when the number of disputes over land was increasing and land values were, as a result, decreasing. American interest in Vanuatu as an area for investment reversed this trend and allowed a number of European planters to sell their properties at prices they otherwise would not have been able to get. In a number of cases, the purchases were made in partnership with New Caledonian, Australian, New Zealand and local businessmen and companies. Peacock purchased six major properties in Vanuatu, which he planned to subdivide and develop as residential communities.[76]

Both residencies opposed the new land rush when it first started. The French were concerned that it would lead to an increase in the number of land disputes, as ni-Vanuatu saw Europeans making high profits on the sale of land which they themselves claimed,[77] while the British opposed any further European expansion into undeveloped areas.[78] The French, however, soon came to view the acquisition of land by Americans as an advantage, since it enabled some of their nationals to dispose of properties they no longer wanted at relatively good prices. Moreover, they welcomed the company they would have in facing the growing number of land disputes.[79] In early 1971, however, the French changed their position again and joined with their British partners to enact regulations taxing subdivisions and thus curbing land speculation in Vanuatu, though the sale of developed properties to outside investors continued throughout the 1970s.

This last change on the part of the French came about when it had become clear that Peacock was going through with his subdivision plans. Extensive clearing of bush and roadwork had been carried out and hundreds of plots sold to investors, primarily in Hawaii.[80] The French finally came to agree that it would not be a good idea to have uncontrolled subdivision of land, bringing in large numbers of immigrants with all that entailed, i.e. demands on government services which did not exist in rural areas.[81] The French, in fact, took the initiative in proposing the tax on subdivisions as a deterrent and agreed to a new regulation, which for the first time gave joint control over the immigration into Vanuatu of people who were neither French nor British.[82] The French must have realized that, while the presence of a few other foreign landowners was useful to them in their struggle against ni-Vanuatu land claims, thousands of non-French immigrants would tip the demographic balance to the point where they would no longer be in the dominant position. By 1971, the French Residency had also become concerned by the increasing number of Anglophones taking up residence in Port Vila as a result of the growth of the Finance Centre, which posed a direct threat to their dominant position in the town.[83]

French Policy

By the late 1960s, officials in the French Residency had ceased almost completely to co-operate with their British counterparts on matters relating to land. The reason for the change in attitude was a direct result of the French Government's decision in the late 1950s — in particular, that of General de Gaulle, who came to power in 1958 — to reverse the trend, which was leading France's colonies in the Pacific towards self-government and possible independence. France's Pacific territories had become important to the Gaullists in their drive to strengthen and enhance France's power and prestige in world affairs. The remote and scattered islands of French Polynesia were ideal for carrying out nuclear tests, when France lost its test-site in the Sahara with the independence of Algeria in 1962. Likewise, New Caledonia's rich mineral deposits were of immense strategic and financial value to France. Thus, moves towards autonomy, which had been gaining strength following the Second World War, had to be brought under control. By the early 1960s, autonomist leaders had been discredited in New Caledonia[84], and a growing dependence on France for its economic livelihood made self-government in French Polynesia an unpopular political goal.[85]

The implications of this new policy for Vanuatu were significant and help to explain the clear change in attitude by French officials regarding co-operation with the British in land matters. Vanuatu was not a French territory, merely an area of joint administration with Great Britain, but in the 1960s the French Government began to implement a policy which was intended to increase French influence at the expense of the British and ultimately allow France to stay in the islands indefinitely — a return to the aim which had guided French Policy since the late 19th century.

The two colonial powers were clearly divided in their goals for the future political development of Vanuatu. The retiring French Resident Commissioner, M. Mouradian, outlined the two positions in a report to the Minister of Overseas Departments and Territories in October 1969: "My instructions from de Gaulle were: 'we are staying'".[86] His role as Resident Commissioner for the previous years had been "simply to implement those instructions".[87] On the other hand, Mouradian noted that:

> More and more openly Britain seeks to lead this territory to independence.... The emphasis is on the necessity of providing the country with a manageable infrastructure, especially in matters of social equipment.... These efforts are directed towards creating unified structures which can easily be handed over to the New Hebrides 'Nation', and at the same time towards putting the brake on French expansion which is particularly marked in the social sector.[88]

Since any significant reforms to the dual system of administration required the agreement of both metropolitan governments, the French could effectively block the British as they did in relation to land matters.

Mouradian described what he considered his achievements:

> The French Residency has not allowed unified structures to be created which could undermine our influence. It has refused to agree to the integration of laws and legal procedures and above all to the extension of Local Councils and their integration at island level.... We already had our education service, we have dug a divide between the two medical services, and we have deliberately rejected, even against the wishes of some of our compatriots, plans dear to the British Residency for a joint hospital. Where political institutions are concerned, we have applied the brakes to the accelerating democratization of the Advisory Council favoured by our partners.... We have avoided universal suffrage while proclaiming that we did not fear it and organizing in the islands a network of school teachers at least as effective as the Protestant pastors.[89]

In other words, French policy was to push ahead with the development of separate French services and block any attempt at integration. At the same time they opposed any moves at political reform which would have led to the emergence of institutions of government which could have begun to challenge their position.

Education was the key element in the French strategy:

> Our efforts are based on what is now a comprehensive network of island boarding schools (Baoufatu, Isangel, Lamap, Norsup, Vilakalaka, Sola) and involve determined penetration of Anglophone areas (Nguna, Banks Islands).... I have helped the Francophone missions to confront their

> obligations by doubling their grant when I arrived and then increasing it by 10% every year.[90]

Mouradian's successor, M. Langlois, explained the philosophy behind France's education policy:

> There is a possibility of lasting political action in spreading our education system. Admittedly the results will not be immediate, but if we can manage to create an elite comparable in size and quality to the Anglophone one, and at the same time deeply penetrate the rural population, yet hardly touched, we shall be able to insure alliances which could be reflected in local community groups and finally in the Advisory Council which for the time being escapes us completely as far as its native members are concerned.[91]

By expanding the French education system, therefore, French officials hoped to create a French-speaking majority which would be reflected in future voting patterns.

It should be noted that until the 1960s, education in Vanuatu was provided primarily by the missions. About 12% of the population was Catholic, thus at the most only 12% of the Melanesian population would have been French-speaking. Until recently, the Catholic Mission was staffed almost entirely by French-speaking clergy. With the exception of a few isolated areas where the missions had not penetrated, the remaining over 80% of the population would have had links with English-speaking missions — Presbyterian, Anglican, Church of Christ and Seventh Day Adventists. Thus, in the 1960s, when the French Government set out to transform Vanuatu into a French-speaking country, Francophonie was almost non-existent. That this policy would produce a deep division among ni-Vanuatu was irrelevant to the French Government. Their aim was to stay in Vanuatu and they were willing to divide and create unnecessary rivalry among ni-Vanuatu in order to achieve it.

Health services was another area on which the French Government concentrated its efforts. Mouradian described Residency 'achievements':

> The recurrent health budget nearly doubled between 1964 and 1969, while the capital budget increased from a little more than 2 million to 36 in 1968.[92]

Like education, health care provided direct penetration into local communities and could produce a deep sense of gratitude towards France among the local population.

Mouradian's report also gave details regarding French efforts to train administrators through the establishment of a police training school, which he described as:

> training personnel who have undergone military-type discipline, have qualifications from CEP [Certificate d'Etudes Primaries — equivalent to Primary Leaving Certificate] and have received instruction in various areas: civics, accounting, typing, mechanical skills, first aid and English.[93]

It is significant that the level was relatively low by French standards. French training did not envisage the emergence of a class of ni-Vanuatu administrators who would eventually take over the running of the country, but instead a group of low level administrative officers, typists and mechanics, who had been educated with "military type discipline" to continue to take orders from French colonial officials.

The French paid ni-Vanuatu well for their loyalty:

> The highest salaries are paid by the French, be it at the French Residency, in commercial firms or recently through openings offered by New Caledonia.... Knowledge of the French language is no longer merely the key to the language of the 'mastas'; it is also and above all the key to the best paid jobs.[94]

The intended effect of this policy was to entice ni-Vanuatu to the French side, create a level of consumption which would exceed what an independent country could afford and thereby develop a degree of dependence on France which would make the idea of independence unthinkable to the local population. The French Resident Commissioner summed up the policy:

> All this means, not only that we are here to stay but also that we now matter enough in the eyes of the people for them to want us to stay.[95]

By the late 1960s, therefore, French officials felt that they had effectively established a policy that would block moves towards independence and in any case, by the creation of a loyalty to France and an extreme dependence on French aid in education and the social services, local people would not want them to leave.

This determination of the French to stay clearly explains the change of attitude apparent by the mid-1960s in their relations with the British regarding land reform. They would have been reluctant to see their dominant economic position eroded at a time when they were attempting to consolidate and expand their influence. Indeed, as Mouradian pointed out, the planter and business communities were very much a part of the overall plan to transform Vanuatu into a permanent French possession:

> We did not... neglect to help our investors and to encourage the dynamism of our settlers. Cattle rearing had made a promising start.... The timber industry has settled down and nothing was spared in helping the Agathis Co. to overcome their initial difficulties. Tourism found me reticent at first, but after examination, I gave all my support to the Lagon enterprise, regretting that M. Bourgeois, who was one of its promoters, should have put himself at the disposal of Qantas and the Australian Bank.[96]

The vast amount of undeveloped land, which made up the biggest portions of most registered titles outside the urban areas, would have been seen as having immense potential value for future economic development and, thus, expanding French influence and power.

Given the principle embodied in the Protocol of 1914, which required both metropolitan governments to agree to any change in the system, the French might indeed have succeeded in their plan to implant themselves permanently in Vanuatu. They were prepared to spend more money than their British partners on building up their system of education and social services, which in the end could have had the desired effect of creating the dependence on and loyalty to France which would have enabled them to stay. What they did not expect, but which soon came to be a far greater threat to their plans than British attempts to keep pace, was opposition by ni-Vanuatu to the Condominium system. The focal point of this opposition was the land problem, which began to intensify in the mid-1960s in the form of a semi-cult movement called Nagriamel, led by Jimmy Moses Stephens, but later evolved into a nationalist movement with the clear goal of independence.

It was a response to the threat of a nationalist movement rooted in ni-Vanuatu dissatisfaction over land — and in particular, concern over the growing influence of Jimmy Stephens — that the French evolved a new land policy designed to buy off the growing number of dissidents. The French Residency came to realize that the land problem was the issue which could undermine all their efforts to expand and implant themselves permanently in Vanuatu and thus it had to be contained in the early stages before it took on political overtones. By 1968, they had come to the conclusion that they could handle Jimmy Stephens by agreeing to hand back to ni-Vanuatu ownership of excess undeveloped portions of SFNH and French State land. As the French Resident Commissioner noted:

> Our establishment is now sufficiently deep-rooted and large, since it is tied up not only with our settlers, cattle and business people, but also with our teachers, medical staff, missionaries and administrators, to enable us to base our rights on something other than the uncertain ownership of vast areas of bushland. Each pupil that we train is worth more for our future presence here than a title deed, since we know in advance what that same pupil will think of it when he will have reached the age of reason.[97]

Many registered titles included vast amounts of uncleared bush land, in addition to developed plantation areas, and the French calculated that by giving up 'dark bush' they could satisfy ni-Vanuatu demands and at the same time retain their economic base.

Bringing the operation of the SFNH under control became a key part of the French Residency's plan to return land to ni-Vanuatu and diffuse the land problem. In 1959, the Company had regained considerable freedom to develop its land holdings through the signing of a convention with the French Government formalizing the transfer to the State of lands which the SFNH had ceded to the French Government as part of the 1934 agreement, i.e. those portions of the original 160,403 hectare grant which had been registered by the Joint Court. In addition, the Company ceded to the French Government an additional 24,500 hectares of land stemming from the earlier agreements of 1894 and 1934; and at the same time, the French Government abandoned its claim to the *zone maritime* for those properties to which the SFNH had been granted title.[98]

By agreeing to the 1959 Convention, the French Government had in effect relinquished control over the business operation of the Company, though it still retained a majority share interest. The SFNH had been given the freedom to develop its properties as it saw fit and had even begun to sell small portions of its holdings as land speculators began to flood the country in the late 1960s.[99] As noted above, however, it was at this same time that the French Government came to realize that the vast land holdings of the SFNH had become more of a liability than an asset.

By the late 1960s, French Residency officials were obviously beginning to regret the new arrangement with SFNH. They were becoming increasingly aware that the conduct and nature of the operations of the SFNH were a growing threat to French interests in the group. The Company's recent land sales, for example, were undermining the efforts of French officials to win the confidence of ni-Vanuatu who for decades had viewed French settlers, and SFNH in particular, as 'land thieves'.[100] In his May 1968 report to the Minister of

Overseas Departments and Territories, the Resident Commissioner noted that the French Residency found itself in the invidious position of having to defend its own nationals in land disputes with ni-Vanuatu, that could and should have been avoided. He noted that the SFNH had recently sold a piece of undeveloped land at Big Bay on Santo to a New Caledonian businessman by the name of Jeanin, which was claimed by ni-Vanuatu who had hunting rights over it. A dispute broke out, ni-Vanuatu were imprisoned and upon their release made another attempt to block occupation by the new owner. "This time the French Residency refused to follow it up."[101] The Resident Commissioner declared that "the time has come to examine on the spot, the complaints and claims of the natives in order to establish the limits within which the natives will be able to settle themselves without being persecuted".[102]

While not abandoning the SFNH or any settler, the French Resident Commissioner had come to the conclusion that ni-Vanuatu claims to alienated land needed to be accommodated, if France's ultimate aim of remaining indefinitely was to be achieved:

> Originally, the Company prided themselves on possessing 800,000 hectares. The enormity of this figure leaves no doubt as to the way that land was acquired, . . . I would, for all that, abstain from making the mistake of discrediting SFNH at all costs. Without them France could not have established herself in the New Hebrides, and we have to go back to the spirit of the time when the taking over paved the way for the supremacy of the European countries over lands to be colonized. However, when the Caledonian Company was liquidated at the end of the last century, Jules Ferry's France had the choice between rescuing Mr. Higginson and sending half a dozen teachers to the islands. The second solution would have been the less costly and the more rewarding.
>
> However, we ended where we should have started and it is certain that the success of our educational system gives us an influence on New Hebrides youth which might be sapped by domanial litigation.[103]

Clearly, Residency thinking had undergone a significant transformation. New directions had been embarked upon which they believed would achieve for the French what had eluded them for decades — total political control over the islands of Vanuatu.

The Minister of Overseas Departments and Territories in Paris, therfore, agreed to a French Residency proposal to hand back undeveloped land, and a Convention was signed between the French Government and the SFNH in November 1973 for the purchase of

73,097 hectares. The Company received 35,801,000 FNH with the stipulation that it be used to improve the remaining 34,672 hectares left in the Company's possession. At the same time, the French State made available 74,998 hectares of its own land to be included with that acquired from the SFNH, thus leaving the French Government with a total of 1,727 hectares of registered land.[104] In total, during the years 1973 to 1976, 148,095 hectares of land were ceded by the SFNH and French State to ni-Vanuatu as follows:

	SFNH	*French State*	*Total*
Santo	37,797 ha.	51,184 ha.	88,981 ha.
Maewo	30	—	30
Nguna	599	—	599
Epi	6,798	10,621	17,419
Malakula	21,838	10,532	32,370
Ambrym	185	—	185
Pentecost	5,850	—	5,850
Efate	—	2,661	2,661
	73,097 ha.	74,998 ha.	148,095 ha.

The effect of the land transfers was to significantly alter the picture of the SFNH and French State in Vanuatu with regard to alienated land. The SFNH retained all of its developed land and the better portions of its undeveloped properties for the future expansion of its operation:

Santo	17,013 ha.
Malo	3,805
Efate	11,245
Epi	2,227
Other islands	382
Total	34,672 ha.

Before 1973, their combined total of registered land and land in the process of registration amounted to over 30% of the total area of the country. Following the transfers, that amount was reduced to 6.3%.[105]

French Residency officials were optimistic about the potential effect of the land transfer programme. Its main objective was:

> to disarm the contest over land — to disarm the political movements which depended on it — by permitting the cession of parcels [of land] by the State to natives for the price of principle, to promote individual ownership and the development of Melanesian agriculture.[106]

The Residency also organized village committees, where land had been returned, under the guidance of the French District Agents in the various administrative districts. The purpose of the 'land committees' was to encourage development using a proposed 90 million FNH fund to be provided by the French Government. The financial support did not eventuate, but the committees had a certain political value and provided an avenue for more effective penetration of the rural areas.[107]

The Land Trust Board

In the 1970s, however, the British had a further opportunity to experiment with returning alienated land to ni-Vanuatu ownership. In 1968, the Australian Government approached the British divesting itself of the land it had received in 1902 from Burns Philp in return for granting the Company a special concession to run a mail service through the islands.[108] The Australian Government was beginning to find its ownership of land in Vanuatu embarrassing at a time when ni-Vanuatu were starting to question the colonial system which had facilitated alienation of much of their best land.[109] Moreover the land always had been a financial and administrative liability, and the legality of the Commonwealth's rights over the properties was always in doubt. In 1909, the Commonwealth Attorney General gave a legal opinion on the 1902 contract to the effect that the Commonwealth was not a competent party to any land claim in Vanuatu, that the purported assignment of lands was not a valid conveyance, and that the Commonwealth merely had a contractual right to direct Burns Philp with respect to disposal of the land. He advised that the Company should undertake to have the titles validated before the Joint Court. Burns Philp was informed of this and that the Commonwealth Government would pay all expenses.[110] For the next ten years, the Commonwealth Government maintained its own surveyors in Vanuatu to survey Burns Philp lands and those of the Presbyterian Mission. A total of 391 surveys were completed involving 49,532 hectares.[111]

Adding to the legal confusion was the fact that all the so-called Commonwealth land was registered by the Joint Court in the name of Burns Philp, which thus possessed indefeasible title. The Commonwealth's only legal right would have been to take personal action in the Australian Courts (or in the case of Burns Philp, in the British National Court in Vanuatu) to compel the Company to execute transfers according to the Commonwealth's direction. The true situation was, therefore, that Burns Philp had complete power over the disposition of the land, even if the Commonwealth still collected the rents from leases and paid the bills.[112]

The Commonwealth Government's income was miniscule compared to the amount expended over the years in administering the lands. The original land lease scheme run by Burns Philp never operated successfully. By 1915, only 19 leases had been granted, of which four had been abandoned. During the whole period of its operation, the scheme granted about 50 leases. In 1976, only 26 leases were still current. Moreover, during the entire period since 1902, the original rental of 1/2d. per acre had never been increased, which meant that the Commonwealth Government only collected about £60 to £80 per year.[113] On the other hand, from 1905 to 1934, the total survey and legal expenses came to £37,806.[114] In addition, the Government kept a solicitor in Port Vila to assist British settlers establish their titles and look after Commonwealth interests, and in the 1960s sent one at various times from Canberra to appear before the Court.[115]

Why the Commonwealth Government maintained its interests in land is not clear, since it accrued substantial losses. It was probably due to the momentum of administrative machinery, which operated mechanically unless directed to do otherwise. After the establishment of the Condominium, the question of Vanuatu was never raised at a sufficiently high level for a review of policy to occur, and thus the situation continued undisturbed.[116]

Due to the difficulties of negotiating with the French on land matters, the British set up their own system for transferring Commonwealth lands to ni-Vanuatu ownership. The Australians preferred a trust, which coincided with British thinking, so a Land Trust Board was created by the British administration under Queen's Regulation no. 14 of 1973, which came into force on 31 October 1973.[117] It created a corporate body with broad powers to acquire and dispose of land with the objective of furthering "the use of such land ... for the benefit of the people of the New Hebrides" (section 7 [1]). The Board was presided over by the British Resident Commissioner, who was an *ex officio* member. There were three official members from the British Residency, including the Attorney General; four unofficial members appointed by the Resident Commissioner, representing each administrative district; and one other unofficial member. Provision was included for the appointment of alternative members for each of the representatives of the four districts. The first members of the Board were: Roger Du Boulay, British Resident Commissioner and Board Chairman; Paul Treadwell, Attorney General; Keith Woodward and Guy Wallington, British Residency officers; John Qarani, Northern District; Sethy Regenvanu, Central District 2; Chief Graham Kalsakau, Central District 1; and Gideon Nambas, Southern District. Wilshire Webb, a local solicitor, was appointed the other unofficial member.[118] In 1976, the Queen's Regulation was amended to give the Board more control over leases, allowing it to intervene to prevent a lessee selling his lease, but in such a case stipulating that the Board should prevent "hardship to any person or persons having a valid claim in custom to land".[119]

At its inaugural meeting on 3 December 1974, a representative of the Australian Government handed over to the Land Trust Board the various certificates of title, plans and leases which it had controlled for nearly three-quarters of a century.[120] The Resident Comissioner expressed the view of the British administration that all the land taken over by the Land Trust Board should one day be returned to the indigenous people.[121] The Board acquired from Burns Philp 53 properties with a total land area of about 10,358 hectares of which 2,853 hectares were leased, mainly to expatriates. Most of the leased properties were in the South Santo area, with other important properties on Ambae, Efate and Epi. Burns Philp retained four properties for its own business operations.

The Board interpreted the long term objective of return of the land to Melanesian ownership rather conservatively. There is no evidence from the documents that it saw its role as a 'clearing house' to facilitate the immediate return of formerly alienated property. Indeed, it began by investigating the various properties — including site inspections — and gradually formulated policies as issues rose. For leased land it adopted a general policy of return to custom owners when it was clear that they could develop it.[122] The Board was inclined to hand over title to land with little potential for development, but the problem of determining the true custom owners made the actual transfer of title difficult.

Thus, for example, the Board agreed to transfer three properties on the island of Moso totalling 150 hectares and of minimal economic value, except for use to village people, but was only willing to agree to granting occupation leases to claimants of the more valuable Elizabeth Bay property on Erromango. Neither transfer took place due to uncertainty as to the 'true' custom owners. The Board's caution is understandable in view of the fact that no precedents existed. A number of small unleased properties (several less than a hectare in size) were not dealt with in detail, since they were already in the hands of ni-Vanuatu, and making an issue of them could have created unnecessary problems.

The leased properties presented different problems, in that

rent money was involved and a number of disputes existed between ni-Vanuatu custom claimants and lessees. The original rental of 1/2d. per acre had never been varied and thus only $A172 was being collected in any one year. The Board, therefore, brought in a team of New Zealand valuers who reassessed the properties resulting in annual rents of A$4,200.[123]

The valuations also enabled the Board to deal with disputed properties. It was decided that the lessees of seven of the properties would be bought out and a request for aid was submitted to the British Government in 1979. The Board offered the following amounts to cover improvements:

Siviri (Efate)	296 ha.	A$30,000
Creek Ai (Efate)	170	500
Narugu (Ambae)	174	48,000
Atzonie River (Santo)	810	18,000
Tasmalum (Santo)	203	5,000
Sanaravo (Malo)	16	1,250
Assuan (Malo)	1	500

The British Government agreed after some delay and all but two lessees accepted. The lessee for Creek Ai decided to simply surrender his lease due to the legal costs and Fred Stephens of Tasmalum did not respond.[124]

The latter case is of special interest in that it involved the family of Jimmy Stephens, who by the late 1970s was a key political figure in Vanuatu and leader of the Nagriamel movement. Fred Stephens had inherited the lease from his father Thomas Stephens, but had abandoned the property in the 1960s, when a tidal wave swept through the plantation. The Board rejected his proposal to sell the lease to Jimmy Stephens, prefering to buy it out to make it available to interested ni-Vanuatu.[125] This may explain to some extent why Jimmy Stephen's considered the French more genuine in their desire to rectify injustices over land than the British, as the French had already begun to transfer SFNH and French State land to ni-Vanuatu. In a letter to the British Residency news sheet, *New Hebrides News*, the MANH Party *(Mouvement Autonomiste des Nouvelles-Hébrides)* and Nagriamel asked why the French Administration had returned thousands of hectares to ni-Vanuatu, while the British had given back none. The official reply was that the British had "never owned large tracts of land — so they had none to give back" and that the Land Trust Board was dealing with land formerly owned by the Australian Government. Moreover, the British reply pointed out that the Land Trust Board was independent and not under the direction of the British Residency.[126]

In reality, of course, the British Residency did influence the Land Trust Board through its official members, and its influence was evident in the Board's policies. Retaining land in trust rather than returning it to customary ownership was encouraged by the British representatives on the Board and the British Government generally as expressed by Simpson, Lawrence and Fleming, the British land tenure advisers during this period. Ni-Vanuatu members of the Board agreed that alienated land which was returned to local people should be properly utilized, but they were keen that transfers should take place. The stipulation that custom owners should develop their land was the compromise settled upon by the Board members.

The British view also felt that the Board had an obligation to lessees. While ni-Vanuatu were not opposed to buying expatriate leases — especially since the money came from abroad — they were less worried about compensation as the lessees had paid negligible rent. At the suggestion of Sethy Regenvanu, it was agreed that part of the compensation money should be paid to the communities to whom the land was to be transferred. The British Government agreed, bank accounts were set up and the Department of Agriculture was given responsibility to assist the communities and distribute the funds.[127]

While the Land Trust Board was the first real attempt to establish a general policy to facilitate the return of developed land —the French were only willing to consider the return of undeveloped land — it fell short of the longer term goal of the British in setting up the Land Trust Board, that of demonstrating a possible approach to the solution of the general problem of disputed alienated land. Clearly, the Land Trust Board had evolved an effective system for meeting the demands of local people for the return of alienated land. The French would not agree to establish a Condominium Land Trust Board — as suggested by Fleming — nor would it accept financial responsibility for the repurchase of properties from French individuals and companies.

Although the chance was missed to institutionalize what could have become a valuable mechanism to deal with alienated properties, benefiting both expatriates and ni-Vanuatu, the trust concept was used by the Presbyterian church in handling the land it had held since the previous century. At the 1955 General Assembly members passed a motion to formalize the church's role as trustee over land which the various missions had acquired.[128] In 1959, a Land Trust

Association was created under Queen's Regulation No. 1 and a Land Trust Committee was established to deal with a number of issues.[129]

The Presbyterian-held land was complicated by the fact that the application for registration of the various church properties had been made by different overseas mission boards which sponsored missionaries in Vanuatu (i.e. the Presbyterian churches of Canada, Scotland, New South Wales, Victoria, Tasmania, South Australia, New Zealand and Otago). The 1961 Assembly agreed that all such land should be transferred to the Presbyterian church of the New Hebrides.[130] Foreign mission land held in trust fell into three categories: land used or to be used by the Presbyterian church in Vanuatu, e.g. land on which churches and schools were built; land used for mission purposes, e.g. land on which mission run institutions such as the Paton Memorial Hospital and Lenakel Hospital had been built; and land held in trust for the people of Vanuatu, e.g. land at Erakor and Erromango. The foreign mission boards agreed to transfer all lands to the Presbyterian Church in Vanuatu,[131] and the British and French governments waived the land transfer fees in 1966.[132] By 1970, therefore, all the land held previously by the various overseas missions of the Presbyterian church was transferred to a Land Trust Association of the Presbyterian Church in Vanuatu. In 1971, the name was changed to the Property Trust Committee.[133]

The Presbyterian church then began to grapple with the next step. One point of view, encouraged by the Australian Presbyterian Board of Missions in 1967, was that individual demands for the return of land should be resisted and the needs, interests and customary rights of the whole community concerned should be ascertained.[134] The implication was that the interests of the church community as a whole was of primary importance. The Presbyterian Church appears to have adopted this position. In 1970, anticipating the closure of the Paton Memorial Hospital on Iririki Island (the new British built hospital opened in Port Vila in 1972), the General Assembly asked its members to recommend what use the church should make of the island and the hospital buildings. At the following General Assembly in 1971, it was reported that a number of suggestions had been received: give the land to Fila Island; keep the building for a conference or church medical training centre; use it for a rest house; lease a portion of the island and the building, with half the proceeds going to the church and the other half to Fila Island; use the buildings for a girls' hostel; or turn the property into an artifact and craft training centre and develop the island as a tourist attraction.[135] No decision was made, and within a few years it had become evident that ni-Vanuatu were becoming impatient with the church's reluctance to return land which it no longer needed for its own immediate operation.[136]

The Presbyterian Church responded positively to pressure from various communities and agreed to transfer unused land to ni-Vanuatu ownership. In two cases, where communities had formed trusts to look after such land, Fila Island and Erakor, the properties were handed over. For the majority of cases, Church lands were transferred to the various regional Presbyteries to handle the final transfers, but the Presbyteries did not process further, and the status of such properties remained in question.[137]

Agreement on Reform

While the British and French governments in the late 1960s each began to evolve their own policies (the British experimenting with the concept of land commissions and repurchase of disputed properties and the French handing over to ni-Vanuatu undeveloped land), ni-Vanuatu continued to press for a genuine programme of land reform. In the new Advisory Council (ADCO) set up in 1969, Dr. John Kalsakau was replaced by George Kalkoa, who in 1980 became Vanuatu's first President, Ati George Sokomanu. He was one of the youngest, best educated and, for the times, most radical of the ni-Vanuatu members and took over from Dr. Kalsakau the role of spokesman for those urging the two governments to deal with the land question before it became unmanageable.

In the October 1969 session of ADCO there was another long discussion on land during which George Kalkoa suggested that an expert be appointed. When assurances had been given that the proposed land adviser would not be looking into the work of the Joint Court, but would assist in finding solutions to existing problems, a motion was passed proposing that "the Government recruit a Commissioner of Lands to make a study of customary land tenure in the New Hebrides and that this be a Condominium post".[138] Ni-Vanuatu members of the ADCO were concerned about the excessive alienation and the problems that it had created, but the best the British could do was to get the French Residency to agree to the appointment of a Land Tenure Adviser to look into the situation, enquire into customary land tenure and make proposals for reform. In other words he was to take up where Simpson had left off in 1964 and with what the British had tried to get through at the 1966 Ministerial Conference: i.e. he was to revive the question of land reform — including the possibility of a single code of land law and an improvement in the system of registration. The emphasis was to be on legislative rather than political reform, but the British hoped that the former would lead to the latter.[139]

In February 1972, before the appointment of the Condominium Land Officer, the British Land Tenure Adviser for the Foreign and Commonwealth Office, Mr. Jerry Lawrence, visited Vanuatu. He saw the need, more than Simpson had, to initiate a programme which would take into account the increasing number of disputes. He considered the root of the problem to be "the maldistribution of land ownership between Europeans and New Hebrideans"[140] and recommended a programme of land repurchase, concentrating on undeveloped land, but including properties which were seriously disputed. He noted that both administrations were moving towards this solution, e.g. the purchase of the Bonkovia property, the decision to return Commonwealth Lands and the repurchase of SFNH land by the French Government for transfer, along with French state land, to ni-Vanuatu. Because of these developments, Lawrence also recommended immediate reforms in respect to land registration which would include ni-Vanuatu and take into account both individual and group ownership. It was his opinion, however, that it would be "impracticable to set up a land commission which purports to review Joint Court judgments" [141] Indeed, the French Government would never have agreed to such a review and pressure to do so could have led to their blocking the limited moves towards reform which had been initiated so far.

In February 1973, Mr. Jim Fleming arrived to take up his position as Condominium Land Officer — the title of his post was redesignated locally as Land Tenure Adviser. His report to the two Resident Commissioners in July contained proposals on registration of title, adjudication of customary land, control of dealings in agricultural land, establishment of a Joint Land Trust Board to acquire, hold or dispose of land vested in it (including native reserves) or purchased by it, and formation of a Lands Department. Fleming then formulated preliminary drafts of legislation covering registration, adjudication and land control and he worked with the Attorney General on amendments to the Protocol, which would be needed as a result of his proposals.[142]

His most controversial proposals related to land transfer. Despite the separate moves by the two governments to bring this about, Fleming recognised that no progress had been made in transferring land owned by private individuals or companies. His solution was an agreed joint approach, with the two administrations providing funds for a Condominium institution, such as his proposed Land Trust Board.[143] While the need for a programme of land transfer to ni-Vanuatu was generally acceptable to both governments, the French wanted finance to be equally shared by both Great Britain and France.[144] Needless to say, the British did not, since the share of land held by British individuals in 1970 was only 23,626 hectares compared with 105,331 hectares by French nationals. Moreover, 'British' land —including that held by the Commonwealth of Australia, the various missions and the British Government itself — only amounted to 51,201 hectares. The French state and the SFNH, on the other hand, held title or claimed 94,649 hectares and 177,840 hectares respectively.[145] The British and French could never agree on a formula for financing a repurchase scheme and thus — except for the programmes of each separate government as discussed above — no progress was ever achieved in this regard.

The French Government also opposed the establishment of a Condominium Land Trust Board, though specific objections were never expressed.[146] The French were reluctant to see a system of land transfer established which, while intended to deal with unused and disputed land, would inevitably lead to a general demand for the return of all alienated land. Since they were still not committed in the mid-1970s to independence for Vanuatu, they could not support policies which would undermine their long-term economic power base there.

The French counterpart to the British Land Tenure Adviser for the Foreign and Commonwealth Office, was Inspector-Generale Robert (later to become the last French Resident Commissioner before independence in 1980) who had visited the islands on several previous occasions to deal with land and other administrative matters. Robert received Fleming's proposals quite favourably when he visited Vanuatu in 1974, even supporting the establishment of a Condominium Land Trust Board, which later proved unacceptable to officials in Paris.[147] Fleming's proposals were discussed at Anglo-French ministerial talks in London on 4 and 5 November 1974, which were a turning point in the political evolution of Vanuatu. The governments of Great Britain and France — represented respectively by Miss Joan Lester and M. Olivier Stirn — agreed to create a Representative Assembly elected by universal suffrage and administrative reforms leading to the unification of the legal system and the establishment of a new system of land tenure.[148]

Both Fleming and Robert were present for the discussion on land matters. Robert supported the Fleming report and suggested that reform should be by Joint Regulation rather than by amendment to the Protocol.[149] Presumably, the French were reluctant to take the radical step of altering the Protocol, since such a move could have cast doubt on the basis of French power — registered titles. M. Stirn had reservations on two of Fleming's proposals: the creating of a Land Trust Board and the immediate need to establish a special office to deal with land. The Ministers agreed in principle with the need to introduce land reform measures and that a "committee of experts" should study the question.[150]

At a meeting in January 1975 in London in which Messrs. Robert, Fleming and Lawrence participated, Fleming's draft legislation was studied. The French accepted the abrogation of the land provisions of the Protocol (Articles 22-27) and the need for Joint Regulations instead. From this point onwards the two powers deferred decisions on land matters, preferring to allow the Representative Assembly, elections for which were scheduled for November 1975, to deal with them.

While the agreement reached at the 1974 London Ministerial Conference and the measures taken subsequently represented a considerable advance, events would show that they did not take into account the political reality of Vanuatu in the mid-1970s. During the build-up to the Representative Assembly election, the position of the political parties on land was hardening. Ni-Vanuatu — and particularly, the New Hebrides National Party — were becoming increasingly preoccupied with excessive alienation and were now demanding the return of *all* land — developed or undeveloped. Indeed, the leaders of the National Party expressed their opposition to Fleming's work because he failed to deal adequately with alienated land. Fleming's draft and reform legislation, which was complete by mid-1976, was never considered by the Representative Assembly. Anglo-French policy had been overtaken by political events (see Chapter 8).

Clearly, the British and French governments had underestimated the groundswell of protest which began in the 1960s against European land alienation and their ability to control and direct the pace of change. While the French finally realized in the face of mounting protest that they could no longer control vast areas of undeveloped land, they did not understand (or were not willing to accept) what the challenge to European control of land symbolized — the desire by Melanesians to regain full control over their lives and their country. The French believed throughout the 1960s and 1970s, as reflected in their handling of the growing number of land disputes, that they could still gain political control in Vanuatu — even when independence became inevitable — by refusing to compromise on the right of their nationals to retain registered title to their properties and attempting to manipulate Melanesians and political events to achieve that objective.

British officials realized much earlier than their French colleagues that land reform was imperative, but following the pattern which had developed since the establishment of the Condominium in 1906, they could do little more than protest and suggest — without French agreement, change was not possible. Moreover, in the crucial mid-1970s, the ability of British Residency officials to manoeuvre was curtailed by the fact that London was not willing to jeopardize the interests of 60 million Britons for the sake of a few thousand Melanesians — Britain's new partner in Europe, following British entry into the Common Market in 1973, could not be offended. Thus, the British were locked into positions and policies which did not take into account the true aspirations of ni-Vanuatu with regard to land, nor as events would show, enable the country to achieve Britain's main long-term goal — progress in an *orderly* way towards independence. France's unwillingness to compromise and Britain's reluctance to 'rock the boat' resulted in the creation of unnecessary divisions and conflict among ni-Vanuatu in their struggle for independence. These would take many years to fully overcome.

5

Nagriamel

In 1951, the Joint Court registered a large property on South-east Santo claimed by the Société Francaise des Nouvelles-Hébrides (SFNH) known as Luganville. The judgment gave the French company title to 13,000 hectares beginning at the Canal and cutting a large rectangle into the bush northwards of the present town area. The Company began to subdivide the underdeveloped portion of the property and lease or sell it to French planters who by the late 1950s had started extending roads and clearing the bush. About this same time, ni-Vanuatu who had moved to the western side of the Sarakata River during the Second World War because of the establishment of United States bases in the area, began to move back. A major dispute developed in the 1960s between Chief Buluk and his people and the French planters who had taken up sections in the Luganville property. Chief Buluk acquired the help of Jimmy Moses Stephens, under whose leadership the dispute developed by the mid-1960s into a protest movement with cargo cult overtones known as Nagriamel, and by the 1970s into a political movement which would significantly influence Vanuatu's progress towards independence.

Land disputes were not new in Vanuatu nor on Santo — there had been violent confrontations between ni-Vanuatu and Europeans off and on during the previous 100 years, and between ni-Vanuatu for millenia before that. The land disputes of the 1960s and 1970s, however, occurred under radically changed circumstances — in the post World War II international context — and became a catalyst for the nationalist movement which would ultimately carry the country to independence in July 1980.

Early Opposition to European Settlement

Santo was one of the first islands in the South Pacific to experience European settlement. Quiros discovered and named the island in 1606 and established a settlement at the mouth of the Jordan River on Big Bay.[1] The settlement did not survive and from that time onwards the island was seldom visited by Europeans. In the early 1800s records show only an occasional visit by whaling boats and traders,[2] and Santo was one of the last islands in the Pacific to have regular contacts with Europeans. Even the missions were late in being established. There were occasional visits, but the first missionary to set up a permanent station, the Rev. J. Anand, did not arrive until 1873.

The event that ended Santo's relative isolation was the discovery in 1853 of substantial stands of good sandalwood by the firm of James Paddon, who had established a trading station on Aneityum in 1843. Other trading firms soon learned of the new find and a mild rush for sandalwood took place on Santo during the years 1856-8. So great was the demand that stations were established and gangs of labourers imported from other islands. The boom was short lived, with only negligible quantities being taken after 1865.

Except for several small holdings acquired in the 1970s along the southeast coast near the Canal and on the neighbouring small islands of Aore and Malo, purchases of land on Santo did not occur to any large extent until the 1880s. Beginning in 1882, however, Santo along with Efate, Epi and Malakula became the focal point for fierce competition between French and Australian companies seeking land. In that year a representative of John Higginson's newly formed Noumea-based Compagnie Caledonienne des Nouvelles-Hébrides (CCNH) made his first voyage to the group and in only 14 days claimed to have purchased more than 95,000 hectares (about one twelfth of the total land area of Vanuatu). Higginson's own purchases plus the claims which he bought from W.E. Morgan's South Sea Speculation Company, gave him control on paper to well over half the land area of Vanuatu. In 1928, the successor to the CCNH, the Société Francaise des Nouvelles-Hébrides (SFNH), filed 17 applications for registration of approximately 1,600 square kilometres on Santo or almost all of the island.[3]

Higginson's Australian competitors, the Australian New Hebrides Company (ANHC) acquired land on all the major islands in the archipelago, but its largest holdings were on Santo (24,000 ha.) where by 1891 they had leased land for plantations to nine Australians.[4] However, when one of the planters was killed by protesting local residents in September 1891, the scheme collapsed and most of the other settlers departed.

The reception Europeans received on Santo depended on the circumstances. In the very early period, there were reports of boat crews being attacked.[5] However, as the nature and scale of the sandalwood trade indicates, Europeans were able to maintain relatively good relations when their presence was seen by local inhabitants as beneficial. During the sandalwood boom — the 1850s and 1860s —Santo people were willing to allow European traders to occupy small sections of land on a temporary basis as trading and transhipment stations.

Disputes over land, however, began to occur with the arrival of European planters in the late 1880s and 90s. One of the most notorious European settlers was George Latour, a British subject, who in the 1880s acquired claims to over 17,800 hectares of land on Aore and the south coast of Santo. In a request for a visit by a British man-of-war to assist him in securing his claims, he reported that he was "now constituted a chief" and that British officers would be "well received".[6] In fact he had become a tyrant and was alleged to have poisoned wells on Aore to get rid of the indigenous population. The following notice was erected near the gates of his plantation:

> "Dogs and Niggers are forbidden to enter inside the Portals of these gates. Any Dogs or Niggers found therein will suffer the Penalty of Death."[7]

Latour was killed in 1890 and three ni-Vanuatu were subsequently executed by a British naval commander for having committed the offence.[8]

The following year Peter Sawyer, a partner in the Powell brothers' plantation at Nalibu — one of the Australian New Hebrides Company's properties — was killed[9] as a result of a land dispute with local inhabitants, who did not accept the sale of the property by a tribe which had subsequently moved to the nearby uninhabited island of Arake. The Powell brothers had been threatened on previous occasions when they deprived residents from the area of access to the property to shoot wild pigs. A British naval commander sent to investigate the disturbance reported that when Powell refused one of the chiefs named Malolo entry into the property he:

> became very threatening saying "Suppose I shoot pigs. What you do? Shoot me," and began gesticulating wildly and

> striking the gate with his tomahawk.... Another native named Boddil or Sebutala came to Mr. Powell's gate some time previously, striking the gate several times excitedly, saying "I have killed white men before and I will drive them all out."[10]

After some delay, a British man-of-war was sent to the area and in reprisal shelled the village of the men involved.[11]

The use of force in incidents appears to have had the desired effect. No further serious acts of violence were reported against Europeans until 1908, when the Greig family was murdered at their property at Big Bay on the other side of the island. Then, in 1923, a plantation owner by the name of R.O.D. Clapcott was killed at Tasmalum on South Santo.[12] The circumstances regarding the Greig murders have remained unclear, but the attack on Clapcott was fully investigated by Condominium authorities and revealed the existence of a cargo cult with anti-European tendencies.

Clapcott had been shot by four ni-Vanuatu, his body mutilated and his possessions taken and distributed throughout the surrounding villages. The instigator was a Santo man named Ronovuro, who had gained prominence due to his reputation of being immortal. He promised to secure the whole island of Santo for his followers with himself as king. Anyone who wished to join the movement was required to pay a fee to bring a 'big ship' to take away the 'whiteman' and leave ni-Vanuatu to enjoy the land undisturbed.[13] His influence spread through much of central Santo, as far as Turtle Bay and Hog Harbour. Prior to Clapcott's death, however, he was regarded by officials as a 'semi-visionary and harmless', his only 'mischievous' action having been to place a tabu on some roads. The British Resident Commissioner had spoken to Ronovuro and convinced him to restrict his activities.[14]

Following a period of greater than usual local mortality due to disease, the movement became more distinctly anti-European. Ronovuro began to speak of a general extermination of Europeans on Santo. At a big *singsing* a few days prior to the murder of Clapcott he announced his intentions and gave instructions on how Clapcott was to be eliminated. Ronovuro's confidence was such that when he was sent for he came willingly. He boasted to his followers that he would tell the Government that he had ordered the killing of Clapcott, that he could not be held and would not be punished. However, Ronovuro and two of his followers, Asapele and Lolorave, were found guilty and executed.[15]

There were reports of the movement's continued existence, but it was not until 1937 that signs of any real disturbance appeared.

At that time the principal character was Avu Avu, who was arrested and died in prison.[16] Again, towards the end of the Second World War in 1944, reports were received of the revival of a cult-like movement, this time under a man named Atori who claimed to be the former assistant of Ronovuro. He predicted the arrival of boats laden with cargo and urged construction of 'docks' (warehouses) to receive it. The Atori cult reveals a direct link between the movements of the 1940s and that of Ronovuro 20 years earlier.[17]

Another cult leader from the Santo bush at about the same time was Tieka, who advocated the destruction of gardens and individual family houses and the institution of a communal existence including the sharing of women.[18] Ni-Vanuatu opposition to the cult was reported to be widespread and had created difficulties within and between a number of villages in the central bush region.[19] The people most concerned by Tieka's activities were Presbyterian missionaries, who saw the movement as a threat to their work on Santo.

One factor which led to the reappearance of cult movements on Santo in the 1940s was the arrival of the American forces who established extensive military bases along the southeast coast. A Presbyterian missionary in the area reported that the presence of the Americans had begun to attract bush people to the coast to sell their produce. However, when a routine police patrol visited some bush villages, the people stopped coming because, it was said, they were frightened of the Government.[20]

Other than these minor cult manifestations, no further incidents related directly to the presence of American forces were reported at that time. Nevertheless, the American presence in Vanuatu during the War had a tremendous psychological impact on the local population and must be seen as a major turning point in its history. From 1942 to 1945, over a quarter of a million American troops passed through or were stationed in Vanuatu. Hundreds of ni-Vanuatu from all over the islands came to Efate and Santo, the locations of the main military installations, where they found employment with the American forces or just observed.[21]

The war brought a boom period to Vanuatu. Wages were high and the population, including ni-Vanuatu, acquired large quantities of surplus military stores and equipment.[22] The effect of large numbers of American troops, extensive installations and logistic support, opened ni-Vanuatu eyes to a world they had never known. Close contact with American military personnel introduced them to a different type of white man. The average American soldier was generous with government supplies and related in a more egalitarian way to local people, compared to the remote colonial administrator or the harsh plantation master. The missionary might have been more humane, but he had little property. Ni-Vanuatu observed for the first time other black men (American soldiers) participating in and enjoying the benefits of the white man's world. And they must also have become aware of the fact through the progress of the war that their colonial masters, the British and French, were not invincible.

It is not, therefore, surprising that with the re-establishment of Condominium rule many ni-Vanuatu were not content to return to their pre-war existence. Many were unwilling to go back to a totally subsistence way of life or to working for low wages on European plantations. They too wanted a share of the immense material wealth of the white man, the existence of which was clearly demonstrated during the American occupation. Furthermore, many ni-Vanuatu quickly came to realise that the one resource they possessed which could give them access to greater material wealth and a higher standard of living was their land. As the world economy began to recover following the war, the demand for primary products brought record high prices for Vanuatu's main export, copra. Ni-Vanuatu had begun planting coconuts for copra production during the 19th century, but following the Second World War their efforts intensified. It was estimated that by the late 1950s up to half of the acreage planted in coconuts was in the hands of ni-Vanuatu and the percentage was increasing every year.[23] As a result, since ni-Vanuatu found it more profitable to work for themselves, European planters experienced great difficulty in getting labour.[24] However, high copra prices did not last and by the mid-1950s Vanuatu was again experiencing an economic slump. In 1959, a severe hurricane damaged plantations and added further economic problems.[25]

As a way out of their economic difficulties European planters turned to beef production. They could run cattle on their plantations with much less labour and were assured of higher and more stable prices for the export of beef than copra. New breeding stock was imported and cold storage facilities built at Vila and Santo. A cannery was opened at Santo and turned out 180,000 cans of beef in 1964. Direct shipments of fresh meat to French Polynesia were also begun.[26] Potential profits seemed so great, in fact, that a number of European planters and companies invested in clearing undeveloped portions of their properties for grazing. Moreover, the resumption of land registration by the Joint Court in the late 1940s established permanent title to a number of very large properties — in particular, on the island of Santo — the status of which had been unclear since the early part of the century. Many of these properties consisted of large sections of virgin bush which the owners had never bothered to fence or otherwise delineate. In the process of extending their plantations, settlers disturbed ni-Vanuatu who were occupying land which they had never known to be alienated and as a result, during the 1960s and 70s, land disputes between ni-Vanuatu and Europeans increased and intensified.

By this time, however, circumstances had changed. The colonial powers — weakened by long years of struggle to win the World War — were less able to resist the demands of people strengthened by a confidence acquired through their own experiences during the war years and a determination to gain access to the material benefits offered by the modern world. The confrontations between the followers of Chief Buluk and Jimmy Stephens and European planters on Santo were little different from those of earlier days, but ni-Vanuatu found that the responses were different and that they could indeed influence events in their own favour.

The Joint Court Judgment

One factor which complicated the issue of ni-Vanuatu rights in the Luganville property was the ambiguity of the 1951 Joint Court judgment. It did not give absolute and unrestricted ownership to SFNH, since it provided that:

> the natives who belong originally to the district may erect buildings and make gardens and plantations on the areas not occupied by the owner company or its assigns, for as long as the said areas remain unoccupied. They shall retain the right to the use of such buildings, gardens and plantations, for as long as these are used or worked by them. They shall have at their disposal such rights of way across said areas as may be necessary for the use of their buildings, gardens and plantations.[27]

Although not a very generous concession to native interest, the judgment did represent a slight change of attitude on the part of the Court and a deviation from its normal procedure of providing for the needs of indigenous people. Instead of delineating a native reserve to be surveyed and registered along with the claimant's portion of the property, the Court allowed the indigenous inhabitants access to any unoccupied areas within the property.[28]

The SFNH was concerned about the provisions "defining the beneficiaries of the right of user and the duration of their right"[29] and requested an interpretative judgment, which was given in June 1959. The Court ruled:

> that the native beneficiaries of the right of user provided in land registration judgment No 442 on the 10th November, 1951 in regard to the 'LUGANVILLE' property shall be those established on 10th November, 1951 within the limits of the said property, as well as their descendants, but such right of user... shall not in any case be enjoyed by any of them for more than ninety-nine years (that is until 10th November 2050) nor after the date on which they may have ceased to use or exploit their buildings and plantations....[30]

The Joint Court, therefore, specified the criteria for Melanesian rights and placed a time limit on them, but did not specify the individuals nor the location of the rights.

The other aspect of the original judgment which could have led to problems was the absence of specific boundaries of native occupancy. The SFNH did not specifically request the Court to deal with this issue in its interpretive judgment, so it is assumed that SFNH officials did not see this as a major problem due to the fact that Southeast Santo had a very small indigenous population. The Company was most likely unaware of any ni-Vanuatu living in or near the area and felt that by defining the duration of occupancy rights, they would be finished with the problem. Since no census was taken, however, neither in 1951 nor 1959, a degree of ambiguity remained.

The Buluk Land Dispute

There is some confusion regarding Chief Buluk's origin and link to the land in question. He claimed to have been born about 1900 at Tanafo,[31] the area in which he and his followers eventually settled on Santo, but this was questioned by M. Gauger, the French District Agent (FDA) who investigated Buluk's original claim. He reported that any trace of the original hamlets in the area had disappeared and that Buluk was established further inland before the war in a village outside the SFNH claim at Tambetsar.[32] Whatever may have been the truth, Chief Buluk claimed custom rights to the land at Tanafo and was supported in his claim by a number of ni-Vanuatu from the area. Given the nature of ni-Vanuatu customary land tenure systems, it is not unusual to find someone with claims to land which he or she may never have occupied. This would be common in a period of declining population in which land rights would pass to the last surviving member of a family or larger kin-group. Indeed, such was the situation on southeast Santo in the pre-war period, where the population had declined dramatically.

In 1956 Buluk and a few followers established a village called

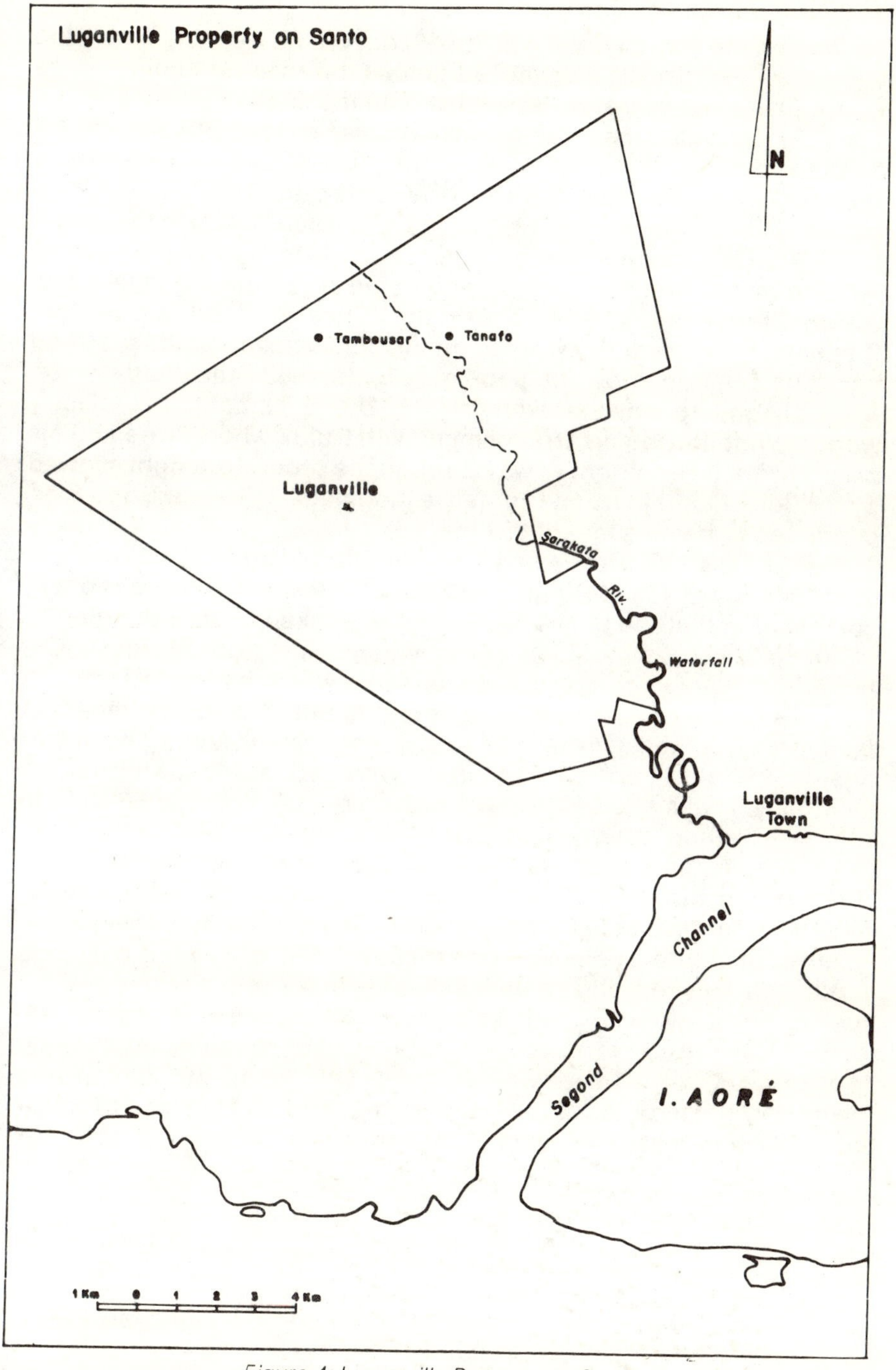

Figure 4: Luganville Property on Santo

Velliara within the Luganville property, but on the western side of the Sarakata River. In 1961 he moved across the river and built a large house just inside the area, which became the subject of the dispute. The FDA attributed the establishment of this house to Buluk's interest in the progress of a road, cleared in 1956-57, which extended a former American road towards the Sarakata River. The FDA's investigation in September 1964 found 87 persons living in the area.[33]

In 1961 the first incident in the dispute took place when a Mr. Simonsen, who was renting land in the area from the SFNH, told Jimmy Stephens that he had no right to use the road in question. Stephens had previously worked on the construction of the road and had thus come to know the people there. In 1962 Buluk and his son were alleged to have broken fences, but a complaint was later withdrawn following an arrangement with Buluk whereby he and his people were given a right of way through the property, a right allowed by the Joint Court in its interpretative judgment.[34] The road, however, continued to be a source of dispute.

The dispute first came to the attention of authorities in Vila in July 1964, when Chief Buluk wrote to both Resident Commissioners complaining that the SFNH had wrongfully taken lands belonging to various native communities. He demanded the restitution of these lands and claimed compensation for cattle which had been removed from his land by Europeans.[35] Later that month Buluk, accompanied by Jimmy Stephens, visited the Native Advocate in Vila to complain against the SFNH and M. Procuruer, who had leased land from the Company. It was at the Native Advocate's request that the FDA made the investigation referred to above.

On 3 March 1965, a meeting took place at the home of Jimmy Stephens, chaired by Chief Buluk and attended by his followers, including Simon Garae (a Church of Christ leader from Ambae) and a number of Santo bushmen. This was the first of several meetings organized by men and their families in the Santo area who were having problems with land. This group would eventually form the core of the Nagriamel movement. As a result of this meeting, the first 'Act of Dark Bush Land' was issued.[36] This manifesto, which was really only the minutes of the meeting, resolved that the land of Buluk and his followers should be kept for native use:

> "Comments from Chief Buluk and other bushmen's chiefs say, our land must be kept to our native families and our relatives. . . ." It was also pointed out that they had been given to understand from their forefathers and the Joint Court ". . . that no French planters could claim the land beyond the cocoa and coffee plantations' end." Nevertheless,

> Messrs Charles and Procuruer had expanded their plantations into the "Dark Bush" without Chief Buluk's permission.[37]

References were made to the destruction of five "heathen villages" by a bulldozer driven by Jimmy Stephens on M. Procuruer's behalf during the construction of the road to the waterfall on the Sarakata River. It was also stated in 1962, that another bulldozer had excavated the graves of Chief Buluk's mother and father.[38]

These references to destroyed villages and graves are important since they imply long habitation by Buluk and his family. Now these people were being deceived, according to the 'Act of Dark Bush Land'. The road which had originally been constructed for public use was being used by French planters to expand their land holdings, "without the permission from the natives of the land".[39]

Another significant aspect of this meeting was a request made to Jimmy Stephens for help:

> Please Jimmy, from today and onwards we are extent [sic] to you our right hand of fellowship that you be with us always as an eye witness and a mouth piece in all property and lands etc. Please in god love and kind act help us.[40]

The complaints spelled out above and this appeal for help were the cries from a people frustrated and bewildered by events which they no longer felt they could control. The man Chief Buluk and his followers had chosen as their spokesman was not a true *man Sānto* by blood. His mother was from Motalava in the Banks Islands and his father was of mixed Tongan and European descent. However, he had attributes which made him attractive as someone who could achieve what they could not. He was well travelled by ni-Vanuatu standards, having worked on a trading vessel which had taken him to Australia. More important, he knew Europeans and their ways and had worked with the American military forces in Santo during the war. One of the names they used to call him was 'American Jimmy'.[41]

According to Jimmy Stephens, one of the jobs he had during the war was to accompany the American officers whose task it was to move ni-Vanuatu out of the bush areas on Santo close to the military camps. Stephens says he was with the American officers and helped to explain to the bush people that they would have to move. He reports they were told that the land was not being taken permanently, that after the war the natives could have it back. This was the basis for the claim which Chief Buluk and others had to the land in the Santo bush near Luganville town. If this did occur, as Jimmy Stephens tells it, his involvement would have made him the ideal person to help

Buluk and his followers. This is the reason which Jimmy Stephens says the people used to persuade him to help them in their struggle over land.[42]

Furthermore, although Jimmy Stephens was not a *man Santo* by blood, he was born on Santo at Tasmalum on the south coast and had close links with the people involved in the Clapcott murder. His father had worked on a trading boat belonging to Clapcott. According to Jimmy Stephens, at the time of his birth in 1926, his mother was assisted by a woman named Vehaii who was the niece of Ronovuro. Stephens called Vehaii his 'second mother'.[43] The precise date is not clear, but some years later his father left Tasmalum with his family in search of work elsewhere. Stephens later returned to Tasmalum and in discussions with local residents found out the details of the Clapcott incident. A year later he left Tasmalum again when government officials returned and ordered the plantation workers to move back into the interior of the island because of all the troubles which had taken place.[44]

There is, therefore, clear evidence that a direct link existed between the Nagriamel movement of the 1960s and 1970s and that of the 1920s, which had resulted in the murder of Clapcott. The first was Atori, the key figure in one of the cargo cults of the mid-1940s, who claimed to have been one of Ronovuro's assistants and to have stayed with Vehaii at the same time as Jimmy Stephens. Even more significant was Jimmy Stephens' link to the troubles at Tasmalum through his relationship with Ronovuro's family and friends.

While the March 1965 meeting marked the formal beginning of Nagriamel, the movement and Jimmy Stephens' association with it had been growing for a number of years. According to Jimmy Stephens, Chiefs Buluk, Varikara and Tora had approached him for help in the late 1950s, when they ran into opposition from Europeans as the displaced Santo people attempted to re-establish themselves on the land claimed by SFNH west of the Sarakata River. At that time, Jimmy Stephens owned a small trading vessel which he used to transport goods between New Caledonia, Australia and Vanuatu. One of the trade items was guns, which eventually got him arrested after a group of ni-Vanuatu complained that he had taken their money and not delivered the goods. However, according to Jimmy Stephens, he was released from gaol when the people who had ordered the guns realised that he would be of use to them in their struggle to regain possession of their land and asked that the charges be dropped.[45]

In 1960, a meeting took place attended by the above mentioned chiefs and Jimmy Stephens at which the Santo people again asked him for help. According to Jimmy Stephens, he asked them what power they had which would help them to hold onto the land:

> They replied that they had nothing but their traditional customs. But they didn't know how best they could utilise their custom, and looked to me for an answer.[46]

Custom to these people was symbolised by two leaves, *namele* and *nagria*. The *namele* leaf represented custom law and the *nagria*, the people, in particular 'women', who traditionally in time of war were exchanged to establish peace.[47] Stephens says he was impressed by their explanation and told them that they should unite behind their common custom, i.e. "grip the *namele* and *nagria* together", as the means to win back and hold their land.

He then sent representatives to the nearby islands in the North of Vanuatu to seek wider support. August Maliu went around Santo, Sam Wells around Ambae and others went to Malakula and Pentecost. Each man was instructed to ask the people they met whether they knew the two leaves and accepted them as representing their custom. According to Jimmy Stephens, within a few weeks the men returned with baskets of *namele* and *nagria* leaves, which people from the different islands had given his representatives. This symbolized their acknowledgement of custom and their unity with the people of Santo in their struggle over land.[48]

About this time Chief Buluk and his people moved across the Sarakata River and established at Tanafo. Shortly thereafter the first incident of trespass took place. Encouraged by the initial support, Jimmy Stephens sent out more of his followers to make contact with ni-Vanuatu seeking to regain alienated land. During the next few years groups of supporters were established in all islands of northern Vanuatu from the Torres Islands as far south as Pele and Nguna.

On 20 November 1965 a second meeting was called by Chief Buluk and his followers and another 'Act of Dark Bush' issued in which Jimmy Stephens was authorised to visit Vila to make representations to the Joint Court on their behalf. It was resolved also that the land should be returned "entirely to the Santo Bushmen's descendants from this time onwards".[49] Shortly after this meeting Jimmy Stephens and several others called on the officers concerned with land questions in the British and French Residencies and explained the complaints. However, there is no evidence that they made any attempt to see the Joint Court judges.

Following the trip to Vila, still another meeting took place in Santo on 15 January 1966, this time attended by over 600 men, women and children, including some from other islands. At the meeting Jimmy Stephens and Chief Buluk were introduced as the two head chiefs of Santo. Stephens addressed the meeting and stated that he did not intend to fight or oppose anyone, but to get everyone to work together to improve conditions in Vanuatu. In future, if anyone had problems with land, they were to see Jimmy Stephens or Chief Buluk.[50]

What had begun as the frustrated efforts of a small group of Santo bushmen was solidifying into a substantial movement with clear goals and a defined leadership. A growing feeling of confidence appeared among the people involved that they could effect their own solutions to their problems. They had received no satisfaction from their approaches to government and the visits of their leaders to Vila had produced nothing. It is, therefore, perhaps no coincidence that at about this time reports were received by police in Santo of several cases in the Luganville area of ni-Vanuatu squatting or illegally planting gardens on European registered land. The police were called and minor confrontations between Europeans and ni-Vanuatu began to take place.[51]

The lack of positive response from government led Stephens and Buluk to seek help from outside Vanuatu. In February 1967, Stephens wrote on behalf of Chief Buluk to the High Commissioner of the Western Pacific in Honiara, explaining that they had reported the intrusion of white men into the "dark bush land" to the two Resident Commissioners but had received no response. He described further intrusions that had resulted in the burning of houses and the destruction of gardens.[52] A reply was eventually sent by the High Commssioner, but only after months of delay.

In the meantime Jimmy Stephens wrote to the Secretary General of the South Pacific Commission and made two submissions to the United Nations. The first, dated 2 June 1967, was merely a copy of the letters sent to the two Resident Commissioners and to the Western Pacific High Commissioner.[53] The second, dated the following month, included more details about the land problems of Santo bushmen and a copy of the latest 'Act of Dark Bush'.[54]

The incidence of trespass and confrontation continued to increase. In November 1967 it was reported that Buluk and Stephens had attempted to settle some Ambrym people on land owned by a Frenchman, Edouard Allegre, who was in the process of selling his land to a ni-Vanuatu, William Ezra. Buluk and Stephens visited Ezra and argued that only Chief Buluk had authority to allocate land and that any arrangements made with Europeans or government had no effect. They warned him that if he continued to clear the boundary and failed to recognize the authority of Buluk, they would evict him.

The situation became tense when survey markers were removed and fences cut.[55] In late November, Buluk, Stephens and the Ambrymese whom Buluk had tried to settle on Allegre's land were convicted of trespass and sentenced to three to five months in prison. Stephens appealed and with the help of the Fiji lawyer, Mr. Karam Ramrakha, had his sentence reduced to two months which he served from March to April 1968, plus paying a fine of $50.[56]

Anglo-French Reaction

Soon after the two Resident Commissioners first became aware of the Buluk land dispute in July 1964, contact was established through the two District Agents on Santo, but no reply was sent to Stephens' letter from either residency. The first public mention of the movement came at the end of 1968 in the joint statement of the two Resident Commissioners at the opening of the sixteenth session of the Advisory Council:

> . . . a re-settlement operation now being carried out by some New Hebrideans in the Vanafo area of Santo. Whilst in some respects e.g. their desire to develop the land for agriculture and cattle with the help of modern equipment — these people are forward-looking, in others they seem to be pre-occupied with the past in as much as they talk a great deal about custom law. Although it was necessary earlier this year to punish some of the people involved in the Nagriamel movement for illegal entry onto land we are watching its activities with interest and we shall not oppose any desirable project which will not disturb good relations between the various communities.[57]

Until this point no mention had been made of the movement or its leaders either in the two residencies' information bulletins or on the radio. In the early stages officials tried to avoid encouraging its leaders by giving them official recognition.

Throughout 1965 and 1966 the two residencies did not understand or were not willing to accept the significance of the Buluk/Stephens affair, despite reports from both District Agents on Santo detailing the rapid growth of the movement. As late as February 1967 the French Resident Commissioner referred to comments from the British District Agent (BDA) who saw the claims by ni-Vanuatu over land on Santo as a generalized phenomenon and not an organized movement. He admitted that Buluk and Stephens were a nuisance, but felt "the claims would develop into nothing and that giving into them would be a regression".[58] Although some officials in the British

Residency were concerned about the land situation, some still felt (as the French clearly hoped) that by ignoring it, the Buluk/Stephens problem would simply fade away.

In anticipation, however, that harsher measures might be necessary, and as the incidents increased in the first half of 1966, the two residencies agreed to strengthen the trespass law. A joint regulation was passed providing for a fine of up to $50 and/or imprisonment of not more than six months.[59] Several ni-Vanuatu were subsequently convicted for trespass on the Jeanin property at Big Bay. It was suspected that they had been incited by Buluk and Stephens.[60] The official reaction to this incident and that of trespass involving the attempted settlement by Buluk and Stephens of Ambrym people on M. Allegre's land which lead to the conviction and eventual prison sentence, indicates a hardening on the part of the two residencies and a willingness to confront Buluk and Stephens.

The British Resident Commissioner reported to the Western Pacific High Commissioner that he had tried to convince his French counterpart that the problem would not disappear and that positive action was needed.[61] However, the incidence of trespass increased in 1966 and involved attempts at taking permanent possession of portions of registered properties through illegal squatting and planting. The British Residency reported that the French had assumed a stance of immovability.[62] Both residencies now agreed that firm action, while not solving the problem, was necessary to prevent it from getting out of control. Initially, however, the British were not prepared to press for the arrest and conviction of Buluk and Stephens, but wanted the two governments to deal with the underlying issue which had led to the trespass — the future of undeveloped land in European ownership.

By late 1967, the British had become firmly convinced that the joint administration:

> was drifting into a dangerous position in which New Hebrideans, because they have received no satisfactory reply to their representations about land grievances, are beginning to think that their only remedy is to take the law into their hands.[63]

In a letter to the French Resident Commissioner on 23 November, the British Resident Commissioner proposed that the two governments should establish a working party to advise on a modern comprehensive land code and suggest improvements in the procedure for registration of title, "with a view to facilitation of title on behalf of New Hebrideans" and to advise on a single land code to govern all transactions in registered land. He also suggested that Buluk and Stephens be informed that the two Resident Commissioners were prepared to set up a land commission to investigate their grievances, but would not tolerate their taking the law into their own hands.[65]

While convinced of the need for land reform, the British wanted to avoid a situation, similar to what happened in Solomon Islands in the 1950s when long standing grievances began to manifest themselves in a semi-cult movement called Marching Rule. One of the aims of Marching Rule had been to set up a native administration in opposition to the colonial government.[66] Furthermore, the British were concerned about "a political movement of an unbalanced kind owing its origin to a grievance".[67] It was obvious to the British that a clearly defined grievance was already taking on a cargo cult tinge. Continued inaction could only lead to its growth and spread. The French, however, totally opposed the British suggestion of a land commission, either to look at the general problem or at specific cases.

Despite the reluctance of the British, the prosecution of Buluk and Stephens went ahead. Their conviction and subsequent two month prison sentence had a result which probably neither government expected. While in prison, French Residency officials talked to Jimmy Stephens about the land problem. As a result, the French came to believe that it might be possible to negotiate settlements as they had begun to elsewhere:

> If Stephens is convinced of the possibility of relying on administrative action to settle those of his problems which are most pressing and real, it is not impossible that solutions of the kind reached elsewhere could be found soon in Santo.[68]

By the time of Stephens' release in May, the French had concluded that indeed he and his movement could be contained:

> His theme is as follows: Melanesians never sold land to Europeans. Owing to this he categorically refuses to recognise any registration of undeveloped land which might have been approved by the Joint Court.... He accepts only the old agreements valid for the right to use the land which according to Melanesian custom are the only rights recognised; the ownership rights remain theirs.... He abstains from claiming developed parcels since in this case, the occupation rights have been used.... He does not at all intend to prevent the economic development of this country by the settlers or the companies, but when he refers to occupation of undeveloped land or the cultivation of fallow

> parcels, the right to use the land must be subjected to new agreements and must not be based on permanent ownership, which to him and his kind is an alien way of thinking.[69]

The French had achieved a certain understanding of the land problem in Vanuatu. The discussions with Jimmy Stephens confirmed their earlier thinking that French land interests could be preserved by negotiating agreements with individuals and communities whereby undeveloped portions of registered properties or claims under application for registration could be handed back in exchange for acceptance of permanent alienation of developed areas.

French officials had been extremely frightened of Jimmy Stephens and his movement when confrontations between his followers and European plantation owners began in the late 1960s. Since the vast majority of alienated land in Vanuatu was held or claimed by French nationals and companies they were most vulnerable to attacks from ni-Vanuatu pressing for reform. The French Resident Commissioner expressed this fear in August 1968:

> Whatever the future of the movement shall be, a string of claims has emerged and we have to consider it. It is urgent to find a solution to the land litigations if we want to prevent them from growing into disputes which would diminish our influence at the moment it is increasing.[70]

Thus when French officials found they could negotiate with Jimmy Stephens, the cultivation of his support for French policy and his co-operation in settling land disputes involving French plantation owners became a major aspect of French strategy in Vanuatu until the country became independent in 1980. They agreed to build a primary school as a means to "gain a foothold at Fanafo"[71] and extended the road to Tanafo through to Big Bay which provided access into an area in which French investors were interested, but at the same time gave Stephens access to his supporters in the north of Santo.

At a meeting held at Tanafo shortly after his release from prison, Stephens indicated that he had taken seriously the offer of negotiated settlements made by French officials:

> Stephens told the story of his detention... and ... the contacts he had made. His tone and his speech remained restrained. No doubt this calm attitude indicates a wish to spare the administration from whom positive action is expected. It will remain for as long as the hope of settling the dispute will last.... The meeting of the 5th of June allowed a

> few of its members to state claims which Stephens collected and will present to us.[72]

The plan to transfer French State and SFNH land to ni-Vanuatu individuals and communities was eventually approved in Paris and a land adviser sent to help prepare the transactions. The first transfers were made in 1973, and by the end of the 1970s, almost 150,000 hectares of land were handed over in this way.

Another aspect of French strategy in dealing with the Nagriamel movement was to encourage links between Jimmy Stephens and the millionaire French businessman from Noumea, Andre Leconte. The French Residency learned in late 1968 that Leconte had contacted Stephens about the possibility of acquiring a large piece of land on Santo for development as a cattle station. Mouradian, the French Resident Commissioner reported:

> I encouraged him (Leconte). I am convinced that a resistance to Stephens' action can be found in exploiting virgin land, on the condition that the natives are informed of these projects and that they benefit, for instance, through technical assistance. A kind of co-operation can bind them to the fate of European enterprise and turn them away from paralysing claims.... M. Leconte intends to provide his native neighbours with help in clearing some land and in making roads.... I do not entertain hopes about Stephens' and his kind's good faith, but if such a method allows a period of calm, long enough to develop a profitable rearing station and some lull in the land claim movement through the clearing of bushland for native development, we will then be able to look on it as a success and a test.[73]

The French obviously had their doubts about the reliability of Stephens as a partner in working out a permanent solution to the land problem, but the link with Leconte was seen as a way to divert Stephens from the issue of permanent alienation. Leconte's proposal was appealing, since it provided the opportunity to prove to Stephens and his followers that they could benefit from a European presence.

The agreement provided for Leconte to gain control over 10,000 hectares of Santo bush land. He would receive one hectare of land in exchange for supplying one hour's clearing of bush or road work with heavy equipment (i.e. bulldozers, graders, etc.). Jimmy Stephens consulted a local law firm and was informed that the agreement was "entirely unsatisfactory from the point of view of you and your friends...."[74] The legal adviser pointed out that the agreement did not provide for leasing, but outright sale of the land; that the land was to be handed over immediately upon signing the agreement

Jimmy Stephens and Nagriamel members at Pekoa Airport, Santo, awaiting the arrival of the French High Commissioner, M. [illegible] (Photograph from ***Nakamal****, No. 51, March 1974)*

before any work had been done for the original landowners; and the agreement was vague about what Leconte was to do, since nothing was included regarding size of equipment or amount of work to be accomplished in an hour.[75] It is not certain whether Jimmy Stephens took the advice of his legal adviser to renegotiate new terms. In any case, an agreement was signed, Leconte was reported to have purchased cattle for the scheme and bush clearing was in process by May 1970.[76]

The British were suspicious of Leconte from the beginning and considered the agreement "dangerous politically".[77] Once details of the project were known it was clear to both residencies that the Leconte deal was no better than the land transactions of the last century which involved unscrupulous speculators taking advantage of inexperienced land owners. The French, however, hoped that Jimmy Stephens' involvement with Leconte would lead to his decline:

> This businessman recently sent him a 'little bus' in a poor state of repair and is going to do some clearing at his own expense for the benefit of Fanafo village. But one day, the people of Nagriamel (sic) will have to be told that each hour of the bulldozer's work will have to be paid for by giving up the 'rights' over one hectare of land. It may be an advantageous agreement, but not very much in keeping with the doctrine of the Act of Dark Bush which was meant to keep Europeans within the limits of the land they had already developed. Naive as they may be, the followers will come to suspect a collusion between M. Leconte... and Stephens. In the meantime, I hope Leconte will have acquired and developed the land he is coveting. If that went together with a backward step of the Nagriamel (sic), the result of the operation would be very positive.[78]

The French Residency continued to support and advise Leconte,[79] who did not follow through with his promises. Very little land was ever cleared at Tanafo and by the mid-1970s he had fallen out with Jimmy Stephens and ceased his operation on Santo.

Leconte was, however, only one aspect of the French Residency strategy to influence and control Jimmy Stephens. In the early 1970s, working through their District Agents, the French set out to build a network of political groupings to counterbalance the National Party by capitalizing on existing differences within the Melanesian community. On Tanna, the French District Agent, M. Pouillet, concentrated on welding together the conservative, custom-oriented groups into a political alliance against their traditional rivals who had retained links and continued to work with the administration and the missions and were strong National Party supporters. On Santo, Jimmy Stephens was successfully manoeuvered into an alliance with the MANH Party (Mouvement Autonomiste des Nouvelles-Hébrides) and Tabwemasana. MANH, which was formed in 1974, was a coalition of French colon and business interests plus the Francophone mixed race community on Santo focused in Luganville. Tabwemasana was a small Francophone-oriented party based in Port Orly. In the 1975 Representative Assembly election these three political groups combined to oppose the National Party. Although Nagriamel and Tabswemasana fell out following the election, the French were able to pull the groups together again into a loose alliance known as the Union of 'Moderate' Parties, which functioned until independence in 1980.

The American Connection

By the early 1970s, Jimmy Stephens had become involved with a far more dangerous group of speculators: Americans eager to establish a permanent base in Vanuatu to take advantage of the country's status as a tax-free haven. Jimmy Stephens' association with the U.S. military during the war, which inclined him to view Americans as generous friends who had saved Vanuatu from the Japanese, made him the ideal partner. When the joint administration moved to block plans by certain Americans to subdivide their land into residential lots for sale to overseas investors, they rallied behind Jimmy Stephens' Nagriamel movement and his French supporters on Santo in an attempt to subvert the Condominium Government by fostering secession and rebellion. Jimmy Stephens was too gullible and, unfortunately for the country, realized too late that he was being used by his American associates to achieve their own unscrupulous objectives.

Jimmy Stephens was first reported to have made contact with American businessmen in late 1969 in connection with a proposal to develop banana plantations on Santo.[80] Two businessmen were involved: an American named Hunter and his New Zealand partner, Macassey. Jimmy Stephens travelled to Suva to meet them regarding the proposal in April 1970,[81] but there is no further mention of the project in the documents. Hunter and Macassey subsequently acquired properties on Malakula and Santo, though it is not clear whether Jimmy Stephens was involved.

Jimmy Stephens made several trips to Suva during 1970-71 to consult his lawyer, Karam Ramrakha, who during a visit in February 1971 helped him to draft a petition on behalf of Nagriamel to the

United Nations Committee of 24 on Decolonization. In the petition he condemned the Condominium administration and requested that a team be sent to determine whether or not the people wanted independence. If so, he proposed that it should take place immediately. He also wanted a UN commission of inquiry into land matters and was quoted in the *Fiji Times* as saying: "Natives are being imprisoned and in many cases they have been terrorised off the land."[82] Neither of the administrations were concerned about the petition; the French attributed it to Jimmy Stephens being manipulated by Fijian nationals.[83]

Jimmy Stephens' trip to Suva in February 1971 and the UN petition may have been far more important than the officials realised. While in Suva Jimmy Stephens made contact with an American businessman, Michael Oliver, alias Moses Olitsky, who had visited Vanuatu in May 1970 to explore the possibility of acquiring land[84] and in July of the same year concluded arrangements to buy a 503 hectare property on North Malakula.[85] In February 1971, Oliver was back in Vanuatu exploring the possibility of developing land on Erromango as a joint venture involving Macassey, Burns Philp, the Presbyterian Church and ni-Vanuatu landowners.[86] In June 1971, the French Residency learned that Jimmy Stephens had had discussions with Oliver in Suva, regarding plans for the development of a coconut oil mill, schools, dispensaries, roads and wharf facilities in return for the cession of a large amount of Nagriamel-controlled land.[87] While suspicious of Oliver, who was reported to have had links with the Mafia,[88] officials remained unconcerned about his link with Jimmy Stephens. The French Resident Commissioner dismissed the plan as "not to be taken seriously".[89]

French officials were unconcerned about Jimmy Stephens' contacts with American businessmen. Furthermore, there is no evidence that the French decision to join with the British in blocking Oliver and his associate, Eugene Peacock, in 1971, by the enactment of Joint Regulations limiting sub-divisions was due to any apprehension regarding Jimmy Stephens' links with American business interests. However, Jimmy Stephens' association with Michael Oliver was to have far-reaching consequences. The joint move against the subdivision schemes provided the basis for an even closer relationship between Jimmy Stephens and his American friends.

With the enactment of the joint regulations controlling subdivision of land, American interest in Vanuatu declined over the next few years. Only Peacock, who had made a substantial financial investment, remained active. In November 1971, he closed his hotel at Lokalee Beach on Santo[90] and in 1973, began to negotiate the sale of property near Vila to Australian interests.[91] At the same time he instituted litigation against various top officials in the British administration, whom he considered primarily responsible for the subdivision regulations.

Michael Oliver, the other key American, temporarily turned his attention elsewhere. In the mid-1960s he had been involved in the ultra-conservative libertarian movement in the United States, which was convinced that the American economy was headed towards a major collapse and the country was becoming a fascist/socialist dictatorship. In 1968, Oliver published a book entitled *A New Constitution for a New Country* in which he outlined the decline of the American system, his plan of action for founding a "new country" and its constitution. Oliver viewed human freedom and *laissez-faire* capitalism as one and the same and advocated the establishment of a "new country" where he could escape the "coming collapse" and "onslaught of totalitarianism".[92]

Oliver's proposed constitution reflected his fear of government control and infringement of individual rights and was mainly concerned with outlining what the future government of his "new country" could *not* do. It could not for example, issue money, levy taxes, regulate relations between employers and employees, limit the ownership of weapons, provide financial support for educational institutions, become involved in or subsidize any business. All services such as posts and communications, transportation and even roads were to be operated by private individuals or companies. While forbidding discrimination based on race or religion, it also guaranteed individuals the right to segregate or integrate without government interference. Payment for such government services as military or police protection was to be made voluntarily by those wishing for services.[93] Freedom for Oliver was above all the freedom to make money. The individual was to be 'free' to be uneducated — or to die — if he couldn't find the necessary cash to do otherwise.[94] Oliver's problem was where to establish his "new country". As one of three directors of his newly founded 'Ocean Life Research Foundation', he planned to reclaim up to 400 acres of the Minerva Reef, 200 miles southeast of Tonga and 400 miles southeast of Fiji. The flag of the 'Republic of Minerva' was raised on the atoll on 20 January 1972. Oliver's plans were foiled, when on 15 June 1972 the King of Tonga declared Tongan sovereignty over Minerva Reef and set up a refuge station.[95]

Having failed to establish his "new country" in uninhabited regions, Oliver turned to the Bahamas, which had become independent in 1973 and contained on the island of Abaco a group of white settlers who opposed the new government and had tried to secede before independence. Promising substantial grants of land to the settlers and lesser amounts to the native inhabitants in return for their support, Oliver created the 'Abaco Independence Movement' and the operations necessary to seize control of the island which were "disguised as the uprising of an autonomous, locally organized independence movement". He organised the training and arming of an insurgency force, set up a high-powered radio station and a despatch centre for handling air cargo using a small sea plane, wrote a constitution based on that in his book and prepared for a unilateral declaration of independence on 1 January 1975. To prevent the Nassau Government turning to Great Britain for assistance, Oliver was able to extract an assurance from the British Government through the House of Lords using an associate in his pay, Robert Hamilton (Lord Belhaven), that Britain would not intervene in the internal affairs of the Bahamas. The Nassau Government, however, came to realise what was happening and banned the movement, prohibited the immigration of its organizers and seized weapons bound for the island.[96]

Following the failure of the attempted takeover of Abaco, Oliver created the Phoenix Foundation in June 1975, which published a regular newsletter and whose aim was to promote his philosophy and facilitate the founding of a "new country". Using the good offices of a young British lord, the Foundation approached the Government of the Gilbert and Ellice Islands Colony (now Kiribati and Tuvalu) regarding the possible purchase of one of the Line Islands. The offer was rejected when enquiries revealed the true origin of the request.[97] About this time Oliver turned his attention again to Vanuatu, where political events appeared to have made the situation rife for a takeover bid similar to that of Abaco. It is not clear whether Peacock was associated with Oliver before, but in 1975 they joined forces and, working through Nagriamel, began an offensive designed to split Santo from the rest of Vanuatu and create a separate independent "new country" along the lines espoused by Oliver and his associates.

For Peacock, the situation provided the possibility of validating his subdivision and recouping his investment. He had been on good terms with Nagriamel for some time — close allies in fact. In August 1974, when confronted by supporters of the Natui Tano party opposing the subdivision scheme, he was backed by Nagriamel members, who openly guaranteed to allow settlement on the Peacock estate.[98] Oliver did not have the same investment on Santo, but must have recognized the greater possibility for success in the case of Santo than Abaco, given the fact that Vanuatu was not independent and was experiencing a difficult period of political change. He noticed, "in contrast to Abaco, we found that the people of Nagriamel have been exceptionally well organised..."[99] The situation was rife for political manipulation.

The event which provided Oliver and Peacock with the opportunity to increase their political involvement was the National Party's surprise victory in the election for the first Representative Assembly in November 1975, when it won over 59% of the popular vote and all six Santo seats. Claims of voting irregularities on both sides resulted in the Joint Court invalidating the results for five of the six Santo seats. In the re-elections in October 1976 two MANH/ Nagriamel candidates were elected, one of whom was Jimmy Stephens who, enraged by the defeat of Nagriamel in the 1975 election, turned to Oliver and Peacock for support. As Oliver said, "Nagriamel asked for advice and I gave it".[100]

The Nagriamel movement became the Nagriamel Federation, which included the islands of Espiritu Santo, all the small surrounding islands, all the islands of the Banks and Torres group and any other settlements wishing to join the Federation.[101] Meetings of Nagriamel supporters took place at Tanafo, organized with the help of Oliver and Peacock, the latter providing transport, culminating in a rally in Luganville on 27 December 1975 of MANH, Tabwemasana and Nagriamel supporters estimated at 3,000. At the meeting, Jimmy Stephens announced a declaration of independence for his newly formed Nagriamel Federation, scheduled for 1 April 1976 and later postponed to 10 August. In addition, in a joint letter to the two Resident Commissioners, the contents of which he revealed at the meeting, he demanded that the British administration should leave Santo by 1 April 1976 and that the French administration should take up the joint (Condominium) services.[102] Jimmy Stephens did not intend Vanuatu to become totally independent at this time. He wanted Nagriamel to be free from the Joint Administration, with France looking after general services.

Oliver and Peacock moved quickly to capitalize on the situation. They supplied Nagriamel with a 125 watt transmitter, allowing daily broadcasts of Radio Tanafo, and a second transmitter to provide Stephens regular contact with his American friends overseas.[103] In addition, with American support, Stephens sent two emissaries to the United Nations, James Garae and Timothy Wells, in an attempt to get international recognition for the new break-away state. They were accompanied by Michael Oliver and Ratu Osea Gavidi from Fiji. On their way back the two representatives stopped off in Suva to make contact with the Fiji Government.[104] James Garae,

Foreign Minister of the Nagriamel Foundation, told the *Fiji Times* that his Government wanted to attract investors and land developers. It had abundant land and the Government would offer 99 year leases to developers.[105] They also displayed samples of gold coins minted at the Fletcher Mint in California,[106] a Nagriamel passport and their new flag. Oliver provided the "new country" with its constitution and Stephens announced that all members of the Nagriamel Federation would be issued with Land Share Certificates. The Phoenix Foundation supplied Gavidi with a plane which it was alleged was intended for arms smuggling, but the Fiji Government grounded it for 'technical' reasons.[107] The similarity to Abaco is striking.

The British and French agreed to declare Oliver, Peacock and their associates prohibited immigrants. A number of Americans assisting Jimmy Stephens at Tanafo, including technicians operating the illegal radios, had their residence permits revoked and were forced to leave. A light plane carrying several wealthy American businessmen attempting to fly illegally to Santo was refused permission to land and compelled to return to Nadi.[108]

The two Resident Commissioners could not, however, agree on how to deal with Jimmy Stephens. The British began almost immediately after the December demonstration to press for the arrest of Stephens and the confiscation of the illegal transmitters of Radio Tanafo. The French Resident Commissioner admitted in March 1976 that "the indictments for breach of the Joint Regulation on law and order are not lacking".[109] Moreover:

> All the parties, moderate or not, are agreed in condemning the present action of Nagriamel, are asking that a stop be made to its broadcasting and are requesting the administrating powers to clear the New Hebrides of its subversive strangers.[110]

Yet, except for the restrictions on Oliver and Peacock and the departure of Jimmy Stephens' other American advisers, the French refused to join their partners and the British would not act alone. Thus Jimmy Stephens remained free to continue flaunting his disregard for the joint administration. Radio Tanafo continued to operate until independence in July 1980.

The French reluctance to act was based on their belief that they still enjoyed a favoured position in the eyes of Jimmy Stephens and his followers and that once he had been stripped of his American support, he could be enticed back into the Francophone fold: "Jimmy Stephens considers that French authorities in the New Hebrides cannot but support him . . ."[111] Moreover, they feared that too strong a reaction could push Stephens into the arms of their greatest adversaries, the National Party:

> If we manage to cut off Jimmy Stephens from his American protection, his enterprise can rapidly be jeopardised and no doubt, it will be easier to bring him back to reason. There is, however, a snag that has to be avoided, namely that disappointed in his expectation, his sympathy may turn towards the National Party... That is why... the French Residency's attitudes must remain supple towards a still recoverable and numerically important Nagriamel.[112]

For the French, political objectives clearly outweighed any concern for long-term peace and stability.

The unwillingness of the governing powers to take decisive action to control the illegal activities of certain political elements did much to undermine their credibility among the population as upholders of law and order — an obligation assumed by Great Britain and France with the 1914 Protocol. The French Resident Commissioner noticed that:

> the National Party, who one must admit were able to keep apparently calm during the last three months, are now beginning to show surprise publicly about the forbearance the administrating powers have towards the Fanafo movement which deliberately showed its contempt of the law and its will to reject the two Condominium authorities.[113]

The refusal of French Residency officials to join with the British to put down acts of lawlessness in Vanuatu, when their own supporters were involved, and the unwillingness of the British to exert the necessary pressure to force their partners to fulfil their obligations, became standard practice and was a major contributing factor leading to the rebellions on Tanna and Santo at the time of independence. In 1980, the rebels felt confident to move, knowing from past experience that they were unlikely to face significant opposition from the governing powers.

At this time French officials had their first hint of the extent to which the settler and business community might resort to extra-legal activities to protect their interests:

> The concern shown in this sector... is not without some interest, fed with the situation of the Comoros — in particular Mayotte. The fate of this island seems to incite many European elements, persons of mixed race or close to Nagriamel of Santo to think that this would be a way to follow.[114]

There is no evidence that the Francophone community in 1975 made any definite plans to turn Santo into a second Mayotte.[115] Instead, through their political party, MANH, they adopted a strategy of encouraging future political development along the lines of a federal system with a weak central government elected indirectly through strong regional assemblies.[116] This concept of federalism — and in particular, the idea of a regional assembly for Santo — was attractive to Jimmy Stephens and was one of the factors which enabled the French Residency, working through the MANH Party, to keep Jimmy Stephens as an ally. He participated in the elections of 1976 and 1977, in which he won seats in the Representative Assembly, under the apparent belief that through national politics he could influence the course of events and achieve his goal of autonomy for Nagriamel on Santo.

Following the 1975 election and the declaration of semi-independence, therefore, Jimmy Stephens was diverted somewhat from his American friends. However, the moves in January 1976, which blocked Oliver and Peacock from Vanuatu, did not cut off contact completely. Financial assistance continued to flow. Only two months after Oliver and Peacock were declared prohibited immigrants, another allocation of funds was despatched from California.[117] And up to the time of independence, various Americans and other nationals working directly or indirectly for Oliver visited Stephens at Tanafo, despite the tighter immigration control of the two residencies. Oliver had not given up his plans for Santo.

Cargo Cult or Political Movement

Jimmy Stephens' success in dealing with alienated land cost him two months in jail, but resulted in a rapid increase in support for Nagriamel throughout much of northern and central Vanuatu. In 1969 it was reported that Nagriamel had 10,000 members.[118] By 1971, Jimmy Stephens claimed 22,000,[119] and much of this increased support came from areas where there was little alienated land e.g. West Ambae, North Malakula, North Ambrym and Pentecost. Furthermore, Nagriamel did not attract support in a number of areas where alienated land remained a problem. Tautu Village on Malakula, for example, had seen much of its best land taken in the 1920s by a French company with the aid of a gunboat. In the early 1960s the dispute broke out again and continued through the next decade. The people of Tautu, however, did not join Nagriamel and became staunch National Party supporters.

Thus, while the struggle over alienated land initially galvanized support behind Jimmy Stephens, it was not always the primary motivating factor among the rural population. The vast majority of his followers were attracted more by what his success in dealing with the land problem symbolized — a victory for ni-Vanuatu in their confrontation with the European power structure. Jimmy Stephens sensed from the start that land was only the superficial reason for the frustration of those who appealed to him for help. Their goal was what land meant to rural people — access to material wealth and a higher standard of living through its development.

The first evidence of Jimmy Stephens' appeal in areas where alienated land was *not* a serious issue came in 1967, when he made contact with the Church of Christ community on West Ambae. This was viewed with concern by British and French officials, since the people of that part of Ambae had a history of hostility towards the colonial administration dating from the early part of the century.[120] West Ambae had also experienced one of the most rapid transitions of any rural community in Vanuatu from a subsistence to a cash economy, which in the process had undermined the traditional political system whereby graded titles (*na hungwe*) were acquired through the exchange and sacrifice of pigs.[121] The impetus for the change came after the turn of the century, from the Church of Christ missionary resident at Nduindui by the name of Waters, who encouraged planting of coconuts to give local people access to the range of trade goods available from local stores. The situation on West Ambae was unusual in that relations between missionaries and traders in most of Vanuatu were hostile, but at Nduindui, Waters and an Australian trader together laid the foundation for a Christian community based on cash-cropping.[122]

Hostility towards the colonial administration developed from an incident related to rivalry between Christian converts and the remaining pagan elements. In 1911, with the approval of the British Resident Commissioner, the Christians installed one of their new converts, Sale Bani, as a 'Christian Chief' to assist the mission and the administration in maintaining order in the community. The French Resident Commissioner received complaints in 1914 from French traders in the area that Bani was preventing local people from going to their stores and had become extreme in enforcing the new code of conduct which had been formulated as part of his installation as Chief. The French Resident Commissioner despatched a warship to arrest Bani and held him in prison in Vila for two years without being charged. He was finally released after protests from Church of Christ and Anglican missionaries.[123] The leader of the disaffected group on West Ambae in the 1960s — Jimmy Stephens' main contact — was Abel Bani, Sale Bani's son.

Michael Allen, an anthropologist who worked at Nduindui in 1960-61, reported that the people of West Ambae still used this incident to rationalize their unwillingness to co-operate with European officials. Church of Christ people on West Ambae, for example, refused to participate in the Local Council which the administration had set up in 1962. Allen quotes local people as saying, "the Government gave us chiefs and then put them in jail and told us the chiefs are no good. It is good that we do not listen to what the Government says".[124] The disaffection with European society and institutions extended to the mission. While not rejecting Christianity, Church of Christ members effectively took over the running of the church on West Ambae. European missionaries were still present in the 1960s, but they played almost no part in the government of the Churches of Christ.[125]

Given this history of contact with European culture — rapid conversion to Christianity and adoption of a cash economy, followed by disenchantment and rejection of the colonial administration — it should not be surprising that the Church of Christ community on West Ambae would come to exhibit cargo cult tendencies. The occasion was the establishment of the huge American base on Santo during the Second World War — a short trip by launch from Nduindui. It was not uncommon for half or more of the population to be in Santo at any one time, either working for or just observing the Americans.[126] Allen reported that in 1960-61 there was a widespread belief that when the Americans withdrew from Santo they landed a plane on Ambae and took Tagaro, the creator deity, back to America where he still resided. The Americans were teaching him all they knew and that one day Tagaro would return to share it with the people of Ambae.[127]

Jimmy Stephens' attraction to the Church of Christ community, who felt isolated and oppressed, is understandable. The circumstances were ideal for the arrival of a hero-messiah to restore their prosperity and prestige. However, there appears to have been more practical motives for the link with Nagriamel. A representative from the British Residency, Mr. J.F. Yaxley, reported after discussions with Abel Bani and others in July 1967 that:

> the Nduindui people, most of whom came from Malo to colonise West Ambae in the last century, are intending in the long run to settle their surplus population back on Malo, possibly Tutuba and also the east coast of Santo. The alliance with Buluk/Stephens may improve the chances of

> their move into Santo where they already have a foothold in the Canal and at Kole.[128]

Indeed, Jimmy Stephens had already invited groups of supporters from other islands to settle at Tanafo and there were thousands of hectares of sparsely populated land in the interior of Santo to which he had access through his influence over the bush people. Thus, while alienated land was not a serious problem for the people of West Ambae, it would seem that land was an underlying issue leading to the link between the Church of Christ and Nagriamel, which was formalized on 29 June 1967, when Jimmy Stephens was baptised into the Church at a ceremony attended by an estimated 3,000 people, including 300 from West Ambae. At the same time, a Church of Christ building was dedicated at Tanafo.[129]

Another area of support for Jimmy Stephens was in the central islands, south of Santo, where a cargo cult tradition owed its origin to administrative action taken to suppress the John Frum movement on Tanna. In 1941, tensions which had been building up within Tannese society for years were manifest in a rejection of the mission way of life and a return to 'custom' practices — dancing, *kava* drinking and living in dispersed family hamlets instead of concentrated Christian villages. The situation began to get out of hand when men began to proclaim themselves John Frum, one of whom organized a labour force to build an airport for American planes and threatened the British District Agent with an armed guard. The administration reacted by arresting a number of the movement's leaders. Several, considered too dangerous to be held on Tanna, were moved to Port Sandwich on Malakula, where they quietly continued to preach their message, spreading the John Frum movement throughout most of the central islands, especially Ambrym, Paama and Epi.[130] There is no evidence of any organized cult movement arising directly from this implantation of John Frumism but it can be assumed that its introduction created a psychological environment which would make the area receptive to similar manifestations.

One such movement infected the area several years after the John Frum incident. In 1939, several men from around Matanvat village in the north of Malakula had organized a co-operative movement to increase copra production. With the help of a local planter, the co-operative succeeded in expanding plantations and marketing copra.[131] However, contact between members of the co-operative and American forces in Santo during the war, changed the character of the movement. Shortly after the War, pro-American demonstrations were staged and an American flag was raised at Matanvat village. The French District Agent arrested three of the leaders: Ragrag Charley from Malakula, Paul Tamlumlum from Ambae and Bule John from Pentecost.[132]

Following their release, the movement continued to pick up momentum. Ragrag Charley planned to build an airport for planes loaded with cargo promised him by Captain Otto, an American he met during the war in Santo. In 1947 Bule John began constructing a new road on Pentecost, which again landed him in jail at the hands of the French District Agent. And in 1949, the co-operative installed the son of one of its leaders in Santo as agent to oversee its operation. The Malakula Native Company (Malnatco), as it came to be called, had as a result acquired a clear organisational structure, which began to extend its links beyond North Malakula to other islands. Trade in copra and cargo developed, especially with certain villages on Pentecost and Ambrym as well as other locations on Malakula. Company members received a plaque stamped with their membership number and the company's inscription — Malnatco.[133]

Ragrag Charley continued to be involved with the movement, having made contact with the John Frum exiles at Port Sandwich, and was linked to rumours that alcohol, arms, ammunition and a black flag were to be acquired by the Company. In 1951, sensing that such talk would lead to repressive measures from the government, members of the company expelled Ragrag Charley and he left for New Caledonia. Thereafter, the movement settled back into a basically co-operative organisation which ceased to arouse concern among Condominium administrators.[134] It is significant, however, that the villages which had links to Malnatco in the early 1950s were also Nagriamel strongholds, along with a number of others, two decades later.

It is clear, therefore, that to many of his supporters, Jimmy Stephens was the hero whose coming is awaited in so many Melanesian communities who feel oppressed and look for someone to restore their prosperity and prestige. Indeed, Jimmy Stephens adopted some of the trappings of a cult hero. It is not coincidence that he accepted "Moses" as one of his names — the culture hero of another age, who led his people out of the wilderness into the promised land. The name "Moses" was given to him when he was baptised into the Church of Christ in 1967.[135] He also found it useful to emphasize his links to Ronovuro and the Clapcott affair at Tasmalum. The wooden walking-stick he carried was said to have belonged to Ronovuro and his birth at Tasmalum and close ties to

Ronovuro's family would have made him in the eyes of the Santo bush people a natural successor to their own earlier cult hero.[136]

Jimmy Stephens was not, however, the classical cargo cult leader. He did not claim psychic powers, nor feed his followers with dreams of ships arriving laden with cargo. His emphasis on custom as the fundamental force behind the movement may appear conservative and backward-looking, but there is no evidence that Jimmy Stephens aimed to return to the pre-contact past. On the contrary, he viewed custom as the force to unite ni-Vanuatu for positive action against the European power structure and as the basis on which to build a new socio-economic order:

> Nagriamel is not the party. Nagriamel is not the politic. It's the people's heart, it's the people's custom. But to lift it up again ... you must use it in the proper way... Nagriamel is been before me. But to reform him again — grip it together and put it on the flag and we fly it up. That's my job. People ask me — we want our Nagriamel to be fly... and for our coming children. I said I will do my best and Nagriamel will be for you black pikinini.[137]

This emphasis on custom as the source of strength for a revitalized Melanesian society gave Nagriamel its appeal outside Santo and continued to unite Stephens' followers within once the land problem appeared solved, i.e. once ni-Vanuatu rights to undeveloped bush had been recognised.

Unfortunately, most officials and observers dismissed Nagriamel in its early stages as simply a cult movement. It exhibited all the usual characteristics: the tendency towards collective action, a large village as symbolic 'custom headquarters', the attempt to imitate Europeans in plantation development and the emphasis on money as "the key to cargo".[138] It is difficult to comprehend, however, why such features should have been singled out as evidence of a cult movement, when almost every other society in the world exhibits similar traits. Why for example, should the collective action of Jimmy Stephens and his followers to oppose the Condominium system be seen as somehow less legitimate than any other political movement or grouping? Why should Tanafo be perceived as any different from London or Paris, which are also important centres of culture and tradition for the people of Great Britain and France? Most agriculture departments in developing countries emphasize the need for rural people to adopt modern techniques to improve production — Nagriamel members' desire to imitate the European plantation would seem to be, therefore, quite progressive. And clearly, if the emphasis on money as "the key to cargo" is to be interpreted as evidence of a cult movement, Nagriamel must be seen as insignificant compared to the capitalist cargo cults of Europe and North America.

A few officials in the British Residency sensed that Nagriamel represented something far more significant than a passing cult phenomenon. Mr. J.F. Yaxley, special adviser in the late 1960s at the time of the first census, travelled throughout Vanuatu and was able to meet with various leaders of the movement. He noted that Nagriamel:

> might fizzle out ... it might develop into a bizarre and dangerous politico-religious organization... or with luck it might even become a suitable vehicle for future economic social and political progress which the Administration might be prepared to aid and encourage in much the same way as it helps the more orthodox units of local government. May I suggest that the best policy to pursue would seem to be for the Administration to keep open, and if possible, extend sympathetic lines of communication with Abel Bani, Buluk and Jimmy Stephens.[139]

According to Jimmy Stephens, however, the only official who ever made an effort to understand Nagriamel was Keith Woodward, Political Adviser in the British Residency in the 1960s and 70s:

> He always said, "Come into my office. I like to talk some story Jimmy. Tell me all about what is you think to do or what is your plan to do." ... But those government, no they just said get out — they tell me to out, out — that's only thing they said. Get out ... But Woodward, every time he called me to his office and he said, "Sit down young man and tell me your story. What do you want?" And I explain almost everything ... and he said, "Oh, great pity, but I think you take your way it's very wrong. Or it's very hard to get this ground back" .... He's got chance to talk, but not the government and not the mission ... But only one English fellow, he like to talk to me, he like to listen, but he cannot do much, but he like to listen — that's Mr Woodward.[140]

The British were reluctant to act in dealing with Jimmy Stephens and were extremely cautious with regard to Nagriamel due to their earlier experiences with such movements in Solomon Islands. The course of action Jimmy Stephens followed, which led him into association with unscrupulous foreign businessmen and increasingly unlawful activities, was at least partly due to the attitude of the two residencies. It is to the discredit of most British and French officials that they were unable to see Jimmy Stephens as anything but a cult leader. Had they made an effort to guide and educate him along lines which could have brought the results he desired — to view him as a positive force for change — they could perhaps have saved the country from the violence and disruption which accompanied independence in 1980.

Jimmy Stephens' desire for positive change can be seen in the administrative structure he created for Nagriamel, using custom as the basic foundation.[141] The most important institution was the 'Land Committee' consisting of 21 custom chiefs from Santo, representing different tribes. Its main function was to discuss proposals made to it by individuals and companies wishing to acquire access to land for development. Outsiders were expected to negotiate through the 'Land Committee' rather than directly with landowners. If a proposal was considered worthwhile, the 'Land Committee' would consult with the landowner and help negotiate lease arrangements. The sale of land was forbidden by custom and the maximum term for a lease was set at 45 years, with the possibility of renewal by mutual agreement. The 'Land Committee' was also authorized to investigate land disputes, though final settlement rested in the hands of the 'Ten Head Committee' (see below).

The next level of administration was the 'Upper Committee', which consisted of 15 members, one each from the 15 islands which recognized Nagriamel. Its function was to oversee projects which had been approved by the 'Land Committee', to organize the building of roads and water supplies and to authorize and monitor surveying. Representatives from islands outside could be chosen to the 'Upper Committee' after they had resided five years at Tanafo learning village rules and how to negotiate in land dealings. It was not possible to determine to what extent the power of the 'Upper Committee' was accepted in the other islands, but the presence of non-Santo people on it seems to indicate that it was perceived as a regional administrative structure for Nagriamel. In 1977, when Jimmy Stephens outlined this structure in an interview, there was no evidence as to the actual functioning of the structure but it does indicate that he saw Nagriamel as uniting a wide group of ni-Vanuatu with similar aspirations and problems.

The third and highest administrative body was what Jimmy Stephens called the 'Ten Head Committee', membership of which was limited to people who had achieved chiefly grade. As with the 'Upper Committee', only people who had resided at Tanafo for at least five years could be chosen. It is not clear to what extent the power of the 'Ten Head Committee' was accepted in the other islands, but its membership indicates that it was intended to have influence beyond Santo. Its main function was to deal with matters of custom, e.g. land problems, where families had died out and the results of investigations were referred to it by the 'Land Committee', and custom issues pertaining to marriage. Working with the 'Upper Committee', it also formed committees to look after day-to-day matters pertaining to the Nagriamel community at Tanafo, e.g. womens' interests, children, communal work and small business projects.

It was beyond the scope of this research to investigate how and to what extent the structure as described above actually functioned. However, from discussions with Jimmy Stephens and observations during a visit to Tanafo, it was clear that Nagriamel was more than a figment of his imagination. It was physically well organized and included an office complex and meeting hall and several well developed agricultural projects including forestry, oil palm and peanut production. The degree of Jimmy Stephens' support in the islands, while difficult to measure, appears to have been substantial up to the time of independence. This can be seen in the results of the November 1979 election for the new Representative Assembly when, despite their overall loss, 'Moderate' party candidates with Nagriamel support won 38% of the total vote cast in the Northern and Central Islands. Moreover, the intensity of the support was demonstrated in the willingness of Nagriamel members to take up arms in the Vemarana Federation of the Northern Islands secessionist movement which emerged in the June and July leading to independence.

Further evidence of Jimmy Stephens' basically moderate position can be seen in his reluctance in 1977 to push Nagriamel as the future governing structure for an independent Vanuatu. His position was that he did not want to involve Nagriamel in the political struggle which the Vanua'aku Pati was carrying on against the 'Moderate' party alliance. In fact, while supporting the idea of independence, his earlier declaration of independence in 1975 did not mean that the Europeans should leave but that ni-Vanuatu (at least his people) should be independent of the white man's control:

> I want my people to come out from the joint regulation — not independence to push out the white man, but the people should be out from under their control.[142]

Nagriamel was, to Jimmy Stephens, therefore, not a form of government, but a system for ordering Melanesian society based on custom, which the government of Vanuatu — both the Condominium and a future independent government — had to recognize. According to Jimmy Stephens, "law must co-operate with custom"[143] otherwise it is meaningless.

He expressed the opinion that "the two governments must put the land problem straight before independence".[144] He noted that as ni-Vanuatu were becoming aware that they were likely to regain control of a substantial amount of European-owned land — and had already done so through the return of SFNH and state land by the French Government — the number of disputes over custom ownership was increasing. He was especially concerned about the number of ni-Vanuatu who had "left custom" to be educated and work with the European establishment who might now try to regain rights to land which, through their rejection of the traditional way of life, they had in his opinion forfeited. What this reveals is his concern that the new, educated ni-Vanuatu elite — both Anglophone and Francophone — would simply take over from the Europeans and perpetuate the existing system, which excluded the vast majority of the local population from participating in the development of their islands, and as a result prevent them from enjoying the benefits such economic advances could bring. He felt that it was the obligation of the colonial administration to solve this problem before they turned over control to an independent government, which Stephens must have realized would be dominated by ni-Vanuatu far more experienced than he or any of his followers. In other words, Jimmy Stephens wanted recognition of Nagriamel by the Colonial administration before independence in order to legitimize his position and the administrative structure he had created in order to ensure its continuation in the future.

For Jimmy Stephens, therefore, it was possible for the two worlds — European and Melanesian — to exist side by side if Europeans accepted the right of ni-Vanuatu in the islands to conduct their own affairs as they wished, recognized their control over undeveloped bush land and assisted them in developing it. He was not anti-European in a racial sense. He resented European domination, but at the same time viewed the European presence as necessary to assist in administration for the country as a whole and as a source of expertise and capital to enable ni-Vanuatu to develop their land and thereby progress materially. A priority was that landowners should "eat something from their land",[145] i.e. if landowners had excess land and wanted to develop it, they should be given the opportunity and should receive the economic benefit. For this reason he was willing to give foreign businessmen access to Nagriamel controlled land.

Jimmy Stephens' role in facilitating suoh land deals was not unrewarded. Landowners were expected to give half the lease money received to the 'Land Committee', but could designate how it should be distributed — Jimmy Stephens often received a share. Moreover, it was recognized that a portion of any profits from the development of the land should also go to Nagriamel. No specific percentage was given — probably due to the fact that little development had taken place on land which had been leased. Another source of income for Nagriamel was through the sale of produce from gardens at Tanafo and for wages paid to Tanafo residents working outside the village. Nagriamel members were expected to contribute ten percent of their wages to the organization.

The means by which Nagriamel financed its activities — in particular Jimmy Stephens' share of the income and his general behaviour — have been used by many to discredit the movement and its leader. He has been described as "the most corrupt individual in Vanuatu and everyone knows it".[146] While openly courting his support, French officials held him in contempt:

> Stephens' behaviour, his costly journeys, his mistresses (who are honoured in the movements' calendar as "ladies who gave themselves to the cause"!) are giving the slow-thinking Melanesians doubts as to his integrity and the sincerity of his concern for the interests of his half-brothers by race. As for me, I am not in a hurry to see him disappear from the scene, as there is the danger of his being replaced by tougher, more sincere leaders who will not have the same weaknesses of greed, venality and knavery, which make him in the end, a valuable party to deal with for investors who are not excessively worried by moral scruples.[147]

As early as 1971, it was reported that Nagriamel members were beginning to wonder what had happened to the dues they had been paying: $2.00 per man, $1.00 per woman and $0.20 per child. This money was intended for development projects, but appeared to have gone to finance political activities and the promotion of Jimmy Stephens.[148] And in 1975, questions were raised by Olsen Kai — a rival from Ambrym — who used finance and other issues to strengthen his position within the movement vis-a-vis Jimmy Stephens.[149]

Without records for analysis, it is difficult to make a fair judgment of Jimmy Stephens' handling of Nagriamel finances.[150] Moreover, before simply dismissing Jimmy Stephens as a "corrupt" politician, it is necessary to examine whether his conduct could be termed more dishonest than any other individual in a similar position of power, and the degree to which he made seemingly unethical decisions based on ignorance and inexperience, rather than out of a conscious effort to deceive or defraud.

For example, it would seem unjust to criticize Jimmy Stephens for expecting landowners, whose land had been leased, to contribute something to the organization which had made this possible. Moreover, his acceptance of money from foreign business interests, who could expect to make high profits from the development of land leased at low rates from custom owners, is not an unusual arrangement, given the high investment required to develop virgin bush land. It could be argued that Jimmy Stephens was taking advantage of his position as intermediary between foreign business interests and his uneducated and less experienced followers for his own personal gain. However, since almost none of the foreign controlled projects got under way, it is not possible to judge the extent to which the land owners or Jimmy Stephens would have shared the profits of such ventures. If there is reason to be concerned about how well indigenous interests would have been safeguarded, it should be that Jimmy Stephens was totally inexperienced in negotiating such business ventures (as was evident in the Leconte deal), not that he was preparing some massive swindle.

Although Jimmy Stephens would have been far more skilled in dealing with foreigners than most of his supporters, his knowledge of modern business practices was extremely limited. The only model for development he would have known was the exploitation of land by private individuals and companies with little indigenous participation. It should not be surprising, therefore, that he would have agreed to offers made to him by American and French friends. He had, after all, corrected what appeared to him and his followers, as the main iniustice — the uncontrolled expansion of European plantations into undeveloped bush land — while gaining European recognition of indigenous ownership of such land and the assurance that ni-Vanuatu would be paid for its use in any future development. There is nothing to indicate that Jimmy Stephens would not have responded favourably to such ideas as joint ventures or profit sharing — the current models advanced by developers as providing the most advantageous arrangement for indigenous landowners to share in the wealth produced from their land.

If by "corrupt" it is meant that Jimmy Stephens made excessive personal gain out of his deals with foreign investors, there is significant lack of evidence. His life-style was by no means extravagant. Stephens lived in a thatched house, usually drove a pick-up truck and dressed and ate simply. It would appear that the large grants received from abroad were spent primarily on running the organization and assisting Nagriamel members with small development projects rather than the personal comfort of its leader. Indeed, with his numerous wives and children he would have had higher than average living expenses, which could only have been met with financial support from Nagriamel — his age, poor health and commitments as President of the organization would not have enabled him to produce his own food or grow cash crops. In any case, it should not be surprising that his followers, numbering more than 20,000 would have wanted to support their leader and give recognition to his status by providing him with a basic livelihood. Indeed, the common pattern is that political leaders often find it difficult to live up to their ideals once they get into a position of power. The interesting thing about Jimmy Stephens is that his daily requirements seem to have remained so moderate.

Jimmy Stephens also faced criticism from segments of the local Anglophone community, especially expatriate missionaries and some ni-Vanuatu, who were concerned about his emphasis on custom and his appeal to local people to reject existing institutions in favour of Nagriamel. The Anglican Bishop of Vanuatu, Derrick Rawcliff, was one of his greatest antagonists. In an Advisory Committee Meeting in late 1969, he spoke strongly against statements he had heard from Nagriamel supporters urging people to reject the government, local councils and the missions:

> people have been told, by whom I don't know, but have been told not to join local councils, not to allow their children to go to school, not to have anything to do with co-operatives and so on, because Nagriamel is going to provide all their things... another thing which is worrying ni-Vanuatu is the fact that Jimmy Stephens appears to have taken several wives and claims that he is allowed to do this.[151]

Bishop Rawcliff expressed concern about Jimmy Stephens' deal with Leconte and collection of money from members of the movement with no proper accounting of how it was spent.[152] Rawcliff was supported by George Kalkoa, who expressed a common feeling that "The followers of this movement are illiterate. I think someone is taking advantage of this fact. We call for action and it must be now."[153] In the late 1960s, therefore, Jimmy Stephens was viewed as a disruptive force in the country. While severai young ni-Vanuatu members of the Advisory Council had begun as early as 1960, quite independent of Nagriamel, to question the joint administration on the land issue, nationalist feelings had not yet jelled into an organized force to challenge the European power structure.

Although many of the members of the New Hebrides National Party (later Vanua'aku Pati) did not agree with the tactics of Jimmy

Stephens, there were many issues which they held in common — the most important in the early 1970s being land. It is significant that the National Party did not attack Nagriamel openly in its newspaper — *New Hebrides Viewpoints* — until 1976, when it printed a statement by the Natui Tano party with which it had close links. The article attacked Jimmy Stephens' declaration of Santo independence, his opposition to non-Santo people living in Santo and his challenging of the election results for the Representative Assembly.[154] It was Jimmy Stephens' involvement in national politics in alliance with the French-backed parties which finally brought the two movements into conflict. Although there were continued contacts between Jimmy Stephens and the Vanua'aku Pati leadership, when the possibility of joining forces was discussed, no agreement was ever reached.

Jimmy Stephens confirmed when interviewed in 1977, that on most issues he and the Vanua'aku Pati were in agreement:

> For me with Vanua'aku Pati, all these big people like Walter Lini, Barak Sope, George Kalkoa, they're ni-Vanuatu with me. I always talk with them. We been friend together for long time. But I never against Vanua'aku Pati, and I don't think they ever against Nagriamel too. But I think sometime what they say — I heard from Barak Sope — he ask me... "How now you go join with Frenchman?" I said, "I try to tell Frenchman to do something, to pay some of his problem — pay something out, do something for the people. But I don't join them nothing.... Today it's look like Nagriamel is against National Party. No, but sometime talk — sometime way of action.[155]

After 1975, the fundamental issues which kept the two parties apart had become power and independence. While the Vanua'aku Pati began pressing for an early independence, Jimmy Stephens lagged behind — hoping to consolidate his position as leader of the people based on a common regard for custom. Moreover, the Vanua'aku Pati would have represented to him the very group of ni-Vanuatu whom he described as having "left custom" and joined the white man. It would have been, therefore, ideologically difficult in Jimmy Stephens' mind to combine with the Vanua'aku Pati. And he must also have realized that he would have been overshadowed by the Pati's far more sophisticated and better educated leadership.

6

Tautu Village Dispute

The first major land dispute to come to the notice of the joint administration after the Second World War occurred in the Norsup area on the eastern coast of Malakula. In early 1962, the Joint Court handed down three interim decisions covering a complex set of claims involving two French companies — Plantations Réunies des Nouvelles-Hébrides (PRNH) and Société Francaise des Nouvelles-Hébrides (SFNH) — the French State, the Presbyterian and Seventh Day Adventist Missions, a number of individual planters and ni-Vanuatu interests, as represented by the Native Advocate, M. Pujol. Final registration of the claims was withheld pending the surveying of boundaries. Once completed, and the interested parties having been given the chance to comment, the Court would then give its final judgment. Surveys were completed in early 1963, and several final judgments handed down in 1969, but the issue of ownership was never settled, due to the opposition of ni-Vanuatu from nearby villages, especially Tautu.

The Interim Judgments

The first judgment, handed down on 18 March 1962, involved the Corlette Estate, PRNH and various ni-Vanuatu claims. It confirmed the ownership of a small parcel of land purchased by the inhabitants of Norsup Island from the Corlette Estate, the right of

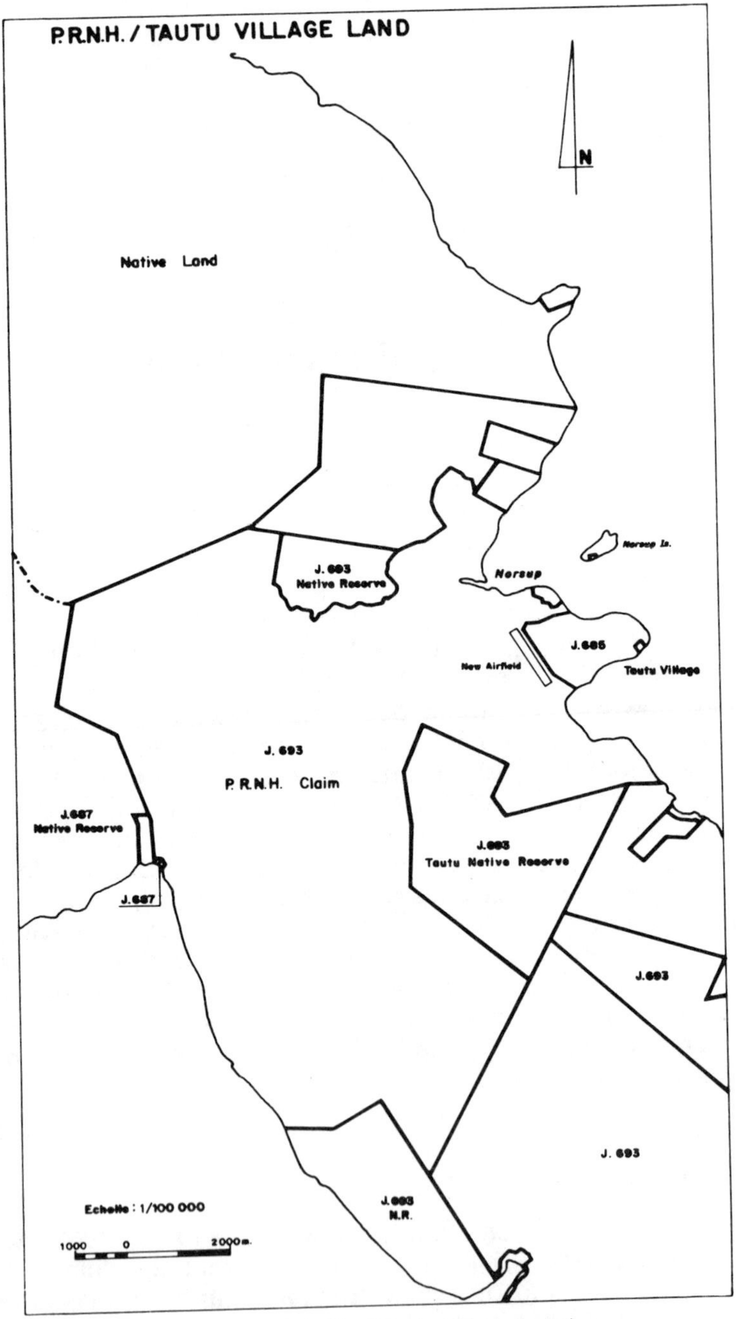

Figure 5: P.R.N.H./Tautu Village Land

ownership of PRNH to 180 hectares of developed plantation land and established the *zone maritime* of the French State along the shore. In addition, Judgment 685 created two native reserves: one for the villages of Mahe, Bethel and Norsup Island consisting of 1,040 hectares and a second smaller reserve of 70 hectares for Tautu village.[1]

On 22 March 1962, the Court handed down a second judgment, which concerned land on the opposite side of Malakula, but extending close to the Norsup area, since at that point the island narrows considerably. It established a large native reserve of over 23,000 hectares, the area inhabited by the Big Nambas people, and confirmed title to several smaller sections for the Presbyterian Church of Vanuatu, the Seventh Day Adventist Mission, the French State and the PRNH.[2]

The third Joint Court judgment relating to land in the Norsup area was handed down on 25 April 1962. It involved the French State, PRNH, SFNH, the Presbyterian Church of Vanuatu, the Seventh Day Adventist Mission and several individual planters or their estates. It established native reserves for Tautu and several other ni-Vanuatu villages and confirmed a large PRNH claim, which included parts of its existing plantation and a considerable area of undeveloped bush land. The Tautu Reserve, which totalled 3,350 hectares, consisted of two parts: Tautu Point, site of the present village, and a separate area several miles distant in the interior.[3]

As with most Joint Court decisions at that time concerning land on Malakula, the above three judgments had been preceded by negotiations between the Native Advocate and the various parties. This reflected the concern of the two residencies that land problems would increase on Malakula, if the large sections of claimed land were registered without taking account of the needs of local inhabitants. At their urging the Native Advocate visited Malakula personally to view the situation and negotiate with the various institutions and individuals. The French Resident Commissioner, in particular, played an important role in making land previously claimed by the French State and the SFNH available for native reserves, and attempted to put pressure on other French claimants to do likewise. Some private individuals and institutions were willing to surrender portions of their claims, but the PRNH refused to compromise and insisted on the registration of its extensive claims which consisted of large areas of undeveloped bush land in addition to its plantation at Norsup.

Historical Background

The origin of the dispute in the Norsup area goes back to the 1920s, when the Société Contonière established its plantation "by force of arms... against the general opposition of the inhabitants"[4] using Vietnamese labourers. According to Chief David of Tautu, the problem began when the people tried to stop the Company expanding its planting onto land which it had not purchased.[5] The people of Tautu acknowledged that a small piece of land called Wolumera had been sold, but not the huge area eventually claimed by the Company. Indeed, the sale of land was contrary to custom, thus the transaction was probably seen by the original Tautu people involved as a temporary arrangement rather than permanent alienation.[6]

Another factor which complicated the situation in the Norsup area was that ni-Vanuatu staying at Tautu but originating from such places as Wala and Uripiv allegedly allowed Europeans to use land or sold land to which they did not have primary rights.[7] European claimants would argue, therefore, that ni-Vanuatu had created the problem by selling land illegally. These purported land sales by non-Tautu people became an issue after independence between several ni-Vanuatu communities, since it tended to indicate that other villages in the area also had rights to portions of the land on which the Company was established. Given the close proximity of other villages and the huge expanse of the plantation, it would indeed seem possible that several communities would have legitimate rights to the land in question, though clearly the claims of Tautu would be the most significant.

In the early 1920s, it was the people of Tautu who first opposed the Company, since it was land which they were using at the time that was threatened. Tautu people argue today that the reason why the PRNH is the largest plantation in Vanuatu and was developed so quickly — the main part of the plantation had been planted in coconuts by 1928 — was because the Company simply took land which was being used by their forefathers and thus was already cleared. The relatively uniform height of a major portion of the coconut trees on the plantation, which indicates that they were planted at about the same time, would tend to substantiate the claim.[8] Indeed, it would not have been possible to plant such a vast area, if it had been necessary to clear 'dark bush'.

When, in the early 1920s, the people of Tautu tried to stop the expansion of the Company onto their land, they were threatened and the manager, M. Caillard, was said to have told his Tonkinese labourers to kill any *man Tautu* who entered the plantation or tried to seek Government assistance.[9] Contact was, however, made with the British District Agent at Bushman's Bay, Mr. Adam, and with Mr. Corlette, who was owner of the plantation there, but the chief of the village was told that nothing could be done. The only help the people of Tautu received was from the Presbyterian missionary, Mr. Barton, who was based at Tisman. With his assistance — he negotiated with the Company's manager — the people of Tautu were left to reside on the small peninsula known as Tautu Point, which was used originally by the villagers for keeping pigs.[10]

In November 1927, at the request of the Company Manager, the administration sent the French naval vessel *Cassiopée* to Norsup to support the Company's operation against opposition from local inhabitants.[11] The next year, further trouble erupted, but this time with another group, the Small Nambas tribe from the interior of the Island.[12] Trouble again flared in 1947, when a further attempt was made to prevent the company from expanding the area planted in coconuts. The opposition to the Company's activities again came from the Small Nambas, who were led at this time by a chief called Bonbon. He was denounced by Caillard, as "a dangerous character" and as a result of his opposition, "was shot down by the British District Agent", who lost his job as a result.[13]

The PRNH succeeded the Société Contoniere after it was bought by the Banque de l'Indochine, and the difficulties which the PRNH had in the 1960s and 70s with the people of Tautu village had their origin in the violent incidents described above. The Melanesians who most consistently disputed the land claims of the PRNH were the people of Tautu. However, the dispute was more complex in that other local groups also opposed the expansion of the Company's operations and, in part, the claims of the people of Tautu as well.

Indeed, Tautu village faced the greatest hardship. They lost a large portion of their land close to the coast and were confined to a small peninsula, separated by the PRNH plantation from their remaining garden land several hours' walk away. Furthermore, as in a number of areas in Vanuatu, Tautu people were never fully aware of the extent of European land claims, since the pre-war period development had been confined to relatively small areas along the coast. They were suddenly made aware of these claims with registration, the surveying of boundaries, and the attempt in the 1960s to expand into undeveloped bush areas. Indeed, Chief David mentioned that when the Native Advocate, M. Page, visited Tautu in 1960 or 1961, accompanied by the Chief Surveyor, M. Pujol, they first came to realize the extent of the land claims of the PRNH and began to consider ways to halt the expansion of the plantation.[14]

Renewal of Dispute

The first official hint that problems over land were again heating up in the Norsup area came from the British District Agent in May 1963. He reported to the British Residency that the natives of Tautu had complained to him that the main reserve allotted to them as part of Judgment 693, though providing them with a large area of land, had given the best of the land to the PRNH. What remained to them was a mountainous and inaccessible region with valleys, which the villagers considered useless for gardening. In particular, they complained that their best gardening land, named Jinarur, had been included in the PRNH claim.[15]

The District Agent held discussions with the Tautu people and M. Tanguy, the manager of the PRNH plantation, and suggested an exchange of land to preserve the Jinarur gardening area for native use. According to the District Agent's report, this idea was acceptable to the Tautu people, but the Company Manager said he would have to look into it more carefully.[16] At this point, therefore, the Tautu people took a fairly moderate position in view of subsequent developments in the dispute. In 1963, there was no hint of any challenge to the legitimacy of the PRNH developed plantation, merely the demand that long existent gardening rights be recognized.

During 1964, at the suggestion of the British District Agent, the Tautu people and PRNH met and worked out an agreement whereby the company erected a fence across the contested area. This agreement was rejected later by the Tautu people as having been concluded under pressure from the Company. Thus, although the issue was not raised in 1964, it had not been solved.

It was in 1964 as well, that Chief David made contact with Nagriamel. He went to a meeting in Santo and contributed $200 to the organization. Links were, however, broken off with Jimmy Stephens and his followers when in 1967, Chief David was asked to sign a paper giving Nagriamel control over all Tautu land.[17]

The dispute heated up again in late 1965. This time it focused on land allocated to the Company on the western side of the island at Lesinwa village, which was the subject of Judgment 687, and involved attempts by the Company to begin further development of its lands in that area. When materials were taken to the site on the west coast in order to construct several buildings, a delegation of local people appeared and said that the land belonged to them. They claimed that the land had been sold in the last century to Mr. Gillan, the then resident Presbyterian Missionary at Uripiv. The manager of PRNH agreed to hold off the construction of the buildings until the matter could be resolved.[18]

The ni-Vanuatu delegation then appeared at the British District Agent's office and told him that they could not accept the Joint Court judgment as the land had been sold to Gillan to ensure that it was not taken over by Europeans. They pointed out that there were living witnesses, the grandchildren of the man who had sold the land, and also that they had not been consulted or informed when the interim judgment was made. They also pointed out that in the judgment, the arable land had been included in the section allocated to the PRNH, while the mountainous, stony portion had been given to them, i.e. to the Mission.[19]

The District Agent reported that he felt the claims were partially justified in view of the existence of gardens and mature coconut trees on the land in question. He blamed the Presbyterian Mission for the predicament, since their advocate had negotiated the settlement resulting in the division of the land as laid down in the Joint Court judgment. However, he pointed out that even though the Mission was directly responsible, the joint administration was the culprit in the eyes of the Melanesian communities involved. He recommended that the whole matter should be looked into before final judgment was given by the Joint Court and that the PRNH be urged to abandon the part of the claim in question.[20] PRNH, however, was not willing to negotiate and the Court went ahead and handed down several final judgments covering the various lands in question.[21]

In 1964, the communities in the area had agreed to assist the PRNH in the construction of a transinsular road from Norsup to Lesinwa. In October 1965, however, it was reported by the British District Agent that they had refused to allow the bulldozer working on the road to continue.[22] They must have realized that, although the road would have been of benefit to them, it would also have allowed the Company to extend its operations further into their undeveloped land. In the 1920s, such opposition resulted in violent counteraction. Now the people of Tautu found that not only was it possible to restrain the activities of their European rivals, but they could even have their point of view listened to and taken into consideration. Moreover, in late 1965, the British District Agent reported that Tautu people were demanding that PRNH abandon "all of the undeveloped land which they claimed",[23] indicating that they had now taken the offensive.

These events reveal the gradual awakening of Melanesians to the changing power structure of the post-war period. In the 1960s, the people of Tautu, like many other ni-Vanuatu throughout the archipelago, began to test the strength of the old order and found that they had regained the power to influence areas which Europeans had dominated in the past. Furthermore, the land conflicts of the 1960s and 70s, like that of Tautu Village, reflect rising Melanesian expectations and populations. It is not surprising that land was the subject on which they would come into conflict with Europeans, as it was the source of Melanesian wealth and power, and the key to their greater participation in economic development.

In 1965, Chief David expressed these feelings very clearly. In a letter to the two Resident Commissioners he wrote:

> we are not agree to the mark which the spear line had put on our land.
>
> The spear line did without us and didn't even let us to know this before they marked the land. Several Nakamals for the people of Tautu have marked out into the PRNH side. So we cannot again let it free to the PRNH. For surely this Company has taken away the best of our land.
>
> Plenty business you are teaching us the people of the New Hebrides, such as Co-operative Society, coconut plantation, cocoa and Farming. And we people from Tautu, where we gone to do these things? If the French Co. takes this again.
>
> Surely they have stolen all our best, the flat good ground around Tautu . . . . What will happen to the people of Tautu in the future.[24]

The "spear line" refers to the surveyed boundaries, which the Tautu people felt were incorrect. Chief David's argument, which would be heard again and again in Vanuatu, was that Europeans had stolen their land and the administration had validated this theft through its surveys, without consulting the people involved.

Chief David also described how in 1965 attempts were made to buy him off. Officials in French Residency offered him a job in Vila with high pay, a house and a vehicle. In addition, an offer was made to provide 100 head of cattle and a bulldozer to clear Tutu land. The villagers responded to all of this by cutting fences belonging to the PRNH.[25]

Although the dispute subsided during 1966, it had not been resolved. It appears to have been a time of consolidation and assessment, during which the people of Tautu formed the 'Tautu Landing Committee' to protect their lands. In early 1967, they began to reassert their claims by more direct action; reports of trespass on PRNH land were received in October.[26]

In 1967, the administration tried to get the PRNH management and Tautu village to negotiate a settlement. The position of the Company, however, had changed very little.[27] He suggested a joint venture between the Tautu villagers and the PRNH, whereby the villagers supplied the labour in return for which the Company would fence and make available certain paddocks to them. There was no mention, however, of a re-evaluation of the Company's land claims.

At the same time, Melanesian opinion was hardening. At a meeting at Tautu village on 19 October 1967, Chief David emphasized that the Tautu people claimed all the bush land, including the portions fenced by PRNH in 1964. One of the main issues at that meeting was the trespass on the land fenced by PRNH. He rejected the Company's allegation that no objection was made to the fence being erected in 1964 and stated that acceptance of the fence had been pressed upon the then Chief (David became Chief in 1965).[28]

The following month the people of Tautu were informed that it was likely that a Land Advisory Commission would be formed to investigate the causes of the dispute and to try to find a basis for settlement. The British District Agent reported that the villagers of Tautu replied that "the land in dispute belonged to them and therefore there was no need for a commission".[29] The idea of such a commission came from the British Residency. It had been tried once in the case of the Bonkovia dispute on Epi, but the French generally opposed such a strategy for fear of raising the whole question of registered land. They were suspicious of British aims in such matters, believing that the British were prepared to sacrifice planter interests to Melanesian claims. The French must have viewed the British handling of this dispute as inimical to their own position. They would also have resented British involvement in what was to them a French problem, since it involved French land. But it was to the British District Agent that the Melanesians in the dispute turned initially, and most often, for help and advice.

By late 1967, however, the French position regarding the PRNH/Tautu dispute had softened, as evidenced by their willingness to discuss the possibility of setting up an ad hoc Land Advisory Committee. It was reported that the French Resident Commissioner was prepared to tell PRNH to abandon all idea of maintaining their position over undeveloped land on the Norsup property.[30] A land commission was not convened, but by this time the way in which the settlement was reached prior to the interim judgments of 1962, came to be known. The French Resident Commissioner at that time, M. Deloney, had arranged for the original 10,000 hectare claim to be shared: 3,000 hectares as native reserve and the remainder to the company. The French Resident Commissioner in 1967, M. Mouradian, admitted that this action had been hasty, since it had become apparent that when PRNH wished to develop the area "the local inhabitants had not understood what was being done, not all those who were concerned had been consulted and not everyone had given their agreement".[31] The French hoped to arrange an exchange of their own state lands as a possible means of persuading the PRNH to shift its stance but no agreement to this proposal was ever reached.

In 1968, a more flexible attitude was evident from the PRNH management, most likely due to pressure from the French Residency. Several compromise proposals were presented to the Tautu people during the year. One was that the undeveloped land desired by the Company could be transferred to the Tautu people and then leased to PRNH for a nominal fee. This would lead eventually to developed land being transferred to the Tautu people.[32] Another alternative suggested was that 1,500 hectares should be sold back to Tautu village and then repurchased by PRNH at a higher price.[33]

By this time, however, the people of Tautu were not interested in any such proposals, which would have meant the prolonged alienation of their land, whether by sale or lease. In August 1968, it was generally accepted that the negotiations had broken down.[34] Both French and British officials must have realized that the first step in any solution would have been for PRNH to transfer all undeveloped land back to native owners with no strings attached. Since the Company was unwilling to make this concession, the dispute remained unresolved with PRNH activities confined to their developed properties only.

During 1969 and 1970, PRNH made its own attempts to improve relations with the Tautu people in the hope of bringing about a settlement. It was reported, for example, that the Company provided an interest-free loan to Chief David to buy a vehicle. Work also began again, without incident, on the transinsular road, which by this time had become vital to the Melanesian community's own plans for economic development.[35] In February 1970, however, PRNH threatened to stop work on the road, which transversed the undeveloped portion of their property, unless the Resident Commissioners guaranteed that the road would not result in the alienation of PRNH property and that *bona fide* negotiations be opened to settle the Company's dispute with the Tautu people.

The shift in positions since the dispute had broken out again in 1962 is striking. In 1965, ni-Vanuatu had stopped work on the road, fearing that its completion would strengthen the Company's hold on the as yet undeveloped bush land through which the road passed. By 1970, the people of Tautu were so confident of their ultimate success in regaining control of these undeveloped portions of the PRNH claim that the Company contemplated trying to block them.

The Airport Dispute

Ten years after the dispute had started up again the positions of the two sides had hardened and there appeared to be little chance of a settlement being reached in the near future. Then in February 1974, a new phase began. Reports reached Vila that 40 angry Tautu men at the site of the proposed new airport at Aop near Norsup had stopped the work of the bulldozer and were replanting coconuts knocked down the day before.[36] The land in question was part of the main PRNH plantation, close to the native reserve in which Tautu village was located.

The issue this time was the right of PRNH to sell developed land to the Condominium Government. This was the first time the Tautu people actually protested about the developed portions of the PRNH holdings, and represented a further shift in their position. Although they had never fully accepted the alienation of the land which PRNH had developed, Tautu people had not challenged the Company's right to continued use of the plantation. This reflects the common Melanesian attitude that an individual, in this case the Company, has the right to the fruits of his labour. Custom usually accepts that trees belong to those who plant them, while the land remains the property of the original landowners. PRNH violated this principle when it sold a portion of its plantation to the Condominium Government for the construction of the airstrip.

The sale of land to the Condominium, even though it was for a project which would have benefited Tautu people, was the incident that most undermined the Company's position and its prospects for continued operation of its plantation. The action of PRNH confirmed to the people of Tautu that the Company did not recognize their traditional rights to the land, nor the argument that it had been 'stolen' from them in the past. Moreover, by the mid-1970s, land had become the most important political issue of the growing nationalist movement. Tautu people received outside support in their struggle over the airport, when representatives from the New Hebrides National Party (later Vanua'aku Pati) visited the village in February to advise them and give encouragement.

The people remained firm in their opposition to the construction of the airport and finally in December 1974, the British and French Resident Commissioners reached an agreement authorizing the establishment of a Commission to enquire into objections that had been raised to the proposed siting of the new airfield to be constructed at Norsup in North Malakula.[37] The Commission consisted of the members of the Special Committee on Communications of the Condominium Advisory Council and the French and British District Agents from Central District 2. The Commission visited Norsup twice, on 7 and 22 January and submitted its final report on 23 January 1975.[38]

The solution decided upon by the Resident Commissioners, which the people of Tautu had agreed to, was that the Condominium Government would sell to the people of Tautu the original 20 hectares it had purchased from the PRNH for a sum of NHF 1.00 (one New Hebridean Franc). The people of Tautu would in turn lease back to the Condominium administration ten hectares — later increased to 12 hectares to accommodate a terminal building — required for the airstrip, for an initial period of 25 years at an annual rent of NHF 40,000 (A$400), subject to review and increase every five years. The village people would also retain the right of use of a footpath across the airfield and preference woud be given to the people of Tautu regarding employment in the construction, maintenance and operation of the facility.[30] The airport was eventually completed according to the arrangements agreed upon, though final signing of the lease did not take place until May 1977.

The agreement represented a compromise on both sides. The people of Tautu were allowed to regain control of land but their willingness to repurchase the land, even though payment was only a token amount, implied a recognition on their part that the land had originally been sold. While the people of Tautu benefited most from the agreement, they had clearly demonstrated their willingness to negotiate solutions to their long-standing land dispute. Unfortunately, the PRNH was never willing to carry on the process of negotiating an equitable solution to the dispute, despite pressure from the French Residency. Thus, although no further major confrontations occurred between the Company and the people of Tautu, the problem remained unsettled until the time of independence in 1980.

7

Urban Land Problems

Beginning in the last half of the 19th century, Europeans began to acquire land around Vila harbour, much of which was part of the traditional landholdings of the residents of Fila Island. These acquisitions occurred at a very chaotic time — a period of population decline, accompanied by considerable movement of people into the Vila area from elsewhere on Efate and Vanuatu. It was also a time when ni-Vanuatu were relatively ignorant of European attitudes and customs relating to land, and of the long term value of their land in relation to European material goods and technology which they desired.

These factors help to explain, at least in part, the rapid loss over a few decades of significant portions of land which Fila Islanders used for subsistence in the past. Fila Islanders would have been willing to allow Europeans temporary use of unneeded land, especially since the close proximity of Europeans gave them access to European goods and employment to ensure their regular supply. However, most Fila Islanders at that time would not have understood that to a European, the giving of a bit of tobacco, cloth or an axe meant the permanent acquisition of the rights to land. There is evidence that Europeans were aware that native custom did not allow for the permanent alienation of land and thus Fila Islanders would argue today that most Europeans took advantage of the ignorance of their forefathers in this regard.

It is also likely that many of the claims by Europeans were

based on the sale of land by ni-Vanuatu who, in fact, had no rights to the land concerned. Fila Islanders today say that they were told of some land sales to Europeans, but many of the claims are based on sales by people they had never heard of. It is likely, therefore, that the presence in the Vila area of many ni-Vanuatu who did not have legitimate land rights also contributed to the confusion over land alienation.

Another way, common throughout Vanuatu, in which some Europeans played upon the ignorance of indigenous landowners was by claiming larger portions of land than the original owners intended or were by custom entitled to transfer. The boundaries described in many of the early deeds were very imprecise, often including areas so large that the indigenous signers of the deeds could not possibly have had the right to transfer permanent title without the consent of a much larger group. Again, there is evidence that some Europeans were aware of this aspect of indigenous custom, but chose to ignore it. Fila Islanders became aware of this practice when the Joint Court began to register European land claims in the late 1920s. They were luckier in one way than most other ni-Vanuatu in that they lived close enough to the centre of colonial administration, and in particular the Joint Court, to have learned what was happening. Fila Islanders were, in fact, one of the few groups to have gained enough knowledge of the Joint Court system to have been able to use it in the registration of their own lands and to oppose European applications for title. However, they never succeeded in preventing the registration of a single claim they opposed.

Early Opposition to Registration

In 1928, the Joint Court began granting titles, most of which involved uncontested claims in the Vila area. Included among these were the Island of Iririki and a small section of land on Fila Island, registered in the name of the Presbyterian Church of Victoria. In addition, a small section of land located along the south shore of Vila harbour, which was sold by Chief Kalsakau to Burns Philp, was registered and a number of small pieces of land in the area on the east side of the harbour where Vila town had begun to develop.

Fila Islanders did not contest the registration of land in the name of the Church, since they must have seen its presence as having direct benefit to them. In the case of the Burns Philp land, since the sale had occurred only recently and had involved the then Chief of Fila Island, there could have been little reason for dispute. Regarding the applications for registration of land in the Vila town area, one can only assume that they were advised by the Native Advocate not to challenge the claims, since there was little chance of successfully opposing registration where considerable investment and development had occurred. This was, in fact, the attitude prevalent among many Fila Islanders in the late 1970s, that where development had taken place, alienation could be accepted, though traditional ownership should be acknowledged by the giving of a small *Nasaotonga* or gift as a form of voluntary compensation.

In 1929 and 1930, however, several caveats were lodged on behalf of the people of Fila Island against applications for title, the registration of which threatened their interests. The land involved was on the fringes of the zone of urban development and Fila Islanders regularly used much of it for subsistence. The pattern of opposition followed by Fila Islanders in the early period was reasonable. Although they may not have agreed with the registration of land, particularly in the town area, they concentrated their efforts on trying to prevent permanent alienation of land required for their own immediate use.

The first caveat lodged on behalf of Fila Islanders was against an application for the registration of the Rodin Estate, a 28 hectare property at the south end of Vila harbour known by the native name of Otonga. It extended from Vila harbour over the ridge to the Erakor lagoon. It had been inherited by the sons of Jack Rodin, who had acquired it in 1872. It was later sold to the Kerr Brothers.

The caveat lodged on behalf of two men then living in Fila Island, Litas Kaltaki and Sekia, who were the sole survivors of a tribe living at Wanagire (the area of the Rodin estate), argued that Jack Rodin had occupied the land merely as a tenant-at-will and only to protect it for the native owners.[1] At the same time that Rodin arrived, Mr. McKenzie, the Presbyterian missionary living in the area, had taken over title in the name of the Presbyterian Mission to land at Erakor, which the Mission was to hold in trust for the people of that village. Fila Islanders claim that Rodin led them to believe that he was doing the same thing for them with regard to the land in question, and they signed documents under this understanding.

The Court rejected the caveat on the grounds that the allegations were not supported by acceptable legal proof and that Rodin and his children had lived on the land since 1872, had developed it at their own expense, and that neither they nor their grantee, the Kerr Brothers, had ever had their occupancy challenged.[2] The Court, therefore, based its judgment on Article XXII, paragraph 3 of the Protocol, which dealt with claims involving title deed coupled with occupation, and ruled that the deed was valid.

The Native Advocate lodged several more caveats on behalf of the Fila Islanders during this period. All were rejected. Among them was a further claim involving a portion of the Rodin estate adjoining the section described above,[3] and a very important series of claims relating to the Anabrou plantation, at the northeast end of Vila harbour and comprising over 100 hectares of coconut palms and gardening land. Despite claims by Fila Islanders that they had not sold the land, the Court ruled in favour of the European applicants, basing its judgment on Article XXII, paragraph 6(A), subsection (b) of the Protocol, which allowed the exclusion of all challenges to a claim, no matter what evidence of sale had been presented, if the land had been sold and then re-sold in good faith between non-natives prior to 1 January 1896.[4] In several other cases involving land on Malapoa Point, caveats were lodged, but withdrawn when it became apparent from the demonstrated policies of the Court, that there was little likelihood of their being upheld.[5]

One of the most complicated challenges mounted by the Native Advocate on behalf of Fila Islanders concerned an application by the SFNH and a number of other claimants with smaller holdings, for the registration of a large section of land between the Tagabe and La Colle rivers, running from the coast to the site of the present airport, Bauer Field. The claim was based on an original sale of land in 1872 by two natives — Naarawah (sometimes translated as Narrowby) and Frubaway — to William Bassett, who in turn sold the land to Donald McLeod, a well known early trader who at times worked with Higginson. Very soon thereafter, in 1890, McLeod sold the land to the Compagnie Calédonienne des Nouvelles-Hébrides (CCNH) and the Société Francaise des Nouvelles-Hébrides (SFNH) lodged the application as the successors of CCNH. In addition to a caveat lodged by the Native Advocate on behalf of the people of Fila Island, there were six caveats lodged by various planters against the claim of SFNH, who had acquired small pieces within the larger section.

The Native Advocate based his case on a number of different points, the first being the imprecision of boundaries. In the original deed of sale the boundaries of the land were described as "... running back towards the mountain for a distance of four miles on the north and less on the south (more or less)".[6] The Native Advocate pointed out the vague terms used and emphasised that, if the original purchaser had been clear about the extent of the land involved, he would have designated the Tagabe River as the southern boundary, which would have been the logical thing to do, but this was left unclear. The Native Advocate questioned how the eastern boundary was determined, given the fact that the southern point was unfixed.[7]

The strongest part of the Native Advocate's case concerned occupancy. He pointed out that on the original plan prepared by the surveyors and directors of the CCNH, specific areas within the property were identified as 'native reserves' or 'native lands', but that these areas had since been occupied by settlers under the authorization of the company. Moreover, this occupation was accompanied by protests from the indigenous population then present on the land. He referred the Court to documents prepared between the settlers and the native occupants, relating to the use of the land by each party. One agreement in particular, that between Chief Kalsakau and M. Frouin, designated a specific portion of the disputed land to be occupied on a provisionary basis by Fila Islanders. He also called attention to a recent protest filed by the Native Advocate himself on behalf of the indigenous occupants of part of the land against one claimant, M. Bladinieres. The Native Advocate based his case against registration on the fact that the claimants were unsure of the boundaries and were taking possession of land which they themselves admitted was occupied by ni-Vanuatu. The aim of the Native Advocate in lodging the caveat was to secure a native reserve on at least part of the land. He argued that 300 inhabitants of Fila Island depended for their existence on the cultivation of land at Tagabe and that a minimum of two hectares of land *per capita* was necessary for their subsistence.[8]

The Court ruled in favour of the SFNH claim with certain exceptions (it granted title to parts of the land to the six settlers who had also lodged caveats) and rejected the Native Advocate's request for a native reserve of 600 hectares within the Narrowby property on the grounds that "the natives already own 400 hectares more or less of land on the left bank of the Tagabe river". It also noted the argument of M. Frouin, that when he agreed to allow Fila Islanders to use part of the land, they did not occupy it but leased it to a Chinese. Finally, the Court noted that, when asked for further information about lands available for use by Fila Islanders, "the Native Advocate was unable to reply". Nor could the Native Advocate substantiate "that the Fila natives have need of further land for their subsistence over and above the lands now at their disposal on the left bank of the Tagabe river". The Court, therefore, rejected the native caveat.[9]

However, in a move entirely outside its jurisdiction as laid down in the regulations governing registration of land, the Court "assigned to the natives of Fila a reserve of land known as Malapoa on the left bank of the Tagabe river".[10] The reserve was created, not out of land which was the subject of the application, but out of an adjacent piece. The Court must have seen this as the easiest way to satisfy both the European claimants and the Fila Islanders. In creating the Malapoa Reserve, the Court would be protecting native interests by preventing subsequent applications for registration of title in respect of that land. Having satisfied itself that it had provided adequate land for the native population, which may have been the case at that time, the Court then felt free to register the land under application without having to probe very deeply into boundaries.

What may have seemed a reasonable solution to the Court in 1930, however, simply postponed having to deal with the real problem. To this day, Fila Islanders maintain that the Joint Court unjustly deprived them of land to which they were entitled. The eviction of Fila Islanders in the 1930s by Europeans, accomplished by turning cattle into their gardens, became part of the oral history of the community. Although the Fila Island people acknowledge the sale of a small piece of land, they refused to accept the amount registered by the Joint Court:

> The land called "Marope" is a small piece of land situated near the Beach at the southern side of the bridge "La Cole" and that was the only piece, sold to a British subject, by a Native of Fila Island named Narewa [sic]. We know the boundary very well, but we cannot understand why our other pieces of land are included through this name, "MAROPE", and some of these claimed lands of ours are now sold to other people.[11]

The section which became one of the focal points of Fila Island protest in the 1970s, although they claimed rights to other parts of the Narrowby land as well, was that piece which bordered directly on the Malapoa Reserve, belonging to the descendants of M. Frouin.

It is clear that in the Narrowby case the Court acted on insufficient evidence regarding the amount of native land available. While the creation of the Malapoa Reserve did save a valuable piece of land for the use of Fila Islanders, the court acted outside its jurisdiction and failed to note the clear evidence of native occupancy on the land under application for registration. Moreover, it failed to come to terms with a common problem relating to land claims in Vanuatu, that in which an area of land included in a transaction between a European and an illiterate native vendor, through various changes of hands, grew into a much larger parcel than the original owner intended.

The last attempt by residents of Fila Island to prevent the

registration of land which they felt had been illegally acquired, concerned an application for title to a further portion of the Rodin estate. Application No. 177, lodged by the SFNH, concerned 73 hectares of land at Maltaurik, to the west of that previously registered by the Joint Court. Accompanying the application was a deed of sale, dated 20 September 1882, between the natives of Fila Island and Ferdinand Rodin. The deed had been registered in Noumea and the land had been purchased by the SFNH on 28 July 1923.

The Native Advocate's caveat argued as before, that the land had been given in trust to Ferdinand Rodin, the son of Jack Rodin. The Court ruled, however, that the original deed of sale made no mention of a trust clause and decided, therefore, in favour of the Compagnie Francaise des Nouvelles-Hébrides (CFNH), which had purchased part of the original estate, under Article XXII, Paragraph 6(B) of the Protocol.[12]

Fila Islanders were gardening on part of the land included in the application, so the Court set aside about 12 hectares of it as a native reserve. Part of this property was transferred to the Condominium Government in the 1960s for the construction of the new Vila wharf. Although Fila Islanders claimed all the Rodin land, this portion remained a focal point of contention.

Revival of Claims in the 1960s

For 30 years Fila Islanders remained relatively silent on land matters, at least on an official level. With the increase in native population and a shift in political 'weight', however, it was only a matter of time and opportunity before the Joint Court's decisions, which so reduced the amount of land available for their use, would be challenged. Limited land for subsistence, which remained important to Fila Islanders, was clearly a factor which motivated Chief Graham Kalsakau and other elders to write to the Resident Commissioners in 1964, raising once again their claims to portions of the Narrowby land. That letter marked the beginning of a new period of Fila Island opposition to the permanent alienation of land, which by the mid 1970s led to violent protests.

Land for subsistence, however, was not the only factor behind the increasing resistance of Fila Islanders to decisions of the Joint Court. As the pace of economic development began to quicken in the 1960s and 1970s, like many ni-Vanuatu, they came to realize the value of land. However, accompanying the rising expectations was the realization that decisions made several decades before, despite their protests, left much of their most valuable land in foreign hands.

Fila Islanders became more acutely aware and resentful of this loss as they witnessed the new owners reaping huge profits from sub-division and re-sale of what were their traditional lands. Chief Graham Kalsakau wrote to the two Resident Commissioners in 1964:

> we are not happy to see other people getting money from our land by selling it. We accept anyone to be in our land, providing that they should rent or pay for it, and to pay to us the owners.[13]

The land Chief Graham was referring to specifically was that of M. Frouin and the Narrowby land settlement. His letter reopened the question of Fila Island rights to registered land. Throughout the period of protest the most important factor explaining the attitude of Fila Islanders was their resentment of profits being made on land which they believed to be rightfully theirs.

The Resident Commissioners expressed understanding and sympathy but made it clear that there was no possibility of changing any decision of the Joint Court.[14] The Resident Commissioners asked for information about the land possessed and used by Fila Islanders, and offered the possibility of acquiring additional land elsewhere, if they were satisfied "that the people of Fila Island are not only short of land but are willing to cultivate what they have more efficiently and can make good use of additional land for gardens or cash crops . . . ."[15] The Fila Islanders did not reply, since the Resident Commissioners would only help with garden land, whereas their main concern was the land which they felt had been unjustly taken from them and was being developed. Other methods would have to be found to bring about change.

Fila Islanders also tried to reopen the question of alienated land through the Advisory Council. One of its members, Dr. Kalsakau of Fila Island and brother to Chief Graham, proposed in the following year the setting up of a lands commission to investigate the issue of registered land in Vanuatu.[16] Dr. Kalsakau hoped that through negotiation, future trouble could be avoided:

> many of these lands were not sold and we are afraid that the young generation, when they understand these things, will try to cause some trouble, especially to our friends who are already working on these lands.[17]

The British Resident Commissioner commented on the "spirit of amity" shown in the motion,[18] but Dr. Kalsakau's suggestion of a land commission was not mentioned and was never agreed to by the governments.

As the pace of development quickened in the late 1960s,

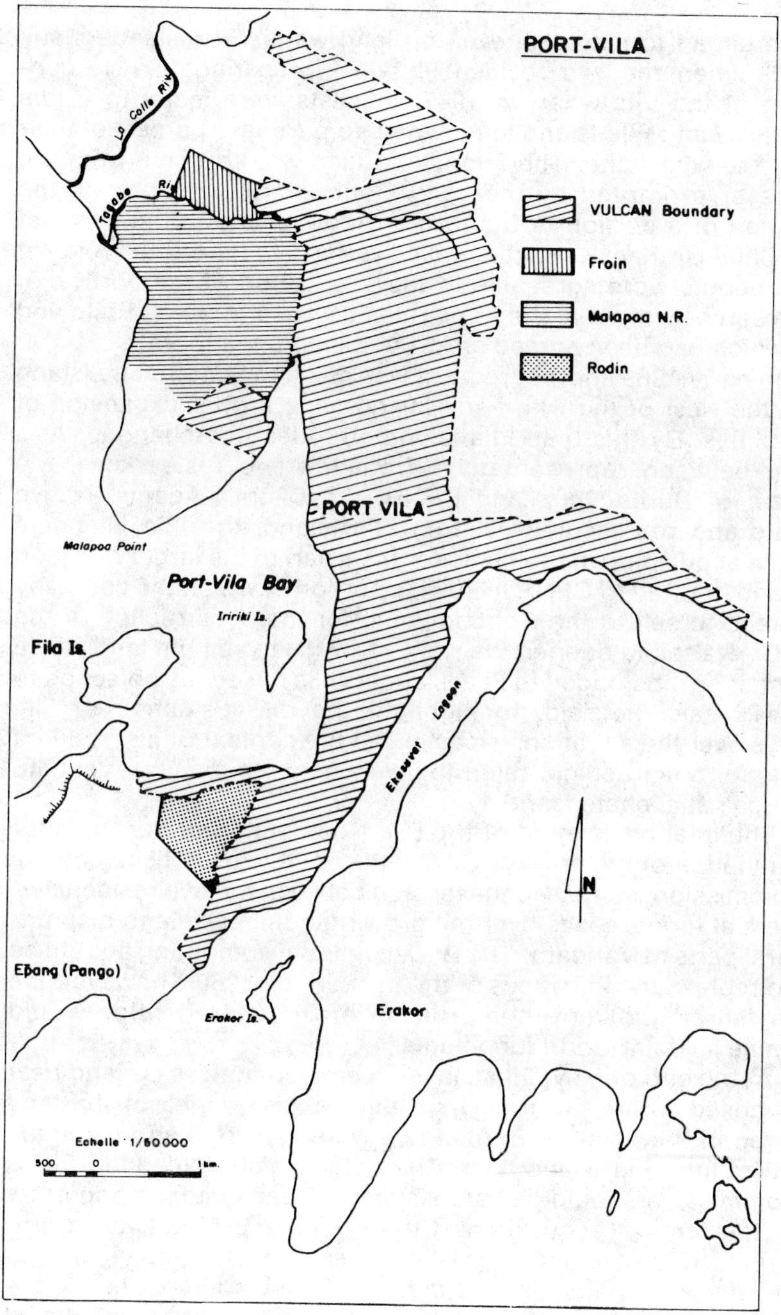

PORT-VILA
VULCAN Boundary
Froin
Malapoa N.R.
Rodin
La Colle Riv.
Tagabe Riv.
PORT VILA
Malapoa Point
Port-Vila Bay
Iririki Is.
Fila Is.
Ekasuvat Lagoon
N
Eβang (Pango)
Erakor Is.
Erakor
Echelle 1/60 000
500
0
1 km.

pressure began to increase, even on land which Fila Islanders still retained. When the two residencies were preparing for the construction of the Vila wharf in 1967, requests were made to Burns Philp, CFNH and Fila Island landowners to purchase parcels of their land for the wharf site. The Fila Island land was to come from the native reserve granted by the Joint Court in 1934, as part of the registration of a portion of the former Rodin estate in the name of CFNH. Chief Graham Kalsakau replied verbally to the written request that his people were agreeable to the acquisition of the portion of native reserve involved at the same rate accorded to Burns Philp and CFNH which had been agreed at A$1 per square metre.[19]

In early 1969 another request was made to acquire Fila Island land to the west of the wharf site for possible further expansion of port facilities. By this time Fila Island attitudes had changed. At a meeting between representatives from the two residencies, the managers of Burns Philp and CFNH, the District Agents, Native Advocate and representatives from Fila Island, the Fila Islanders linked the acquisition of their land for the wharf to the larger question of the land granted to CFNH in 1934, a portion of which the company had agreed to sell to the Condominium for the construction of the wharf. Dr. Kalsakau queried the right of CFNH to sell the land, since he maintained it belonged to Fila Islanders. He raised the objection to the CFNH sale, he said, to highlight the dissatisfaction of Fila Islanders over the situation, especially in the context of his frequent requests for a land commission to investigate the many ni-Vanuatu claims against alienated land.[20]

The change of mind of the Fila Islanders, their demands for re-examination of the original CFNH title and the establishment of a land commission increased the tension between the two residencies, who were at loggerheads over the growing number of land disputes in several parts of Vanuatu. The British felt that something should be done to redress the injustices of the past. In the 1960s, however, the French feared that any compromise on registered titles would undermine all Joint Court judgments.

At the end of May, Fila Islanders erected notices on land near the proposed wharf site implying that the boundaries of the land registered in the name of Burns Philp were incorrect and extended over 100m into Fila Island land. The notices also demanded that a land commission should be established to investigate, among other claims, the original acquisition of the Rodin land. The two governments refused to accept the Fila Island claim. Despite their inability to gain satisfaction on the land claims, the Fila Islanders agreed to the construction of the wharf on the land which had been negotiated earlier, i.e. the portion of the native reserve. However, to emphasize their dissatisfaction, they refused payment for the land until the dispute with CFNH had been settled.

After almost two years of inactivity, the dispute began to heat up again when it was learned that the CFNH intended to sub-divide the remaining undeveloped portion of its property near the wharf site. In response, Islanders began to make more forceful protests. In late October 1971, they removed survey markers and erected notices on the land, but as a result of a visit to Fila Island by the French Resident Commissioner, Chief Graham agreed to have the survey markers replaced and to begin direct negotiations with the Company. CFNH agreed to relinquish about half a hectare free of charge to Fila Island and to make 35 plots in the subdivision — about eight hectares — available to Fila Islanders at a special rate. Fila Islanders then requested a loan from the Condominium Loans Board to purchase the land, which was agreed.

By 1974, the CFNH/Vila wharf dispute had been reduced to a few minor issues. However, in a meeting in September that year between representatives of the two residencies and members of the Fila Island Land Committee, which had been established in 1973 to handle Fila Island land problems, the point was made that until the Joint Administration dealt with the remaining problems, the Fila Island community would not discuss other pressing land issues in the Vila area, which had arisen since the agreement with CFNH had been reached in 1971. It was agreed that a footpath requested by Chief Graham in 1967 would be constructed, that piped water would be supplied to Fila Island (also an earlier request), and the canoe landing at the wharf would be enlarged. These arrangements were agreed to as compensation to Fila Islanders for the pollution that the new wharf would create in one of their traditional fishing grounds. Registration of reclaimed land at the wharf site and payment of landowners was discussed, and the Government was reminded that the loan had not yet been received, nor had the title to the land granted by the CFNH been transferred. The Fila Island representatives also mentioned that they were now ready to be paid the A$1 per square metre for the wharf land, agreed to earlier.[21]

In April 1976, a letter from the British Residency asked the Fila Island Land Committee which customary owners should receive the money for the purchase of the land and how the reclaimed land associated with the wharf's construction should be registered.[22] No formal reply was ever sent, due to disagreement among Fila Islanders regarding custom rights. The loan was finally granted, but never repaid. Fila Islanders ceased to push the issue of the remaining portion of the Rodin land. They did not drop their claim to the land, but shifted their efforts to other areas of disagreement.

Evidence that Fila Islanders still felt strongly about their traditional rights to the CFNH land can be seen in an incident at the Vila wharf on 11 September 1977. Returning to Fila Island from an evening at a local nightclub, a small group of young men passed through the wharf area, where a number of vendors' stalls had been set up to sell local handicrafts and curios to tourists from the cruise ship in port that weekend. The stalls were owned mainly by Tongans and Chinese. The men set fire to one stall and threw another into the harbour. A confrontation with police resulted in minor injuries on both sides. Two men were arrested; the others returned to Fila Island.

The following morning at about 5.30, a contingent of British and French police arrived on Fila Island to arrest the other men involved in the incident. They were reluctant to give themselves up and Barak Sope and Kalpokor Kalsakau, prominent Fila Islanders who attempted to mediate, told the police that they would not allow the men to be arrested until the Condominium settled Fila Island land claims. A compromise was reached — the men agreed to go to police headquarters to make statements and a meeting was organized with the two Resident Commissioners. Four Fila Islanders were given prison sentences.

Two similar attacks by Fila Islanders on vendors' stalls at the wharf had occurred the previous year. The motivation, as explained by one of the men involved, was the long-standing dispute between Fila Islanders and the CFNH, who had sold land to the Condominium which was claimed by Fila Islanders. The young men said they attacked the stalls because they did not approve of people making money on Fila Island land without having asked permission.

The Frouin Land Dispute

In August 1973, when it came to be known that the Frouin family were intending to sub-divide their property at Tagabe, a dispute broke out which had its beginning over 40 years before at the time of the Joint Court decision to grant title to the land. This was the land which Chief Graham Kalsakau referred to in his letter to the two Resident Commissioners in 1964.

During the last half of 1973, a number of meetings were organized by the French District Agent between representatives of the Frouin family and members of the Fila Island Land Committee, which by this time had begun to take over from Chief Graham in negotiations and decision making relating to land. The Fila Island

Louis Gabriel Frouin and his wife (neē Kuter) in 1910. In centre is Gabriel (Bielo) Frouin, still alive in 1979 (from ***Nabanga,*** *No. 112, 9 June 1979).*

position was that the land should remain untouched until an agreement had been reached. However, the Frouins ignored the requests, claiming rights by virtue of the Joint Court decision, and began construction of two houses beside the road to Mele village. The Fila Island Land Committee, in a meeting on 9 January 1974, resolved and conveyed to the Frouins:

> That Frouin be removed from the disputed property unconditionally. But if Frouin or anyone else wishes to remain on the land they shall pay rent to the Fila Island people.[23]

Members of the Committee attempted to meet with Frouin the day after their meeting, but were not successful. So they conveyed the above resolution in writing and added that "unless an agreement is obtained from your side we will be forced to take militant action against you".[24] In a subsequent meeting organized by the French District Agent, the spokesmen of the Committee turned down a suggestion that a 20 hectare section could be turned over to Fila Island with Frouin being compensated with property elsewhere. They reiterated their claim to the whole property and intimated that Fila Island rights extended as far as Bauer Field, and that the return of the Frouin property was only the first stage of their claim.[25]

Following two months in which no progress was made towards a settlement, the Fila Islanders used the occasion of the first visit of the French High Commissioner, M. Eriau, to Vanuatu to stage a demonstration involving direct action against the Frouin property. A large crowd of Fila Islanders and other ni-Vanuatu sympathizers marched to the Frouin property at Tagabe and constructed a fence around the portion on which the houses were being constructed. The demonstrators stopped the High Commissioner's car on the way from the airport and confronted him with ni-Vanuatu grievances relating to land. The following day, as part of a joint plan by the two Residencies to maintain law and order, 50 French *gardes mobile* were flown into Port Vila from Noumea to reinforce local police. The fence was removed from the Frouin property and police were stationed nearby to prevent further action. Building on the property was, however, suspended pending renewed negotiations.

In a speech before the two Resident Commissioners shortly after the demonstration, a representative from Fila Island read a statement spelling out their position:

> The fence was both a symbolic gesture, and a warning. It was symbolic in that it was to show the governments that they haven't bothered to deal with our problems....
>
> It was a warning in that we New Hebrideans cannot sit down

*Barak Sope with French Governor Erian: Fila Island land demonstration about Frouin land at Tagabe (from **Nakamal,** No. 51, March 1974).*

> and hold our frustration for so long. We cannot sit down and watch others build houses, roads, waterfronts and wharves on our land.
>
> We know that the Frouin family hold the title to that piece of land — but we also know that our forefathers did not sell that land. For that reason we do not believe in the Joint Court decision concerning that piece of land and many more.
>
> We will assure you now that no further demonstrations will be staged if the Governments can also assure us that:
> 1. The Frouin family will return our land.
> 2. That the Frouin family stop the construction of buildings or any other sort of developments on that land until the dispute has been settled.[26]

In meetings which followed the demonstration, an agreement was worked out which met at least part of the demands. All construction was halted on the Frouin property and an offer made to hand back nearly all the Frouin land to the Fila Island community except a small area along the main road upon which buildings had already been constructed. The Frouin family was to be compensated by the Condominium with a gift of land of approximately equal value.

The proposed settlement was accepted by the Fila Islanders, but not by the Frouins, who demanded over A$800,000 in compensation, while two independent valuations produced figures of A$500,000 and A$450,000. In early 1975, the two residencies decided they could not meet the demands of the Frouin family and the problem was left in abeyance.[27] The Frouins made no further attempt to sub-divide or develop the property and the Fila Islanders made no further direct moves to occupy the disputed land.

The Seafront Dispute

Another area of dispute between Fila Islanders and the Condominium Government, which erupted in the mid-1970s, concerned reclaimed area along the Vila seafront. In early 1975, Fila Islanders began to voice opposition to the construction of a covered market and filling station/shop complex on the land. The reclamation had been carried out by the Condominium at a cost of around A$900,000 and the governments intended to recover the costs by making the land available for various commercial ventures. Demonstrations by Fila Islanders held up the construction for six months until an agreement was worked out that would guarantee Fila Islanders' participation in the economic ventures planned for the site. Fila Islanders also used the opportunity to raise their old demands.

The response of the two governments to the new demands reflects the increasing power of the Fila Islanders — both projects were completed by mid-1976. The dispute, however, threatened to break out again, since the real issue of ownership had not been dealt with. Just before the covered market was about to be handed over to the Vila Municipal Council, the Fila Island Land Committee threatened to disrupt the ceremony and future operation of the facilities:

> neither yourselves nor Shell Company have a right to hand over buildings to the Municipality, when such buildings are on our land without our approval. Should the buildings be handed over as planned, we will do our uttermost to prevent the orderly use of these buildings.[28]

Fila Islanders were not willing to allow the use of the seafront land for any development that did not begin by recognizing them as the rightful owners of the land. They did not oppose development *per se*, but would welcome the use of the seafront once their claim was recognized and if there was adequate participation by the Fila Island community.

The Fila Island Land Committee made it clear they were not objecting to the market, but to the other buildings and the proposed arrangements for operating them. The agreement made with the Fila Islanders the previous year had been overlooked and the franchise for the filling station awarded to another party rather than to the Fila Islanders as earlier agreed. Further negotiations between the Fila Island Land Committee and Shell resulted in an agreement which allowed Shell to operate the filling station for five years at an annual rent for the site of $600 to be paid to the Ifira Trust, which had been set up to manage land belonging to the Fila Island community as a whole. The Shell Company agreed to employ and train people from Fila Island in running the facility and the Land Committee assured the Company that "it is our expressed intention to co-operate and work together with Shell Company".[29]

The issue of the covered market was more complicated, since the people of Erakor village also claimed rights to some of the land on the seafront and threatened to intervene if Fila Islanders tried to prevent its opening, which was re-scheduled for September 1977. To prevent a confrontation, a meeting took place between the elders of the two villages, in which the representatives from Erakor explained that they did not oppose Fila Islanders' rights, but only their contention that they held exclusive rights to the land in question. They pointed out that some people in Erakor also had traditional links to the seafront land and that if this were recognized by Fila Island,

The main wharf in Port Vila was built on land which Fila Islanders claimed had been unjustly registered by the Joint Court.

In the early 1970s, the reclaimed seafront and covered market in Port Vila became a focus in the Fila Island drive to regain their traditional land rights.

Iririki Island in Port Vila harbour was registered in the name of the Presbyterian Mission. It was the site of the Paton Memorial Hospital and the residence of the British Resident Commissioner.

then their objections would be withdrawn. This point was accepted at the time by the Fila Island Land Committee and the tension subsided.

Part of the Erakor concern was also based on the fact that the women of that village are extensively involved in growing fresh produce for sale in Port Vila and would have benefited from the construction of proper market facilities. Moreover, the dispute broke out at a time when ni-Vanuatu were becoming increasingly polarized politically into opposing Anglophone and Francophone camps. The fact that Erakor was a stronghold of the Union of 'Moderate' Parties and Fila Island firmly National Party, indicates clear political motives behind the dispute as well.

Further evidence of Francophone interest in attempting to exploit the market issue for political purposes was the public position taken by the Vila Municipal Council, which was controlled by French expatriates. The Council pressed Condominium officials to go ahead with the opening of the market and transferring the site to the Council. The Fila Island Land Committee reacted to the proposal to transfer seafront land, because the title was still in dispute. They threatened to retaliate by refusing to allow the Council the continued use of Fila Island land for the city dump and requested that a water pipe that crossed their land be disconnected.[30] To avoid a confrontation the two residencies delayed the formal opening of the market again and the Mayor, M. Remy Delaveuve, requested a meeting with the representatives of Erakor and Fila Island villages. The situation was clarified without Fila Islanders having to press their position further. However, while the dispute subsided, it was by no means settled. The two residencies did not pursue an application to register the reclaimed land, originally filed in the Joint Court in 1974, but decided instead to leave settlement of the issue of land rights to the new Legislative Assembly. The issue of land, however, was never debated and thus the dispute remained unsettled.

Iririki Island

In 1928, the Joint Court granted title to Iririki Island in Vila harbour to the Presbyterian Church of Victoria. It was the Court's first judgment and was easy as there were no caveats lodged against it. Until 1972, part of the island was used by the Presbyterian Mission's Paton Memorial Hospital. The northern portion, leased to the British Government for 999 years, had become the permanent residence for the British Resident Commissioner. In 1975, the Fila Island Land Committee began negotiations with the Presbyterian Church for the return of the island to Fila Island ownership. The church had no immediate use for the land, since its hospital facilities had been closed with the construction by the British Government of the new Vila Base Hospital. Fila Islanders saw the potential income which might accrue to them through leasing the island for development purposes, if title could be regained.

There was initial resistance from the church and suggestions among its leadership that the island might be used for a Bible College or some similar training facility. There was concern on the part of the church about what sort of purposes the island might be used for, if they relinquished title, and requested proposals from the Fila Island Land Committee. However, the Committee felt the church had no business trying to influence how the land would be used and refused to co-operate in this regard. The church then put a price of $100,000 on the land, which the Committee rejected. In 1976, after an initial offer of half the island, the Church Assembly — which met at Southwest Bay on Malakula in August with representatives of the Fila Island Land Committee in attendance — finally agreed that the whole island would be returned to Fila Island on the condition that the church would not have to return the land which it had originally received from the British Government in Vila town in exchange for the lease of part of the island. It also stipulated that the British Residency would be permitted to stay on Iririki until independence. It was decided by the Land Committee that Iririki would become part of the IFIRA Trust, rather than go back to individual landowners.

The Pattern of Fila Island Protest

Although the two governments refused to negotiate on the question of registered titles, Fila Islanders achieved some success during the 1960s and 70s. They regained rights to some land, forced the curtailment of the sub-division and development of others, and obtained the acceptance from the two residencies that the issue of registered titles was a subject for discussion, if not at present, then under an independent Vanuatu government. With the realization that it was not possible to change official policy regarding the status of titles, the intensity of protest had subsided by the mid-1970s. Moreover, it became clear in 1974, when reinforcements were called in from Noumea, that the Joint Administration was prepared to use force to defend the existing order. What must also have acted as a restraining force in the events of 1974 was that Fila Islanders could no longer count on the British Administration to act as a moderating force on the French. At the height of the crisis there were those in the British Residency who appealed for action which would not impair the British reputation "... as the upholders of justice and reform in the New Hebrides".[32] However, the Resident Commissioner, Mr. Du Boulay, allowed public statements at that time by the French High Commissioner, Mr. Eriau, which expressed clearly the joint nature of the police action undertaken.

It might be argued that the British had no choice but to support the French then, if they hoped to have any influence over them in the long run. However, it is obvious from the reports sent to the Foreign and Commonwealth Office in London, that the predominant attitude in the British Residency had become unsympathetic to the Fila Island position. The British Resident Commissioner reported:

> This development coincided with the return from University of Barak Sope and Kalkot Matas-Kele, both members of the dispossessed and unsatisfied factions in Fila Island, and both looking for causes on which to exercise their newly-learned revolutionary fervour and student militancy. After a trial run on 27th December on an extraneous issue, they turned their attention to exploiting this most promising vein. It seemed to have everything. A genuine injustice had been committed and perpetuated in the 1930s. The present beneficiaries were white, and French at that. Successful prosecution of the claim would bring rich financial rewards. And Barak Sope's own political position would be assured. Thus motives of avarice, racism, xenophobia and personal advancement were allied with a burning sense of injustice to form the basis of a genuinely popular cause.[33]

After years of fruitless protests and entreaties, to blame the frustrations manifested in the Frouin land demonstration simply on youthful idealism and ambition, shows a distinct lack of understanding of the history surrounding Fila Island problems.

An examination of the chain of events leading to the 1974 confrontation reveals, on the contrary, a clearly reasonable approach. Fila Islanders genuinely felt that the land called Narrowby, of which the Frouin land was a part, had been wrongly taken from them. Their caveats against the application for registration in 1930 had been rejected. Chief Graham Kalsakau's letter to the Resident Commissioners in 1964 protesting against the alienation and other rather tame protests had no more effect than the moderately expressed demands of Dr. John Kalsakau and other members of the Advisory Committee in 1965 and 1967 for an investigatory land commission. Moreover, the erecting of notices and removal of survey markers on the CFNH land in 1969 and 1971 could hardly be termed violent.

The concessions they were able to win regarding the CFNH land may have encouraged Fila Islanders to use more direct methods of protest and taught them that their views would only be listened to when they committed some physical act. However, putting up a fence would seem to be an understandable course of action given the long history of seemingly unshakable indifference on the part of the joint administration.

There was, indeed, a change in leadership in Fila Island during the period leading up to the confrontation in 1974, which may have been a factor in determining the course of action. In August 1973, two residents of Fila Island, Arthur Kalchichi and Kalbeau Kalsakau, proposed the formation of a committee to deal with land matters, when Chief Graham Kalsakau refused to go along with their efforts to stop Frouin from developing the property at Tagabe. Membership was to be based along *naflak* (family) lines and to include educated members of the community. The initial membership came to 12, including Barak Sope and Kalkot Matas-Kele, when they returned from their studies in late 1973. It is significant that they were not involved in the founding of the Land Committee, which had its origin among a group of ordinary Fila Islanders with whom these two younger, more outspoken individuals came to be allied.

The final break with Chief Graham on the land issue occurred in a meeting in late February 1974, after attempts by members of the Committee to meet with Frouin had failed and plans were being made for the demonstration. The Chief's refusal to agree to the fencing of Frouin's land, it is said, resulted in a heated discussion in which the view was expressed that Fila Islanders had lost confidence in his ability or willingness to represent them effectively in land matters. The Chief went to the Resident Commissioners after the demonstration to disassociate himself from the action, but from that time the joint administration dealt primarily with members of the Committee on land matters, in effect, recognizing the change of leadership in this regard.

Chief Graham's initial reaction to the new line of protest is understandable, since he belonged to the generation which had been forced to accept the fact that Fila Islanders had no way to oppose the colonial administration. As a young boy, he would have witnessed the destruction of the gardens of his fellow Fila Islanders as Europeans cut fences and drove cattle onto properties which the Joint Court had registered in their favour. As Chief of Fila Island, he would have seen his responsibility as that of looking after the best interests of his people. It is not surprising that he wanted to avoid a confrontation with Condominium authorities which he knew from his own experience could not be won. Within a short time, however, Chief Graham changed his position completely and gave full support to the Fila Island Land Committee and its policies.[34]

After achieving the aim of preventing the development of the Frouin property and gaining assurances from the administration that efforts would be made to return the land to Fila Island through an exchange of land with Frouin, the Land Committee adopted a conciliatory attitude. However, it continued to press the two residencies for the settlement of a number of outstanding issues, often holding out the possibility of moderation or concessions in one area, for agreement to Fila Island demands in another.

By late 1976, Fila Islanders were eager to solve the major outstanding land problems. It was at the request of the Committee that meetings were called in November 1976 with the two Resident Commissioners and in March 1977 with the two High Commissioners during their joint visit to Vanuatu. At the latter meeting, for example, the Committee expressed its willingness to accept only token compensation, accompanied by recognition of traditional Fila Island ownership rights, in regard to the land in Vila Town.

Although it has not been expressed by Fila Islanders, one reason which may have given the Land Committee an incentive to seek speedy solutions to their problems was the pace of political development in 1976/1977. The first elected Legislative Assembly met twice during 1976, and although the Vanua'aku Pati opposed its composition and the vague pronouncements from the two governments regarding constitutional development, it was evident by 1977 that Vanuatu was beginning to move towards independence. Moreover, the two residencies had taken the position on a number of occasions that they could not make decisions relating to basic issues of land policy and that these would be better dealt with by the Representative Assembly or an independent Vanuatu government. The Natural Resources Committee, which had been set up by the first Representative Assembly, had discussed the land problem in its meeting on 3 and 4 January 1977, and although no policy was decided, the issues were given a thorough airing. During these discussions, the similarities and differences in view between the Vanua'aku Pati, some of the top officials of which were also leaders in the Fila Island Land Committee and the Union of 'Moderate' parties (a coalition of Francophone Melanesian groups) became clear. It may have occurred to Fila Islanders involved in these meetings that they were more likely to achieve their goals before independence than after, when the need for compromise between fellow ni-Vanuatu would be greater and increasingly more difficult.

Furthermore, by the end of 1976, the French Government had completed the last phase of its handing back to ni-Vanuatu of large sections of primarily undeveloped bush land, formerly owned by the SFNH and French State. Although most of the land involved was already in the hands of ni-Vanuatu by virtue of long occupation and neither the SFNH nor the French State could have attempted to develop it without local opposition, the act improved the image of the French regarding land matters and did much to diffuse the land issue nationally. Under the changed circumstances in which the issue of land had become a problem primarily for only isolated groups, there would be less enthusiasm in an independent Vanuatu for the repudiation of registered titles to the degree envisaged by Fila Islanders. Moreover, in an independent Vanuatu, Port Vila would cease to be the colonial headquarters, but would become instead the nation's capital, which would entitle all ni-Vanuatu to a say in its affairs.

However, because of the close ties between the Fila Island Land Committee and the Vanua'aku Pati — two leading figures in the Vanua'aku Pati, Barak Sope and Kalkot Matas-Kele, were from Fila Island and members of the Land Committee — Fila Islanders were certain of continued support. The party's unequivocal stand on registered land, which called for the re-examination of all titles granted by the Joint Court, meant in the late 1970s that Fila Islanders would eventually have the opportunity to seek redress for the injustices which they felt they had suffered in the past, if the Vanua'aku Pati were able to form the first ni-Vanuatu Government.

8

Land, Politics and Independence

On 19 August 1971, a group of ni-Vanuatu led by Fr. John Bani — members and supporters of the newly formed New Hebrides Cultural Association — staged a peaceful demonstration in Port Vila. Their action was in support of Joint Regulations 15 and 16 of 1971, limiting sub-divisions, which had come into effect earlier in the month. The demonstrators held a vigil outside the meeting place of the Advisory Council Standing Committee, which had convened a special sitting to receive a submission from a 'Citizens Committee' — representing *colon* and business interests in Port Vila and Santo — recommending amendments to the Joint Regulations.[1] Following the demonstration, the New Hebrides Cultural Association reconstituted itself as the New Hebrides National Party (NHNP) and in so doing marked the birth of national politics in Vanuatu.

The Cultural Association had been founded the previous June when a small group of ni-Vanuatu working in Santo decided to publish a newspaper to increase awareness among the Melanesian population on important issues relating to the future development of their country. The founding members of the Association were: Donald Kalpokas, a teacher; and two Anglican priests, Fr. John Bani and Fr. Walter Lini, who became Vanuatu's first Prime Minister in 1980. The aims of the New Hebrides Cultural Association were:

> To promote, to preserve, to revive and to encourage New Hebridean culture. To seek the advancement of the New Hebrideans socially, educationally and politically in relation with New Hebridean culture and Western civilization.[2]

The first issue of the Association's newspaper, the *New Hebrides Viewpoints*, of which only about 25 copies were printed, produced a significant response from ni-Vanuatu throughout the country. Within a short time membership had spread to Port Vila and other centres in the archipelago.[3]

The issue which had brought about the transformation of the Cultural Association's supporters from a concerned group of individuals to a political party was land:

> Our aims in forming a National Party are to preserve the New Hebridean people; their culture and their ways of life are in immediate danger of large scale settlement by Europeans. Already large areas of land had been bought at Hog Harbour, Cape Queiros and Palekula all on Santo. Without mentioning other places these pieces of land have been subdivided and resold. This means a lot of Europeans will be coming to settle on them . . .
>
> We are facing a danger which means we must act now before it is too late. The present government set up provides little hope of getting things done in the interest of the New Hebrideans. Once the National Party is set up we can advise the government of the New Hebrides on how to work steadily towards independence. We must bring pressure on the 2 Governments to stop this settlement before it is too late.[4]

While supporting the Joint Regulations, it is clear that members of the Cultural Association did not feel that the Condominium Government could or would protect the interests of ni-Vanuatu. The long-term solution for the NHNP was, therefore, independence.

Alienated land was not a new issue in 1971. The number of land related confrontations between ni-Vanuatu and Europeans had been increasing throughout the 1960s. However, the moderate requests made by ni-Vanuatu representatives on the Advisory Council for land reform, i.e. that the two governing powers should take seriously the growing discontent and seek to deal with Melanesian grievances over land by establishing a land commission, had been ignored. Only Nagriamel, which had been prepared to physically confront plantation owners and the Condominium administration, succeeded in its aim of halting the further expansion of European settlement on undeveloped land. What made 1971 different from earlier ni-Vanuatu protests was that for the first time the land issue took on a national political dimension when it was coupled with demands for political change. The demonstration and founding of the NHNP were a declaration to the colonial powers that some Melanesians were no longer willing to accept their almost total exclusion from the decision-making process which governed Vanuatu. The National Party took up the land problem, because it symbolized the fundamental issue confronting ni-Vanuatu at that time — their lack of power to influence the present and the future directions of their country.

The Politics of Land

The advent of the New Hebrides National Party — and in particular, the demonstration held in August 1971 — had a profound and immediate effect. Commenting on the impact of the demonstration on the local European population, the then French Resident Commissioner, M. Langlois, noted:

> Although the demonstration held for about two hours by just a few dozen natives was absolutely calm, its impact on the Europeans was gripping. Unable to believe that natives could adopt an attitude that had not been dictated to them, the European population pinned this fear down to the activity of the British Residency, the Presbyterian Mission, the Anglicans, etc. . . . It is evident that the British were delighted to see an awakening of civic consciousness in the natives, who wished to have their say in the settlement of affairs bearing on general interests. It is none the less certain that this awakening has been spontaneous, its occurrence having been hastened by the attitudès of the Europeans, yet it had been lying in wait for a coherent and organised movement.[5]

In December 1971, the members and supporters of the Citizens' Committee who had been confronted by National Party demonstrators several months earlier responded by founding the Union de la Population des Nouvelles-Hébrides (UPNH).[6]

The most important support for this new political party came from well established European plantation owners and business interests — primarily French, but not exclusively. They were the most conservative group within the party, "the guardians of the Condominium status quo", and remained in the background, leaving a more moderate faction to the forefront.[7] The aims of the UPNH were as follows:

> 1. To uphold the Condominium system until the evolution of the archipelago enables the determination of a new, rational

and realistic orientation.
2. The creation of the position of a Secretary-General of the Condominium Administration.
3. To increase the possibilities of the individual ownership of land and to eliminate as far as possible property litigations.[8]

The third aim was a rather indirect statement to the administration to do something to stem the increasing number of challenges to European titles, i.e. "to uphold the Condominium system".

The more moderate faction of the UPNH, including the Party's President, M. Philippe Delacroix, were inclined to support modification of the Condominium system, including the participation of some ni-Vanuatu in the political process. M. Langlois, French Resident Commissioner in 1971, noted before the August demonstration that:

> Certain Europeans, such as M. Delacroix, think that it is time to organize young Melanesians into political groupings which would permit the inevitable evolution of their behaviour to be guided.[8]

Langlois, however, was skeptical of such notions:

> I fear that they [Europeans like Delacroix] delude themselves with illusions and I rather believe that these political regroupings which will certainly take place will be undertaken by the natives themselves, as soon as a small thinking elite, capable of representing the masses will have been formed. All we hope for is that this elite will be Francophone, trained in our own way of thinking.[10]

Efforts were made by the UPNH to attract ni-Vanuatu support by advocating the concept of a trade union. Vila taxi drivers, in particular, found this appealing due to problems they were having at the time over the issuing of licences to non-Melanesians. It was estimated that they and other ni-Vanuatu UPNH members numbered about 150.[11]

The reactionary attitude of many of the UPNH's European members was, however, in direct opposition to the interests of most ni-Vanuatu. By the end of 1972, it had become apparent that the Party leadership had no real concern for ni-Vanuatu worker welfare and Melanesian membership declined. Nevertheless, the UNPH did not disappear completely. It continued to exist, more in name than in substance, until 1974.[12] In that year, it was supplanted by a new party, the Union des Communautés des Nouvelles-Hébrides (UCNH), which included some of the former members of the UPNH and attracted significant ni-Vanuatu support.

Following the founding of the NHNP in 1971, there had been an initial surge of interest and enthusiasm among ni-Vanuatu — especially Anglophones — but then the growth of the Party had slowed. Most of its members were civil servants and church leaders concentrated in the urban and administrative centres. The Party's leadership was dispersed geographically, which limited its ability to formulate and sustain an active policy. The first Chairman, Aiden Garae, was based in Santo. Fr. John Bani was chosen Vice-Chairman and worked in Port Vila with a strong committee including Donald Kalpokas, Peter Taurakoto and George Kalkoa, who became President Ati George Sokomanu in 1980. Fr. Walter Lini edited and published the *New Hebrides Viewpoints* from Lolowai on Ambae.

Barak Sope, who became Secretary General of the Party in 1974, returned to Vanuatu from Fiji in early 1973, during which time he undertook research on the issue of land and politics as part of his university studies. With regard to the NHNP he noted:

> the party had no definite policies for the achievement of its objectives. This was mainly because of the lack of organisation and the lack of people dedicated enough to sacrifice their time for the party.[13]

In addition, according to Sope, the Party had not followed through and capitalized on the one issue that could have unified the Melanesian people into a strong political force — the land problem. Writing again in 1973, he noted:

> the unity of many New Hebrideans is possible if based on a common struggle for the regaining of alienated land.... For the New Hebrideans land is also a tool that can help to bridge the educated-uneducated and the urban-rural gaps.[14]

Sope's visit in early 1973 and discussions with NHNP leaders seems to have had an effect. In mid-1973, the headquarters of the NHNP was shifted from Santo to Vila and it was decided that the Party should be led by a President. Fr. John Bani was elected. At the same time, the publication of the *New Hebrides Viewpoints* was shifted from Ambae to Vila. The Party leadership was also aware of their weakness in the rural areas and took steps to overcome this by establishing a system of sub-committees in each of the four districts.[15]

Local churches also began to play an active role in politics at this time. The 1973 Presbyterian Assembly held on Tanna, for example, passed a resolution supporting independence.[16] Indeed, church membership became an important factor in determining which of the two metropolitan powers and languages ni-Vanuatu identified with and hence what political affiliation they developed.

Father Walter Lini speaks at National Party rally at Togabe on 5 May 1974. George Kalkoa (President Ati George

Anglicans and Presbyterians, who made up over 60% of the total population of Vanuatu, were Anglophone and for the most part, staunch National Party supporters. Members of the smaller Anglophone churches — Seventh Day Adventists and Apostolics — also tended to support the National Party. The Church of Christ was, however, divided. One faction was affiliated with Nagriamel, while the remainder joined the National Party grouping. Moreover, it is significant that most Nagriamel members who claimed membership in one of the Christian churches were Anglophones. Ni-Vanuatu Catholics, who numbered only about 12% of the population, tended to join the various political parties opposed to the NHNP, especially the UCNH.

In addition to the administrative changes to the NHNP, several important political events took place in 1973 which began to move the Party forward again. At the request of Fr. Lini, a group representing various Pacific churches agreed to hold a conference in Port Vila to discuss future trends and developments in the region. In January 1973, the Pacific Council of Churches organized what it called the SPADES (South Pacific Action for Development and Economic Strategies) Conference in Port Vila and, much to the displeasure of the French Residency and the embarrassment of the British, supported in its resolutions, independence for still dependent territories and "where there is alienated land, problems of land tenure, an independent land board be set up".[17] The SPADES Conference encouraged NHNP members and in August the Party took its first major policy step by petitioning the United Nations to intervene in Vanuatu to bring about independence.[18]

The most important action taken by the NHNP in 1973, in terms of political impact, was a demonstration held in Vila on 27 December 1973 to protest the arrest of two ni-Vanuatu — the Rarua brothers — for allegedly assaulting a policeman. The two had been arrested in Santo by a French *gendarme* and detained in jail until a letter was smuggled to the NHNP notifying members of their plight. The Rarua family, who were from Tongoa and NHNP supporters, operated a nightclub in Santo and were disliked and regularly harassed by the French and French mixed-race residents of the town, who resented their success, their party affiliation and the fact that they were not from Santo. At the demonstration, a petition was presented to French officials demanding the immediate release of the Rarua brothers and reform to the legal system governing the powers of the police and the rights of ni-Vanuatu before the courts. The French, with the agreement of the British, responded by releasing the men and agreeing in principle to the other demands. The speed with which the administration gave in to NHNP demands was received with anger and dismay by the Francophone planters and business community in both Vila and Santo and was a major factor leading to the establishment of a new *colon* party in Santo — the Mouvement Autonomiste des Nouvelles-Hébrides — MANH.[19]

Problems of Party administration and a strategy of political action were the subject of the NHNP Congress held at the end of January 1974 in Port Vila. One of the administrative changes agreed to was that the President should work full-time for the Party. Fr. Walter Lini was elected and given leave by the Anglican Church to pursue his political activities. Barak Sope, who had returned to Vanuatu after completing his university studies, was elected Secretary General. With a full-time working President, the NHNP was in a position to tackle what members like Sope had seen as a major shortcoming — the building of strong support for the Party among the rural Melanesian population. The establishment of committees in the islands was extended with village representatives forming area committees.

A number of important policy decisions also emerged from the January 1974 Party Congress, including specific proposals for land reform:

> 1. That all land owned by expatriates (by registered title) be returned eventually to the people of the New Hebrides as Nationalized land.
> 2. That all land owned by New Hebrideans (in registered title) whether it was bought from New Hebrideans or Expatriates, remain as title to its present New Hebridean owners.
> 3. That all bush land (uncultivated, unsettled, undeveloped or uncleared land) owned by expatriates in Registered Title be returned to the New Hebrides people as New Hebridean Custom Trust Land.
> 4. That the National Party recognizes the various New Hebridean Customary titles, rights, claims and tenure to and over the land.[20]

The demand that all alienated land should be returned to ni-Vanuatu ownership was the most significant aspect of the NHNP policy and created the strongest reaction among opposition groups.

While the January 1974 Congress served as a watershed for the NHNP in terms of clarifying its aims and objectives and creating a new sense of commitment and unity of purpose, it also had the effect of revitalizing the Party's main opposition. In early February, only a few days after the NHNP published its new policy objectives, the more conservative elements of the UPNH founded the Union des Communautés des Nouvelles-Hébrides (UCNH). The Party's birth was seen by NHNP leaders as a direct result of the publication of their new land nationalization policy and indicated a consolidation of the "foreign community", which a NHNP spokesman predicted would lead to "open conflict between the planters and the National Party" in the future.[21] In fact, the UCNH grew out of an association of UPNH members, which had formed the previous December as a result of concessions made by the Condominium Government to the National Party in the Rarua brothers incident. The first President was Remy Delaveuve, a long time French resident and senior civil servant in the Condominium Survey Department. Two ni-Vanuatu Francophones, Jean-Marie Léyé and Fr. Gérard Leymang (a Catholic priest) were elected respectively Vice-President and Secretary. Another prominent ni-Vanuatu member was Vincent Boulekone, who along with Léyé and Leymang, had been invited as observers to the NHNP Congress two weeks earlier.[22]

The decision of Boulekone, Léyé and Leymang to become members of the UCNH rather than the NHNP — their attendance at the NHNP Congress is an indication that they saw joining the Party as at least a possibility — illustrates clearly the growing polarization of Melanesians along Condominium lines, i.e. Anglophone and Francophone. Boulekone himself attributed his decision to join the UCNH to the alienation he felt as a Francophone from the Anglophones of the NHNP:

> The National Party was born on the English side and it therefore influenced the Anglophones. The Francophone Melanesians were not interested in this, and didn't understand too well why the National Party had been born. At the same time they understood that the New Hebrides must undergo reform — institutional, administrative, etc.[23]

While agreeing with the goal of independence, Boulekone felt that the NHNP was moving too quickly.[24]

There is no reason to doubt his commitment to this point of view, but had he been aware of the French Government's strategy for maintaining their position in Vanuatu by manipulating Melanesians through education and limited land reform, his position in 1974 might have been different. As later events would reveal, the split between Anglophone and Francophone Melanesians on many issues was often disagreement on detail rather than substance. This was especially true on the land issue. In time, the Melanesian members of the UCNH would come to realize that even the bond of Francophonie was not strong enough to reconcile the differences between themselves and the *colon* group, whose main aim was to block reform and movement towards independence. By 1977, the most important ni-Vanuatu members had left the UCNH to form their own party.

In the aims of the UCNH, formulated at its first meeting, the Party sought to "bring to the attention of the administration their past failures"[25] — a considerable contrast to the NHNP's harsh criticism of the whole Condominium system. Law reform was the only area singled out as requiring immediate attention and reflected the presence in the Party of Vincent Boulekone, who was a trained lawyer. No mention was made of land, but the fourth aim, which called for "taking action considered necessary to ensure the maintenance of respect for law"[26] was a veiled threat that any activity directed against the established order would be opposed.

The second *colon* party to emerge at this time was based in Santo and called itself Mouvement Autonomiste des Nouvelles-Hébrides (MANH). The instigator, a Frenchman by the name of Michel Thevenin, was the son of a planter on Pentecost. It attracted support from French nationals and second and third generation mixed-race settlers on Santo who held French passports, identified closely with France and who would have felt especially threatened by the National Party's challenge to the continued existence of their entrenched interests. Land, however, was not the immediate issue which led to the formation of MANH. The new Party was born at the time in December 1973 of the National Party's demonstration over the imprisonment of the Rarua brothers. A counter demonstration was staged in January out of which emerged MANH. In a petition presented to the British and French authorities at the time, MANH demanded the re-imprisonment of the Rarua brothers, that they be prevented from leaving the country and that they remove their business from Santo.[27]

The Party's formal goals, which were announced later, advocated evolution towards "autonomous status", the establishment of a "Territorial Assembly type of government" and of "municipal councils as the basis of political awareness and management".[28] The emphasis placed on the evolution of regional units reflects clearly the attitude of the *petits colons* of Santo, who identified closely with the island and felt that Port Vila had been developed at their expense. There was, therefore, resentment among MANH supporters towards French *colons* in Vila, which helps to explain to some extent the factionalism which existed within the opposition to the National Party throughout the 1970s. MANH, in fact, quickly allied itself with Nagriamel — an association which would last until 1980 — since

Jimmy Stephens by this time had accepted the idea of continued European occupation of developed land. The two organizations complemented each other well. Nagriamel provided MANH with the grassroots Melanesian support it lacked, while MANH in return gave Jimmy Stephens access to a sympathetic group of Europeans who could assist him in ways which his limited education made difficult. The only other Melanesian support for MANH came from North Malakula, the home of Aimé Maleré, another of the Party's leaders.

In April 1974, another party entered the political fray — Natui Tano or 'children of the land' — which was focused on the Anglophone Presbyterian village of Hog Harbour on Santo. It was basically an extension of the NHNP and grew up in reaction to the consolidation of planter interests in the foundation of the MANH Party and its links to Nagriamel. Natui Tano, in fact, set itself up in direct opposition to Nagriamel with its call for "Santo for *man Santo*" and claimed that Jimmy Stephens and his followers at Tanafo were mostly from other islands and thus had no right to speak for them. Moreover, they were opposed to what they interpreted as a sell-out by Jimmy Stephens to foreign interests, particularly his willingness to compromise on the question of alienated land and his deals with Americans.[29] Natui Tano hoped to attract to its ranks followers of Nagriamel who wished to pursue tougher lines in land matters than their leader. The Party was successful at first in attracting support from a number of areas, including lapsed Nagriamel Catholics from Port Orly. In time, however, the Catholic followers drifted away and Natui Tano remained as a predominantly Protestant movement clearly allied with the National Party.

By early 1974, therefore, the political situation in Vanuatu was becoming tense as the various communities and factions within the country began to organize themselves for what appeared to be an inevitable showdown. On the one side was the NHNP and its ally on Santo, Natui Tano, who were clearly following through with their strategy to use the land issue to challenge the Condominium structure and force the joint powers to instigate political change. In opposition stood the two planter based parties — UCHN, focused in Port Vila, and MANH, allied with Nagriamel in Santo. The real issue was political power, but the spark that could set off the conflagration, which the NHNP had come to believe was inevitable, was land.

Beginning in the second half of 1973, the number of land disputes between ni-Vanuatu and Europeans had indeed begun to increase. On Efate incidents related to attempts by Europeans to sell or sub-divide undeveloped registered land led to increased tension, e.g. Fila Islanders claim to the Frouin land in Port Vila. By this time, ni-Vanuatu were no longer willing to accept the idea of Europeans making high profits on undeveloped land, which local people did not accept as ever having been sold. At Eton Village on North Efate, the removal of survey markers and the blocking of roads used by Europeans to gain access to their properties led a young Frenchman to fire gunshots into the air around the village resulting in a further increase in tension and court cases for both the Melanesians and European involved.[30]

Likewise, on Malakula, transfers of land between Europeans led to increased tension. The people of Uripiv Island pulled out fences and stopped workers on a property near Norsup, which had recently been sold and was for the most part undeveloped. It was in early 1974, as well, that the men of Tautu village blocked construction of the new airstrip at Norsup. The motivation for their action was their opposition to the transfer of land by the PRNH to the Condominium Government, land which they claimed had never been sold. Also on Malakula, at Lamap, the inhabitants of Port Sandwich protested the transfer of land from the SFNH to a European.[31] The significance of the latter case is that the Lamap area is predominantly Catholic and Francophone — Uripiv and Tautu, on the other hand, are Presbyterian and Anglophone. Ni-Vanuatu opposition to continued European control of alienated land was, therefore, a concern for all Melanesian communities, despite differences in religion and language, which might have divided them politically.

At the same time as the number of land disputes began to increase in late 1973 and 1974, decisions made by the two governing powers — both jointly and independently — to diffuse or seek a solution to the problem of alienated land, had or were about to be implemented. In March 1973, Mr. J.T. Fleming arrived in Vanuatu to take up his post as the Condominium Land Tenure Adviser, whose task was initially to produce recommendations for the creation of a single code of land law. By 1973, the French Government had begun to hand back large tracts of undeveloped land to ni-Vanuatu in the hope that demands for the return of alienated land would be satisfied. And in the same year, the British and Australian governments concluded negotiations which would lead to the transfer of Commonwealth lands to a Land Trust Board under the direction of the British Residency with the long-term aim of returning the land to ni-Vanuatu ownership.

The policies of the two governments, however, failed to stem the rising tide of protest over land. Fleming made the unfortunate mistake of not beginning his work in Vanuatu by seeking out the views of important ni-Vanuatu politicians. Instead, he began straight away from his office in Port Vila preparing various draft Joint Regulations.[32] By September he had produced policy proposals, which for the most part would have been acceptable to ni-Vanuatu, but on key issues he failed to take into account local perceptions. Commenting on customary tenure, Fleming noted:

> New Hebrideans have no strong and detailed body of customary land law... [it] is vague and uncertain except in matters of inheritance and there is no sure foundation or authoritative body on which to develop or extend it. There is often a demand arising from a growing sense of nationalism in developing countries to preserve traditional customs and in particular customary law in the face of western or other cultural patterns. I have heard no such demands from the politicians or anyone else whom I have encountered to preserve New Hebridean customary law. The reason for this is that customary land law in these islands, in so far as it exists, is seen to be an obstacle in the way of those seeking to develop their land.[33]

Fleming had obviously not communicated with the National Party nor taken seriously its publication, the *New Hebrides Viewpoints*. Moreover, while Jimmy Stephens may have come to an arrangement with European settlers concerning their continued occupation of developed portions of their properties, he had not abandoned the importance of custom with regard to Melanesian held land.

Fleming appears to have placed too much emphasis on the compromise at which Jimmy Stephens had arrived. In his analysis of the problem of alienated land, Fleming comments:

> There appears to be little antagonism towards the presence of European settlers or their occupation of land which they have developed in the past. The present grievances usually stem from the fact that the settlers are seeking to develop outlying parts of their registered estates for the first time and finding them occupied by squatters who, hitherto, have been left undisturbed.... However, my discussions were usually with the older and presumably more conservative New Hebrideans. It must not be supposed that their successors, a younger generation, will have the same degree of tolerance and understanding which accepts the existence of European settlers.[34]

It is clear that Fleming was also skeptical about the long term prospects of such a compromise and clearly recognized the growing tide of discontent among younger Melanesians.

Despite these doubts, however, Fleming was not willing to confront the problem of registered titles:

> Although the question of alienated land is the most obvious grievance, I declined to discuss the matter at this early stage except for emphasizing the sanctity of title.... the policy at present of purchasing disputed land and handing it back to the New Hebrideans is in my opinion, the only immediate solution to this problem.[35]

Obviously, Fleming had a very difficult task. He was recruited to come to Vanuatu to make proposals for land reform, but in his attempt to strike a position which would not alienate French officials and settlers, he doomed the results of his work from the start.

It could be argued that in 1973, Fleming's position was understandable. The NHNP had not yet come out categorically in favour of the immediate and unconditional return of all alienated land and Jimmy Stephens was making deals with European settlers and foreign investors. But as the politics of land intensified and the NHNP attitude evolved towards the position that all alienated land — developed and undeveloped — should be returned to ni-Vanuatu unconditionally, Fleming stuck to his initial proposals. He should not have been surprised, therefore, when his formula for solving the land problem was described in the *New Hebrides Viewpoints* in 1976 as:

> What a lot of rubbish!
>
> There is no mention of alienated land in New Hebrides whatsoever. This real fact which is the real causing factor of feeling of resentment and frustration — has been left out completely....
>
> To produce a unified system on land matters acceptable to indigenous folks of the islands would require re-examining the judgments passed in the Joint Court.[36]

The NHNP would not participate in the 'working parties on land reform' which Fleming conducted in 1975 to discuss his proposed changes to the joint regulations. By 1976, when his draft reform legislation was complete for consideration by the Representative Assembly, political events had clearly overtaken him and his work. The legislation was never debated in the first Assembly — ni-Vanuatu would deal with land matters in their own way.

The increase in the number of land disputes in 1973 and 1974 also coincided with the start of the French Government's programme of handing back to ni-Vanuatu large tracts of undeveloped French State land and land purchased from the SFNH. Where transfers occurred, land problems between Europeans and Melanesians did in fact subside and the effect was as the French had hoped. Ni-Vanuatu became less resentful of France's presence and, in the case of Jimmy Stephens and his Nagriamel followers, relations with French officials improved. The weakness in the plan was, however, that the French Government was only in a position to hand back land which it possessed or was able to purchase from the SFNH. With few exceptions, private individuals and companies refused to follow the example of the French Government. Thus numerous latent land disputes lay waiting for small unforeseen incidents to cause them to explode. French officials were aware of the potential danger, but could do nothing but deal with each new dispute as it arose. Commenting on the situation in August 1973, the French Resident Commissioner noted:

> at the very moment when the current deal for the buying back of land from SFNH allows us to settle the matter with the native claimants of Santo, new disputes arising in Efate between private owners, French for the most part, and native communities put us in an intermediary position where our natural role of arbitrator can bring criticism on us.... The situation is uncomfortable in as much as the natives can, in this respect, see in us the unconditional defender of European ownership, whereas, the most conservative among the French settlers may accuse us of making unjustifiably great sacrifices in favour of native policy.
>
> For the time being it seems impossible to insure an overall settlement of these disputes. In these circumstances the French Residency tries to settle disputes case by case, sparing at the same time the interest and peace of mind of our nationals, as well as the aspirations of the natives it appears advisable to satisfy. Up to now, the results of this policy resting on a measured amount of flexibility and firmness have been good.[37]

The influence of the relatively small French planter community is clearly evident. The British had suggested a scheme to buy out planters where disputes existed, but the French Government would not agree. They were not willing to sacrifice the interests of their nationals in order to maintain political stability in Vanuatu. Moreover, as events leading up to independence would reveal, the removal of their settlers was never a part of French thinking. The maintenance of the French community in Vanuatu was vital to France as part of its goal to continue to influence and control the future of Vanuatu if independence could in the end not be avoided. Indeed, in 1973 and early 1974, the French Government was still confident that its plan to buy ni-Vanuatu loyalty with land and expanded education and social services would succeed in forestalling independence indefinitely.

The founding of the Land Trust Board in October 1973 to receive and administer Australian Commonwealth land also failed to provide an alternative to the more radical stand on land reform which the NHNP had begun to adopt. Its rather conservative approach to the handing back of land was clearly inappropriate in the political climate of the mid-1970s, even though the concept of land held in trust was also being considered by the NHNP as part of their overall policy. The unconditional return of land was becoming for National Party supporters more and more a symbol of their struggle to regain political control within their own country. Thus, while the approach to land reform introduced by the Land Trust Board may have had merit, it would have to wait to be introduced by an independent ni-Vanuatu Government to become politically acceptable.

Despite these moves by the joint administration to defuse the land issue, by 1974 the NHNP was intensifying its campaign to bring about reform to the Condominium system using land as the primary theme to rally Melanesian support. It would be incorrect to say, however, that the NHNP arbitrarily incited ni-Vanuatu to protest against the occupation of land by Europeans. There was no need — discontent over land had existed for years. What the National Party did was to increase the general awareness of the problem and to create the confidence among ni-Vanuatu that they could do something about it, as the Fila Island and Tautu Village cases clearly illustrate.

In 1974, Party officials began receiving letters from individual ni-Vanuatu seeking advice and assistance in dealing with land disputes, both between Europeans and ni-Vanuatu and also between ni-Vanuatu. The Party's position was to encourage ni-Vanuatu to set up village land committees headed by chiefs and to work out carefully the custom history of the land and the dispute. The Party avoided mediating, though members did sit on committees which were dealing with disputes.[38] The policy followed by the NHNP of encouraging ni-Vanuatu to work out their own solution to land problems — in particular, those in which alienated land was not the issue — remained an important concept in Party thinking up to independence and after. Indeed, it was a wise position to take politically, since it did not necessitate the Party choosing sides at a time when creating unity among rural Melanesians was a primary goal.

Having made land a political issue, however, the NHNP did not hesitate to exploit such disputes to their advantage as they arose —

indeed, that was their strategy. Thus, in February 1974, when the Tautu/PRNH dispute flared anew over the construction of a new airstrip, representatives of the NHNP visited the village to give advice and encouragement. Likewise, the people of Fila Island could count on the full support of the NHNP when, in March 1974, they organized a demonstration to coincide with the visit of the French High Commissioner, M. Eriau, to protest the lack of progress in negotiations to stop the Frouin family subdividing land they claimed. Two of the most influential members of the National Party — Barak Sope and Kalkot Matas-Kele — were themselves Fila Islanders and, at the same time, members of the Fila Island Land Committee.

Despite attempts by the joint administration to stand firm in the face of the rising tide of protest — a contingent of French *garde mobile* was flown to Vila in March following the protest during Eriau's visit — the British and French, came to realize by mid-1974, that political change was unavoidable. Commenting in his confidential monthly report to Paris, the French Resident Commissioner noted:

> There seems to be no hope of finding here a counter attraction to the activity of the National Party. In the face of the offensive of this group — arousing the indigenous masses with issues to which they are especially sensitive — the other political movements [Nagriamel, MANH and UCNH] actually seem paralysed.... It is certain that the status quo cannot be maintained in the end.... In this state of affairs, the absence of initiatives from the French Government benefits only the National Party, who run the chance of representing, as they hope and are pursuing, the big majority of the New Hebridean population.[39]

Reporting on the subject again the following month, Langlois made his position to Paris unequivocal:

> We cannot eternally ignore the political evolution of the spirit and maintain in the Condominium an administrative system that we have judged out of date since 1946 in our other territories.[40]

The problem for the French was how to bring about the political evolution of Vanuatu — which they could no longer avoid — and at the same time preserve their power and influence and protect the interests of their settler and business community.

Of major concern to the French, and clearly a factor contributing to their general anxiety over land, was what they correctly viewed as the British reluctance to intervene in land disputes between ni-Vanuatu and Europeans. Commenting on the increasing number of disputes on Malakula in 1974, the French Resident Commissioner, M. Langlois, noted:

> In every case — the British administration being obviously resolved under any pretext, not to undermine its privileged relationship with the National Party — the burden of maintaining and eventually re-establishing order rests solely with the French Residency...[41]

While Langlois himself had described the advent of Melanesian political activity in 1971 as spontaneous, he and subsequent French officials could never believe that the British Residency was not working actively with the National Party.

Nevertheless, the British had usually been willing to stand with their French colleagues when serious breaches of the law occurred resulting in violence or a breakdown in public order as, for example, in 1968 when Chief Buluk and Jimmy Stephens were imprisoned for trespassing and destroying private property. Indeed, in 1974 the British had agreed to allow the *garde mobile* to be sent to Vanuatu. In fact, by 1974, there is evidence that the British Government had clearly decided to join with the French in controlling the rising tide of political protest. In April, the two powers issued a Joint Regulation for the 'safeguarding of law and order', which placed restrictions on the conduct of public meetings and demonstrations and provided the legal means to prosecute violations.[42] And, in September — reacting to a National Party demonstration in July during which the Condominium office building was temporarily occupied and rumours circulated that the Party had come under the influence of 'Black Power' radicals — the British Resident Commissioner, Mr. du Boulay, spoke out publicly against what he saw as the increasing tendency towards violence and racism. On a visit to the island of Tongoa to open a health centre, he told a crowd of several hundred that:

> Political parties have their part to play.... But when they seek to use force rather than convince by reason, and press their views by frightening rather than persuading others, then their activities are no longer acceptable.... Those who preach violence and hatred and seek to set one man against another, must be rejected.[43]

Du Boulay also stressed in his speech the material benefits which ni-Vanuatu enjoyed because of the joint efforts of Europeans, who had "lived together [with ni-Vanuatu] in harmony for 50 years".[44] As Langlois noted in his September report to Paris: "the Resident Commissioner seems to have decided to play the game"[45]

While the British Government's firm stand on the side of maintaining law and order was consistent with past policy, du Boulay's statement that ni-Vanuatu and Europeans had "lived together in harmony for 50 years" indicated a significant change in attitude and interpretation of historical fact. British officials had remonstrated since the 19th century against abuses perpetrated against ni-Vanuatu by European settlers, and the recent surge of land disputes was clear evidence of a latent hostility and resentment among Melanesians towards European domination. But times had changed. In 1973 Great Britain had become a member of the European Common Market and the Foreign Office rather than the Colonial Office was looking after the remains of the British Empire. A diplomat was now in charge in the British Residency instead of a colonial administrator — an official whose highest priority was the maintenance of good relations with Great Britain's new partner in Europe. By the mid-1970s, the British Government was eager to extricate itself from a colonial situation which clearly threatened its own national interests as never before. Co-operation was the order of the day.

Elections

By the mid-1970s, the colonial powers were clearly in retreat. The decisions made in November 1974 at the London Ministerial Conference to allow political change to proceed was the first step in the process of decolonization. Vanuatu was entering a new period in which the question was no longer if, but when and in what form independence should occur. As part of the general administrative reforms agreed to at the London Conference, the introduction of a new code of land tenure was given a high priority, though there was some slight disagreement on details. After decades of talking about reform, the two governments had finally agreed on basic principles — Fleming's report — and thus the way was clear to proceed. What the British and French did not seem to understand, however, was that their solutions to the problem were too little and too late. In fact, in the latter half of the 1970s, the number of land disputes between ni-Vanuatu and Europeans declined significantly, while confrontations between Melanesians began to increase. Power was still the underlying issue in land disputes, but now the struggle was between ni-Vanuatu. The question ceased to be whether or not Europeans should retain registered developed land, but how land should be controlled by Melanesians in an independent Vanuatu.

In 1975, attention turned to the election of the first Representative Assembly scheduled for November and the Municipal elections for Port Vila and Luganville which were to take place in August, three months earlier. Although the number of land disputes had declined by this time, land did not disappear as a political issue. It ceased, however, to dominate the political centre stage and became instead one of a number of issues discussed as part of the general debate on the future form and policies of an independent Vanuatu. The key issue now was independence itself and, in particular, who would rule afterwards. While Britain and France had agreed in 1974 to allow the political evolution of the country to proceed, the question of what kind of governing bodies and institutions should be established remained to be determined. Moreover, no sequence of steps was laid down to guide the country through an orderly transition from colony to independent nation. In other words, while Britain and France had agreed to political change, there was no firm commitment to speedy progress to independence. Thus, the political debate in 1975 and, indeed, up to independence in July 1980, focused on the all important question of the date.

The position of the NHNP was that independence should come quickly. Following a visit to the United Nations in May 1974, Father Lini demanded that independence should take place in 1977 — the date set down in the official NHNP platform in the campaign for the 1975 election.[46] The National Party's desire for an early independence stemmed largely from their lack of confidence in the Condominium system and distrust of the British and French governments — especially the latter. The National Party had in fact proposed as early as 1973 the abolition of the Condominium and the placing of Vanuatu under the authority of the United Nations.[47]

The 'Moderate' parties, as the opposition to the NHNP came to be called, favoured a slower pace, emphasizing the need to develop the country economically and socially before moving to full political independence. This was also the position of the French Government, which in 1975, was still confident that its plans for building a strong Francophone majority would materialize and provide the support necessary to enable French settlers and businessmen to retain their dominant economic position. If this could be achieved, the French would be able to consolidate and maintain their influence and political control, even if independence itself could not be avoided. Needless to say, the National Party — with its demands for early independence and the return of all alienated land — was the main worry of French officials. Thus, while the land issue had become less important to Melanesian politicians in terms of immediate political goals, it remained for French officials a prime factor which would lead them to attempt political manipulation of elections in order to ensure the defeat of the National Party and, when that failed, to support a secessionist movement on the island of Santo, where French settlers and business interests were heavily concentrated.

The strategy of the French, which they began to implement in the early 1970s, was to build a network of political groupings as a counterbalance to the National Party. By 1972, French Residency officials had come to the conclusion that contact was possible with Jimmy Stephens and his movement and that he could be quieted on the land issue by promising to hand back undeveloped bush land. Nagriamel was seen as: "a barrage strong enough to withstand the activities of the 'evolues' of the National Party in the rural areas".[48] Reporting on political developments in July 1972, the French Resident Commissioner noted that Nagriamel would:

> ...open for us rural areas resistant up to now to our action and thus favour our presence. After all, our policy of settling land problems cannot fail. In fact, positive consequences of change of mind of the natives towards us are already appearing.[49]

In the urban areas, French officials could depend on their own nationals to organize political parties. As discussed above, the UCNH which had been established in Port Vila, also had centres of support in rural areas, especially where the Catholic Church had its mission stations. In addition, on Santo the French had the MANH Party, which was allied with Nagriamel.

In the South, on Tanna, the French District Agent, M. Poullet, concentrated his efforts on welding together conservative, custom-oriented groups into a political alliance against the National Party.[50] The followers of John Frum (based at Sulfur Bay) and a new party, Kapiel, (with its headquarters in the Middle Bush area) were deeply suspicious of the Presbyterians on Tanna, who were strong National Party supporters. The suspicion dated back to the time of 'Tanna Law', when the severe penalties imposed by the Presbyterian Mission on such custom activities as kava drinking and dancing led to the withdrawal by most of the Tannese people from dealings with both the mission and the Condominium administration.

French officials were encouraged by their efforts to influence the new political groupings which began to emerge at this time and, indeed, they enjoyed some success. What they did not fully understand however, was that the political rivalry which they sought to foster was not the real substance of the political awakening which was occurring during the 1970s. They found that early alliances fell apart or were difficult to maintain as other issues, which often were the real basis for the formation of new political groups, came to the surface.

Moreover, the French could not always rely on the ties of Francophonie to guarantee support for their cause. This is clearly illustrated in the emergence of another Santo party — Tabwemasana — which is the name of the highest mountain on the island. The Party was founded in June 1975 by Michel Bernast, a left-wing political activitist originally from New Caledonia, as a counterforce to the ultraconservative MANH Party. He hoped to attract Melanesian support by advocating a policy of preservation of land on Santo for the indigenous inhabitants. His stress on custom and tradition was appealing to a number of Nagriamel breakaways — in particular Catholics from the village of Port Orly, which became the Party's main power base along with several villages close to Luganville.[51] Tabwemasana, therefore, was Francophone and Catholic, the equivalent to the Anglophone/Protestant Natui Tano Party. While opposed to the National Party, it was not, however, able to maintain its initial alliance with MANH and Nagriamel after the 1975 elections.

The Municipal elections in August were a great victory for the French supported parties. In Vila, the UCNH won 18 of the 24 seats to the NHNP's 6 and in Luganville the MANH/Tabwemasana/Nagriamel alliance won 15 of the 16 seats with only one going to the NHNP.[52] The results of the two elections however, did not provide a true picture of the political alignment within the country as a whole and after an analysis of the results, even the French concluded that the 'Moderate' parties were going to have an extremely difficult time in the Representative Assembly elections to follow.[53]

French officials, therefore, began to realize that their strategy was not working. To try to save the situation, the French Residency intervened directly in the campaign leading up to the Representative Assembly elections. Their most difficult task as reported by the Resident Commissioner, was getting the various 'Moderate' parties to put aside their rivalries and differences and to agree on a common strategy:

> For the time being, the agreement between parties on a concerted strategy is still hypothetical, despite the intervention of the French Residency.[54]

Even with the French Resident Commissioner's direct involvement, obtaining unity among the 'Moderate' parties proved difficult:

> MANH leaders, temporarily in Port Vila, remained elusive faced by our reprimands, in spite of the warning I gave them

> that they would receive no help from the Residency if they did not agree to an 'entente' with UCNH.[55]

One of the key strategies was to persuade the various parties to limit the number of candidates to constituencies where they had a chance of winning and to prevent vote splitting in others:

> Reports from delegates and from the Police Station made one fear a resounding defeat of the moderates in North Efate. Individual talks with the leaders of the MANH finally shook their pride. They agreed finally in the last week of October during an ultimate intervention on my part in Santo to withdraw six candidates from MANH and Nagriamel as well as related independents. Among these are Bouletare on Pentecost and Ruru Gratiana on Mallicolo, which will give Vincent Boulekone and Father Leymang a better chance. At the same time the Residency obtained the resignation of Lionel Michel, French candidate of the National Party, thus insuring the election of a French UCNH in the town. These are no small advantages.[56]

In addition, despite the cooling of relations, the French Residency still maintained contact with Jimmy Stephens, though with little tangible success. The French Commissioner intervened personally to get Nagriamel support:

> Despite assurances which he gave to me during my visit to Santo, Jimmy Stephens has done nothing yet or would do nothing towards withdrawing the Ambrym and Epi-Paama candidates.[57]

The difficulty which the French Residency encountered in its attempted manipulation of the 'Moderate' parties shows the degree to which they had overestimated their ability to create a loyalty to France — even among their supporters — when local issues were at stake.

The French Residency, however, carried its manipulation of political events even further — to the extent that French officials attempted to buy votes by authorising direct aid and assistance including the transfer of land to various key groups:

> According to instructions received in the course of a tour of South Pentecost, I have been able to organize certain road jobs in the Melsisi region with the help of the High Commissioner and the armed forces of New Caledonia. This should draw a few hesitant voters towards Vincent Boulekone. On his side, the French District Agent of Santo has been able to proceed to clear rocks from many roads in

> Maewo and the Banks Islands, out of private funds, thus being able at the most opportune moment to keep old promises. On the 14th of October, I handed over publicly to various families and Melanesian communities of Santo, land titles representing more than 3,000 hectares bought back by the State from SFNH.[58]

Yet, despite the wheeling and dealing on the part of the French Residency, the National Party won 59% of the Melanesian votes and 17 of the 29 universal suffrage seats contested.[59] Of the remaining 12 seats, 10 were captured by UCNH and two by the MANH/Nagriamel coalition. An additional four seats reserved for chiefs — one from each of the four districts — were to be elected later and the remaining nine seats were chosen by the Chamber of Commerce and Co-operatives.

Due to allegations of voting irregulaties on both sides, resulting in the invalidation of five of the Santo seats and delays in organizing the election of the four chiefs, the Representative Assembly did not meet in December as originally planned. The National Party in fact boycotted the Assembly over the delays in electing the four chiefs, preventing its sitting until June 1976, when a special meeting was called to consider the issue. National Party members suspected that the colonial powers were attempting to manipulate the elections to undermine the majority they had won in the November election.[60]

By the time the Assembly met for its first official sitting in November 1976, by-elections on Santo had reduced the NHNP's seats by one resulting in a 21 to 21 split in the Assembly, which included the special interest seats as well as those elected by universal suffrage. Thus the National Party found that despite having won 59% of the Melanesian vote and a majority of the universal suffrage seats, it did not have a majority in the Assembly. At its January 1977 Party Congress, at which the New Hebrides National Party was renamed the Vanua'aku Pati (VP), members called for the removal of the six Chamber of Commerce seats and made plans to step up political activity as a sign of their dissatisfaction with the two governing powers over the stalemate in the Assembly. When on 24 February 1977 a tie vote resulted from a VP motion to remove the Chamber of Commerce representatives, the Party decided to boycott the Assembly for good.[61]

The January 1977 Congress was a turning point for the Vanua'aku Pati in that its members clearly resolved to return to the use of more activist political methods in order to force the British and French governments to commit themselves to a clear plan for moving

Vanuatu to independence. Their aim was to force the two governments to agree to the setting up of a ministerial system of government with full executive powers and to begin work on devising a new governmental structure and reformed electoral system.[62] A series of "actions" were proposed including one advocating the taking over of alienated land by making copra and gardens, cutting fences, killing cattle and other animals, organising demonstrations and openly disputing with Europeans. In March it was reported that VP supporters had occupied a French-owned plantation at Southwest Bay on Malakula.[63] Land had become a weapon again at a time when the VP felt the two governments were dragging their feet on the question of political reform. The British and French finally agreed that the only solution was a new election, which was scheduled for 29 November 1977.[64]

At its sixth Congress, held in late October at Labultamata on North Pentecost, the VP refined its stand regarding the forthcoming elections. The Pati issued a communique stating the conditions under which it would agree to participate: majority rule, internal self-government, a referendum on an early date for independence, the right to vote for 18 year olds and the exclusion of non-Melanesians from voting. The communique also stated that if the demands were not met, in addition to boycotting the election, the VP would not recognize the legitimacy of the Assembly if elected, nor would it recognize the British and French governments "to be the guardians of justice and peace over the people of Vanuaaku [sic]".[65] The demands were rejected by the two governments and as a result, on 29 November 1977, the joint administration confirmed by no contest the election of the new Representative Assembly, with George Kalsakau as Chief Minister. The VP had not entered candidates. Members raised the Vanua'aku Pati flag at a number of locations in the islands and declared a People's Provisional Government (PPG). In a number of centres, including Port Vila, the flag-raising provoked 'Moderate' party opposition supporters to retaliate with acts of violence.[66]

The PPG lasted until May 1978 during which time VP supporters throughout the country took control of large sections of various islands. Roadblocks were set up, Government officials were required to have passes to enter Vanua'aku areas, supporters were urged to set up their own island, district and village governments, and taxes were collected.[67] The PPG also continued to move against European owned plantations: at Walafea[68] and Rindove[69] on Epi, Lonorore on Pentecost and elsewhere. In addition, VP supporters occupied a plantation at Wesso on East Malakula belonging to a ni-Vanuatu member of the Assembly, Mr. Amos Andeng, who had purchased the property from a Frenchman. The VP had clearly decided that if the British and French would not negotiate the transfer of power, they would take it.

Land and Independence

Vanuatu's progress towards independence was characterized by a series of political crises, which forced the colonial governments to concede each step, rather than an orderly and planned handing over of the instruments of power. Furthermore, the presence of two colonial powers in Vanuatu with widely differing perceptions of their future role in the country, prevented the nationalist movement, led by the Vanua'aku Pati, from uniting all Melanesians in the struggle for independence. However, while the VP was overwhelmingly Anglophone in its membership, and the Union of 'Moderate' Parties predominantly Francophone, it would be incorrect to conclude that ni-Vanuatu were simply divided into pro-British and pro-French factions. Clearly, the French were seen by the VP leadership as opposed to granting independence and thus the greatest obstacle to achieving their goals, but by the mid-1970s, the British also had begun to lose credibility in their eyes, and this explains to some extent the more extreme position taken by the Pati on certain issues — in particular, land and education. Their proclamation of the People's Provisional Government in November 1977, was a reaction to what they saw as the closing of ranks by the two powers.

While the establishment of the PPG led at first to an increase in violence and a heightening of tension, the longer term effect was to jolt ni-Vanuatu political leaders of all parties to an awareness that steps needed to be taken to bring the two sides together to begin discussions on future political developments if serious problems were to be avoided. While not recognizing the Kalsakau Government, the VP agreed to begin discussions with the opposition resulting, after a number of "meetings of understanding", in the signing of a Joint Communique on 5 April 1978, designed to "set things in motion towards independence".[70] In the communique, it was agreed that special committees should be established to discuss electoral reform, education, law and judicial reform and land.[71] Given the chance to sit down and share points of view, Anglophone and Francophone Melanesians soon began to discover that there was a common basis on which they could move together towards independence.

On 11 August 1978, the French Minister for Overseas Departments and Territories, M. Paul Dijoud, arrived in Vanuatu for a four-day visit. In a press conference he set out the steps which would have to be followed in order to get France to agree to independence for Vanuatu. The Dijoud Plan, as it came to be called, required: the establishment of a Government of National Unity; a new census; writing of the Constitution which guaranteed regionalization, the preservation of French language and culture, the concept of proportional representation in the formation of the National Assembly in recognition of minority rights; and a new election, which would be preceded by the census.[72]

At the news conference during which the plan was presented, Dijoud also set out France's position with regard to the land problem. He expressed the opinion that a solution could be found whereby the greatest portion of the land in the group would be returned to custom owners, while "the exploitation can be entrusted to some Europeans who would bring their experience here".[73] But he pointed out that solutions could not be found quickly — it might take as much as 20 years — but the problem was in the process of being regularized.[74] Dijoud's perception of an independent Vanuatu was clear — that the European (primarily French) planters and businessmen should still retain their privileged position.

Discussions between the opposing political parties finally led to the decision to set up a Government of National Unity (GNU), which was to have an enlarged Council of Ministers, five of whom would be from the Vanua'aku Pati. On 16 December, the Kalsakau Government was defeated in a vote of no confidence and Father Gérard Leymang replaced him as the new Chief Minister and head of the GNU. The VP joined the GNU on the condition that it would only be transitional — the first step towards new elections.[75]

A clear sign of the change which was beginning to take place was the decision of Vincent Boulekone in September 1978 to resign from the UCNH and form a new party. In a letter to the President of the UCNH, Mr. Jean-Marie Léyé, Boulekone described the feeling of political domination and frustration he had experienced as a member of the Party:

> I want to work with my compatriots and not be a tool at their disposal.
> I realize that the members of the UCNH do not support the aspirations of Melanesians who are seeking to work and discuss with their brothers who are not members of the Assembly [i.e. Vanua'aku Pati members].[76]

Boulekone's defection from the UCNH, and that of other prominent Francophone Melanesians, reveals the almost total failure of French Government policy to create a Melanesian majority which they could

Signing of agreement between Vanua'aku Pati Cabinet members, Kalkot Matas-Kele and Barak Sope, and a representative of the New Hebrides Government, Vincent Boulekone. (Photo from ***Nabanga,*** *No. 77, 15 April 1978).*

*Father Walter Lini, French Minister Paul Dijoud, and Father Gerard Leymang (from **Nabanga** No. 99, 24 February 1979).*

manipulate and count on to support their aims of retaining power in Vanuatu for ever.

In a remarkable spirit of unity, given the troubled period Vanuatu had experienced up to 1978, the Dijoud Plan was fulfilled, including the very difficult task of writing the Constitution. The negotiations — which included representatives from all political parties, the churches and chiefs — were long and hard, but the guarantees which Dijoud had demanded were met and agreement reached through a process of negotiating by consensus. On 14 November 1979, elections were held for the new Representative Assembly under United Nations supervision. The Vanua'aku Pati won an overwhelming majority of 62% of the popular vote and a two thirds majority in the 39 seat Assembly.

It is important to emphasize that the provisions in the Constitution relating to land were agreed to by all political parties and accepted by both the British and French Governments. What had become clear during the many meetings of the Constitutional Planning Committee (CPC), which began meeting in April 1979, was that a consensus was emerging between Anglophone and Francophone Melanesians on fundamental issues important to a future independent Vanuatu. The degree to which Francophone Melanesian politicians had moved towards the VP position on land issues can be seen in the resolutions passed by the Ad Hoc Land Reform Committee, made up entirely of representatives from the Union of 'Moderate' Parties, which had been formed in 1978 under the Kalsakau Government to study and make recommendations to the Assembly. By this time Jim Fleming's draft land reform legislation was complete and awaiting consideration by the Assembly , but the Kalsakau Government chose to seek its own solutions. In May 1979, the Assembly discussed the Committee's report and unanimously passed 22 recommendations advocating radical change to the existing Condominium land tenure system.[77]

On the key question of alienated land, the Assembly adopted the Committee's point of view that land is inalienable in Melanesian custom and thus sales of land to Europeans were made by chiefs in violation of custom or by people who were not the owners of the land. The Assembly voted, therefore, not to recognize deeds of purchase (Recommendation 1). Following on from this, was acceptance of the recommendation to invalidate Joint Court judgments granting registered title (Recommendation 2). The Assembly accepted the principle that "custom, family and individual" ownership should apply to rural areas and opposed nationalization of land, recognizing the need for expropriation only for public purposes (Recommendation 3). All formerly alienated land was to be returned to legitimate custom owners (Recommendation 4) — "whether developed or not" (Recommendation 7) — and it was agreed that the metropolitan government of the former purchaser should be obliged to pay compensation (Recommendation 19).

The Committee stipulated that urban land comprised a special category (Recommendation 5), that the land on which administrative buildings stood would become the property of the Government (Recommendation 6g) and that land could be acquired for public purposes (Recommendation 14). Land which had been subdivided and sold was to remain the property of the purchaser, whether fully paid for or not and regardless of nationality (Recommendation 6a and b). This last recommendation was intended to protect the rights of ni-Vanuatu who had purchased town lots in Vila and Santo. The missions were also to retain land required for their operation and land sold or given by the missions to their staff and adherents was to remain the property of those people (Recommendation 8). Subdivided land which had not been sold, plantation land, all undeveloped land and all land registered in the name of the Land Trust Board was to be returned to custom owners (Recommendations 6c, e, f and 10).

The Committee stressed the importance of custom ownership in its proposed land reform. In addition to ownership, land which had been transferred according to custom was to remain the property of the person who had acquired it (Recommendation 17), inheritance in both urban and rural areas was to follow custom procedures (Recommendation 18) and the limit of land ownership should, according to custom, extend to the edge of the reef in rural areas (Recommendation 15).

While recommending the unconditional return of both developed and undeveloped rural land to custom owners, the Committee was also concerned that land should be developed and used efficiently. It, therefore, recommended a land survey programme (Recommendation 12); land registration, but only at the request of custom owners (Recommendation 9) and the development of land "according to its nature" (Recommendation 13). The sale, transfer and subdivision of land was to be prohibited (Recommendation 21), but land could be leased for development purposes with the consent of custom owners as to tenant and terms of agreement. There was no guarantee that existing occupants would be granted leases — it was to be "left to the custom owner whether or not to retain the present occupant or to choose another" (Recommendation 11).

By 1979, therefore, when the Constitutional Planning Com-

*Signing of the constitution by Father Walter Lini and Father Gerard Leymang (from **Nabanga,** No. 128, 6 October 1979).*

mittee met, the land issue had been fully aired, and, as can be seen from the above recommendations, the two sides had arrived at a basic consensus. Nevertheless, the debate over land in the CPC was long and difficult. According to Papua New Guinean lawyer, Bernard Narokobi, who was a member of the CPC as special consultant representing the Vanuatu Christian Council:

> every section of the chapter on land in the Constitution was hotly debated by the CPC members. Although on many issues debate tended to resolve into the Vanuaaku Party view as against the Moderates' view, on the land issue front personal views were expressed across party lines...
> The final wording of [the] nine articles of Chapter 12 of the Constitution went through many drafts, redrafts, understandings and misunderstandings. But it was unanimously adopted as expressing the true feelings of both the anglophone and francophone New Hebrideans.[78]

The underlying issue in the debates over the various provisions was usually the question of who would hold power and/or how it would be exercised rather than on fundamental principles.

Article 71 of the new Constitution incorporated the most important principle relating to land on which both sides had agreed: that "all land in the Republic belongs to the indigenous custom owners and their descendants".[79] With those few words, the framers of the Constitution swept away the rights of foreigners to own land in Vanuatu. However, while there appears to have been little debate on the fundamental principle, there were lengthy discussions on several related issues. According to Narokobi, the words "and their descendants" were omitted from the first draft of Section 71, but were added when fears were expressed that mixed-race children would be excluded by the Constitution from owning land, even though by custom they would be permitted that right.[80] It is significant to note that most of the key members of the CPC were married to Europeans or other Pacific Islanders, thus the land provisions and those for citizenship had a direct bearing on their children. Nevertheless, the Committee adopted the position that a distinction should be made between indigenous citizens — i.e. individuals with four ni-Vanuatu grandparents — and others. With regard to citizenship, provision was made to enable non-indigenous people to apply. In the case of rights to land, the rules of custom would solve the problem in the long term.[81]

Indeed, the CPC laid great emphasis on custom as providing the underlying principles on which the new national land tenure system should be built. It was agreed under Section 72 that "the rules of custom shall form the basis of ownership and use of land in the Republic". Furthermore, the CPC agreed under Section 73, that non-indigenous persons, whether or not they became citizens, could not own land. Perpetual ownership would only be possible for indigenous citizens "who have acquired their land in accordance with a recognized system of land tenure", i.e. through custom. Thus, the Constitution clearly denies the right of non-citizens to own land in Vanuatu because their citizenship is not linked to Melanesian parentage and because the manner in which they acquired land in the past would not be a "recognized system of land tenure".[82]

Article 74 of the Constitution empowered Parliament to enact a national land law to implement Articles 71, 72 and 73 and allowed it to "make different provisions for different categories of land, one of which shall be urban land". Government was also to be empowered to acquire land "in the public interest" (Article 78) and to buy land from custom owners for resettlement of indigenous citizens and communities (Article 79). Alienated land was the subject of Article 76, which empowered Government to hold formerly alienated land temporarily in cases where disputes developed concerning custom ownership. Government was directed, however, to establish institutions based on custom principles to resolve disputes relating to custom land.

Thus, while the power of Government to own land was not extensive, the Constitution did spell out the right — a provision agreed to after much debate — reflecting the fears of some members of the CPC that an independent government might simply take over formerly alienated land and not return it to the rightful custom owners.[83] In fact, Article 71, which states that all land belongs to the "indigenous custom owners and their descendants", places a limit on the government's right to acquire land, which is spelled out clearly in Article 78 and 79.

Article 75, which directs Parliament to compensate foreigners or non-indigenous citizens for the loss of title to land — i.e. "persons whose interests are adversely affected by legislation under this chapter" — was included under pressure from the French Government. The VP members of the CPC wanted no provision for compensation, but VP leaders were informed that the French Government would not accept the Constitution unless such a guarantee were included.[84] It is not clear from available accounts what the position of 'Moderate' party members of the CPC was, on this issue, but it could be assumed that they also would have been reluctant to support this provision, given the fact that Recommendation 19 of the Ad Hoc Land Reform Committee stipulated that the metropolitan government of the former purchasers should be responsible for compensation. The wording of Article 75, however, gave Parliament the right to prescribe its own criteria for assessing compensation and the manner of payment, thus in theory Government would not be bound to allocate an exorbitant amount if it chose not to.

Finally, Article 77 provided for Government control over "land transactions between an indigenous citizen non-citizens or non-indigenous citizens". Government was empowered to block any transaction if it considered it to be prejudicial to the interests of custom owners, indigenous citizens, communities or the national interests of the Republic. The framers of the Constitution were determined to prevent indigenous citizens from again being taken advantage of in dealings with foreigners and non-indigenous people relating to land. It is significant to note, however, that the Constitution does not provide for Government to intervene in transactions between indigenous citizens as long as custom principles are followed. In future, ni-Vanuatu may find that local people can be just as unscrupulous as foreigners and, indeed, more adept at manipulating the system for personal gain than the land speculators of the 19th century.

Having won an overwhelming majority in the new Parliament, and having succeeded in incorporating its basic philosophy regarding land reform into the Constitution, the Vanua'aku Pati was now in a position to implement its policy. The new Government, under the leadership of Father Walter Lini, established a separate Ministry of Lands. Sethy Regenvanu, MP from Malakula and formerly a member of the Land Trust Board set up by the British to deal with the return of Commonwealth land, became the first Minister. He and his staff, who were assisted by a team of three advisers supplied by UNDAT and the University of the South Pacific — Peter Larmour, Bill McGrath and Jim Fingleton — began early in 1980 to formulate a new land policy. On 24 April 1980, the Minister of Lands issued a communique outlining the broad principles on which future policy and legislation would be based.[85]

The Ministry divided land into three categories: rural land, urban land and public land. The communique noted that rural land would be "owned according to custom", while Government would hold a perpetual lease of urban and public land. Custom owners would, however, receive a share of any revenue raised by Government from urban and public lands. They would also be entitled to: retain certain areas of urban land for their own use and development, representation on statutory bodies established to manage land, compensation when land was needed for future urban expansion and the "reservation and protection" of *tambu* places within urban areas and on public land (Section 7). Where more than one group of custom owners claimed land within urban areas, revenue would be divided on the basis of a formula which they themselves would work out (Section 8).

The communique also spelled out the way in which land could be leased by non-indigenous citizens or companies. In the case of rural land, Government consent would be required to ensure that adequate discussions would have taken place with the legitimate custom owners and that the lease arrangement would be in their best interest as well as that of the country (Section 12). The length of leases would depend on what the land would be used for, but normally 30 years would be allowed for rural land and 50 years for urban land (Section 14). Leases would have the backing of Government (Section 13) and they could be bought, sold, sub-let and mortgaged (Section 15). Conditions could also be written into leases relating to land use: rate of development, rates of rent and benefits to owners and consultation with owners before subleasing or transferring of leases to someone else (Section 16). Joint ventures with custom owners were also mentioned as a possible arrangement whereby non-indigenous people and companies could gain access to land. The communique concluded by referring to plans to formulate policies relating to mining and the environment and the legislation which would be forthcoming to implement the policy (Section 17, 18 and 19).

Following the issuing of the communique on Land Policy, meetings and discussions were held between Ministry staff and "all interested parties",[86] including custom owners and representatives from the private sector. This fact was noted in an article published in *Nabanga*, the French Residency newsheet, and was a factor which led to its overall favourable evaluation of the new policy, describing it as:

> a coherent system, capable of responding to very diverse situations and of assuring an equilibrium between at times contradictory rights and interests.[87]

Indeed, while the private sector expressed concern over possible problems in identifying and negotiating with custom owners and the length of leases, the new Land Policy was generally well received. M.R. Elziere, Managing Director of the SFNH, made the point at a Regional Conference on Land Management held in Port Vila in June 1980, that from his point of view, it was "better to have a good lease than a bad title".[88] Coming from the manager of the Company with the greatest amount of land under registered title (over 3% of the total land area of Vanuatu) M. Elziere's comment indicates a remarkable about face and acceptance of the changing political realities of Vanuatu. The small individual plantation owners who had lived and worked on their land for several generations, especially the *petit colon* on Santo, reacted quite differently. Their response was to participate in a rebellion against the democratically elected government of Father Walter Lini with the aim of creating a separate state, including Santo and neighbouring islands, in which their position and land rights would be preserved.

Specific details relating to the administration of urban land and lease arrangements continued under discussion, but the immediate need was for the Ministry of Lands to produce draft legislation for approval by Parliament before independence. This was necessary to allow for the implementation of Chapter 12 of the Constitution — in particular, Articles 71, 72 and 73, which dealt specifically with land ownership. Termination of the Condominium and the provisions of the 1914 Protocol would mean that all registered freehold titles would cease to exist, the land reverting to custom ownership.

While the land provisions of the Constitution were indeed revolutionary, the Lini Government was clearly concerned that independence in Vanuatu should not degenerate into chaos. The Government wanted to prevent the spectacle of Melanesian custom owners rushing into plantations and driving off individuals and families who in some cases had lived on their properties for several generations and were operating businesses which were clearly assets to the nation. The Government was aware that an element existed among the European and mixed-race planter community, who were clearly prepared to resist the land reforms and the potential for disputes between rival ni-Vanuatu claimants of formerly alienated land was very great. At the time of independence, the Vanuatu economy was almost totally dependent on the rural sector for exports and foreign exchange earnings and thus it was important for the future economic well-being of the country that plantations should continue to produce. Moreover, the Government clearly recognized that foreign capital and expertise would be required for many years to develop Vanuatu's rural sector — Article 77 of the Constitution provided for leasing of land by non-citizens — thus the country could not afford a decline in investor confidence, which would result from a violent and chaotic transition from foreign to indigenous land ownership.

The Land Reform Regulation, which came into effect at

independence,[89] therefore, stipulated that a former alienator — the term used to refer to a registered title-holder — would be:

> entitled to remain on land occupied by him on the Day of Independence until such time as either he enters into a lease of the land or a part thereof with the custom owners of the land or receives payment for improvements on that land (Section 3).[90]

Moreover, custom owners were specifically forbidden, under threat of imprisonment and fine, to forceably enter land which they might claim or "attempt to eject any persons occupying that land by force" (Section 21 [1]). However, an alienator could not stop custom owners "peaceably entering the land occupied by him" (Section 21 [3]). At the same time, alienators and custom owners were prohibited from damaging or destroying any improvements on the land (Section 12, no. 22 [1]). The Land Reform Regulation, therefore, included provisions designed specifically to relieve the fears of alienators that independence and the loss of title would result in expropriation of their properties and investments, without being given the opportunity to negotiate some sort of lease arrangement with custom owners, or compensation if such negotiations failed.

A second major area of concern for alienators and possible future investors dealt with by the Land Reform Regulation was the process of negotiation with custom owners for leases. The position of Government was clear. From independence, all existing registered titles would become null and void. All alienators would, however, have to negotiate with custom owners regarding their future occupation and use of land to which they had held registered title in the past — there was no guarantee of an automatic lease. Moreover, negotiations would have to take place between a potential lessee and the custom owners of the land in question. The role of Government would be to facilitate such negotiations — it would not act as agent on behalf of a negotiator.

The new Regulation did, however, stipulate that no alienator or other person could enter into negotiations with any custom land owner without first applying to the Minister of Lands for a certificate to negotiate. An application to become a "registered negotiator" had to include a statement explaining the "object of the negotiations" (Section 6 [2]), thus enabling Government to vet projects as well as potential leases. If Ministry of Lands officials felt a proposed lease was not in the best interests of custom owners and/or the nation, it could refuse to issue a certificate to negotiate. All agreements between non-indigenous citizens and custom land owners would require the approval of the Minister of Lands and have to be registered in the Land Records Office, the establishment of which was authorized under Section 14 of the Regulations.

While requiring alienators of land to negotiate future lease arrangements, the new Regulation guaranteed the continued enforcement of any existing leases on formerly alienated land until such time as such leases expired (Section 26). In addition, any mortgages which might have been negotiated against which formerly alienated land had been given as security would "continue in full force and effect from the Day of Independence" (Section 8 [2]). The effect of the Reform Regulation provided an assurance to those individuals and institutions who had lent money based on the possession of a registered title or lease, that their rights as mortgagees would be protected. Such a guarantee was seen as necessary, if the confidence of future investors and lending institutions was to be maintained.

The Minister of Lands was also given the power to "consent to a substitution of one alienator for another" (Section 8 [2]). The effect of this section was to allow land transactions to continue subject to the provisions of the Constitution and Land Reform Regulations. This was especially important in urban areas where properties change hands more frequently and many ni-Vanuatu had acquired residential properties. As provided for in the Constitution, Government envisaged separate legislation to deal with urban land and did not deal specifically with the issue in the Land Reform Regulation drafted before independence.

Another important part of the Land Reform Regulation designed to deal with the transition of land from foreign to custom ownership was those sections dealing with Public Land. The Condominium Administration and the British and French Governments owned various properties and facilities (e.g. schools, airstrips, clinics, etc.) which at independence would pass to the Government of Vanuatu. The Land Reform Regulation stipulated, therefore, that:

> On the Day of Independence all state land shall vest in the Government and be public land and be held by it for the benefit of the Republic... (Section 9[1]).

Provision was also made for the Government to divest itself of public land (Section 9 [3]) and to acquire more when required subject to payment of compensation to custom owners (Section 9 [3] and [4]).

Government was also empowered to manage land including the right (as described above) to substitute one alienation for another, to grant leases and to take measures to "conserve and protect the land of the custom owners" (Section 8 [2]). The Minister of Lands

nabanga

N° 162 HEBDOMADAIRE D'INFORMATION 28 JUIN 1980

Dernière heure : saisie de notre confrère « Jeune Mélanésie »

*Francophone demonstration in Vila, 25 June in favour of French language and education (from **Nabanga,** No. 162, 28 June 1980).*

could also establish "corporate bodies for the better carrying into effect of this Regulation" (Section 19 [1]). Legislation was being prepared for the establishment of 'urban land corporations' for Vila and Luganville which was passed after independence. The provision also proved useful immediately after independence when it became necessary to provide some managerial institution to administer the properties of a number of foreign nationals, who had been involved in the pre-independence rebellion and had either left the country or been deported.

There was little debate during the passage of the Land Reform Legislation in June 1980, which indicates that general agreement had been arrived at between most political leaders on the land issue. The exceptions were members of the Nagriamel/MANH coalition and members of the custom-oriented parties on Tanna, who by June 1980 had embarked on a new course of action — to secede from Vanuatu before independence and set up their own independent state, including Santo, the northern islands and Tanna. While the major issue at stake was political power, land again appeared as an underlying theme in the debate which emerged in the early months of 1980 as the Lini Government prepared for independence amidst growing opposition from certain elements of the political opposition.

Rebellion

The results of the November 1979 elections had been a blow to the plan of Jimmy Stephens and his allies. The Vanua'aku Pati's victory in 26 of the 39 seats in Parliament — a two thirds majority — would give them the power to make constitutional changes. Jimmy Stephens had himself participated in the Constitutional Planning Committee and, with the support of his allies, had been able to ensure the inclusion of provisions for the establishment of an unspecified number of regional councils. Encouraged by his French friends on Santo, Stephens had embraced the concept of federalism following the 1975 election as the means to consolidate his position and achieve the long-term goal of establishing full control over internal affairs in Santo.

Chapter 13 of the Constitution on decentralization provided for the establishment of an unspecified number of regional councils which would include custom chiefs. Once elected, the councils would negotiate with the central government regarding their administrative powers, legislation for which would have to be approved by at least two-thirds of the members of Parliament.[91] The Constitution also provided as part of its transitional provisions that the regional councils for Santo and Tanna would be elected at the same time as the new Parliament — November 1979.[92]

The vagueness of the provisions relating to decentralization, which deferred defining the powers of the regional councils until after the elections, reflects the difficulty that the framers of the Constitution had in coming to an agreement. The fact that Jimmy Stephens offered himself as a candidate for the Santo Regional Council, rather than for Parliament, indicates that he felt confident that he and his supporters would win the election and thereby be able to consolidate their control.

Thus, an even greater defeat for Jimmy Stephens than his loss in the National elections was the VP victory by a narrow margin (less than 2.25%) in both the Santo and Tanna Regional Council elections. Stephens and his allies claimed that voting irregularities had occurred, despite the fact that a United Nations delegation had observed the election and found no basis for complaint. But Jimmy Stephens refused to co-operate further with the Government until the instances of alleged electoral fraud were dealt with. His immediate reaction upon hearing the results of the elections was to threaten Vanua'aku Pati supporters from other islands living in Santo, whose presence, he claimed, had prevented the people of Santo from achieving their rightful victory. As a result of this intimidation, an estimated 400 people left Santo for their home islands — mainly in the north of the group. Given the fact that Jimmy Stephens himself had gathered around him at Tanafo several hundred non-Santo Nagriamel supporters who were eligible to vote in the election, his accusation lacked real credibility.

Even more significant than the public accusations of electoral fraud and intimidation of Vanua'aku Pati supporters was the decision by Jimmy Stephens and his allies to organize another Santo secession movement. However, unlike the attempt at secession in 1975/76, Jimmy Stephens had, in addition to his old friends Michael Oliver and the Phoenix Foundation, the full support of the French *colon* and business community on Santo and the backing of the French Government. The November 1979 election was, therefore, the catalyst which united the diverse groups of people who had been competing since the 1960s for control of Santo: Jimmy Stephens as leader of the Santo bush people, French and mixed-race planters and businessmen seeking to protect their land-holdings, and right-wing Americans looking for opportunities for speculative capital investment. Moreover, the speed and precision with which events began to unfold in early 1980, reveals clearly that planning had been going on for some time and that the groups involved were preparing to act regardless of the results of the elections.

The first sign that the next few months leading up to independence would not be smooth, occurred in January 1980 with the opening of an office in Luganville by the leaders of what was called Vemarana — a group consisting of Nagriamel supporters and certain French settlers and people of mixed-race. At the same time, they raised the Vemarana flag before a large crowd of supporters. This was followed towards the end of January with the symbolic closing of the District Agency by 200 Santo bushmen — Nagriamel supporters — who barred the door with *namele* leaves. Government authority was quickly restored, but Vemarana continued to hatch its plans.

In late February, the French Government invited Jimmy Stephens and the other 'Moderate' party leaders to France to discuss the political situation and await the arrival of the official Government mission to negotiate post-independence aid to Vanuatu. The aim of the Minister of Overseas Departments and Territories, Mr. Dijoud, was to pressure the Government of Father Walter Lini into making political concessions — i.e., changes to the Constitution — using aid and the date of independence as bargaining chips. After a brief meeting between the two political groups, however, it was decided that further discussions would take place in Vanuatu and the two delegations left Paris for home.

In a communique issued by M. Dijoud after the return of the various delegations to Vanuatu, French ideas about concessions were clearly laid out: inclusion of custom authorities in the fundamental decision-making of the country, further provision for decentralization of power, assurances that the French language and culture would be maintained and further study on the questions of citizenship and land, "leading to solutions acceptable to everyone".[93] In other words, Dijoud demanded a revision of the Constitution, which had been written and agreed to by all political groups in the country and which he himself and the French Government had just approved a few months earlier. One can only assume that the French had agreed to the Constitution in anticipation that the 'Moderate' parties would win the election. So overwhelming was their defeat and, by the same token, so great was the mandate for the Vanua'aku Pati (62% of the votes cast and 26 of the 39 seats in Parliament) that French officials, now more openly than ever, moved to support the opposition as a last resort to preserve their position and influence in Vanuatu.

Dijoud also spelled out what the alternatives were if the Lini Government refused to compromise: the Condominimum could be maintained "long enough to allow the re-establishment of a climate which would permit the realization of a compromise" or the Government would run the risk "that the opposition, with outside support, would create chaos and a civil war following the Condominium [i.e. after independence]".[94] Dijoud knew, therefore, what Jimmy Stephens and his supporters were planning. His assurances that "there is no question of France supporting secessionist movements"[95] ring hollow in view of the actions of the French government in the months to follow.

On his return trip from France, Jimmy Stephens and several other 'Moderates' stopped off in Carson City, Nevada in the United States where they had discussions with Michael Oliver. Although no details from the meeting itself are known, the events that followed over the next few months reveal that the decision must have been made to proceed with plans for an armed uprising intended to bring about the secession from Vanuatu before independence of Santo, the other northern islands and Tanna in the south. Michael Oliver's support for Vemarana and his objectives were similar to those of 1975. Another opportunity had presented itself to establish a 'new country' where the individual would be able to live and make money free of government control. It was to take the form of a loose union of five separate political units to be known as the Confederation of Natakoro, which were themselves federations of smaller sub-units, the boundaries to be determined by custom chiefs. The five political regions were: the Vemarana Federation (Santo and neighbouring small islands), the Banks-Torres Federation, the Nemakiauti Federation (Malakula and neighbouring small islands), the Federation of the Northern Islands (Ambae, Maewo, Pentecost, Epi, Ambrym), and the Tafea Federation (all the islands south of Efate). Constitutions were produced for each of the five political units and one for the Confederation, which was to have very limited powers relating only to such things as defence, foreign affairs and essential government functions (e.g. transportation, communication, etc.).[96]

In April 1980 it was reported that Oliver had organized a meeting in Panama to enlist financial support for his newly formed Vemarana Development Corporation, which was to provide the initial capital base for the 'new country'. Investors were offered the opportunity to purchase shares in the Corporation at a cost of US$2,000 per share for which they would receive, in addition, a 99 year lease on a one acre parcel of Vemarana land for each share purchased. In the first instance, 10,000 shares were to be offered, 5,000 of which would be held by those persons who had previously provided "seed capital in funds and services to help Vemarana",[97] i.e.

Oliver and his associates. The directors and officers of the Corporation were: F. Thomas Eck III (President and Director), Michael Oliver (Secretary/Treasurer and Director) and Dr. John Hospers (Vice-President-Government Relations and Director).[98] Assuming an initial investment of US$10,000,000, the Corporation planned to use the money to improve communications; purchase inter-island trading vessels and cargo planes; upgrade the Santo airport; lease and purchase land for agricultural purposes and for sub-division and make necessary improvements thereon; establish a bank and issue a gold and silver backed currency; establish a private postal service; promote Vemarana world-wide to attract investment, "particularly on land which this corporation is to lease or purchase from private and tribal owners"; and pay salaries.[99] The Corporation also welcomed "native persons as shareholders". They would have the option of receiving "shares rather than money as compensation for land leased or purchased from them".[100]

It is not clear to what extent the "seed capital and services" were to include guns and/or trained mercenaries — as had been the case in the Bahamas — but with Jimmy Stephens' French allies on Santo and their close links to New Caledonia, such support was less urgent compared to the previous attempt at secession in 1975. Moreover, given the heavy involvement of French *colon* and business interests and the French Government itself, the acceptance of American interests as part of Vemarana at this initial stage of the rebellion was most likely a ploy on the part of his Santo allies to ensure Jimmy Stephens' support, rather than a serious plan for the future development of the islands. Had the rebellion succeeded, it is doubtful that the French *colon* and business community would have allowed American interests to dominate.

While Oliver and his associates dreamed about the huge profits to be made in their new venture, the situation in Vanuatu began to deteriorate rapidly. During April and May, the Lini Government arranged three different meetings with 'Moderate' party representatives to try to come to some agreement regarding decentralization of power. By this time, however, those involved in organizing the rebellion had decided against compromising and the discussions produced no positive results.

By mid-May, tension on Tanna between 'Moderate' and Vanua'aku Pati supporters began to increase. Violent confrontations occurred, leading to an attack by the 'Moderates' on 26 May on the Government station at Isangel, during which the ni-Vanuatu Deputy Commandant of Police and the Assistant District Commissioner were taken hostage. The British Mobile Unit (specially trained ni-Vanuatu

John Frum Celebrations at Sulphur Bay, Tanna, 15th February 1980 (from ***Nabanga,*** *No. 147, 23 February 1980).*

police) was sent to Tanna the following day and, confronted with dynamite attacks and rifle fire, made its way to the 'Moderate' camp to free the hostages, who by that time had already escaped. Following this move by the British Mobile Unit on their camp, hostile activity by the 'Moderates' directed towards Government officials and property subsided somewhat. The rebellion, however, was not over and flared again in early June with tragic results.

In the meantime, trouble had broken out on Santo. In the early hours of the morning of 28 May, Vemarana supporters, including local French and mixed-race 'Moderates' and a large number of bushmen sent by Stephens, attacked the British Paddock — residence for many ni-Vanuatu civil servants — and the British police station. Buildings were smashed, private property and personal effects either destroyed or stolen and men, women and children forced to flee into the bush. The ni-Vanuatu police under British command and the District Commissioner, Job Dalesa, were captured, beaten and taken to Tanafo. Another group of Vemarana supporters seized Pekoa Airport, set up roadblocks along the main roads and took over control of Luganville. It is significant to note that the rebels did not touch the French *gendarmerie*, nor did the police under French command make any effort to stop the violence. Moreover, while all Government and private radios were confiscated or put out of action, those at the *gendarmerie* and French Residency headquarters in Santo were untouched and continued to operate throughout the rebellion until independence on 30 July.

The Lini Government reacted to the rebellion by declaring a blockade of Santo and evacuating over 2,000 civil servants and Vanua'aku Pati supporters from the island. The rebels established a provisional Government of the Republic of Vemarana with Jimmy Stephens as President. Without any military forces under its command, and the two metropolitan governments unwilling to move against the rebels, no immediate action was taken to try to regain control over the rebel-held portion of Santo. Life in Luganville returned to normal with Vemarana policemen patrolling the town in stolen British police uniforms and vehicles.

Back on Tanna, however, violence flared again. On the night of 10 June a group of 'Moderates' marched from Sulfur Bay across the island to Isangel where they planned to free their comrades who had been arrested the previous week by the Mobile Force at the time of the assault on their camp. In the early hours of the morning, they attacked the police station. Shots were fired, the prisoners broke out of the cells and in the chaos which ensued, Alexi Iolu — one of the 'Moderate' leaders — was fatally wounded. With the death of Alexi

French Resident Commissioner Robert visits Jimmy Stevens at Pekoa airport, Santo, during the rebellion (from ***Nabanga,*** *No. 160, 16 June 1980).*

Iolu, the 'Moderates' ceased their hostile activities thus ending the rebellion on Tanna.

This new level of violence, however, provoked the British and French governments in Europe into action. Each decided to send a military contingent of their own forces to Vanuatu to prevent the situation from getting any further out of hand. A unit of the French *garde mobile* was flown into Port Vila from Noumea where they took up key positions around the town. However, when the French Government realized that the British were preparing to send troops they quickly withdrew their troops, claiming that all was peaceful and calm. The French obviously hoped this would give the British second thoughts about sending their forces half way round the world. However, on 12 June, 200 British marines arrived in Port Vila where they remained for most of the time until Independence.

The arrival of British troops stabilized the situation in Vanuatu very quickly. Following the initial outbreaks of violence on Santo and Tanna, Government leaders and prominent members of the Vanua'aku Pati in Vila had received death threats and a so-called 'secret army' scattered leaflets and painted anti-Anglophone grafitti around the town. With the arrival of the British marines, the fears of local Vila residents subsided. The studio of the local radio station was bombed, but significant acts of violence never reached the capital. Furthermore, the presence of the British marines made it much more difficult for the French Government to achieve its goal of blocking independence and bringing down the duly elected Government of Father Walter Lini.

There is conclusive evidence that French officials were fully aware of the plans of their own nationals to rebel against the Lini Government and actively encouraged and supported them in their efforts. As noted above, throughout the rebellion French officers and personnel were never attacked and did nothing to constrain the activities of those involved. Moreover, the French Residency was able to maintain contact with the rebels and its officials on Santo by radio which Vemarana allowed to operate throughout the uprising. At his trial after the rebellion had collapsed, Jimmy Stephens stated that:

> French administrators, including the Resident Commissioner, Inspector General Jean-Jacques Robert, promised him 'a lot of things' and that he would never drop him. They also promised to find him support in other countries.[101]

The French Resident Commissioner, Inspector Generale Robert, fully supported the concept of creating an autonomous government for Santo and stated publicly that French forces would be flown in from

Noumea to counter the mobilization of a VP volunteer army.[102] Moreover, on 23 July, prior to the arrival of French and British troops on Santo — it had finally been agreed that Government control should be re-established on Santo prior to independence — Robert assured Santo residents that the presence of the troops would mean continued metropolitan control:

> The French and English governments have, by a joint decision, agreed that if no agreement has been reached (prior to Independence) the French Government representative will stay; the English Government representative will also stay . . . . to my mind the main thing is getting the French troops in here. Once they are here, they have to be taken out again . . . . this decision was taken without the Government's knowledge . . . . that is to say, Lini's government.[103]

It is clear that Robert was in league with Vemarana to create a second Mayotte. It is no mere coincidence that he and his counterpart in Santo, who remained there throughout the rebellion, had both been in Mayotte at the time of the military coup which allowed it to remain under French control after the independence of the Chamorro Islands in 1973.

The proof is, therefore, overwhelming that top officials in the French Residency were fully involved in the secessionist rebellion, especially with the French *colon* and business community and mixed-race population on Santo. They in turn were allied with right-wing elements in New Caledonia, whose ultimate aim was to link the islands of Santo and Tanna with the Loyalty Islands to form a separate buffer state between Vanuatu and New Caledonia. Their intention was to separate off the Loyalty Islands, which are predominantly Melanesian, leaving the business and *colon* community in control of *Le Grande Terre* (the main island), where Kanaks comprise only about 25% of the total population.[104]

It has been alleged by some that the French Resident Commissioner in Port Vila, Inspector Generale Robert, often acted independently of senior officials in Noumea and Paris. However, while his special status as Inspector Generale meant that he reported directly to the President of France, it is hard to believe that the High Commissioner in Noumea and the Minister of Overseas Territories in Paris, M. Dijoud, were uninvolved in the events taking place in Vanuatu.[105] There is clear evidence that French officials in both Noumea and Paris knew what their nationals were planning and actively supported them in carrying out the rebellion. For example, three days before the rebellion broke out on Santo, officials in New Caledonia cleared a light plane carrying Vemarana leaders and, it was suspected, arms and ammunition, for a direct flight from Noumea to Santo without the approval from authorities in Port Vila.[106] During the Government blockade of Santo, the rebel-owned ship — *Vemarana Federation* — was allowed to dock in Noumea to load supplies.[107]

Any doubts that French Government officials were involved in the rebellion were dispelled following independence, when Phillipe Delacroix — one of the rebels, who had been deported — wrote an open letter to Dijoud in one of the local New Caledonian newspapers, criticizing the Minister for not following through with the support he had promised:

> Sir,
>
> After woefully inaccurate statements about Vanuatu that you have seen fit to make quite recently to the National Assembly, are you still able to look at yourself in the mirror without blushing?....
>
> You had been charged by our country's Government to prepare the independence of the New Hebrides. You have failed in this mission. Thus you had to find somebody upon whom you could unload the totality of your errors. That is now an accomplished fact: how easy and tempting it was to burden falsely your compatriots who have been hunted out of Vanuatu.
>
> However M. Dijoud, you have lied....
>
> Do you remember 26 May 1980? Where were you on that date? At Noumea wasn't it? Where, two months before independence, incensed at the fact that Father Lini Chief Minister of the New Hebrides had refused to come to meet you, you practically gave the green light to what was to be wrongly termed the Santo rebellion.
>
> With the agreement of the French authorities, the Provisional Government of Vemarana and the Confederation of the Northern Islands, was proclaimed on 28 May, and you know perfectly well that right up to the last minute, right up to 30 July, we pursued desperately the federal solution, the only viable one in the face of the British Government's stubbornness and the French Government's indecision as it tried to run with the hare and hunt with the hounds.[108]

Clearly, French officials at the highest level were aware of the plans and activities of the secessionists and gave their tacit and at times active support.

At stake for the French Government was its continued influence and power in Vanuatu, which by 1980 depended on the future status of its planter and business allies. The reforms embodied in the new Constitution — of which the provisions on land were some of the most important — written and agreed to by *all* ni-Vanuatu political groups, marked the total failure of the French to create a Melanesian majority which it could continue to manipulate and control. The last option was for the French Government to support the secessionists on Santo and Tanna. Santo, in particular, with its vast, sparsely populated land area could have easily provided the economic base for the continuation of a French colonial presence in the islands.

The turning point in the crisis was the Pacific Heads of Government (FORUM) meeting, held on Tarawa in early July, at which a resolution was passed unanimously supporting 30 July as the date for Vanuatu independence. Even more significant, was the opportunity provided by the meeting for the Prime Ministers of Australia (Malcolm Fraser) and Papua New Guinea (Julius Chan) to meet with the Chief Minister of Vanuatu, Father Walter Lini. Chan and Frazer both agreed that their governments would assist the Lini Government in putting down the rebellion once independence had been achieved. The British and French retained control over the military (mobile forces) and police until independence, but refused to move against the secessionists — to maintain law and order in Vanuatu as required under the Protocol of 1914. Thus Chan's pledge of Papua New Guinea troops and Fraser's agreement to supply logistic support allowed the Lini Government to remain firm on their commitment to 30 July as the date for independence, knowing that afterwards they would have the means to regain those areas held by the rebels.

At mid-day on 30 July 1980, the Vanuatu flag was raised in Port Vila and in those areas under government control. A contingent of British and French marines had gone to Santo on the 27th, but remained in Luganville and made no moves to confront rebel forces. Sela Molisa, Government representative and *man Santo* flew to Santo on the 29th and, guarded by the marines, raised the flag on the 30th. During the following days, when it became clear that Anglo-French control in Vanuatu was indeed at an end the rebels went on a rampage of looting and destruction. Several bridges were blown up, the copra oil mill destroyed and shops and warehouses broken into and goods stolen.

On the 6th of August the first contingent of the Papua New Guinea Mobile Force arrived on Santo, accompanied by members of the Vanuatu Mobile Force. Within days most of the rebels had been arrested, including Jimmy Stephens, and the Government resumed full control. Those foreign nationals who had been involved in the rebellion and had not fled to Noumea on French Government plans, prior to the arrival of the Papua New Guineans, were also arrested. Most chose deportation rather than to stand trial. Ni-Vanuatu involved in the rebellion were also arrested, many being tried and sentenced to prison sentences for various crimes including theft, damaging property, kidnapping and assault. Jimmy Stephens was sentenced to 14 years in prison for his part in the rebellion. It will take many years to heal the wounds created by Vanuatu's unfortunate passage to independence.

The rebellion, which was basically a movement aimed at protecting land-holdings and providing opportunities for capital investment, need never have happened. Had the colonial governments responded positively to ni-Vanuatu demands for reform in the early 1970s, the transition could have been orderly. While ni-Vanuatu political leaders of all parties and factions were for the most part united on the question of ownership of land — i.e. that all alienated land should be returned to custom owners — there was widespread acceptance of the need for foreign participation and assistance in land development. The land provisions in the Constitution and the Land Reform Regulation of 1980, which guaranteed the temporary rights of former title-holders and provided a system for acquiring leases, clearly demonstrated that Vanua'aku Pati leaders were prepared to accept and work with foreign planter and business interests to develop their country. What they wanted and in the end, what they achieved, was to become once again, rulers of their own land.

EPILOGUE

On 30 July 1980, as provided by the Constitution, all formerly alienated land in Vanuatu returned to custom ownership. The Lini Government prepared for this major change of title by passing land reform legislation prior to independence. This laid down the basic principles on which its future land policy would be based and at the same time clarified the rights of former freehold title holders and custom owners during the transitional period required to resolve such questions as custom ownership, leasing arrangements and compensation. During the last half of 1980, the Ministry of Lands continued to work on defining the details of the Government's land policy and the legislation required for its implementation.

In the meantime, in the aftermath of the rebellion, the Government was faced with the problem of what to do with the properties of Europeans and mixed-race people with foreign passports who had been deported for their part in the uprising, or who had simply abandoned their plantations and fled the country rather than face possible legal proceedings against them. In order to restore effective management to these plantations, a Cabinet decision was made in December 1980 to establish a Rural Land Corporation (Land Reform Order No. 14 of 1980) — a power provided to the Minister of Lands, the Hon. Sethy Regenvanu, in the 1980 Land Reform Regulation. The role of the Corporation was to supervize the running of abandoned plantations, for which temporary managers were appointed, until such time as permanent leases could be arranged and custom ownership determined. The Corporation's first meeting was held in Luganville on 5 December 1980 under the ex-officio chairmanship of the First Secretary of the Ministry of Lands. The Government provided an initial loan of vatu 2,000,000 (A$20,000) for its operation, which was matched by a grant of similar amount made available through the Australian High Commission.

By the end of 1980, important decisions were also made with regard to urban land. In the months following independence, the Ministry of Lands came under increasing pressure from local lawyers and real estate agents to produce legislation which would validate dealings in urban land, which had been transacted both before and after freehold titles had been converted to leasehold by the yet to be established Urban Land Corporations. Conflicting interests within Government itself, however, made the task of deciding on a fair and equitable policy difficult. One of the most contentious issues was that of the urban boundary of Port Vila. Cabinet finally approved a municipal boundary which excluded the largely developed de Gaillande sub-division and certain public lands, e.g. the radio station, at Malapoa. These basically urban areas were classified as rural land which meant that existing residents would be required to negotiate for their leases with Fila Islanders as the custom claimants.

Land Reform Order No. 26 of 1981 delineated the boundaries of Port Vila and Luganville and declared these areas to be public land. A separate order — Land Order No. 25 of 1981 — also provided that certain areas cease to be public land. Land Orders No. 30 and No. 118 of 1981 provided for the establishment of the Port Vila and Luganville Urban Land Corporations. The function of the two corporations was to manage urban land for the government. This would involve the leasing of land within the urban boundaries and collecting rents. Custom owners would receive as compensation, as provided for in section 11 of the Land Reform Regulation, a percentage of the annual rents collected.

The other major issue relating to urban land was that of the rate of rental to be charged. Two options were presented to Cabinet: a 'rental rate' system whereby lessees would be charged a certain percentage each year based on the assessed value of the land, or a 'percentage lease' system under which users would be charged according to actual revenue raised from the use of the land and premises constructed thereon. The 'percentage lease' system would have produced considerably more revenue for Government — and also for custom owners who were to receive a percentage of the income collected — but it was rejected in favour of the 'rental rate' system. Cabinet left it to the Vila and Luganville Urban Land Corporations to fix the percentage to be applied, subject to a maximum of 5 percent.

In January 1981, a Cabinet re-shuffle resulted in Sethy Regenvanu moving to Agriculture and being replaced by Thomas Rueben Seru. The decision to change ministers appears to have been due to the increasing pressure felt by the Lini Government from custom owners who, despite independence and pronouncements that all formerly alienated land had been returned to them, found that for the most part expatriates were still physically in possession of their properties and in cases of abandoned or deserted plantations, ni-Vanuatu were prevented from taking over. Thomas Rueben, it was felt, would get things moving.

The dilemma faced by the Government, which the re-shuffle in the end did not solve, was how to satisfy ni-Vanuatu demands for the return of their land and at the same time carry out an orderly transition to custom ownership without disrupting the rural economy and alienating prospective investors. The Ministry of Lands under Sethy Regenvanu had indeed devoted much of its time in 1980 to devising policies to deal with former owners and the transition to custom ownership — a strategy approved by the Government through its passage before independence of the Land Reform Regulation, and as dictated in the Constitution. What, in 1981, was only beginning to loom as the main obstacle to effecting final transfers of title to custom owners was often, in fact, the custom owners themselves. Population decline and movement, plus the fact that many properties had been in European hands for decades, made it extremely difficult to determine who exactly were the true custom owners. In October 1980, Land Reform Order No. 9 had come into effect. This provided the procedure for expatriates and former owners to acquire a 'certificate to negotiate' with custom owners, but the problem then became, with whom should the 'registered negotiator' negotiate?

It had been the policy of the Vanua'aku Pati prior to independence to urge villages to set up land committees to deal with problems of custom ownership and to carry out negotiations. Where such committees existed and villagers could agree that land should be returned to the community as a whole, the problem was reduced. This, for example, enabled the people of Eton village in October 1981, to successfully conclude a lease with the former owner of a 3,000 hectare cattle station on North Efate — the first rural lease signed in Vanuatu. In 1981, such successful negotiations were few and the prospects for resolving the numerous claims and counter-claims by custom owners seemed almost impossible. However, the existence of village land committees did not necessarily mean the end of disputes. The land committees of Fila Island and Erakor, for example, have not been able to agree to a percentage division of the rentals collected on their behalf by the Port Vila Urban Land Corporation. As a result, the money is being held in trust.

One of the first changes which the new Minister of Lands brought about, in what was intended to be a tougher policy towards former owners, was an amendment to the Land Reform Regulation of 1980. The definition of alienator was tightened and undeveloped land, which was formerly part of registered titles, was excluded from properties which alienators could continue to occupy (Amendment No. 6 of 1981). Former owners still in occupation of their properties were, therefore, restricted to developed portions only, though the amendment did not prevent their applying to lease the undeveloped land which had been part of their registered titles before independence.

The amendment also included the provision that, in cases of abandoned properties, the Minister of Lands should have the right of general management and control. A number of properties formerly owned by deportees or prohibited immigrants were being run on their behalf by friends, relatives or agents. The effect of the amendment was to deal with what was seen as an unresolved remnant of the rebellion, i.e. deportees were recorded as alienators, but only for payment of improvements on their properties. They lost all other rights, including that of collecting rents and profits from business operations. In effect, therefore, the amendment legalized the expropriation of all land and properties belonging to people who had been deported as a result of their participation in the 1980 rebellion. They would, however, be eligible for compensation for any improvements.

Despite the appointment of a new Minister of Lands and the tougher stand taken towards former owners, little progress was achieved during 1981 in resolving the question of the future status of formerly foreign owned properties in the rural areas, i.e. how to effect the transfer of such land to the custom owners. The problem, as noted above, was how to determine the true custom owners. The case of the island of Aore illustrates well the complexity of the problem. Before independence, it was commonly believed that there were no survivors left from the island — most having died from disease or been killed off in the last century. However, 19 ni-Vanuatu came forward claiming custom ownership to various parts of the island — most descendants of earlier residents who had moved to or were related in some way to the inhabitants of nearby islands (e.g. Tutuba, Malo and Mavea).

Legislation for the establishment of island courts — which were provided for in the Constitution in the hope that they would make available the legal means to resolve custom land disputes — remained bogged down in the Attorney General's Office in the drafting stage, but was finally passed by Parliament in late 1983. A training programme was begun to effect its implementation as soon as possible in 1984.

Where custom owners could be identified, negotiations with former owners did begin to take place. There was as yet, however, no set policy on terms of leases, thus progress was slow at this time in formalizing agreements. Moreover, the question of compensation had not been dealt with — there were some Government leaders who felt no compensation should be paid for improvements. Thus, custom owners (especially in the rural areas) who would have chosen not to negotiate a lease with former owners found they still could not take over land to which they were entitled. Most would not have had the capital to pay for improvements and in any case, there was no mechanism to determine the amount of compensation due to former alienators. Minister Seru's decision to allow certain claimants to enter properties where disputes as to the true custom owners still existed, led to several violent confrontations between ni-Vanuatu and was one of the factors leading to his dismissal in December 1981. One of Minister Seru's last acts was to establish a new institution for Santo/Malo, the Santo Land Council, which was to deal with land problems in the Santo/Malo Island Council area. The Ministry of Lands was merged with that of Agriculture, Forestry and Fisheries under the leadership of Sethy Regenvanu, the former Minister of Lands.

Minister Regenvanu sought to deal with the growing problem of multiple custom claimants by giving notice in February 1982, that he would use his power as Minister to negotiate leases for selected properties, where custom claimants could not resolve their differences. The Santo Land Council had the power to make such decision in the case of Santo/Malo. Custom claimants were given three months notice to come to an agreement. In several cases, the Minister did in fact negotiate leases — the most important being the large PRV (Plantation Reunies de Vanuatu, formerly the PRNH) at Norsup on Malakula. It is not clear what the long-term effect of such a policy will be, but the position taken by certain prominent Tautu villagers in the 1983 national election seems to indicate that ni-Vanuatu involved in such cases do not accept such imposed solutions. Tautu village had always been staunchly Vanua'aku Pati, but in the 1983 election, the brother of the local Chief stood as an independent, thus drawing votes away from Sethy Regenvanu who comes from the same area and was the Vanua'aku Pati candidate for the constituency.

In April 1982, Parliament passed another significant piece of land legislation, the Bill for the Alienated Land Act, which dealt specifically with the rights of alienators and the procedures relating to negotiations for leases. The amendment to the Land Reform Regulation agreed to in 1981 requiring deportees to hand over their land was included in the Act which came into effect on 1 August 1982. The new Act also stipulated that former owners who had not been granted leases would be required under certain circumstances to leave their land within 60 days, without first having received payment for improvements. This in fact has not often happened. In addition, the Act defined what constituted compensatable improvements and provided for payment over a ten year period. The Alienated Land Act, therefore, was a victory for those in the Government pushing for a quick and final solution to the process of transferring ownership of formerly alienated lands to custom owners.

A second piece of land legislation passed in April 1982 was the Lands Referee Act, which provided for the appointment of an independent person to determine levels of rent or payment for improvements, when negotiations between custom owners and former owners failed to reach an agreement. Government, however, was slow to act on this bill — the post was not filled until the end of 1983 — which reflects their reluctance to give up control over such politically sensitive matters as rent and compensation during this early phase of land policy implementation.

The most recent and important land legislation passed by Parliament is the Land Leases Act of 1983. Consisting of 113 sections, the Act produces in one piece of legislation a law and procedure for establishing and maintaining a register of title to leases of land. The Act authorizes the establishment of a Land Records Office, sets out the Director's powers and lays down regulations for issuance of titles and procedures for dealings in registered leases. It also provides that leases shall not be longer than 75 years. In 1986 the Act was slightly amended to provide that leases may be reviewed not more often than every five years at the request of either party. Under the Act, leases can be transferred, sub-divided, mortgaged and inherited. The Land Records Office opened in March 1984.

By the end of 1983, therefore, Vanuatu had in existence a legal framework to deal with land transactions as provided for under the Constitution. While foreigners and non-indigenous citizens were prohibited from owning land, it was possible to lease land with the assurance that one's investment was protected by law. In February 1984, the Vila Urban Land Corporation announced that it would begin issuing leases to all former owners and those who had been substituted as alienators on properties within the urban boundary. It was also possible to formalize lease arrangements negotiated since independence in rural areas, which numbered more than 100. Vanuatu, therefore, made considerable progress in the first few years after the establishment of the Ministry of Lands in 1979. Clearly, the country's revolutionary land reforms will be achieved more quickly in the towns than in the rural areas, but the Government has shown a determination to seek solutions which protect the rights of indigenous ni-Vanuatu and at the same time deal fairly with former owners — those who chose to accept the terms of the Constitution at independence — and prospective investors. It is remarkable, given the difficult transition to independence, that so much was achieved in so short a time.

NOTES

Chapter 1

1. Kelly, C. *La Australia...* pp. 202-38.
2. Dunmore, J. *French Explorers...* pp. 91-94.
3. Beaglehole, J.C. *The Life of James Cook,* pp. 394-409.
4. Shineberg, D. *They Came for Sandalwood,* p.202.
5. *Ibid.,* p.203.
6. Speiser, F. *Ethnographische Materialien...* p.333 (Vao); Allen, M. 'The Torres, Banks and Northern New Hebrides', p.98 (East Ambae); Guiart, J. 'Societes, rituels et mythes du Nord Ambrym', p.21 (Ambrym); Deacon, A. *Malekula...* p.173.
7. Codrington, R. *The Melanesians...* p.60.
8. Sope, Barak. *Land and Politics...* p.7.
9. Barrau, J. *Subsistence Agriculture in Melanesia.*
10. Crocombe, R.G. *Land Tenure in the Pacific,* pp. 1-4.
11. *Ibid.,* p.14.
12. *Ibid.,* p.21.
13. Codrington, R. *The Melanesians,* p.67 (Banks Islands); Deacon, A., *Malekula...* p.150.
14. Guiart, J. 'Sociétés, rituels...' p.22.
15. Allen, M. 'Descent Groups...' p.16.
16. Guiart, J. In Espirat, J.-J. et al., *'Systeme des Titres...'* p.274.
17. Bonnemaison, J. 'Social and Cultural Aspects of Land Tenure in Vanuatu'. In University of the South Pacific, *Report of the Regional Conference on Land Management,* p.20.
18. The official name for this island is Aoba, but in 1982, the chiefs of the island decided to revert to calling it by an older version — Ambae, which quickly became accepted throughout the country.
19. Allen, M. 'Descent Groups', pp. 10-11.
20. *Ibid.,* p.17.
21. Bonnemaison, J. 'Espace et paysages...' p.231.
22. Allen, M. 'The Torres', pp. 97-8.
23. *Ibid.*
24. Lane, R. In Crocombe, R.G. (ed), *Land Tenure in the Pacific,* pp. 249-53.
25. Deacon, A. *Malekula,* p.172.
26. Guiart, J. *Espiritu Santo,* p.152.

27. *Ibid.*, p.158.
28. Such was the pattern on Fila Island.
29. Guiart, J. *Espiritu Santo*, p.158.
30. Codrington, R. *The Melanesians*, p.64.
31. Bonnemaison, J. 'Social and Cultural...', pp. 20-21.
32. Guiart, J. 'In Espirat, J.-J. et al.', p.273.
33. *Ibid.*, p.274.
34. Bonnemaison, J. 'Social and Cultural', p.21.
35. Guiart, Jean. "In Espirat, J.-J. et al.', p.274 (with the exception of Nguna, Pwele and Emau).
36. *Ibid.*, p.95.
37. *Ibid.*, p.274.
38. Guiart, J. 'Prescriptions matrimoniales...' p.344.
39. Allen, M. 'Descent groups', p.9.
40. Guiart, Jean. 'In Espirat, J.-J. et al.', p.274.
41. See note 22 above.
42. Guiart, Jean. 'In Espirat, J.-J. et al.', p.274.
43. *Ibid.*
44. Codrington, R. *The Melanesians,* p.65 and Allen, M. 'The Torres', p.68.
45. Allen, M. 'The Torres', pp. 109-10.
46. Dillon, P. *Narrative of La Perouse...*
47. Shineberg, D. ...*Sandalwood,* pp. 17-25.
48. *Ibid.*, p.72.
49. *Ibid.*, p.100.
50. *Ibid.*, pp. 129-30.
51. *Ibid.*, pp. 155-7.
52. *Ibid.*, p.100.
53. Western Pacific High Commission [WPHC] — Minute Papers [MP] 112 of 1882. Letter from Capt. Bridge of HMS *Espiegle* to WPHC, 27 July 1882.
54. Morrell, W.P. *Britain in the Pacific Islands*, p.95.
55. *Ibid.*, p.92.
56. *Ibid.*, p.95.
57. *Ibid.*, p.96.
58. Don, A. *Peter Milne*... pp.80-1.
59. *Ibid.*, p.21.
60. *Ibid.*, p.89.
61. *Ibid.*, pp. 26-7.
62. *Ibid.*, p.90.
63. Presbyterian Mission. *1st Annual Report... 1864.*
64. Don, A. *Peter Milne*, pp. 115-6.
65. Langridge, A. *The Conquest of Cannibal Tanna*, pp. 46-7.
66. *Ibid.*, p.58.
67. *Ibid.*, pp. 78-9.
68. WPHC/MP. Land Registry, Book A, Folio 80. See also Thompson, Robert. *Australian Imperialism*... p.29.
69. Thompson, R. *Australian Imperialism*... p.29.
70. *Ibid.*
71. Scarr, D. *Fragments of Empire,* pp.181-2.

72. WPHC/MP. Land Registry, Book A, Folio 6205. See also Scarr, D. *Fragments of Empire,* p.198.
73. Joint Court. Application No. 77.
74. *Ibid.,* Judgment 139.
75. Scarr, D. *Fragments of Empire,* p.181.
76. *Ibid.*
77. Thompson, R. *Australian Imperialism*... p.44.
78. Scarr, D. *Fragments of Empire,* p.181.
79. *Ibid.,* p.176.
80. Quoted in Scarr, D. *Fragments of Empire,* p.197.
81. WPHC/MP 85 of 1883. Letter from Capt. Bridge to High Commissioner [HC], 15 May 1882.
82. WPHC/MP 37 of 1884. See also *Royal Fiji Gazette,* 11 January 1884.
83. *Ibid.,* p.182.
84. *Ibid.*
85. Morrel, W.P. *Britain in the Pacific Islands,* p.199.
86. Higginson, J. *Les Nouvelles-Hébrides*..., p.7.
87. *Ibid.,* p.12.
88. *Ibid.,* p.15.
89. *Des Granges Papers.* Higginson to Minister of Foreign Affairs, 8 June 1885.
90. Scarr, D. *Fragments of Empire,* p.120.
91. Higginson, J. *Les Nouvelles-Hébrides,* p.16.
92. *Des Granges Papers.* Report from V. D'Arbel, 2nd Officer on ship *Calédonienne,* to Governor of New Caledonia, 20 November 1882.
93. Scarr, D. *Fragments of Empire,* p.199.
94. *Des Granges Papers.* Report from D'Arbel to Governor of New Caledonia, 20 November 1882.
95. *Ibid.*
96. *Ibid.,* Captain of cruiser *Fabert* to the Admiral, Commander of Naval Division in the Pacific, 7 April 1888.
97. Scarr, D. *Fragments of Empire,* p.201 and Thompson, R. *Australian Imperialism*... p.133.
98. WPHC/MP. Land Registry, Book A, Folio 16, no.
99. *Ibid.*
100. *Ibid.,* Folio 9, no. 15.
101. Thompson, R. *Australian Imperialism*... p.133.
102. Scarr, D. *Fragments of Empire,* p.202.
103. WPHC/MP 219 of 1887. Letter from Julian Thomas to High Commissioner, 20 July 1887.
104. Residence de France. Synthese Mensuelle. May 1968, Annex II. Letter from Lt. Legrand, Commander of the *Dives,* to the Governor of New Caledonia, 11 April 1886. Hereinafter cited as RFSM.
105. *Des Granges Papers.* Notice of founding of Society.
106. *Ibid.*
107. *Ibid.* Captain of cruiser *Fabert* to Admiral, Commander of Naval Division in the Pacific, 7 April 1887.
108. *Ibid.*
109. WPHC/MP 112 of 1883. Letter from F.R.M. Wilson and John G. Paton to

the Secretary of State for the Colonies, 1 March 1883.
110. Thompson, R. '*Australian Imperialism...*' p.133.
111. WPHC/MP. Land Registry, Book B, Deed 433/137.
112. Joint Court. Judgment 92.
113. Thompson, R. '*Australian Imperialism...*' pp.134-5.
114. *Ibid.*
115. Australian New Hebrides Company Ltd. *Memorandum and Articles of Association of the Australasian New Hebrides Company Ltd.*
116. Thompson, R. '*Australian Imperialism...*' p.135.
117. *Ibid.*
118. Scarr, D. *Fragments of Empire,* p.203.
119. WPHC/MP. Land Registry Book A.
120. Scarr, D. *Fragments of Empire,* pp. 203-5.
121. Thompson, R. *Australian Imperialism,* p.136.
122. Scarr, D. *Fragments of Empire,* p.205.
123. *Des Granges Papers.* Note by Governor of New Caledonia.
124. Scarr, D. *Fragments of Empire,* p.205.

Chapter 2

1. Legge, J.D. *Britain in Fiji...* and France, P. *The Charter of the Land,* pp. 36-91.
2. Thompson, R.C. *Australian Imperialism...*, pp.44-7.
3. *Ibid.,* p.47.
4. Scarr, D, *Fragments of Empire,* p.207.
5. British Foreign Office Documents, c.5648. 'Correspondence Respecting the New Hebrides Joint Naval Commission, 1886-1887', p.3. Hereinafter cited as BFOD, c.5648.
6. Morrell, W.P. *Britain in the Pacific Islands*, p.202.
7. BFOD, c.5648, p.1.
8. *Ibid.*, p.3.
9. *Ibid.*
10. *Ibid.*, p.7.
11. *Ibid.*
12. *Ibid.*, p.14.
13. *Ibid.*, p.17.
14. *Ibid.*, p.24.
15. *IBid.*, p.31.
16. *Ibid.*, p.60.
17. The full text of both the Agreement and the Regulations can be found in BFOD, c.5687, 'Further Correspondence Respecting the New Hebrides Joint Naval Commission', pp.10-1. Hereinafter cited as BFOD, c.5687.
18. BFOD, c.5648, p.62.
19. *Ibid.*, p.62.
20. BFOD, c.5687, pp.3-4.
21. *Des Granges Papers.* Minister of the Navy to Captain of the frigate *Volta,* 14 October 1885. Document entitled: 'Policy to be followed in the New Hebrides'.
22. *Des Granges Papers.* Report to Minister of the Navy, 15 September 1890.

23. WPHC/MP 207 of 1891. 'Memorial on French Aggression in the New Hebrides'.
24. *Ibid.*
25. *Des Granges Papers.* Minister of the Navy to Captain of the frigate *Volta,* 14 October 1885. Document entitled: 'Policy to be followed in the New Hebrides'.
26. Higginson, John. *Les Nouvelles-Hébrides...*, pp.34-5.
27. *Ibid.*, pp.56-9.
28. Scarr, D. *Fragments of Empire,* pp.218-21.
29. British Foreign Office Confidential Print, 8721. 'New Hebrides Commission. Proceedings of the New Hebrides Commission Held at the Foreign Office, London, February 1 to 27, 1906', pp.5-6. Hereinafter cited as BFOCD, 8721.
30. *Ibid.*
31. Scarr, D. *Fragments of Empire,* p.221.
32. British Parliamentary Paper, Cd. 3288. 'Correspondence Relating to the Convention with France, dated 20th October, 1906, Respecting the New Hebrides', p.6.
33. BFOCP, 8721, p.1.
34. *Ibid.*
35. *Ibid.*, p.2.
36. *Ibid.*, pp.9-10.
37. *Ibid.*, pp.10-11.
38. *Ibid.*
39. *Ibid.*, p.14.
40. *Ibid.*, p.11.
41. *Ibid.*
42. *Ibid.*, p.14.
43. *Ibid.*, p.16-17.
44. *Ibid.*, p.9.
45. *Ibid.*, p.17.
46. *Ibid.*, p.18.
47. *Ibid.*, p.19.
48. *Ibid.*
49. *Ibid.*, p.22.
50. *Ibid.*, p.23.
51. *Ibid.*, p.28.
52. *Ibid.*, p.25.
53. *Ibid.*, p.26.
54. BFOD, Cd. 3288, 'Correspondence Relating to the Convention with France, Dated 20th October 1906, Respecting the New Hebrides', pp.14-35. Hereinafter cited as BFOD, Cd.3288.
55. The Torrens System was introduced into Australia in the 1850s to register large areas of unoccupied land, where the boundaries were determined by survey, rather than already defined boundary features.
56. The provision was invoked only twice: in 1964 with regard to Pango Village on Efate and in 1965 with regard to the whole of the island of Togoa.
57. *Des Granges Papers.* Report of M. Picannon. No date.

58. Scarr, D. *Fragments of Empire,* p.230.
59. Politis, N. *Le Condominium. . .,* p.70.
60. *Ibid.,* p.67.
61. *Ibid.*
62. BFOCP, 8721, p.102.
63. *Ibid.,* p.11.
64. Roberts, S.H. *History. . .,* Vol. 2, pp.533-4.
65. Scarr, D. *Fragments of Empire,* p.230.
66. Jacomb, E. *France and England. . .,* pp.77-8.
67. *Ibid.*
68. Scarr, D. *Fragments of Empire,* pp.233-4.
69. *Ibid.*
70. Under the *lois de suris* a judge was allowed to grant leniency for a first offence.
71. 'Proceedings of the New Hebrides Conference, held at the Foreign Office, London, June 10 to August 6, 1914', Vol. 1, pp.26-7. Publisher not given. Hereinafter cited as 'Proceedings of the New Hebrides Conference'.
72. Alexander, G. *From the Middle Temple. . .,* pp.189-91.
73. *Ibid.*
74. 'Proceedings of the New Hebrides Conference', Vol. 1, pp.39-40.
75. Scarr, D. *Fragments of Empire,* p.239.
76. *Le Néo-Hébridais,* no. 48, September 1913.
77. *Ibid.*
78. *Ibid.*
79. 'Proceedings of the New Hebrides Conference', Vol. 1, pp.68-9.
80. New Hebrides Presbyterian Mission Synod, Minutes of June 1913.
81. Scarr, D. *Fragments of Empire,* pp.239-41.
82. *Ibid.,* pp.241-8.
83. Letter from British Delegates to New Hebrides Conference of 1914 to Sir Edward Grey, 15 September 1914, p.2. Included as separate document following 'Proceedings of the New Hebrides Conference', Vol. II. Hereinafter cited as 'Letter from British Delegates to New Hebrides Conference'.
84. *Ibid.*
85. 'Proceedings of the New Hebrides Conference', Vol. 1, p.27.
86. *Ibid.,* pp.27-8.
87. *Ibid.*
88. *Ibid.,* p.30.
89. *Ibid.*
90. *Ibid.*
91. *Ibid.,* p.37.
92. *Ibid.,* Vol. II, p.20.
93. *Ibid.,* Vol.I, pp.67-8.
94. *Ibid.*
95. *Ibid.*
96. *Ibid.,* Vol. II, Annex IV, Text of Convention showing the Amendment adopted by the Conference, pp.29-92.
97. *Ibid.,* p.87.

98. Letter from British Delegates to New Hebrides Conference, p.12.
99. *Ibid.*

Chapter 3

1. Commonwealth of Australia, 'Records Relating to the Pacific', A1108, Vol. 5. Letter from A. Vigoureux on behalf of the SFNH to the President and Judges of the Joint Court, 7 December 1914. Hereinafter cited as COA.
2. Great Britain. 'Foreign Office Records', 371, A2021/308/51. French Ambassador in London to Secretary for Foreign Affairs, 20 March 1921. Hereinafter cited as FOR 371.
3. *Ibid.*, A8882/308/51. Colonial Office to Foreign Office, 29 November 1921.
4. Article in *Matin*, 'La Société Francaise des Nouvelles-Hébrides aurait offert ses concessions á l'Australie'. Included in FOR 371, A8600/308/51.
5. Article in *Temps*, 17 March 1928, 'La Colonisation Francaise aux Nouvelles-Hébrides'. Quoted in FOR 371, W2890/63/17. Letter from British Ambassador to Colonial Office (CO), 22 March 1928.
6. FOR 371, A9198/308/51. French Chargé d'Affairs to British Government, 8 December 1921.
7. *Ibid.*, A1513/211/51. French Ambassador to British Government, 1 March 1922.
8. Ibid., A9573/308/51. British Resident Commissioner [BRC] to High Commissioner [HC], 20 October 1921.
9. *Ibid.*, A2829/23/51. Report on the Work of the Joint Court during 1923 from the Acting President, H.H.T. Goeman Borgesius, 16 January 1924.
10. *Ibid.*, A9699/40/51. Count de Buena Esperanza to Under Secretary of State, Foreign Office (FO), 14 December 1921.
11. *Ibid.*, W3868/2/17. CO to FO, 6 May 1926.
12. *Ibid.*, W5383/2/17. BRC to CO (Message from President of Joint Court), 14 June 1926.
13. *Ibid.*, W5680/2/17. Count de Buena Esperanza to CO, 24 April 1926.
14. *Ibid.*, W7679/2/17. Telegramme from HC to Secretary of State for the Colonies, 17 July 1926.
15. *Ibid.*, W1716/646/17. Joint Order of 2 December 1926.
16. *Ibid.*, W8070/646/17. Anglo-French Agreement on the New Hebrides, signed 18 August 1927.
17. Joint Court Records.
18. Roberts, S.R. *A History*. . ., Vol. 2, p.541.
19. *L'Océanie Francaise*, 'Les intérets francais dans le Pacifique', no. 59, October-December 1921, p.100.
20. Roberts, S.R. *A History*. . ., Vol. 2, p.542.
21. COA A981, no.74. Copy of letter from British Embassy, Paris, to Prime Minister's Office, London, 1 June 1926.
22. Article in *L'Univers Financier*, 'Société immobilère des Nouvelles-Hébrides', 5 November 1924. Cited in FOR 371, W9679/9339/17.
23. Article in *L'Océanie Francaise*, 'Les intérets francais aux Nouvelles-

Hébrides', no. 137, July-August 1934, pp.66-71. Cited in COA A981, no.74.

24. New Hebrides Condominium. 'Rules of Procedure for the Registration of Land'.
25. *Protocol Respecting the New Hebrides signed at London on August 6, 1914, by the representatives of the British and French Governments,* Article XVII, section 3. Hereinafter cited as *Protocol.*
26. FOR 371, A4284/26/51. British Embassy Paris to Ministry of Foreign Affairs, 7 July 1923.
27. *Ibid.*, A6104/26/51. Ministry of Foreign Affairs to British Embassy, 12 October 1923.
28. Western Pacific High Commission, Confidential File 4/65, MP 405, no. 1a. Note to French Resident Commissioner [FRC] from President of Joint Court, 28 December 1927. Hereinafter cited as WPHC, CF 4/65.
29. *Ibid.*, MP 3096, no. 1. BRC to HC, 4 October 1928.
30. *Ibid.*
31. *Ibid.*, no. 2. HC to BRC, 3 December 1928.
32. *Ibid.*, no. 7. BRC to HC, 13 February 1929.
33. *Ibid.*, MP 1909, no. 1. BRC to HC, 2 July 1929.
34. *Ibid.*
35. *Ibid.*, no. 10a. BRC to FRC, 12 February 1929.
36. *Ibid.*, no. 16a. FRC to BRC, 13 December 1930.
37. *Ibid.*, no. 10. BRC to HC, 14 November 1929.
38. FOR 371 W1463/200/17. Secret Memorandum to the HC regarding Count de Buena Esperanza from the Acting BRC, 15 June 1931.
39. *Ibid.*
40. COA A981, no. 63. Letter from A. Larney to the BRC, 7 May 1928. Quoted in confidential report on 'The Joint Court and its Surveys' from F.E. Wallace to J.C. McLaren, Secretary to the Prime Minister, Canberra, 6 July 1931, p.3. Wallace was a solicitor appointed by the Government of the Commonwealth of Australia to deal with Commonwealth affairs — in particular, to handle the registration of Commonwealth land.
41. *Ibid.*
42. *Ibid.*, p.9.
43. FOR 371, W3001/247/17. BRC to HC, 20 December 1929.
44. *Ibid.*
45. WPHC, CF 4/65, MP 253, no. 6. BRC to HC, 20 January 1931.
46. *Ibid.*, no. 6c.
47. COA A981, no. 63, p.10.
48. *Ibid.*
49. *Ibid.*, Enclosure no. 2. Original letter from Mr. A. Larney to Mr. F.E. Wallace, 3 July 1931.
50. *Ibid.*, Enclosure no. 1. Copy of a letter from the President of the Joint Court, Count de Buena Esperanza, to Mr. A. Larney, Chief Surveyor, Joint Court, 18 May 1931.
51. *Ibid.*, pp.1-12.
52. *Ibid.*
53. *L'Océanie Francaise,* 'Les intérêts francais aux Nouvelles-Hébrides', no.

137, July-August 1934, p.67.

54. *Le Néo-Hébridais,* 'Le Crédit National: son aide á la Colonisation Franco-Néo-Hébrides', no. 157, May 1931, pp.1-2. See also, FOR 371, W4689/20/17. BRC to HC, 24 February 1933, for details on distribution of loans and repayment requirements.
55. *Ibid.*, 'Convention entre le Ministre des Colonies représentant l'État francais et la Société francaise de Nouvelles-Hébrides', Annex to *L'Océanie Francaise,* 'Les intérets francais aux Nouvelles-Hébrides', no. 137, July-August 1934, pp.66-71.
56. FOR 371, W8608/108/17. 'Report of the New Hebrides Committee', 22 July 1931. The committee was set up by the Imperial Conference of 1930 to examine the question of British interests in the New Hebrides and suggest possible options for the Government to follow.
57. Joint Court Records.
58. FOR 371, W7181/200/17. BRC to HC, 14 April 1932.
59. *Ibid.*
60. *Ibid.*, W362/2/17. Count de Buena Esperanza to CO, 9 February 1926.
61. *Ibid.*, W580/2/17. Count de Buena Esperanza to CO, 24 April 1926.
62. Joint Court. Judgments 116, 117, 118 and 120.
63. WPHC, CF4/65, MP 253, no. 5. Report of the President of the Joint Court to the Secretary of State for the Colonies, 15 January 1931.
64. *Ibid.*, MP 1283, no. 7a. Count de Buena Esperanza to Secretary of State for the Colonies, 15 October 1931.
65. *Ibid.*, no. 21. BRC to HC, 23 April 1932.
66. *Ibid.*, MP 1365, no. 48. Ministre des Affaires Etrangeres to Secretary of State for Colonies, 7 August 1932.
67. FOR 371, W12290/20/17. Report of conversation between representatives of British Embassy in Paris and the Ministre des Affaires Etrangeres, 24 October 1933.
68. *Ibid.*, A6196/2375/51. Count de Buena Esperanza to Under Secretary of State, FO, 20 December 1920.
69. *Ibid.*, W7414/63/17. British Ambassador in San Sebastian to FO, 2 August 1928.
70. *Ibid.*, W8077/10/17. BRC to HC, 31 May 1929. See also, W8047/247/17. British Embassy, Brussels to FO, 5 August 1930.
71. *Ibid.*, W9857/63/17. British Embassy, Brussels to FO, 11 October 1928.
72. WPHC, MP 2293, no. 1a. Secretary of State for Foreign Affairs, 'Exchange of Notes between His Majesty's Government in Britain and the French Government, modifying the Agreement of 18 August 1928 in regard to the New Hebrides', Paris, 1929.
73. *Ibid.*, MP 1368, no. 6. Secretary of State to HC, 7 September 1936.
74. FOR 371, W10796/10/17. Ministre des Affaires Etrangères to the British Ambassador in Paris, 20 September 1933.
75. *Ibid.*, W3682/2010/17. HC in Suva to HC in Noumea, 30 November 1931.
76. COA A981, no. 17. Letter from Ballard (Commonwealth Solicitor in Vila) to Secretary, Department of External Affairs, 14 September 1936.
77. FOR 371, W10713/2145/50. Report by M: Cruyl, Acting President of the Joint Court on the Work of the Court, July 1933, 27 July 1934.
78. *Ibid.*, W7152/111/50. British Embassy, Brussels to FO, 13 August 1935.

79. Joint Court Records.
80. WPHC, CF4/65, MP 1365, no. 25a. French Ambassador in London to Secretary of State, 17 November 1936.
81. *Protocol*, Article XXII, section 5.
82. *Ibid.*
83. *Ibid.*, Article XXIV, section 3.
84. *Ibid.*, Article XXVII, section 8.
85. Rules of Procedure for the Registration of Titles to Land, Articles 33, 35, and 44.
86. WPHC, CF4/65, MP 1365, no. 4. Despatch from Acting BRC to HC, 15 June 1931.
87. *Ibid.*
88. New Hebrides Presbyterian Mission Synod. 'Correspondence, 1927-1948'. Pacific Manuscripts Bureau, microfilm no. 561 (reel 1). Letter from Clerk of Synod (Basil Nottage) to the BRC, 24 August 1934. See also WPHC, CF4/65, MP 1836, no. 9a.
89. *Ibid.*, Letter from Nottage to BRC, 5 August 1936.
90. *Ibid.*, Letter from Nottage to Rev. F.B. Barton (President of Presbyterian Church of New Zealand), 21 August 1935.
91. Joint Court Records.
92. *Ibid.*, Judgments 25, 28, 74, 84, 10, 188, 189.
93. *Ibid.*, Judgment 333.
94. *Ibid.*, Judgments 30, 128, 129, 199.
95. *Ibid.*, Judgment 130.
96. *Ibid.*, Judgments 134, 116, 149, 201.
97. *Ibid.*, Judgment 134.
98. Louis, Simon. 'The Protection of 'Native' Interests in Applications for Registration of Titles Before the Joint Court', unpublished paper, p.37.
99. *Ibid.*, p.38.
100. Joint Court Records. Judgment 342.
101. *Ibid.*, Judgment 279. Except for six hectares registered in favour of the Presbyterian Church of Victoria, the remaining 1942 hectares of the island of Aniwa were made into a native reserve.
102. British Parliamentary Paper, Cd. 3288. 'Report by the High Commissioner for the Western Pacific on a visit to the New Hebrides — June-August, 1906', to Secretary of State, received 15 September 1906, Appendix, p.75.
103. WPHC, MP 1365, no. 11b. British Judge, W.D. Carew to BRC, 1 August 1935.
104. *Ibid.*
105. *Ibid.*, MP 637, no. 1a. 'A New Scheme for the Rapid Determination of Land Claims in the New Hebrides', January 1939.
106. *Ibid.*
107. FOR 371, Z1403/145/17. Foreign Office to M. Rene Pleven, Free French Headquarters, 29 March 1941.
108. *Ibid.*
109. *Ibid.*,MP 1365, no. 15b. French Judge (R. Janvier) to Judge Carew, 4 October 1935.
110. *Ibid.*, MP 637, no. 1a.

111. *Ibid.*, MP 1365, no. 31. Notes by BRC for discussion with HC, June 1937.
112. *Ibid.*, no. 33. Joint Court Order regarding new methods of survey, 26 September 1939.
113. FOR 371, W7181/200/17. BRC to HC, 14 April 1932.

Chapter 4

1. FOR 371, W7871/2236/50. Foreign Office to British Ambassador in Paris, 5 June 1939.
2. *Ibid.*, Z1403/145/17. Foreign Office to M. Rene Pleven, Free French Headquarters, 29 March 1941.
3. *Ibid.*, Z2987/145/17. Gen. de Gaulle to FO, 12 April 1941.
4. FOR 371, Z8817/8817/17. Senor Bosch Barrett to FO, 20 June 1945.
5. *Ibid.*, FO to British Ambassador in Paris, 30 January 1946.
6. *Ibid.*, Z5727/673/17. Ministre des Affaires Etrangères to British Ambassador, 7 June 1947.
7. References were made in the documents to correspondence relating to this issue, shown at F.O. 371 Z5727/1382/17, but they were missing from the Public Records Office archives.
8. Joint Court Records.
9. British Residency. Miscellaneous Papers. Letter from BRC to HC, 13 January 1962.
10. *Ibid.*, Letter dated 28 July 1960, quoted in Report from British and French District Agents, Central District 1.
11. *Ibid.*, Report from British District Agent, Central District 1, p.1.
12. *Ibid.*, pp.7-13.
13. *Ibid.*, Report from British District Agent, Northern District, p.3.
14. *Ibid.*, Report from British District Agent, Central District 1, p.7.
15. *Ibid.*, Letter from BRC to HC, 13 January 1962.
16. *Ibid.*
17. *Ibid.*, p.4.
18. *Ibid.*, Letter from BRC to FRC, 7 November 1961.
19. *Ibid.*
20. *Ibid.*
21. *Ibid.*
22. *Ibid.* Notes of Discussions between BRC and FRC, 17 November 1961.
23. *Ibid.*
24. *Ibid.*
25. Keith Woodward. Personal interview.
26. *Ibid.*
27. *Ibid.*
28. Joint Court Records.
29. *Ibid.*
30. Keith Woodward. Personal interview.
31. Joint Court Records.
32. Simpson, R. 'Memorandum on Land in the New Hebrides', pp. 1-2.
33. *Ibid.*, p.13.
34. *Ibid.*
35. *Ibid.*

36. *Ibid.*, p.14.
37. *Ibid.*, p.9.
38. *Ibid.*, p.14.
39. *Ibid.*, p.4-8.
40. Keith Woodward. Personal interview.
41. Advisory Council. Session 11, 10 December 1965, p.225.
42. *Ibid.*
43. *Ibid.*
44. *Ibid.*
45. Keith Woodward. Personal interview.
46. Advisory Council, Session 11, 10 December 1965, p.207.
47. *Ibid.*, p.227.
48. *Ibid.*
49. Keith Woodward. Personal interview.
50. *Ibid.*
51. British Residency Confidential Files, 275/7 Bonkovia, no. 9. Acting BRC to FRC, 15 June 1966. Hereinafter cited as BRCF 275/7.
52. *Ibid.*
53. *Ibid.*, Comment by Keith Woodward.
54. *Ibid.*
55. *Ibid.*, No. 70. Summary of Bonkovia Land Dispute.
56. Joint Court. Judgment 342.
57. BRCF 275/7 Bonkovia, No. 70. Summary of Bonkovia Land Dispute.
58. *Ibid.*
59. *Ibid.*, No. 26. Letter from FRC to BRC, 23 August 1966.
60. *Ibid.*
61. *Ibid.*, No. 28. BRC to FRC, 15 September 1966.
62. *Ibid.*, No. 48. BDA to BRC, 28 January 1967.
63. *Ibid.*, No. 69. BRC to Foreign and Commonwealth Office, 26 February 1970.
64. Keith Woodward. Personal interview.
65. *Ibid.*
66. BRFC 272/11 Buluk/Stephens (Vol. II), No. 8.
67. *Ibid.*
68. *Ibid.*
69. *Ibid.*, No. 7.
70. *Ibid.*
71. *Ibid.*
72. *Ibid.*, No. 9.
73. *Ibid.*, No. 22.
74. Résidence de France. Synthese Mensuelle, February 1967, p.4. Hereinafter cited as RFSM.
75. *Ibid.*
76. BRCF 355/77, No. 4, 4 July 1972.
77. RFSM, April 1968, p.7.
78. *Ibid.*, July 1969, Annex: Letter from BRC, Colin Allan, to FRC.
79. *Ibid.*, September 1969, p.2.
80. *Ibid.*, March 1971, p.8.
81. Keith Woodward. Personal interview.

82. There was always control over the entry of British subjects, but not over French nationals. The French argued that under the French Constitution their nationals could not be kept out of any French territory despite the fact that Vanuatu was not a French territory, but a region of joint administration with the British.
83. RFSM, September 1971, p.7.
84. Thompson, V. and Adloff, R. *The French Pacific Islands*, pp. 307-18.
85. *Ibid.*, p.66-77.
86. RFSM, October 1969.
87. *Ibid.*
88. *Ibid.*
89. *Ibid.*
90. *Ibid.*
91. *Ibid.*, July 1972.
92. *Ibid.*, October 1969.
93. *Ibid.*
94. *Ibid.*
95. *Ibid.*
96. *Ibid.*
97. *Ibid.*, April 1968.
98. Société Francaise des Nouvelles-Hébrides. Typed information sheet given to me by M. Elziere, Director of SFNH, outlining company structure and history.
99. RFSM, May 1968.
100. *Ibid.*
101. *Ibid.*
102. *Ibid.*
103. *Ibid.*
104. French Residency., *Compte Rendu d'Execution de la Convention passée entre la SFNH et l'Etat Francais le 19 November 1973*, pp.4-7. Personal copy. The Convention is included in this report on the total project.
105. *Ibid.*, pp. 31-2, 47.
106. *Ibid.*, pp. 4-5.
107. *Ibid.*, pp. 8-9, 34.
108. Ballard, B.C., 'Australian Land Interest...', p.286.
109. *Ibid.*
110. Commonwealth of Australia, 'Records Relating to the Pacific', A 1108, Vol. 6, Minute Paper from Attorney General: Commonwealth of Australia, 21 December 1909. Hereinafter cited as COA.
111. BRCF 211/7, 'New Hebrides Land Trust Board', Background Paper.
112. *Ibid.*
113. *Ibid.*
114. COA A 981, No. 59. 'New Hebrides Land: Court fees and related financial matters', May 1934, p.24a.
115. A Mr. Woolcott arrived in 1910, followed by Mr. F.G. Wallow in 1912 and Mr. B.C, Ballard in 1934, who was involved up to the 1970s.
116. BRCF 211/7. 'New Hebrides Land Trust Board'.
117. Ballard, B.C. 'Australian Land Interests...' p.287.
118. Stober, W. 'The Land Trust Board', in Peter Lamour (ed), *Land Tenure in*

Vanuatu, p.6.

119. Great Britain. Queens Regulation No. 7 of 1973, 'To Amend the Land Trust Board Regulation of 1973'.
120. Ballard, B.C. 'Australian Land Interests...' p.287.
121. BRCF 211/7. 'New Hebrides Land Trust Board'. Opening speech of the British Resident Commissioner', 3 December 1974.
122. Stober, W. 'The Land Trust Board', pp. 36-41.
123. *Ibid.*, pp.41-2.
124. BRCF 211/7, No. 30. Annex to note on Agenda item 7 of Land Trust Board meeting of 17 May 1976.
125. Stober, W. 'The Land Trust Board', pp. 40-1.
126. *New Hebrides News*, No. 44, 12 January 1977.
127. Stober, W. 'The Land Trust Board', pp.42-3.
128. Presbyterian Church. General Assembly Minutes of 1955, p.18.
129. *Ibid.*, 1959, pp. 37-8.
130. *Ibid.*, 1961, pp. 24-5.
131. *Ibid.*, 1965, p.26.
132. *Ibid.*, 1966, p.27.
133. *Ibid.*, 1971, p.14.
134. *Ibid.*, 1967, pp. 34-5.
135. *Ibid.*, 1971, p.48.
136. Discussion with Barak Sope, Secretary General of the Vanua'aku Pati and member of the Fila Island Land Committee.
137. Discussion with Sethy Regenvanu, former member of the Property Trust Committee and Minister of Lands from 1980 to 1982 and 1983.
138. Advisory Council — Session 17, 2 October 1969, pp. 55-63.
139. Keith Woodward. Personal interview.
140. Lawrence, J. 'Report of visit to the New Hebrides from 20-26 February 1972,' dated 12 April 1972.
141. *Ibid.*
142. Lawrence, J. 'Report of visit to the New Hebrides from 9-16 March 1975', dated 28 April 1975.
143. Fleming, J. 'Land Tenure in the New Hebrides: Policy Proposals' paragraphs D24-40 and E1-3, September 1973. Cyclostyled.
144. Lawrence, J. 'Report of visit... 9-16 March 1975'.
145. *Ibid.*
146. *Ibid.*
147. *Ibid.*
148. Record of 'Anglo-French Ministerial Talks on the New Hebrides between the Parliamentary Under-Secretary of State and the French Minister of Overseas Departments and Territories, held at the Foreign and Commonwealth Office on 4 and 5 November 1974'. Personal copy.
149. *Ibid.*
150. *Ibid.*

Chapter 5

1. Kelly, C. *La Australia Del Espiritu Santo*, pp. 202-38.
2. Shineberg, D. *They Came for Sandalwood*, p.130.

3. Western Pacific High Commission (WPHC). Confidential File 4/65, Minute Paper (MP) 3096, No. 1. British Resident Commissioner (BRC) to High Commissioner (HC), 4 October 1928.
4. Scarr, D. *Fragments of Empire*, pp. 203-4.
5. WPHC. Inward Correspondence 1892, MP 88 — Report from Lt. Com. Bremer to Admiral Scott, 28 March 1892.
6. WPHC. Inward Correspondence 1887, MP 205. Letter from G. de Latour to Rear Admiral Fairfax, 10 March 1887.
7. Scarr, D. *Fragments of Empire*, p.203.
8. *Ibid.*
9. Thompson, R.C. *Australian Imperialism...*, p.137 and Deryck Scarr, *Fragments of Empire*, p.215.
10. WPHC. Inward Correspondence 1892, MP 88.
11. WPHC. Inward Correspondence 1892, MP 133. Correspondence relating to Sayer murder.
12. Guiart, J. 'Forerunners of Melanesian Nationalism', p.86.
13. Commonwealth of Australia (COA), 'Records Relating to the Pacific', A981, No. 65. Report from the acting Commandant of the Constabulary to the British Resident Commissioner, 20 August 1923.
14. *Ibid.* Letter from the British Resident Commissioner to the Western Pacific High Commissioner, 14 September 1923.
15. *Ibid.* Report from the acting Commandant of the Constabulary to the British Resident Commissioner, 20 August 1923.
16. Guiart, J. 'Forerunners...', p.86.
17. Hours, B. '... Le Nagriamel', p.235.
18. Miller, J.G. 'Naked Cult...' pp. 330-2.
19. *Ibid*, pp. 332-5.
20. Presbyterian Mission Synod Correspondence. PMB 561(2). Report from Santo to British Resident Commissioner, 16 July 1944.
21. Geshin, Y. 'Les Américans...', pp. 245-86.
22. Great Britain. *Condominium of the New Hebrides, Colonial Office Report,* 1949/50, p.31.
23. *Ibid*, 1957/58, p.25.
24. *Ibid.*
25. *Ibid.*, 1961/62, p.5.
26. *Ibid.*, 1963/64, p.37.
27. Joint Court Records. Judgment 442, 10 November 1951.
28. *Ibid.*
29. *Ibid.*, Interpretative Judgment, 17 June 1959.
30. *Ibid.*
31. Tanafo is sometimes called Fanafo and Vanafo.
32. British Residency Confidential File (BRCF), 272/11 (Vol. 1), No. 6.
33. *Ibid.*
34. *Ibid.*
35. BRCF 272/11 (Vol. 1), No. 1.
36. *Ibid.*, No. 12.
37. *Ibid.*
38. *Ibid.*
39. *Ibid.*

40. *Ibid.*
41. Interview with Jimmy Stephens. October 1977.
42. *Ibid.*
43. Hours, B. 'Leadership et Cargo cult...' p.211.
44. *Ibid.*, pp. 210-1.
45. Interview with Jimmy Stephens. October 1977.
46. Plant, C. (ed). *New Hebrides...*, p.35.
47. *Ibid.*, p.36. Also see Hours, B. 'Un Mouvement...', pp. 233-4.
48. Interview with Jimmy Stephens.
49. BRCF 272/11 (Vol. 1), No. 18a.
50. *Ibid.*, No. 22.
51. *Ibid.*, No. 26.
52. *Ibid.*, No. 36a.
53. *Ibid.*, No. 59.
54. *Ibid.*, No. 78.
55. *Ibid.*, No. 97.
56. BRCF 272/11 (Vol. 11), No. 29a.
57. Advisory Council, Session 16, 19 December 1968, p.5.
58. Résidence de France. Synthese Mensuelle (RFSM), January 1967, p.6.
59. Joint Regulation No. 27 of 1966.
60. BRCF 272/11 (Vol. 1), No. 49.
61. *Ibid.*, No. 74.
62. BRCF 272/11 (Vol. 1), No. 52.
63. *Ibid.*, No. 100.
64. *Ibid.*
65. *Ibid.*
66. Laracy, H. 'Marching Rule...', pp. 96-114.
67. BRCF 272/11 (Vol. 1), No. 91.
68. RFSM, April 1968, p.2.
69. *Ibid.*, May 1968, pp. 2-3.
70. *Ibid.*, August 1968, p.1.
71. *Ibid.*, July 1968, pp. 3-4.
72. *Ibid.*, June 1968, p.3.
73. *Ibid.*, November 1968, p.7.
74. British Residency, Miscellaneous Papers — M. Wilshire Webb to Jimmy Stephens, 1 August 1969.
75. *Ibid.*
76. RFSM, May 1970, pp. 8-9.
77. *Ibid.*, June 1969, p.6.
78. *Ibid.*, February 1969, p.4.
79. *Ibid.*, May 1970, pp. 8-9.
80. *Ibid.*, November 1969, p.7.
81. *Ibid.*, April 1970, p.4.
82. *Fiji Times*, 6 March 1971.
83. RFSM, March 1971, p.3.
84. *Ibid.*, May 1970, p.9.
85. *Ibid.*, July 1970, p.6.
86. *Ibid.*, February 1971, p.6.
87. *Ibid.*, June 1971, p.8.

88. *Ibid.*, January 1971, p.7.
89. *Ibid.*, June 1971, p.8.
90. *Ibid.*, November 1971, p.5.
91. *Ibid.*, July 1973, p.5 and September 1973, p.8.
92. Oliver, M. *A New Constitution...*, pp. 11-26.
93. *Ibid.*, pp. 89-94.
94. Plant, C. 'The Nagriamel...', p.52.
95. *Fiji Times*, 22 June 1972.
96. Plant, C. 'The Nagriamel...', p.53, 6-8.
97. Confidential private source.
98. RFSM, August 1974, p.4.
99. Plant, C. 'The Nagriamel...', p.54.
100. *Ibid.*, p.55.
101. Plant, C. (ed). *New Hebrides...*', p.88.
102. *Ibid.*, p.88 and RFSM, December 1975, pp. 5-6.
103. RFSM, January 1976, pp. 6-7.
104. *Ibid.*
105. *Fiji Times*, 16 January 1976.
106. *Ibid.* In 1973 the Fletcher Mint also sold gold coins to the Prime Minister of Solomon Islands, Solomon Mamaloni, resulting in a vote of no-confidence being passed against him by Parliament.
107. Plant, C. 'The Nagriamel...', p.55.
108. RFSM, March 1976, pp. 1-12.
109. *Ibid.*, p.6.
110. *Ibid.*, February 1976, p.3.
111. *Ibid.*, March 1976, pp. 6-7.
112. *Ibid.*, January 1976, pp. 6-7.
113. *Ibid.*, March 1976, p.1.
114. *Ibid.*, December 1975, p.3.
115. When the Chamorro Islands gained their independence from France in 1973, the French community on the Island of Mayotte — supported by the French military — seceded and remained under French Government control.
116. Sawer, M. and Jupp J. 'The New Hebrides...', p.26.
117. RFSM, March 1976, p.7.
118. *Pacific Islands Monthly*, July 1969, p.23.
119. *Ibid.*, July 1971, p.39.
120. RFSM, January 1967, p.6 and BRFC 272/11 (Vol. 1), No. 67.
121. Allen, M. '... Christianity and Cash-cropping...', p.42.
122. *Ibid.*, pp. 34-6.
123. *Ibid.*, pp. 37-8.
124. *Ibid.*, p.44.
125. BRFC 272/11 (Vol. 1), No. 77.
126. Allen, M. '... Christianity', p.45.
127. *Ibid.*, p.46.
128. BRFC 272/11 (Vol. 1), No. 77.
129. RFSM, June 1967, pp. 5-6.
130. Guiart, J. 'Forerunners...', pp. 87-8; 'John Frum...', pp. 165-77; 'Culture Contact...', pp. 105-16; Rice, E., *John Frum You Come.*

131. Guiart, J. 'Le Mouvement Cooperatif...', p.244.
132. *Ibid.*
133. *Ibid.*, pp. 245-6.
134. *Ibid.*, p.247.
135. Interview with Jimmy Stephens.
136. Hours, B. 'Un Mouvement...', pp. 210-11.
137. Interview with Jimmy Stephens.
138. Hours, B. 'Un Mouvement...', p.239.
139. BRCF 272 (Vol. 1), Comment 77.
140. Interview with Jimmy Stephens.
141. *Ibid.*
142. *Ibid.*
143. *Ibid.*
144. *Ibid.*
145. *Ibid.*
146. Guiart, J. 'La situation politique...', p.3.
147. RFSM, June 1970, p.3.
148. *Pacific Islands Monthly*, July 1971, p.39.
149. RFSM, January 1975, p.6.
150. Nagriamel files were seized in 1980 following the collapse of the rebellion, but these were not available to the public at the time this was written.
151. Advisory Council, Session 18, 16 December 1969, pp. 327-8.
152. *Ibid.*
153. *Ibid.*
154. *New Hebrides Viewpoint*, No. 16.
155. Interview with Jimmy Stephens.

Chapter 6

1. Joint Court Records. Judgment 685.
2. *Ibid.* Judgment 687.
3. *Ibid.* Judgment 693.
4. Guiart, J. 'Les Nouvelles-Hébrides...'
5. Interview with Chief David and Kenere Williams of Tautu Village.
6. *Ibid.*
7. *Ibid.*
8. *Ibid.*
9. *Ibid.*
10. *Ibid.*
11. Guiart, J. 'Les Nouvelles-Hébrides...'
12. *Ibid.*
13. *Ibid.*
14. Interview with Chief David and Kenere Williams.
15. British Residency Confidential File [BRCF] 278/6, No. 1. Touring Notes on British District Agent, 5 May 1963.
16. *Ibid.*
17. Interview with Chief David and Kenere Williams.
18. BRCF 278/6, No. 5. Report from British District Agent to British Resident Commissioner, 3 September 1965.

19. *Ibid.*
20. *Ibid.*
21. Joint Court Records. Judgments 959, 689, 980-983.
22. BRCF 278/6, No. 8. Report from British Agent to British Resident Commissioner, 7 October 1965.
23. *Ibid.*, No. 12. British District Agent to British Resident Commissioner, 27 October 1965.
24. *Ibid.*, No. 9. Letter from Chief David of Tautu village to British and French Resident Commissioners, 10 October 1965.
25. Interview with Chief David and Kenere Williams.
26. BRCF 278/6, No. 25. Report from British District Agent to British Resident Commissioner, 16 October 1967.
27. *Ibid.*, No. 20. Letter from Manager of PRNH to the British and French Resident Commissioners, 20 September 1967.
28. *Ibid.*, No. 28. Notes on a meeting held at Tautu village, 19 October 1967.
29. *Ibid.*, No. 37. British District Agent to British and French Resident Commissioners, 22 November 1967.
30. *Ibid.*, No. 38. British Resident Commissioner to British District Agent, 9 December 1967.
31. *Ibid.*, No. 39. Notes on discussion between British and French Resident Commissioners, 122 December 1967.
32. *Ibid.*, No. 46. Report of a meeting at the French Residency between Chief David and M. Tanguy, manager of PRNH, 3 February 1968.
33. *Ibid.*, No. 52. Report on meeting with Tautu people, March 1968.
34. *Ibid.*, No. 61. Notes on meeting between French and British Resident Commissioners, 7 August 1968.
35. *Ibid.*, No. 67. Report from British District Agent, November 1969.
36. *Ibid.*, No. 86. British District Agent to British Resident Commissioner, 6 February 1974.
37. BRCF 215/2/5. Joint Communique by the Resident Commissioners of France and Britain, 28 January 1975.
38. *Ibid.*
39. *Ibid.*

Chapter 7

1. Joint Court Records. Judgment 27.
2. *Ibid.*
3. *Ibid.* Judgment 42.
4. *Ibid.* Judgments 32, 40, 47, 50 and 51.
5. *Ibid.* Jdgments 33, 35 and 43.
6. *Ibid.* Judgment 57.
7. *Ibid.*
8. *Ibid.*
9. *Ibid.*
10. *Ibid.*
11. British Residency Confidential File (BRCF) 271/39, No. 3. Letter from Chief Graham Kalsakau and other officials of Fila Island to the two Resident Commissioners, 4 November 1964.

12. Joint Court Records. Judgment 247.
13. BRCF 271/39, No. 3. Letter from Chief Graham Kalsakau and other officials of Fila Island to the two Resident Commissioners, 4 November, 1964.
14. BRCF 271/39, No. 9. Letter from British and French Resident Commissioners to Chief Graham Kalsakau, March 1965.
15. *Ibid.*
16. Advisory Council. Session 11, 10 December 1965, pp. 225-6.
17. *Ibid.*
18. *Ibid.*
19. BRCF 271/17, No. 10. Joint letter from British and French District Agents of Central District 1 to the Resident Commissioners, 2 September 1967.
20. *Ibid.*, No. 64. Note on discussion concerning land for Vila wharf, 19 April 1969.
21. BRCF 214/2/3, No. 20. Notes on meeting between representatives of the two Residencies and members of the Fila Island Land Committee, 3 September 1974.
22. BRCF 214/2/4, No. 9. Letter from W. Stober of the British Residency to Mr. B. Sope, 1 April 1976.
23. BRCF 271/39, No. 39. Copy of letter from B. Sope for the Fila Island Land Committee to Frouin. Not dated.
24. *Ibid.*
25. BRCF 271/39, No. 40. Report of meeting between the French District Agent and members of the Fila Island Land Commitee from British District Agent to British Resident Commissioner, 10 January 1974.
26. *Ibid.*, Report of Speech before the two Resident Commissioners.
27. BRCF 214/2/4. Report on Fila Island Land Problems, 21 September 1977.
28. *Ibid.*, No. 20. Letter from Fila Island Land Committee to the Shell Co. Ltd., confirming agreement reached, 7 September 1976.
29. *Ibid.*, No. 45. Letter from Fila Island Land Committee to the Shell Co. Ltd. confirming agreement reached, 7 September 1976.
30. *Ibid.*, Letter from Fila Island Land Committee to Mayor and Councillors of Port Vila, 26 October 1977.
31. *Ibid.*, 10. Notes on a meeting between the High Commissioners of Great Britain and France and representatives of the Fila Island Land Committee, 17 March 1977.
32. BRCF 217/39, Comment 63. Analysis of the situation regarding the occupation of Frouin land by Fila Islanders, 6 March 1974.
33. *Ibid.*, No. 46. Telegramme from the British Resident Commissioner to the Foreign and Commonwealth Office, 12 March 1974.
34. Discussions with Barak Sope.

Chapter 8

1. Plant, Chris (ed). *Nouvelles Hebrides*..., p.24.
2. *Ibid.*
3. Lini, Walter. *Beyond Pandemonium*..., pp. 24-5.

4. Vanua'aku Pati Files (VPF) circular sent to interested people in August explaining the aims of the New Hebrides National Party.
5. Residence de France. Synthèse Mensuelle (RFSM) — August 1971.
6. Plant, Chris (ed). *New Hebrides*, p.26.
7. *Ibid.*
8. *Ibid.*
9. RFSM. January 1971.
10. *Ibid.*
11. Plant, Chris (ed). *New Hebrides*, p. 26-7.
12. *Ibid.*
13. Sope, Barak. *Land and Politics*. . ., p.34.
14. *Ibid.*, p.33.
15. *Ibid.*, p.35.
16. RFSM, January 1973. Text of final Resolutions of the SPADES Conference, 11 to 26 January, 1973.
17. *Ibid.*
18. Sope, Barak. *Land and Politics,* p.36.
19. Plant, Chris (ed). *New Hebrides*, pp. 30-1.
20. New Hebrides National Party policy published in *Nakamal*, No. 46, 14 February 1974, p.3.
21. Matas-Kele, Kalkot. "A Political Groundswell in the New Hebrides", *Pacific Islands Monthly*, May 1974, p.42.
22. *Ibid.*, pp. 28-9.
23. *Ibid.*, p.47.
24. *Ibid.*, pp. 48-9.
25. *Ibid.*, p.29.
26. *Ibid.*
27. *Ibid.*, pp.30-1.
28. *Ibid.*
29. RFSM, May 1974.
30. *Ibid.*, September — November 1973.
31. *Ibid.*, November 1973.
32. Interview with Keith Woodward.
33. British Residency Miscellaneous Papers. "Land Tenure in the New Hebrides: Policy Proposals", by J.T. Fleming, September 1973, pp. 6-7.
34. *Ibid.*, p.3.
35. *Ibid.*, pp. 3-4.
36. *New Hebrides Viewpoints*. "Unifying Land Laws in the New Hebrides", No. 17, July 1976.
37. RFSM, August 1973.
38. Discussion with Kalkot Matas-Kele, September 1977.
39. *Ibid.*, July 1974.
40. *Ibid.*, August 1974.
41. *Ibid.*, July 1974.
42. *New Hebrides News,* No. 11, 9 April 1974.
43. *Ibid.*, 10 September 1974.
44. *Ibid.*
45. RFSM, September 1974, p.5.
46. Woodward, Keith. *Historical Summary*. . ., p.76.

47. *Ibid.*
48. RFSM, May 1972.
49. *Ibid.*, July 1982.
50. *Ibid.*, June 1974.
51. Woodward, Keith. *Historical Summary*, p.8. See also RFSM, June 1975.
52. *New Hebrides News.* No. 38, 29 August 1975.
53. RFSM, October 1975.
54. *Ibid.*, September 1975.
55. *Ibid.*, October 1975.
56. *Ibid.*
57. *Ibid.*
58. *Ibid.*
59. *New Hebrides News.* No. 43, 24 November 1975.
60. Plant, Chris (ed). *New Hebrides*, pp. 77-87.
61. Woodward, Keith. *Historical Summary*, pp. 30-1.
62. *Ibid.*, p.29.
63. Vanua'aku Pati Files. "National Party Actions", 5th Party Congress, January 1977.
64. Woodward, Keith. *Historical Summary*, pp. 47-9.
65. *Ibid.*, pp. 62-5.
66. *Ibid.*, p.75.
67. *Vanuaaku Viewpoints*, Vol. 8, No. 1, p.9.
68. *Ibid.*, Vol. 8, No. 2, p.11.
69. Woodward, Keith. *Historical Summary*, p.67.
70. *Vanuaaku Viewpoints*, Vol. 8, No. 3, p.9.
71. *New Hebrides News*, No. 97, 8 April 1978.
72. *Nabanga*, No. 86, 22 August 1978.
73. *Ibid.*
74. *Ibid.*
75. Molisa, Grace, et.al. "Vanuatu...", pp.91-2.
76. RFSM, September 1978. Copy of letter from Vincent Boulekone to the President of the UCNH, Annex II. See also, *New Hebrides News*, No. 109, 23 September 1978.
77. "Report of the Ad Hoc Land Reform Committee Recommendations to the Representative Assembly". Included in *Representative Assembly Summarized Record of Proceedings*, May 1979.
78. Narokobi, Bernard, in Peter Larmour (ed). *Land, People and Government*, p.150.
79. *Constitution of the Republic of Vanuatu.* Chapter 3.
80. Narokobi, Bernard, p.151.
81. *Constitution of the Republic of Vanuatu.* Chapter 3.
82. Narokobi, Bernard, p.152.
83. *Ibid.*, p.154.
84. Discussion with Barak Sope.
85. Ministry of Lands. "Communique: Land Policy". Included in University of the South Pacific, *Report of the Regional Conference on Land Management.*
86. *Nabanga*, No. 157, 20 May 1980, p.11.
87. *Ibid.*

88. University of the South Pacific. *Report of the Regional Conference on Land Management*, p.54.
89. Ministry of Lands. Land Reform Regulation.
90. This section was amended in 1981 to effect that undeveloped portions of registered properties were excluded from the and which a former alienator was entitled to occupy.
91. *Constitution of the Republic of Vanuatu*. Chapter 13.
92. *Ibid.*, Chapter 15, Section 94[1], p.20.
93. *Nabanga*, No. 152, 29 March 1980, p.2.
94. *Ibid.*
95. *Ibid.*
96. The same constitution was produced for each of the federations, while that for the Confederation of Natakoro provided a loose structure linking all five political units.
97. Vemarana Development Corporation. "An Investment in the Vemarana Federation", p.2.
98. *Ibid.*, p.3.
99. *Ibid.*, p.4.
100. *Ibid.*, p.5.
101. MacClancy, Jeremy. "From New Hebrides...", p.95.
102. *Ibid.*, p.98.
103. Translation from French of Inspector General Robert's speech to Santo residents, 23 July 1980.
104. Guiart, Jean. "The Vanuatu Experience...", pp. 9-13.
105. MacClancy, Jeremy. "From New Hebrides...", p.103.
106. Molisa, Grace, et. al. "Vanuatu...", p.97.
107. *Ibid.*, p.100.
108 .*La Presse Calédonienne.* 10 November 1980. Letter from Philippe Delacroix to Dijoud.

BIBLIOGRAPHY

Official Documents

British Residency. Confidential Files.
CF211/7 New Hebrides Land Trust Board
CF214/2/3 Vila Wharf/Fila Island Land Matters
CF214/2/4 Fila Island Land Matters General
CF271/17 Fila Wharf & Rodin Land. 3 Vols.
CF271/39 Lands: Narrowby
CF272/11 Buluk/Stephens. 2 Vols.

———. Miscellaneous Papers Relating to Land Matters.

Commonwealth of Australia. Records Relating to the Pacific. Australian Archives, Canberra.
A981 Correspondence Files, c.1927-42, New Hebrides
A1108 Correspondence and papers relating to external affairs assembled by Director of the Pacific Branch, Major E.L. Piesse

———. Report of Royal Commission on Mail Services and Trade Development between Australia and the New Hebrides. Victoria: Parliament, 1915.

Des Granges Papers. Microfilm. Vanuatu Cultural Centre.

Fiji Government. *Royal Fiji Gazette.*

Great Britain. Foreign and Colonial Office Printed Documents.
'Correspondence Respecting the New Hebrides Joint Naval Commission, 1886-87'. C.5648.
'Further Correspondence Respecting the New Hebrides Joint Naval Commission, January-February, 1988'. C.5687.
'New Hebrides Commission: Minutes of the Proceedings of the New Hebrides Commission, Held at the Foreign Office, London, February 1 to 27, 1906'. C.8721.
'Correspondence Relating to the Convention with France, Dated 20th October 1906, Respecting the New Hebrides'. Cd.3288.

'Exchange of Notes between The United Kingdom and France. Arrangements under Article X, Section 4, of the Convention of October 20, 1906, Respecting the New Hebrides'. Cd.3876.

'Proceedings of the New Hebrides Conference, held at the Foreign Office, London, June 10 to August 6, 1914'. 2 Vols. No number given.

'Notes Exchanged between the British and French Governments Respecting the New Hebrides Protocol of August 6, 1914'. Cmd.1827.

_______. *New Hebrides Condominium: Colonial Office Reports.* Published every two years from 1949 to 1974.

_______. Foreign Office Records. F0371 Political. Public Records Office, London.

_______. Queen's Regulation No. 14 of 1973, 'TO PROVIDE for the establishment of a Land Trust Board'. Published at the Office of the Resident Commissioner for the New Hebrides, 31 October 1973.

_______. Queen's Regulation No. 7 of 1976, 'TO AMEND the Land Trust Board Regulation of 1973'. Published at Resident Commission of the New Hebrides, 2 July 1976.

New Hebrides Condominium. Advisory Council Minutes.

_______. Census of the Population and Housing of Vila and Santo, 29 October 1972. 2 Vols. Vila: Bureau of Statistics, 1973.

_______. Joint Court Records.

_______. *Joint Regulations of the New Hebrides: comprising a consolidated edition of the Joint Regulations in force on the 18th day of October 1973.* Prepared under the authority of the Resident Commissioners. 3 Vols.

_______. *New Hebrides Condominium Gazette.*

_______. *Protocol Respecting the New Hebrides signed at London on August 6, 1914, by representatives of the British and French Governments, Ratifications exchanged at London, March 18, 1922.* Treaty Series No. 7, His Majesty's Stationary Office, London 1922.

_______. Representative Assembly Summarised Record of Proceedings.

_______. 'Rules for the Registration of Titles to Land'. A photocopy of a typed version was provided by the Registrar of Titles at the Joint Court. The entire set of rules has been reproduced as Annex V in Howard Van Trease, *The History of Land and Property Rights in Vanuatu*, PhD Thesis, USP, 1984.

Presbyterian Church. Assembly Minutes. Located at Presbyterian Church Office, Port Vila.

_______. Miscellaneous Correspondence Relating to Land, 1945-62.

Microfilm: PMB566.
______. Mission Council Minutes, 1949-66. Microfilm: PMB562.
______. Mission Council Reports, 1950-56. Microfilm: PMB563.
Presbyterian Mission. Land and Titles Committee. Located at Presbyterian Church Office, Port Vila.
______. Reports of the Mission Ship *Dayspring*. Nos. 1-38 (1864-1902).
Presbyterian Mission Synod. Correspondence, 1927-48. Microfilm: PMB561. 3 reels.
______. Minutes, 1857-1938. Microfilm: PMB31.
Résidence de France. Synthèse Mensuelle. Confidential monthly reports from the French Resident Commissioner to the Minister for Overseas Departments and Territories. Vanuatu National Archives, Port Vila.
Vanuatu Government. *Constitution of the Republic of Vanuatu.*
______. Ministry of Lands. Miscellaneous documents.
______. *Report on the Census of Population 1979.* Vol. 1: Basic Tables. Port Vila: National Planning and Statistics Office, 1983.
Vanua'aku Pati Files.
Vemarana Federation. 'An Investment in the Vemarana Federation'. Vemarana Development Corporation, 1980.
______. Constitution of Banks and Torres Federation.
______. Constitution of Confederation of Natakoro.
______. Constitution of Tafea Federation.
______. Constitution of Vemarana Federation.
Western Pacific High Commission.
Inward Correspondence, General. Files seen: 1875-1914.
Register of Land Claims, Books A, B and C.
Confidential File 4/65. Correspondence relating to the establishment of the New Hebrides Condominium Land Court, land registration procedures and protection of native rights, 1928-1939. Microfilm. London: Foreign and Commonwealth Office Library.

Unpublished Manuscripts

Allen, Michael R. 'Report on Aoba: Incidental Papers on Ndui Ndui District, Aoba Island, New Hebrides'. Papers resulting from research work from 1958 to 1961 and written for the British Residency. Edited by Caroline Leaney.
Bennett, A.M. 'A Historical Survey of Land Transactions on Iririki Island, Efate, New Hebrides'. Essay submitted as part of a University of the South Pacific course. Vila, 1976.

Bonnemaison, Joel. 'Territorial Control and Mobility within New Hebridean Society'. ORSTOM, 1976. (Cyclostyled).

Fleming J. 'Land Tenure in the New Hebrides: Policy Proposals'. September 1973. Cyclostyled, Personal Copy.

Guiart, Jean. 'La situation politique aux Nouvelles Hebrides'. Unpublished paper dated 15th February 1980, Paris.

_______. 'Race Relations in the New Hebrides'. 1980. (Cyclostyled).

Lawrence, Jerry. 'Report of visit to the New Hebrides from 20-26 February 1972'. Dated 12 April 1972. Personal Copy.

_______. 'Report of visit to the New Hebrides from 9-16 March 1975'. Dated 28 April 1975. Personal Copy.

Lindstrom, Lamont. 'Structure in Name Only (Tanna, Vanuatu)'. Unpublished paper dealing with research on Tanna 1978/79.

Louis, Simon. 'The Protection of Native Interests in Applications for Registration of Titles Before the Joint Court'. USP, 1974.

Philibert, Jean-Marc. 'La Bonne Vie: Le Reve et la Realite. Changements Socio-culturels aux Nouvelles-Hebrides'. PhD thesis. University of British Columbia, 1976.

Rodman, Margaret. ' A Semiotic Approach to Customary Land Tenure: The Grounding of Self in Longana, Vanuatu'. Department of Anthropology, University of Waterloo, Canada, 1982.

_______. 'Custom and Illusion: Traditional Land Tenure and New Forms of Social Inequality in Vanuatu Peasantry'. Department of Anthropology, University of Waterloo, Canada, 1982. Thompson, Roger C. *Australian Imperialism and the New Hebrides, 1862-1922*. PhD Thesis. Australian National University, 1970.

Simpson, R. 'Memorandum on Land in the New Hebrides'. Personal Copy.

Van Trease, Howard. 'The History of Land and Property Rights in Vanuatu'. PhD Thesis, USP, 1984.

Woodward, Keith. 'Historical Summary of Constitutional Advance in the New Hebrides, 1954-1977'. Port Vila: British Residency, 1978. (Cyclostyled monograph).

Newspapers and Journals

Bulletin de Residence de France.

Fiji Times.

Le Néo-Hébridais. Nos. 1-314. Dec. 1909 — Dec. 1944. Published by L.G. Frouin, Port Vila.

L'Océanie Francaise.

Nabanga. French Residency.

Nakamal. Port Vila.

New Hebrides News. British Residency.

New Hebrides Viewpoints. New Hebrides National Party.

Vanuaaku Viewpoints. Vanua'aku Pati.

Pacific Islands Monthly.

The New Hebrides Magazine: A Journal of Missionary and General Information regarding the New Hebrides. Nos. 1-41. Oct. 1900 — Oct. 1911. New Hebrides Presbyterian Mission Synod.

Published Works

Alexander, Gilchrist, 1927. *From the Middle Temple to the South Seas.* London: John Murray.

Allen, Michael R., 1967. 'The Torres, Banks and Northern New Hebrides'. In *Male Cults and Secret Initiations in Melanesia,* pp. 92-119. Melbourne: University Press.

———, 1968. 'The Establishment of Christianity and Cash-Cropping in a New Hebridean Community', *JPH,* Vol. 3, pp. 25-46.

———, 1971. 'Descent Groups and Ecology Amongst the Nduindui, New Hebrides'. In Hiatt, L.R. and C. Fayawardena (eds). *Anthropology in Oceania: Essays Presented to Ian Hogbin,* pp. 1-25. Sydney: Angus and Robertson.

Archimbaud, Leon, 1931. *Exposition Coloniale Internationale de Paris: blissements Francaise du Pacifique austral.* Paris: Societe d'Editions Geographiques.

Aubert de la Rue, Edgar, 1945. *Les Nouvelles-Hébrides: Iles de Cendre et de Corail.* Montreal: L'Arbre.

Australasian New Hebrides Company, Ltd., 1893. *Memorandum and Articles of Association of the Australasian New Hebrides Company, Ltd.* Sydney: Batson & Co.

Baker, J.R., 1928. 'Notes on New Hebridean Customs, with Special Reference to the Intersex Pig', *Man,* Vol. XXVIII, pp. 113-8.

———, 1935. 'Espiritu Santo, New Hebrides', *Geographical Journal,* Vol. 85, pp. 209-33.

Ballard, B.C., 1976. 'Australian Land Interests in the New Hebrides; Their Acquisition and Disposal: A Note', *Australian Journal of Politics and History,* Vol. 22, No. 2, pp. 283-7.

Barrau, J., 1955. *Subsistence Agriculture in Melanesia.* Noumea: South Pacific Commission.

Beaglehole, J.C., 1974. *The Life of James Cook.* London: Adam & Charles Black.

Beasant, John, 1980. 'The Vanuatu Experience: (1) Countdown to

Nationhood', *South Pacific Business News,* pp. 5-8.

Belshaw, Cyril S., 1954. *Changing Melanesia: Social Economics of Culture Contact.* Melbourne: Oxford University Press.

______, 1950. *Island Administration in the South West Pacific: Government and Reconstruction in New Caledonia, the New Hebrides, and the British Solomon Islands.* London: Royal Institute of International Affairs.

Bennett, J.M., 1957. 'Vila and Santo: New Hebridean Towns', *Geographical Studies,* Vol. IV, No. 2. pp. 116-28.

Benoist, Hubert, 1972. *Le Condominium des Nouvelles-Hébrides et la Société Melanesienne.* Paris: Pedone.

Biggs, Bruce, 1975. *A Mele-Fila Vocabulary.* Auckland: Linguistic. Society of New Zealand.

Bonnemaison, Joel, 1974. 'Espaces et Paysages agraires dans le nord des Nouvelles-Hébrides: L'exemple des iles d'Aoba et de Maewo'. *JSO,* Vol. XXX, No. 44, pp. 163-232 and No. 45, pp. 259-81.

Bourge, Georges, 1906. *Les Nouvelles-Hébrides de 1606 a 1906.* Paris: Augustin Challamel.

Bourgeau, Jean, 1955. *La France du Pacifique: Nouvelle-Calédonie et Dépendences Wallis et Futuna — Nouvelles-Hébrides — Etablissements Francais de l'Océanie.* Paris: Editions Maritimes et Coloniales.

Bowman, Robert G., 1946. 'Army Farms and Agricultural Development in the Southwest Pacific', *Geographical Review,* Vol. XXXVI, No. 3, pp. 420-46.

Brunet, Auguste, 1908. *Le Régime International des Nouvelles-Hébrides: Le Condominium Anglo-Francais.* Paris: Arthur Rousseau.

Buckley, K. and Klugman, K., 1981. *The History of Burns Philp: The Australian Company in the South Pacific.* Sydney: Burns Philp & Company Ltd.

Campbell, F.A., 1873. *A Year in the New Hebrides, Loyalty Islands, and New Caledonia.* Melbourne: Geelong, George Mercer.

Capell, Arthur, 1958. *The Culture and Language of Futuna and Aniwa, New Hebrides.* Oceania Linguistic Monograph No. 5. Sydney: University of Sydney.

Cheeseman, Evelyn, 1933. 'The Island of Malekula, New Hebrides', *Geographical Journal,* Vol. LXXXI, No. 3, pp. 193-210.

Codrington, R.H., 1972. *The Melanesians: Studies in their Anthropology and Folk-lore.* New York: Dover. Originally published by The Clarendon Press, Oxford, 1891.

Coombe, Florence, 1911. *Islands of Enchantment: Many-sided Melanesia.* London: Macmillan.

Coulter, John Wesley, 1946. 'Impact of the War on the South Sea

Islands', *Geographical Review*, Vol. XXXVI, No. 3, pp. 409-19.

Crocombe, R.G., 1971. *Land Tenure in the Pacific.* Melbourne: Oxford University Press.

Daville, E., 1899. *Guide Practique du Colon aux Nouvelles-Hébrides.* Paris: Librairie Africaine & Coloniale.

Deacon, A. Bernard, 1934. *Malekula, a Vanishing People in the New Hebrides.* Edited by Camilla H. Wedgwood. London: George Routledge & Sons.

———, 1927. 'The Regulation of Marriage in Ambrym', *JRAI*, Vol. LVII, pp. 325-42.

De Jong, Josselin, 1966. 'Ambrym and other Class Systems'. In *Bijdragen: Tot de Taal, Land en Volkenkunde*, pp. 63-81. Stockholm: Gravenhage.

Dillon Peter, 1972. *Narrative of La Perouse's Expedition.* 2 Vols. Amsterdam: N. Israel. Reprint of original publication of 1829.

Don, Alexander, 1927. *Peter Milne (1834-1924): Missionary to Nguna, New Hebrides, 1870-1924 from the Presbyterian Church of New Zealand.* Dunedin: Foreign Missions Committee, P.C.N.Z. Reprinted by Maropa Bookshop, Vila, New Hebrides, 1977.

D'Orliac, Jehanne, 1930. *Les Iles au Parfum de Santal: Nouvelle-Calédonie, Nouvelles-Hébrides.* Paris: Baudiniere.

Doucere, V., 1934. *La Mission Catholique aux Nouvelles-Hébrides.* Paris: Librairie Catholique Emmanuel Vitte.

Dunmore, J., 1965. *French Explorers in the Pacific.* Oxford: Clarendon Press.

Erskine, Capt. John Elphinstone, 1853. *Journal of a Cruise among the Islands of the Western Pacific, including the Feejees and others inhabited by the Polynesian and Negro Races, in Her Majesty's Ship Havannah.* London: John Murray.

Espirat, Jean-Jacques; Jean Guiart, Marie-Salome Lagrange, Monique Renaud, 1973. *Systeme des Titres dans les Nouvelles-Hébrides centrales D'Efate aux Iles Shepherd.* Paris: Institut D'Ethnologie — Musée de L'Homme.

France, Peter, 1969. *The Charter of the Land: Custom and Colonization in Fiji.* Melbourne: Oxford University Press.

Garanger, Jose, 1972. *Archéologie des Nouvelles-Hébrides: contribution a la connaissance des iles du centre.* Paris: Societe des Oceanistes.

Godden, Ruth, 1967. *Lolowai: The Story of Charles Godden and the Western Pacific.* Sydney: Wentworth Press.

Gray, William, 1894. 'Some Notes on the Tannese', *Internationales Archiv fur Ethnographie*, Vol. VII, pp. 227-41.

Great Britain, 1952. Colonial Office. *An Annotated Bibliography on Land Tenure in the British and British Protected Territories in South East*

Asia and the Pacific. London: H.M. Stationary Office.
Grimshaw, Beatrice, 1907. *From Fiji to the Cannibal Islands.* London: Evelaigh Nash.
Guiart, Jean, 1950. 'L'apres-guerre a Ambrym (Nouvelles-Hébrides)', *JSO,* Vol. VI, No. 6, pp. 238-41.
______, 1951. 'Forerunners of Melanesian Nationalism', *Oceania,* Vol. XXII, No. 2, pp. 81-90.
______, 1951. 'John Frum Movement in Tanna', *Oceania,* Vol. XXII, No. 3, pp. 165-77.
______, 1951. 'Le Mouvement Cooperatif dit Malekula Native Company aux Nouvelles-Hébrides', *JSO,* Vol. VII, No. 7, pp. 242-7.
______., 1951. 'Sociétés, rituels et mythes du Nord Ambrym', *JSO,* Vol. VII, No. 7, pp. 5-103.
______, 1952. *L'Organisation Sociale et politique du Nord Malakula.* Extract from the *JSO,* Vol. VIII, No. 8, December, pp. 149-230. Paris: Musée de l'homme.
______, 1956. 'Culture Contact and the John Frum Movement on Tanna, New Hebrides', *Southwest Journal of Anthropology,* Vol. 12, pp. 105-16.
______, 1956. *Un Siecle et demi de Contacts Culturels a Tanna Nouvelles-Hébrides.* Publications de la Sociéte de Oceanistes (No. 5), Paris.
______, 1958. *Espiritu Santo.* Paris: Plon.
______, 1961/62. 'The Social Anthropology of Aniwa, Southern New Hebrides', *Oceania,* Vol. XXXII, No. 1, pp. 34-53.
______, 1964. 'Marriage Regulations and Kinship in the South Central New Hebrides', *Ethnology,* Vol. III, pp. 96-106.
______, 1973. 'Prescriptions matrimoniales négatives aux Nouvelles-Hébrides', *JSO,* Vol. XXIX, No. 41, pp. 339-67.
______, 1975. 'Les Nouvelles-Hébrides apres les accords de Londres', *JSO,* Vol. XXXI, No. 46, pp. 91-5.
______, 1975. 'La fondation du 'National Party' aux Nouvelles-Hébrides, *JSO,* Vol. XXXI, No. 46, pp. 95-6.
______, 1975. 'Le mouvement 'Four Corner' a Tanna (1974)', *JSO,* Vol. XXXI, No. 46, pp. 107-11.
______, 1977. 'Les Nouvelles-Hébrides avant l'indépendance', *JSO,* Vol. XXXIII, No. 54-5, pp. 93-103.
______, 1980. 'The Vanuátu Experience: (2) Cancer of the Colon', *South Pacific Business News,* November, pp. 9-13.
Harrison, Tom R., 1936. 'Living with the People of Malekula', *Geographical Journal,* Vol. 88, pp. 97-127, 243-61, 332-41.
______, 1936. 'Living in Espiritu Santo', *Geographical Journal,* Vol. LXXXVII, No. 3, pp. 243-61.

———. 'The New Hebrides People and Culture', *Geographical Journal,* Vol. LXXXVII, No. 3, pp. 332-41.

———, 1937. *Savage Civilisation.* London: Victor Gollancz.

Hendrick, John D. and Karen Goodrich Hendrick, 1975. 'An Expedition to the New Hebrides', *Expedition: The Magazine of Archaeology and Anthropology,* Vol. 17, No. 13, pp. 7-15. Published by the University Museum of the University of Pennsylvania.

Higginson, John, 1926. *Les Nouvelles-Hébrides: Mémoire de John Higginson.* Edited by A. Auvray. Paris: J. Bellee.

Hogg, James Edward, 1908. 'French and English Land Law', *Comparative Legislation,* Vol. IX, No. 1, pp. 64-8.

Hours, B., 1974. 'Un mouvement politico-religieux néo-hébridais: Le Nagriamel', *Sciences Humaines,* Vol. XI, No. 3-4, pp. 227-42. Published by ORSTOM.

———, 1976. 'Leadership et cargo cult: L'irrésistible ascension de J.T.P.S. Moise', *JSO,* Vol. XXXII, No. 51-2, pp. 207-31.

———, 1976. 'Melanesia: the three miracles', *South Pacific Bulletin,* First Quarter, pp. 35-40.

Huchet, Catherine D., 1976. 'Fete funéraire a Lendombwey (Centre-Sud Malekula)', *JSO,* Vol. XXXI, No. 53, pp. 293-8.

Humphreys, C.B., 1926. *The Southern New Hebrides: An Ethnological Record.* Cambridge: University Press.

Jackson, Bud., 1973. 'The Development Strategy of a Social Movement. In May, R. (ed), *Priorities in Melanesian Development.* Port Moresby and Canberra: University of Papua New Guinea and Australian National University. Paper delivered at the Sixth Waigani Seminar, 1972.

Jacomb, Edward, 1914. France and England in the New Hebrides: *The Anglo-French Condominium.* Melbourne: George Robertson.

Kelly, C. (ed & trans), 1966. *La Australia Del Espiritu Santo. The Journal of Fray Martin de Munilla O.F.M. and other documents relating to the Voyage of Pedro Fernandez de Quiros to the South Sea (1605-1606) and the Franciscan Missionary Plan,* Vol. 1. Cambridge: Hakluyt Society at University Press.

Lamb, Robert, 1905. *Saints and Savages: The Story of Five Years in the New Hebrides.* Edinburgh: William Blackwood.

La Nauze, J.A., 1965. *Alfred Deakin: A Biography,* Vol. 2. Melbourne: University Press.

Lane, Robert and Barbara, 1956. 'A reinterpretation of the 'Anomalous' Six-Section Marriage System of Ambrym, New Hebrides', *Southwestern Journal of Anthropology,* Vol. 12, pp. 406-14.

———, 1958. 'The Evolution of Ambrym Kinship', *Southwestern*

Journal of Anthropology, Vol. 14, pp. 107-35.

Langridge, A.K., 1934. *The Conquest of Cannibal Tanna: A Brief Record of Christian Persistency in the New Hebrides Islands.* London: Hodder and Stoughton.

Laracy, Hugh, 1971. 'Marching Rule and the Missions', *Journal of Pacific History,* Vol. 6, pp. 96-114.

Larmour, Peter (ed), 1984. *Land Tenure in Vanuatu.* Institute of Pacific Studies and the Vanuatu Extension Centre of the University of the South Pacific. Suva.

Larsen, May and Henry, 1961. *Black Sand New Hebrides: Its People and Places.* Edinburgh: Oliver and Boyd.

Layard, John W., 1928. 'Degree Taking in South West Bay, Malekula', *JRAI,* Vol. 31, pp. 139-223.

______, 1936. 'Atchin Twenty Years Ago', *Geographical Journal,* Vol. LXXXVIII, No. 4, pp. 342-51.

______, 1942. *Stone Men of Malakula: Vao.* London: Chatto & Windus.

Le Chartier, Henri, 1885. *La Nouvelle-Calédonie et les Nouvelles-Hébrides.* Paris: Furne et Jouvet.

Leder, Jean, 1981. *Les Cent Jours Du Bout Du Monde: Autopsie D'Une Tragedie.* Noumea.

Legge, J.D., 1958. *Britain in Fiji, 1858-1880.* London: Macmillan.

Levi-Strauss, Claude and George Guilbaud, 1970. 'Le systeme parental et matrimonial du Nord Ambrym', *JSO,* Vol. XXVI, No. 26, pp. 9-32.

Lini, Walter, 1975. 'New Hebrides National Party Petition to the Governments of Great Britain and France', *JSO,* Vol. XXXI, No. 46, p.101.

______, 1980. *Beyond Pandemonium: From the New Hebrides to Vanuatu.* Edited by Hilda Lini. Wellington: Asia Pacific Books and the Institute of Pacific Studies of the University of the South Pacific.

______. et al., 1980. *Vanuatu: Twenti wan tingting long taem blong independens.* Suva: Institute of Pacific Studies of the University of the South Pacific.

Liversage, V., 1945. *Land Tenure in the Colonies.* Cambridge: University Press.

Loffler, Lorenz G., 1960. 'The Development of the Ambrym and Pentecost Kinship Systems', *Southwestern Journal of Anthropology,* Vol. 16, pp. 442-62.

Lynch, Bohun (ed.), 1923. *Isles of Illusion.* London: Constable.

MacClancy, Jeremy, 1980. *To Kill a Bird with Two Stones: A Short History of Vanuatu.* Port Vila: Vanuatu Cultural Centre.

______, 1981. 'From New Hebrides to Vanuatu, 1979-80', *JPH,* Vol.

XVI, pp. 92-104.

MacDonald, D., 1898. *The Mythology of the Efatese.* Sydney: Australasian Association for the Advancement of Science.

McArthur, Norma and J.F. Yaxley, 1968. *Condominium of the New Hebrides: A Report on the First Census of the Population, 1967.* Sydney: Government Printers.

Matas-Kele, Kalkot, 1974. 'A Political Groundswell in the New Hebrides', *Pacific Islands Monthly,* May, p.42.

Mayer, Elizabeth A., 1937. *Vers les Mysterieuses Hebrides: Notes de Bord.* Paris: Les Editions de la Bourdonnais.

Meek, C.K., 1949. *Land Law and Custom in the Colonies.* London: Oxford University Press.

Miller, Graham J., 1948. 'Naked Cult in Central West Santo', *JPS,* Vol. 57, pp. 330-41.

Molisa, Grace; Nikenike Vurobaravu and Howard Van Trease, 1982. 'Vanuatu: Overcoming Pandemonium'. In Crocombe, R. and A. Ali (eds). *Politics in Melanesia.* Suva: Institute of Pacific Studies of the University of the South Pacific.

Morrell, W.P., 1960. *Britain in the Pacific.* Oxford: Clarendon Press.

Muller, Karl, 1971. 'Le saut du Gol, dans le sud de l'ile Pentecote aux Nouvelles-Hébrides', *JSO,* Vol. XXVII, No. 32, pp. 219-33.

———, 1972. 'Field notes on the Small Nambas of the New Hebrides', *JSO,* Vol. XXVIII, No. 35, pp. 153-67 and No. 36, pp 239-51.

———, 1974. 'Funerary rituals among the Mbotgote South-Central Malekula, New Hebrides', *JSO*, Vol. XXX, No.s 42/43, pp. 71-7.

———, 1975. 'Agriculture and food preparation in Bunlap (New Hebrides)', *JSO,* Vol. XXXI, No. 47, pp. 213-21.

Murray, A.W, 1863. *Missions in Western Polynesia: Historical Sketches of these Missions, from their Commencement in 1839 to the Present Time.* London: John Snow.

———, 1885. *The Martyrs of Polynesia. Memorials of Missionaries, Native Evangelists, and Native Converts, who have died by the Hand of Violence from 1799 to 1871.* London: Elliot Stock.

Narokobi, Bernard, 1981. 'Land in the Vanuatu Constitution'. In Larmour, Peter (ed). *Land, People and Government.* Suva: Institute of Pacific Studies of the University of the South Pacific.

New Hebrides National Party, 1975. 'Constitution of The New Hebrides National Party', *JSO,* Vol. XXXI, No. 46, pp. 96-101.

———, 1975. 'Resolutions of the New Hebrides National Party Governing Council: 8th-11th November, 1974', *JSO,* VOl. XXXI, No. 46, pp. 102-7.

O'Connell, D.P., 1968/69. 'The Condominium of the New Hebrides', *The British Year Book of International Law,* pp. 71-145.

O'Reilly, Patrick, 1958. *Bibliographie des Nouvelles-Hébrides.* Paris: Société des Océanistes.

_______, 1957. *Hebridais Repertoire bio-bibliographique des Nouvelles-Hébrides.* Paris: Sociéte des Océanistes.

_______, 1972. 'Me Gabriel Gomichon des Granges, 1940-1971', *JSO,* Vol. XXVIII, No. 34, pp. 86-90.

Oliver, Michael, 1968. *A New Constitution For A New Country.* Fine Arts Press, Reno.

Paton, Frank H.L., 1903. *Lomai of Lenakel. A Hero of the New Hebrides. A Fresh Chapter in the Triumph of the Gospel.* London: Hodder and Stoughton.

Paton, John G., 1890. *John G. Paton Missionary to the New Hebrides. An Autobiography.* London: Hodder and Stoughton.

Paton, Maggie Whitecross, 1895. *Letters and Sketches from the New Hebrides.* London: Hodder and Stoughton.

Pelleray, E., 1922. 'Les Nouvelles-Hébrides', *L'Océanie Francaise,* No. 61 (March 1922), pp. 25-64.

Plant, Chris (ed,), 1977. *New Hebrides: The Road to Independence.* Suva: Institute of Pacific Studies, University of the South Pacific.

_______, 1977. 'The Nagriamel Federation: New Country, Old Story', *Pacific Perspective,* Vol. 6, No. 1, pp. 49-57.

Poirier, Jean. 'Les Mouvements de Liberation Mythique aux Nouvelles-Hébrides', *JSO,* Vol. V, No. 5, pp. 97-103.

Politis, Nicholas, 1908. *Le Condominium Franco-Anglais des Nouvelles-Hébrides.* Paris: A. Pedone.

Radcliffe-Brown, A.R., 1927. 'The Regulation of Marriage in Ambrym', *JRAI,* Vol. LVII, pp. 343-8.

Rice, Edward, 1974. *John Frum You Come.* New York: Doubleday.

Rivers, W.H.R., 1915. 'Descent and Ceremonial in Ambrym', *JRAI,* Vol. XLV, pp. 229-33.

Roberts, Stephen Henry, 1929. *History of French Colonial Policy (1870-1925),* Vol.2. London: P.S. King.

Rozier, Claude, 1966. 'Un essai de mission catholique a Anatom (Nouvelles-Hebrides), 14 mai 1848 — fin fevrier 1850', *JSO,* Vol. XXII, pp. 1-10.

Sawyer, Marian and James Jupp, 1980. 'The New Hebrides prepares for independence', *Current Affairs Bulletin,* April, pp. 22-30.

Scarr, Deryck, 1967. *Fragments of Empire: A History of the Western Pacific High Commission 1877-1914.* Canberra: Australian National University Press.

Seligman, Brenda Z., 1927. 'Bilateral Descent and the Formation of Marriage Classes', *JRAI,* Vol. LVII, pp. 349-76.

Shineberg, Dorothy, 1967. *They Came for Sandalwood: A Study of the*

Sandalwood Trade in the South West Pacific 1830-1865. Carlton, Victoria: Melbourne University Press.

Sope, Barak, 1974. *Land and Politics in the New Hebrides.* Suva: South Pacific Social Sciences Association.

Speiser, Felix, 1923. *Ethnographische Materialen aus den Neuen Hebriden und den Banks-Inseln.* Berlin: C.W. Kreidel.

St. George, Andrew, 1977. 'The Amazing New-Country Caper', *Esquire,* February, pp. 60-4, 151-4.

Thompson, Roger, 1980. *Australian Imperialism in the Pacific: The Expansionist Era, 1820-1920.* Melbourne: University Press.

Tonkinson, Robert, 1968. *Maat Village, Efate: A Relocated Community in the New Hebrides.* Oregon: Department of Anthropology, University of Oregon, Eugene.

______, 1977. 'The Exploitation of Ambiguity: A New Hebrides Case'. In Michael D. Lieber (ed). *Exiles and Migrants in Oceania.* Honolulu: University Press of Hawaii.

Tryon, D.T. and R. Gely, 1979. *Gazetteer of New Hebrides Place Names.* Canberra: Department of Linguistics, Research School of Pacific Studies, Australian National University.

Turner, Rev. George, 1861. *Nineteen Years in Polynesia: Missionary Life, Travels and Researches in the Islands of the Pacific.* London: John Snow.

University of the South Pacific, 1981. *Report of the Regional Conference on Land Management.* Port Vila: Vanuatu Extension Centre and Institute of Pacific Studies of the University of the South Pacific. The Conference was held in Port Vila from 1 to 5 June, 1980.

Ward, John M., 1948. *British Policy in the South Pacific (1786-1893): A study in British policy towards the South Pacific islands prior to the establishment of Governments by the Great Powers.* Sydney: Australasian.

Watt, Agnes C.P., 1896. *Twenty-five Years Mission Life of Tanna, New Hebrides.* London: R. Parlane, Paisley.

Wilson, J.S.G., 1966. *Economic Survey of the New Hebrides.* London: Her Majesty's Stationery Office.

Woodburn, M. Kathleen, 1944. *Backwash of Empire.* Melbourne: Georgian House.

Zorgbibe, Charles, 1981. *Vanuatu, Naissance D'Un Etat.* Paris: Economica.

INDEX

Europeans ix, 14, 59; European occupation of land, acceptance of 11;